Research and Development in Intelligent Systems XVI

Springer

London
Berlin
Heidelberg
New York
Barcelona
Hong Kong
Milan
Paris
Santa Clara
Singapore
Tokyo

Max Bramer, Ann Macintosh
and Frans Coenen (Eds)

Research and Development in Intelligent Systems XVI

Proceedings of ES99, the Nineteenth SGES International Conference on Knowledge-Based Systems and Applied Artificial Intelligence, Cambridge, December 1999

 Springer

Max Bramer, BSc, PhD, CEng
Faculty of Technology, University of Portsmouth, Portsmouth, UK

Ann Macintosh, BSc, CEng
International Teledemocracy Centre, Napier University, Edinburgh, UK

Frans Coenen, PhD
Department of Computer Science, University of Liverpool, Liverpool, UK

ISBN 1-85233-231-X Springer-Verlag London Berlin Heidelberg

British Library Cataloguing in Publication Data
Research and development in intelligent systems XVI :
    Proceedings of ES99, the nineteenth SGES International
    Conference on Knowledge-Based Systems and Applied
    Artificial Intelligence
    1. Expert systems (Computer science) – Congresses
    I. Bramer, M. A. (Max A.), 1948-   II. Macintosh, Ann
    III. Coenen, Frans
    006.3'3

Library of Congress Cataloging-in-Publication Data
A catalog record for this book is available from the Library of Congress.

Typesetting: Camera ready by contributors
Printed and bound at the Athenæum Press Ltd., Gateshead, Tyne and Wear
34/3830-543210 Printed on acid-free paper SPIN 10747125

ACKNOWLEDGEMENTS

ES99 CONFERENCE COMMITTEE

Dr Frans Coenen, University of Liverpool *(Conference Chairman)*
Dr Robert Milne, Intelligent Applications Ltd *(Deputy Conference Chairman)*
Dr Ian Watson, Salford University *(Tutorial and Workshop Co-ordinator)*
Professor Max Bramer, University of Portsmouth *(Technical Programme Chair)*
Ann Macintosh, Napier University *(Deputy Technical Programme Chair)*
Richard Ellis, Crew Services Ltd *(Application Programme Chair)*
Mike Moulton, University of Portsmouth *(Deputy Application Programme Chair)*

TECHNICAL PROGRAMME COMMITTEE

Max Bramer *(Chair)*
Ann Macintosh *(Deputy Chair)*
Frans Coenen
Ian Watson
Richard Wheeler

TECHNICAL PROGRAMME REFEREES

Andreas Abecker (DFKI, Kaiserslautern)
Samir Aknine (University of Paris)
Rosy Barruffi (University of Bologna)
Andrew Basden (University of Salford)
Max Bramer (University of Portsmouth)
Frans Coenen (University of Liverpool)
Stephane Coulondre (University of Montpellier)
Susan Craw (Robert Gordon University, Aberdeen)
Fredrik Dahlstrand (Lund Institute of Technology)
Alex Freitas (PUC-PR, Brazil)
Hermann Kaindl (Siemens Austria, Vienna)
Brian Lees (University of Paisley)
Hui Liu (Birkbeck College, London)
Peter Lucas (Utrecht University)
Ann Macintosh (Napier University)
David McSherry (University of Ulster)
Robert Milne (Intelligent Applications Ltd, Scotland)
Arnaud Ragel (University of Caen)
Derek Sleeman (University of Aberdeen)
Ian Watson (University of Salford)
Richard Wheeler (Starlab Research Laboratories, Belgium)
Michael Wooldridge (Queen Mary and Westfield College, London)

CONTENTS

SESSION 4: KNOWLEDGE ENGINEERING

SESSION 5: KNOWLEDGE REPRESENTATION AND REFINEMENT

TECHNICAL PROGRAMME CHAIRMAN'S INTRODUCTION

M.A.BRAMER
University of Portsmouth, UK

This volume comprises the refereed technical papers presented at ES99, the Nineteenth SGES International Conference on Knowledge Based Systems and Applied Artificial Intelligence, held in Cambridge in December 1999, together with an invited keynote paper by Professor Yorick Wilks. The conference was organised by SGES, the British Computer Society Specialist Group on Knowledge Based Systems and Applied Artificial Intelligence.

The papers in this volume present new and innovative developments in the field, divided into sections on learning, knowledge discovery, case-based reasoning, knowledge engineering, and knowledge representation and refinement.

The refereed papers begin with a multi-authored paper on the KRAFT architecture for knowledge fusion and transformation by a joint team from the Universities of Aberdeen, Cardiff and Liverpool and BT Laboratories. This paper was judged by the technical programme committee to be the best refereed paper submitted to the conference.

It is a reflection of current trends in the field that the next three sections are devoted to papers on a variety of aspects of machine learning. There are four papers on learning, followed by four on knowledge discovery and four on case-based reasoning.

The remaining papers are devoted to knowledge engineering, representation and refinement and include papers on such important emerging topics as knowledge management and web-based knowledge servers.

This is the sixteenth volume in the *Research and Development* series. The Application Stream papers are published as a companion volume under the title *Applications and Innovations in Intelligent Systems VII*.

On behalf of the conference organising committee I should like to thank all those who contributed to the organisation of this year's technical programme, in particular the programme committee members, the referees and our administrators Linsay Turbert and Thelma Williams.

Max Bramer
Technical Programme Chairman, ES99

TECHNICAL KEYNOTE ADDRESS

Can we make Information Extraction more adaptive?

Yorick Wilks and Roberta Catizone

The University of Sheffield, Department of Computer Science

Regent Court, 211 Portobello Street, Sheffield, UK

Abstract

It seems widely agreed that IE (Information Extraction) is now a tested language technology that has reached precision+recall values that put it in about the same position as Information Retrieval and Machine Translation, both of which are widely used commercially. There is also a clear range of practical applications that would be eased by the sort of template-style data that IE provides. The problem for wider deployment of the technology is adaptability: the ability to customize IE rapidly to new domains.

In this paper we discuss some methods that have been tried to ease this problem, and to create something more rapid than the bench-mark one-month figure, which was roughly what ARPA teams in IE needed to adapt an existing system by hand to a new domain of corpora and templates. An important distinction in discussing the issue is the degree to which a user can be assumed to know what is wanted, to have pre-existing templates ready to hand, as opposed to a user who has a vague idea of what is needed from a corpus.

We shall discuss attempts to derive templates directly from corpora; to derive knowledge structures and lexicons directly from corpora, including discussion of the recent LE project ECRAN which attempted to tune existing lexicons to new corpora. An important issue is how far established methods in Information Retrieval of tuning to a user's needs with feedback at an interface can be transferred to IE.

1 Introduction

Information Extraction (IE) has already reached the level of success at which Information Retrieval and Machine Translation (on differing measures, of course) have proved commercially viable. By general agreement, the main barrier to wider use and commercialization of IE is the relative inflexibility of the template concept: classic IE relies on the user having an already developed set of templates, as was the case with US Defence agencies from where the technology was largely developed (see below), and this is not generally the case. The intellectual and practical issue now is how to develop templates, their subparts (like named entities or NEs), the rules for filling them, and associated knowledge structures, as rapidly as possible for new domains and genres.

This paper discusses the quasi-automatic development and detection of templates, template-fillers, lexicons and knowledge structures for new IE domains and genres, using a combination of machine learning, linguistic resource extrapolation and human machine interface elicitation and feedback techniques.

2 Background: The Information Extraction Context

Extracting and managing information has always been important for intelligence agencies, but it clear that, in the next decade, technologies for these functions will also be crucial to education, medicine, and commerce. It is estimated that 80% of our information is textual, and Information Extraction (IE) has emerged as a new technology as part of the search for better methods of finding, storing, accessing and mining such information.

IE itself is an automatic method for locating important facts in electronic documents (e.g. newspaper articles, news feeds, web pages, transcripts of broadcasts, etc.) and storing them in a data base for processing with techniques like data mining, or with off-the-shelf products like spreadsheets, summarisers and report generators. The historic application scenario for Information Extraction is a company that wants, say, the extraction of all ship sinkings, recorded in public news wires in any language world-wide, put into a single data base showing ship name, tonnage, date and place of loss etc. Lloyds of London had performed this particular task with human readers of the world's newspapers for a hundred years.

The key notion in IE is that of a "template": a linguistic pattern, usually a set of attribute value pairs, with the values being text strings, created by experts to capture the structure of the facts sought in a given domain, and which IE systems apply to text corpora with the aid of extraction rules that seek those fillers in the corpus, given a set of syntactic, semantic and pragmatic constraints.

IE as a modern language processing technology was developed largely in the US. but with strong development centres elsewhere [18], [19], [30], [34], [27] Over 25 systems world wide, have participated in the recent MUC competitions, most of which have a generic structure [34] and previously unreliable tasks of identifying, names, dates, organizations, countries, and currencies automatically – often referred to as TE, or Template Element, tasks – have become extremely accurate (over 95% accuracy for the best systems).. In interpreting MUC figures, it should also be borne in mind that the overall recall and precision of human-provided IE information as a whole is estimated to be about 20% worse [16], [14], [15] than the best human performance; it was measured by how well intelligence analysts perform the task manually when compared to a "gold star" experienced intelligence analyst.

Adaptivity in the MUC development context has meant the one-month period in which competing centres adapt their system to new training data sets provided by DARPA; this period therefore provides a benchmark for human-only adaptivity of IE systems.

This paper describes the adaptivity problem, to new domains and genres, that constitutes the central problem to the extension and acceptability of IE, and to increase the principled multi-linguality of IE systems, which we take to mean extending their ability to extract information in one language and present it to a user in another.

3 Previous work on ML and adaptive methods for IE

The application of Machine Learning methods to aid the IE task goes back to work on the learning of verb preferences in the Eighties by Grishman & Sterling [31] and Lehnert [40], as well as early work at MITRE on learning to find named expressions (NEs) [5]. The most interesting developments since then have been a series of extensions to the work of Lehnert and Riloff on Autoslog [49], which was called an automatic induction of a lexicon for IE, but which is normally described as a method of learning extraction rules from <document, filled template> pairs, that is to say the rules (and associated type constraints) that assign the fillers to template slots from text. These rules are then sufficient to fill further templates from new documents.

No conventional learning algorithm was used but, since then, Soderland has extended the work by attempting to use a form of Muggleton's ILP (Inductive Logic Programming) system to that task, and Cardie [13] has sought to extend it to areas like learning the determination of coreference links. Muggleton's [36] learning system at York has provided very good evaluated figures indeed (in world wide terms) in learning part of speech tagging and is being extended to grammar learning. Muggleton also has experimented with user interaction with a system that creates semantic networks of the articles and the relevant templates, although so far its published successes have been in areas like Part-of-Speech tagging that are not inherently structural (in the way template learning arguably is).

Grishman at NYU [7] and Morgan [43] at Durham have done pioneering work using user interaction and definition to define usable templates, and Riloff [50] has attempted to use some form of the user-feedback methods of Information Retrieval, including user-marking of negative and positive <document, filled template> pairings. Collier at Sheffield [17] tried to learn the template structure itself directly (i.e. unsupervised) from a corpus, together with primitive extraction rules, rather than how to fill a given template.

4 UDIE: what would it be like to have a User-Driven IE system?

User Driven IE is a concept only at the moment: its aim is to address several areas of research such as how to use machine learning techniques to allow a system to be adapted to a new domain without expert intervention, and how the user will interact with the system. Below we discuss the structures that must be learned and proposed strategies for learning them, and the proposed interaction with users that we envision will be necessary to customize a system to a particular application.

A number of issues arise in connection with designing user-driven IE. First, the quality of the system depends partly on the quality of the training data it is provided with (cf. the above figure on the low-quality of much of the human MUC data, compared with the best human data). This makes the provision of tools to involve users in this process as part of their normal work-flow important see e.g. [24]. Secondly, the type of the learned data structures impact the maintainability of the system. Stochastic models, for example, perform well in certain cases, but cannot be hand-tailored to squeeze out a little extra performance, or to eliminate an obvious error. This is an advantage of error-driven transformation-based learning of patterns for IE with a deterministic automaton-based recognition engine, such as the work of the team at MITRE [1], following the work of Brill [9], as well as for all work done in the ILP paradigm.

4.1   Supervised template learning

Brill-style transformation-based learning methods are one of the few ML methods in NLP to have been applied above and beyond the part-of-speech tagging origins of virtually all ML in NLP. Brill's original application triggered only on POS tags; later [8] he added the possibility of lexical triggers. Since then the method has been extended successfully to e.g. speech act determination [39], and a template learning application was designed by Vilain [54].

A fast implementation based on the compilation of Brill-style rules to deterministic automata was developed at Mitsubishi labs [51] (see also [20]). The quality of the transformation rules learned depends on factors such as:

1. the accuracy and quantity of the training data;

2. the types of pattern available in the transformation rules;

3. the feature set available used in the pattern side of the transformation rules.

The accepted wisdom of the machine learning community is that it is very hard to predict which learning algorithm will produce optimal performance, so it is advisable to experiment with a range of algorithms running on real data. There have as yet been no systematic comparisons between these initial efforts and other conventional machine learning algorithms applied to learning extraction rules for IE data structures (e.g. example-based systems such as TiMBL [23] and ILP [44].

Such experiments should be considered as strongly interacting with the issues discussed below (section 3 on the lexicon), where we propose extensions to earlier work done by us and others [4] on unsupervised learning of the surface forms (subcategorization patterns) of a set of root template verbs: this was work that sought to cover the range of corpus forms under which a significant verb's NEs might appear in text. Such information might or might not be available in a given set of <document, template> pairs–e.g. would NOT be if the verbs appeared in sentences only in canonical forms. Investigation is still needed on the trade off between the corpus-intensive and the <document, filled template> pair methods, if templates have not been pre-provided for a very large corpus selection (for, if they had, the methodology above could subsume the subcategorization work below). It will be, in practice, a matter of training sample size and richness.

4.2 Unsupervised template learning

We should remember that there is also a possible unsupervised notion of template learning, developed in a Sheffield PhD thesis by Collier [17], one that can be thought of as yet another application of the old technique of Luhn [42] to locate, in a corpus, statistically significant words and use those to locate the sentences in which they occur as key sentences. This has been the basis of a range of summarisation algorithms and Collier proposed a form of it as a basis for unsupervised template induction, namely that those sentences, if they contained corpus-significant verbs, would also contain sentences corresponding to templates, whether or not yet known as such to the user. Collier cannot be considered to have proved that such learning is effective only that some prototype results can be obtained.

4.3 User input and feedback at the interface

An overall aim of UDIE would be to find the right compromise for a user of IE between automatic and user-driven methods. An important aspect of UDIE that supplements the use of learning methods is a user interface quite different from developer-orientated interfaces such as GATE [22]. There will be a range of ways in which a user can indicate to the system their interests, in advance of any automated learning or user feedback, since it would be foolish to ignore the extent to which a user may have some clear notions of what is wanted from a corpus. However, and this is an important difference from classic IE descending from MUC, we will not always assume in what follows that the user does have "templates in mind", but only that there are facts of great interest to the user in a given corpus and it can be the job of this system interface to help elicit them in a formal representation.

It is crucial to recall here that one of the few productive methods for optimising traditional IR in the last decade has been the use of user- feedback methods, typically ones where a user can indicate from a retrieved document set that, say, this ten are good and this ten bad. These results are then fed back to optimise the retrieval iteratively by modifying the request. It is not easy to adapt this methodology directly to IE, even though now, with full text IR available for large indexed corpora, one can refer to sentence documents being retrieved by IR, documents of precisely the span of a classic IE template, so that one might hope for some transfer of IR optimisation methods.

However, although the user can mark sentences so retrieved as good or bad, the "filled template" part of the <document, filled template> pairings cannot be so marked by a user who, by definition, is not assumed to be familiar with template formalisms. In this section of the work we shall mention ways in which a user can indicate preferences, needs and choices at the interface that contribute to template construction whose application he can assess, though not their technical structure.

Doing this will require the possibility of a user marking, on the screen, key portions of text, ones that contain the desired facts; as well as the ability to input, in some form of an interface language (English, Italian etc.), concepts in key facts or template content including predicates and ranges of fillers). This aspect of the paper is complementary to supervised learning methods for templates, lexicons and KR structures, none of which need assume that the user does have a full and explicit concept of what is wanted from a corpus.

5 Adapting system lexicons for a new domain

Virtually all IE use systems use lexicons, and there is universal agreement that lexicons need to be adapted or tuned to new user domains. The disagreement is about what tuning implies and whether there is real IE benefit in terms of recall and precision. Those in the Information Retrieval tradition of information access are usually skeptical about the latter, since statistical measures tend to bring their own internal criterion of relevance and semantic adaptation. Researchers like Strzalkowski [53] and Krovetz [38] have consistently argued that lexical adaptation, taken as far as domain-based sense tagging, does improve IE. In this paper we intend to adapt and continue our work on lexical tuning to provide some evaluable measure of the effectiveness or otherwise of lexical tuning for IE. That term has meant a number of things: the notion (as far back as Wilks 1972 [56]) has meant adding a new sense to a lexicon on corpus evidence because the text could not be accommodated to an existing lexicon. In 1990 Pustejovsky used the term to mean adding a new subcategorization pattern to an existing sense entry from corpus evidence. In the IE tradition there have been a number ([48], [32]) of pioneering efforts to add new words and new subcategorization/preference patterns to a lexicon from a corpus as a prolegomenon to IE.

5.1 Background on lexical acquisition by rule-based methods

Lexical Tuning (LT) is closely related, but fundamentally different from, a group of related theories that are associated with phrases like "lexical rules"; all of them seek to compress lexicons by means of generalizations, and we take that to include DATR [25], methods developed under AQUILEX [10], as well as Pustejovsky's Generative Lexicon [45] and Buitelaar's more recent research on under-specified lexicons [12]. All this work can be traced back to early work by Givon [29] on lexical regularities, done, interestingly to those who think corpus and MRD research began in the 1980s, in connection with the first computational work on Webster's Third Dictionary at SDC in Santa Monica under John Olney in 1966.

All this work can be brought under the heading "data compressio" whether or not that motive is made explicit. Givon became interested in what is now called "systematic polysemy", and distinguished from homonymy (which is deemed unsystematic), with key examples like "grain" which is normally given an PHYOBJ sense in a dictionary, dated earlier than a mass noun sense of "grain in the mass", and this lexical extension can be found in many nouns, and indeed resurfaced in Briscoe and Copestake's famous "grinding rule" [10] that added a mass substance sense for all animals, as in "rabbit all over the road". The argument was that, if such extensions were systematic, they need not be stored individually but could be developed when needed unless explicitly overridden. The paradigm for this was the old AI paradigm of default reasoning: Clyde is an elephant and all elephants have four legs BUT Clyde has three legs. To many of us, it has been something of a mystery why this foundational cliche of AI has been greeted later within computational linguistics as remarkable and profound.

Gazdar's DATR is the most intellectually adventurous of these systems and the one that makes lexical compression the most explicit, drawing as it does on fundamental notions of science as a compression of the data of the world. The problem has been that language is one of the most recalcitrant aspects of the world and it has proved hard to find generalizations above the level of morphology—those to do with meaning have proved especially elusive. Most recently, there has been an attempt to generalise DATR to cross-language generalizations which has exacerbated the problem. One can see that, in English, Dutch and German, respectively, HOUSE, HUIS and HAUS are the "same word"–a primitive concept DATR requires. But, whereas HOUSE has a regular plural, HAUS (HAUESER) does not, so even at this low level, significant generalizations are very hard to find.

Most crucially, there can be no appeals to meaning from the concept of "same word": TOWN (Eng.) and TUIN (Dut.) are plainly the same word in some sense, at least etymologically and phonetically, and may well obey morphological generalizations although now, unlike the HOUSE cases above, they have no relation of meaning at all, as TUIN now means garden. Perhaps the greatest missed opportunity here has been any attempt to link DATR to established quantitative notions of data compression in linguistics, like Minimum Description Length which gives a precise measure of the compaction of a lexicon, even where significant generalizations may be hard to spot by eye or mind, in the time honoured manner.

The systems which seek lexical compression by means of rules, in one form or another, can be discussed by particular attention to Buitelaar, since Briscoe and Pustejovsky differ in matters of detail and rule format (in the case of Briscoe) but not in principle. Buitelaar continues Pustejovsky's campaign against un-structured list views of lexicons: viewing the senses of a word merely as a list as some dictionaries are said to do, in favour of a clustered approach, one which, in his terms, distinguishes "systematic polysemy" [12] from mere homonymy (like the ever present senses of BANK). Systematic polysemy is a notion de-riving directly from Givon's examples, though it is not clear whether it would cover cases like the different kinds of emitting and receiving banks covered in a modern dictionary (e.g. sperm bank,blood bank, bottle bank etc.)

Clustering a word's senses in an optimally revealing way is some- thing no one could possibly object to, and our disquiet at his starting point is that the examples he produces, and particular his related attack on word sense disambiguation programs (including the present author's) as assuming a list-view of sense, is misguided. Moreover, as Nirenburg and Raskin [47] have pointed out in relation to Pustejovksy, those who criticise list views of sense then normally go on in their papers to describe and work with the senses of a word as a list!

Buitelaar's opening argument against standard WSD activities could seem ill conceived: his counter-example is supposed to be one where two senses of BOOK must be kept in play and so WSD should not be done. The example is "A long book heavily weighted with military technicalities, in this edition it is neither so long nor so technical as it was originally".

Leaving aside the question of whether or not this is a sentence, let us accept that Buitelaar's list (!) of possible senses (and glosses) of BOOK is a reasonable starting point (with our numbering added): (i) the information content of a book (military technicalities); (ii) its physical appearance (heavily weighted); (iii) and the events involved in its construction (long) (ibid. p. 25). The issue, he says, is to which sense of BOOK does the "it" refer, and his conclusion is that it cannot be disambiguated between the three.

This seems to us quite wrong, as a matter of the exegesis of English. "heavily weighted" is plainly metaphorical and refers to content (i) not the physical appearance (ii) of the book. We have no trouble taking LONG as referring to the content (i) since not all long books are physically large–it depends on the print etc. On our reading the "it" is univocal between the senses of BOOK in this case. However, nothing depends on an example, well or ill-chosen and it may well be that there are indeed cases where more than one sense must remain in play in a word's deployment; poetry is often cited, but there may well be others, less peripheral to the real world of the Wall Street Journal.

The main point in any answer to Buitelaar must be that, whatever is the case about the above issue, WSD programs have no trouble capturing it: many programs, and certainly that of (Stevenson and Wilks, 1997) that he cites and its later developments, work by constraining senses and are perfectly able to report results with more than one sense still attaching to a word, just as some POS taggers result in more than one tag per word in the output. Close scholars of AI will also remember that Mellish [28], Hirst [33] and Small [52] all proposed methods by which polysemy might be computationally reduced by degree and not in an all or nothing manner. Or, as one might put it, under-specification,

Buitelaar's key technical term, can seem no more than an implementation detail in any effective tagger!

Let us turn to the heart of Buitelaar's position: the issue of systematicity (one with which other closely related authors' claims about lexical rules can be taken together). If he wants, as he does, to cluster a word's senses if they are close semantically (and ignoring the fact that LDOCE's homonyms, say, in general do do that!) then what has that desire got to do with his talk about systematicness within classes of words, where we can all agree that systematicness is a virtue wherever one can obtain it??

Buitelaar lists clusters of nouns (e.g. blend, competition, flux, transformation) that share the same top semantic nodes in some structure like a modified WordNet: act/evt/rel in the case of the list just given(which can be read as action OR extent or relation). Such structures, he claims, are manifestations of systematic polysemy but what is one to take that to mean, say by contrast with Levin's [41] verb classes where, she claims, the members of the class share certain syntactic and semantic properties and, on that basis, one could in principle predict additional members. That is simply not the case here: one does not have to be a firm believer in natural kinds to see that the members of this class have nothing systematic in common, but are just arbitrarily linked by the same "upper nodes". Some such classes are natural classes, as with the class he gives linked by being both animate and food, all of which, unsurprisingly, are animals and are edible, at least on some dietary principles, but there is no systemic relationship here of any kind. Or, to coin a phrase, one might say that the list above is just a list and nothing more!

In all this, we intend no criticism of his useful device, derived from Pustejovsky, for showing disjunctions and conjunctions of semantic types attached to lexical entries, as when one might mark something as act AND relation or an animal sense as animate OR food. This is close to older devices in artificial intelligence such as multiple perspectives on structures (in Bobrow and Winograd's KRL [6]), multiple formulas for related senses of a word in Wilks [55], and so on. Showing these situations as conjunctions and disjunctions of types may well be a superior notation, though it is quite proper to continue to point out that the members of conjuncts and disjuncts are, and remain, in lists!

Finally, Buitelaar's proposal to use these methods (via CoreLex) to acquire a lexicon from a corpus may also be an excellent approach. Our point here is that that method (capturing the content of e.g. adjective-noun instances in a corpus) has no particular relationship to the theoretical machinery described above, and is not different in kind from the standard NLP projects of the 70s like Autoslog [49] to take just one of many possible examples.

5.2   Another approach to lexical acquisition

We now have developed a set of modular techniques in joint work between Rome University and Sheffield (under the EC-funded ECRAN project) with which to implement and evaluate lexical adaptation in a general manner, and in the context of a full pattern-matching IE system, one not yet fully evaluated in competition:

1. a general verb-pattern matcher from corpora;

2. a Galois Lattice [3] developed as a sorting frame for corpus sub-categorization frames for individual verbs to display their inclusion properties;

3. a general word sense disambiguation program that produces the best results world-wide for general text [57];

4. measures of mapping of the subcategorization patterns (with sense disambiguated noun fillers) at lattice nodes against an existing lexicon of verbs by subcategorization patterns (LDOCE).

These are now sufficient tools to experiment systematically with the augmentation of a lexicon from a corpus with (a) subcategorization and preference patterns and (b) the determination of a novel sense from lattice nodes whose pattern set falls outside some cluster measure for sense.

This aspect of the paper should be seen as interacting strongly with the section above on unsupervised learning of trial template structures from a corpus (Section 4.2 above): in that work a template is induced, seeded only by corpus-significant verbs. In this lexicon-adaptation development, the verbs are explicit seeds and what is sought is the corpus variety of subcategorization patterns within which template fillers for those verbs are to be found and partially ordered. It will be an experimental question whether the subcategorization variety located by the method of this section can be learned and generalised by any of the ML techniques of (Section 3 above).

6   Adapting Knowledge Structures for a new domain

It is a truism, and one of IEs inheritances from classical AI, that its methods, however superficial some believe them, are dependent on extensive domain knowledge; this takes the form of, at least, hierarchical structures expressing relationships between entities in the domain world of the user. These are often shown as hierarchies in the classical manner but the relationship between child and parent nodes may be variously: part- of, membership, subset, control-over and so on. The simplest sort of example would be an upper node representing Company X, and lower children being Division-A, Division-B, Division-C, which could have relationship conventionally to be described as part-of (in that the divisions are part of the company) but which some might prefer to insist were really set membership relations over, say, employees (in that, any employee of Division-A is also an employee of Company-X—all these are matters of the interpretation of simple diagrams).

There is little dispute such structures are needed for sophisticated IE systems; the interesting questions are can they be acquired automatically for a new domain and are they distinct from lexical knowledge? As to the latter question, the types of knowledge cannot be entirely distinct. When systems like [11] attempted to locate genus hierarchies for LDOCE from parsing the definitions in the dictionary, the resulting hierarchies could be seen equally well as lexical knowledge, or as ISA-hierarchies in the world (a daisy is a plant which...etc.). Pattern matching work on corpora (Pustejovsky [46] [50] to establish and augment such relations was presented as lexicon adaptation but the results could equally well have been claimed as knowledge structure discovery. One could (over)simplify a complex philosophical area by saying that the differences–between lexical and KR interpretations of such hierarchical structure–are in part about:

- interpretation: KR hierarchies can be interpreted in a number of ways, whereas as lexical structures they are normally seen only as naive concept inclusion (e.g. the concept Plant covers the concept Daisy);

- transitivity of structure: KR hierarchies are concerned with inference and hence the transitivity of the interpretations of the ISA and part-of etc. links. This is not normally an issue in local lexical relations.

- scope/intensionality etc.: simple KR hierarchies of the sort we have suggested need to support more complex logical concepts (e.g. scope or the question of interpretation as a concept or role, as in "The President must be over 35" which is both about a current US President like Clinton and about any US President as such). Again, these are not issues in lexical relations as normally described.

Simple trial KR hierarchies for new domains could be inferred from combining for example:

1. Initial inference of the ontological population of a new domain by standard IR concepts of significant presence of a set of words compared to standard texts.

2. Attempting to locate partial KR structures for any members of that set that take part in existing EWN or other semantic hierarchies, using a word sense disambiguation program first if applicable to filter inappropriate senses from the existing hierarchy parts so selected.

3. Using some partial parser on domain corpora to locate "significant triples" over all instances of the word set selected by (i) in the manner of Grishman and Sterling [31].

4. Developing an algorithm to assign these structures (whose non-significant words will be sense-tagged and located in hierarchies, chunks of which can be imported) in combination to a minimum domain-appropriate KR structure that would then have to be edited and pruned by hand within a user-interface.

7 Adaptivity to text genre

Another strand of investigation we believe to be of great concern to users of IE is the adaptation, for a given domain, to a new text genre, such as moving from informal messages to formalised reports, without changing domain, and the issue of whether or not templates and their extraction rules need retraining. This was faced as a hand-crafting task in early MUCs when the genre was US Navy messages which had a jargon and syntactic forms quite unlike conventional English. Khosravi [37] has investigated whether an IE-like approach to speech-act and message matching can transfer between dialogue and email messages and found a substantial degree of transfer, of the order of 60It has long been known that certain lexical forms are distinctive of register and genre, as in certain languages (Czech is often cited) there are still "formal dialects" for certain forms of communication. In cases like these, standard techniques (n-grams and language-recognition methods) would be sufficient to indicate genre. These could be augmented by methods such as the ECRAN-like method (see above) of adapting to new subcategorization patterns and preferences of verbs of interest in new text genres.

8 Multilingual IE

Given an IE system that performs an extraction task against texts in one language, it is natural to consider how to modify the system to perform the same task against texts in another. More generally, there may be a requirement to do the extraction task against texts in an arbitrary number of languages and to present results to a user who has no knowledge of the source language from which the information has been extracted. To minimise the language-specific alterations that need to be made in extending an IE system to a new language, it is important to separate the task-specific conceptual knowledge the system uses, which may be assumed to be language independent, from the language-dependent lexical knowledge the system requires, which unavoidably must be extended for each new language.

At Sheffield, we have adapted the architecture of the LaSIE system [26], an IE system originally designed to do monolingual extraction from English texts, to support a clean separation between conceptual and lexical information. This separation allows hard-to-acquire, domain-specific, conceptual knowledge to be represented only once, and hence to be reused in extracting information from texts in multiple languages, while standard lexical resources can be used to extend language coverage. Preliminary experiments with extending the system to French and Spanish have shown substantial results, and by a method quite different from attaching a classic (monolingual) IE system to a machine translation (MT) system.

The M-LaSie (multilingual) system relies on a robust domain model that constitutes the central exchange through which all multilingual information circulates. The addition of a new language to the IE system consists mainly of mapping a new monolingual lexicon to the domain model and adding a new syntactic/semantic analysis front-end, with no interaction at all with other languages in the system.

The language independent domain model can be compared to the use of an *interlingua* representation in MT (see, *e.g.*, [35]). An IE system, however, does not require full generation capabilities from the intermediate representation, and the task will be well-specified by a limited 'domain model' rather than a full unrestricted 'world model'. This makes an *interlingua* representation feasible for IE, because it will not involve finding solutions to all the problems of such a representation, only those issues directly relevant to the current IE task.

A French-Spanish-English prototype of this architecture has been implemented and successfully tested on a limited amount of data. The architecture has been further developed in the AVENTINUS project [21].

9 Conclusion

This has been not so much a paper as a disguised research proposal and compares very unfavourably therefore with those described above who have been prepared to begin the difficult work of making IE adaptive. Another important area not touched on here (though it is to be found in Cardie [13]) is the application of ML methods to the crucial notion of co-reference (e.g. [2]), and particularly its role in relating documents together: or cross-document management, a form of data-fusion between information about individuals in different documents, who may in fact be different although they have the same names.

References

[1] J. Aberdeen, J. Burger, D. Day, L. Hirschman, P. Robinson, and M. Vilain. MITRE - Description of the *Alembic* System used for MUC-6. In *Proceedings of the Sixth Message Understanding Conference (MUC-6)*, pages 141–156, 1995.

[2] S. Azzam, K. Humphreys., and R. Gaizauskas. Using corefernece chains for text summarization. In *Proceedings of the ACL '99 Workshop on Corefernce and its Applications*, Maryland, 1999.

[3] R. Basili, M. Pazienza, and P. Velardi. Aquisition of selectional patterns from sub-langauges. *Machine Translation*, 8, 1993.

[4] R.and R. Catizone Basili, M.T. Pazienza, M. Stevenson, P. Velardi, M.Vindigni, and Y.Wilks. An empirical approach to lexical tuning. In *Workshop on Adapting Lexical and Corpus Resources to Sublanguages and Applications, LREC, First International Conference on Language Resources and Evaluation*, Granada, Spain, 1998.

[5] D. Bikel, S. Miller, R. Schwartz, and R. Weischedel. Nymble: a High-Performance Learning Name-finder. In *Proceedings of the Fifth conference on Applied Natural Language Processing*, 1997.

[6] D.G. Bobrow and T. Winograd. An overview of krl, a knowledge representation language. *Cognitive Science 1*, pages 3–46, 1977.

[7] A. Borthwick, J. Sterling, E. Agichtein, and R. Grishman. Description of the mene named entity system as used in muc-7 muc-7. In *Proceedings of the MUC-7 Conference*, NYU. Proceedings available at http://muc.www.saic.com/.

[8] E. Brill. Some Advances in Transformation-Based Part of Speech Tagging. In *Proceedings ofthe Twelfth National Conference on AI (AAAI-94)*, Seattle, Washington, 1994.

[9] E. Brill. Transformation-Based Error-Driven Learning and Natural Language. *Computational Linguistics*, 21(4), December 1995.

[10] T.. Briscoe, A. Copestake, and V. De Pavia. Default inheritance in unification-based approaches to the lexicon. Technical report, Cambridge University Computer Laboratory, 1991.

[11] R. Bruce and L. Guthrie. Genus disambiguation: A study in weighted preference. In *Proceesings of COLING-92*, pages 1187–1191, Nantes, France, 1992.

[12] P. Buitelaar. A lexicon for underspecified semantic tagging. In *Proceedings of the ACL-Siglex Workshop on Tagging Text with Lexical Semantics*, Washington, D.C., 1997.

[13] Claire Cardie. Empirical methods in information extraction. *AI Magazine*, 18(4), 1997. Special Issue on Empirical Natural Language Processing.

[14] N. Chinchor. The statistical significance of the MUC-5 results. In *Proceedings of the Fifth Message Understanding Conference (MUC-5)*, pages 79–83. Morgan Kaufmann, 1993.

[15] N. Chinchor and Sundheim B. MUC-5 Evaluation Metrics. In *Proceedings of the Fifth Message Understanding Conference (MUC-5)*, pages 69–78. Morgan Kaufmann, 1993.

[16] N. Chinchor, L. Hirschman, and D.D. Lewis. Evaluating message understanding systems: An analysis of the third message understanding conference (muc-3). *Computational Linguistics*, 19(3):409–449, 1993.

[17] R. Collier. *Automatic Template Creation for Information Extraction*. PhD thesis, UK, 1998.

[18] J. Cowie, L. Guthrie, W. Jin, W. Odgen, J. Pustejowsky, R. Wanf, T. Wakao, S. Waterman, and Y. Wilks. CRL/Brandeis: The Diderot System. In *Proceedings of Tipster Text Program (Phase I)*. Morgan Kaufmann, 1993.

[19] J. Cowie and W. Lehnert. Information extraction. *Special NLP Issue of the Communications of the ACM*, 1996.

[20] H. Cunningham. JAPE – a Jolly Advanced Pattern Engine. 1997.

[21] H. Cunningham, S. Azzam, and Y. Wilks. Domain Modelling for AVENTINUS (WP 4.2). LE project LE1-2238 AVENTINUS internal technical report, University of Sheffield, UK, 1996.

[22] H. Cunningham, R.G. Gaizauskas, and Y. Wilks. A General Architecture for Text Engineering (GATE) – a new approach to Language Engineering R&D. Technical Report CS – 95 – 21, Department of Computer Science, University of Sheffield, 1995. Also available as http://xxx.lanl.gov/ps/cmp-lg/9601009.

[23] W. Daelemans, J. Zavrel, K. van der Sloot, and A. van den Bosch. TiMBL: Tilburg memory based learner version 1.0. Technical report, ILK Technical Report 98-03, 1998.

[24] D. Day, J. Aberdeen, L. Hirschman, R. Kozierok, P. Robinson, and M. Vilain. Mixed-Initiative Development of Language Processing Systems. In *Proceedings of the 5th Conference on Applied NLP Systems (ANLP-97)*, 1997.

[25] R. Evans and G. Gazdar. DATR: A Language for Lexical Knowledge Representation. *Computational Linguistics*, 22(2):167–216, 1996.

[26] R. Gaizauskas. XI: A Knowledge Representation Language Based on Cross-Classification and Inheritance. Technical Report CS-95-24, Department of Computer Science, University of Sheffield, 1995.

[27] R. Gaizauskas and Y. Wilks. Information Extraction: Beyond Document Retrieval. *Journal of Documentation*, 1997. In press (Also available as Technical Report CS-97-10).

[28] G. Gazdar and C. Mellish. *Natural Language Processing in Prolog*. Addison-Wesley, 1989.

[29] T. Givon. Transformations of ellipsis, sense development and rules of lexical derivation. Technical Report SP-2896, Systems Development Corp., Sta Monica, CA, 1967.

[30] R. Grishman. Information extraction: Techniques and challenges. In M-T. Pazienza, editor, *Proceedings of the Summer School on Information Extraction (SCIE-97)*, LNCS/LNAI. Springer-Verlag, 1997.

[31] R. Grishman and J. Sterling. Generalizing automatically generated patterns. In *Proceedings of COLING-92*, 1992.

[32] R. Grishman and J. Sterling. Description of the Proteus system as used for MUC-5. In *Proceedings of the Fifth Message Understanding Conference (MUC-5)*, pages 181–194. Morgan Kaufmann, 1993.

[33] G. Hirst. *Semantic Interpretation and the Resolution of Ambiguity*. CUP, Cambridge, England, 1987.

[34] J.R. Hobbs. The generic information extraction system. In *Proceedings of the Fifth Message Understanding Conference (MUC-5)*, pages 87–91. Morgan Kaufman, 1993.

[35] W.J. Hutchins. *Machine Translation: past, present, future*. Chichester : Ellis Horwood, 1986.

[36] Stephen Muggleton James Cussens, David Page and Ashwin Srinivasan. Using inductive logic programming for natural language processing. In *Proceedings of in ECML*, pages 25–34, Prague, 1997. Springer-Verlag. Workshop Notes on Empirical Learning of Natural Language Tasks.

[37] H. Khosravi and Y. Wilks. Extracting pragmatic content from e-mail. *Journal of Natural Language Engineering*, 1997. submitted.

[38] R. Krovetz and B. Croft. Lexical ambiguity and information retrieval. *ACM Transactions on Information Systems*, 10(2):115–141, 1992.

[39] S.Carberry K.Samuel and K.Vijay-Shanker. Dialogue act tagging with transofrmation-based learning. In *Proceedings of the COLING-ACL 1998 Conference*, volume 2, pages 1150–1156, Montreal, Canada, 1998.

[40] W. Lehnert, C. Cardie, D. Fisher, J. McCarthy, and E. Riloff. University of massachusetts: Description of the CIRCUS system as used for MUC-4. In *Proceedings of the Fourth Message Understanding Conference MUC-4*, pages 282–288. Morgan Kaufmann, 1992.

[41] B. Levin. *English Verb Calsses and Alternations*. Chicago, Il, 1993.

[42] H. P. Luhn. A statistical approach to mechanized encoding and searching of literary information. *IBM Journal of Research and Development*, 1:309–317, 1957.

[43] R. Morgan, R. Garigliano, P. Callaghan, S. Poria, M. Smith, A. Urbanowicz, R. Collingham, M. Costantino, and C. Cooper. Description of the LOLITA System as used for MUC-6. In *Proceedings of the Sixth Message Understanding Conference (MUC-6)*, pages 71–86, San Francisco, 1995. Morgan Kaufmann.

[44] S. Muggleton. Recent advances in inductive logic programming. In *Proc. 7th Annu. ACM Workshop on Comput. Learning Theory*, pages 3–11. ACM Press, New York, NY, 1994.

[45] J. Pustejovsky. *The Generative Lexicon*. MIT, 1995.

[46] J. Pustejovsky and P. Anick. Autmoatically acquiring conceptual patterns without an annotated corpus. In *Proceedings of the Third Workshop on Very Large Corpora*, 1988.

[47] Nirenburg S.and V. Raskin. Ten choices for lexical semantics. Technical report, Computing Research Lab, Las Cruces, NM, 1996. MCCS-96-304.

[48] E. Riloff. Automatically contructing a dictionary for information extraction tasks. In *Proceedings of Eleventh National Conference on Artificial Intelligence*, 1993.

[49] E. Riloff and W. Lehnert. Automated dictionary construction for information extraction from text. In *Proceedings of Ninth IEEE Conference on Artificial Intelligence for Applications*, pages 93–99, 1993.

[50] E. Riloff and J. Shoen. Automatically aquiring conceptual patterns without an annotated corpus. In *Proceedings of the Third Workshop on Very Large Corpora*, 1995.

[51] E. Roche and Y. Schabes. Deterministic Part-of-Speech Tagging with Finite-State Transducers. *Computational Linguistics*, 21(2):227–254, June 1995.

[52] S. Small and C. Rieger. Parsing and comprehending with word experts (a theory and it's realiastion). In W. Lehnert and M. Ringle, editors, *Strategies for Natural Language Processing*. Lawrence Erlbaum Associates, Hillsdale, NJ, 1982.

[53] Jin Wang T.Strzalkowski, Fang Lin and Jose Perez-Caballo. *Natural Language Information Retrieval*, chapter Evaluating Natural Language Processing Techniques in Information Retrieval, pages 113–146. Kluwer Academic Publishers, 1997.

[54] Mark Vilain. Validation of terminological inference in an information extraction task. In *Proceedings of the 1993 ARPA Human Language Workshop*, 1993.

[55] Y. Wilks. *Grammar, Meaning and the Machine Analysis of Meaning*. Routledge and Kegan Paul, 1972.

[56] Y. Wilks, L. Guthrie, J. Guthrie, and J. Cowie. *Combining Weak Methods in Large-Scale Text Processing, in Jacobs 1992, Text-Based Intelligent Systems*. Lawrence Erlbaum, 1992.

[57] Y. Wilks and M. Stevenson. Sense tagging: Semantic tagging with a lexicon. In *Proceedings of the SIGLEX Workshop "Tagging Text with Lexical Semantics: What, why and how?"*, Washington, D.C., April 1997. Available as `http://xxx.lanl.gov/ps/cmp-lg/9705016`.

BEST REFEREED TECHNICAL PAPER

The KRAFT Architecture for Knowledge Fusion and Transformation

Alun Preece, Kit Hui

Department of Computing Science, University of Aberdeen
Aberdeen, UK

Alex Gray, Philippe Marti

Department of Computer Science, Cardiff University
Cardiff, UK

Trevor Bench-Capon, Dean Jones

Department of Computer Science, University of Liverpool
Liverpool, UK

Zhan Cui

Intelligent Business Systems Research, Advanced Communications Research
BT Labs, UK

Abstract

This paper describes the KRAFT architecture which supports the fusion of knowledge from multiple, distributed, heterogeneous sources. The architecture uses constraints as a common knowledge interchange format, expressed against a common ontology. Knowledge held in local sources can be tranformed into the common constraint language, and fused with knowledge from other sources. The fused knowledge is then used to solve some problem or deliver some information to a user. Problem-solving in KRAFT typically exploits pre-existing constraint solvers. KRAFT uses an open and flexible agent architecture in which knowledge sources, knowledge fusing entities, and users are all represented by independent KRAFT agents, communicating using a messaging protocol. Facilitator agents perform matchmaking and brokerage services between the various kinds of agent. KRAFT is being applied to an example application in the domain of network data services design.

1 Introduction and Motivation

Most modern organisations have a number of on-line knowledge sources, distributed among the nodes of their information systems networks. To exploit these knowledge sources to the fullest extent, organisations need to be able to combine knowledge from disparate sources in a highly dynamic way: we call this *knowledge fusion*. There has been an enormous amount of work in distributed information management on the topic of distributed database querying. An important feature of these systems is that they use some kind of *integration schema* to provide a common representation across the entire distributed system. Individual data sources must map between their local schemas and the integration schema in order to combine information in a common form.

A distributed database query retrieves *data instances*, but this is not enough for knowledge fusion. To combine information in a meaningful way, data instances need associated knowledge of their context: how they should be interpreted and how they can be used. This kind of knowledge can often be thought of as "small print", and is typically expressible in the form of *constraints*. As an example, consider a distributed design system for Personal Computers. One on-line resource may be a database of information on available PC operating systems. With a distributed database query, we could discover that one of the available OSes is called "Windows NT"; however, to use this OS instance in a PC design, we would also need to know the "small print" constraint: "Windows NT requires a minimum of 32MB of RAM".

In a knowledge fusion system, the information instances and associated constraints need to be mapped to a common representation to allow meaningful fusion. This requires a *common language* for representing instances and constraints, and a common set of definitions of the *terminology* of the knowledge domain: a *shared ontology* [12].

Consider the following small print constraint, which says that "all PC operating systems called 'winNT' need at least 32MB of RAM":

```
constrain each o in pc_os such that name(o)="winNT"
    to have memory_requirement(o) >= 32
```

This constraint is expressed in CoLan [2], which can serve as a relatively readable, common constraint language. The terminology used (for example, the concept pc_os, meaning all PC operating systems, the attributes of this concept, name and memory_requirement) must be defined in the shared ontology for the PC design domain. Note that, to allow data instances to be represented, the shared ontology must have schema-level information in addition to conceptual-level definitions. For example, the ontology defines the concept pc_os as a sub-concept of pc_software, which is in turn a sub-concept of software. It also defines pc_os as having a name attribute, the value of which is represented as a string data structure. This is schema-level information which permits instances of pc_os to be represented, stored, manipulated, and transmitted across the network.

Constraints such as the example above will not generally be stored in this form within the individual resource. They could appear as database integrity constraints, rules in a rule-based system, slot value restrictors in a frame-based system, or constraints in some other constraint language. Similarly, the terminology used within the individual resource will generally not conform to the shared ontology. For these reasons, knowledge in individual resources needs to be *transformed* to the common language and shared ontology, before it can be fused.

1.1 Operations on a Knowledge Fusion System

There are two main kinds of operation users would wish to perform on a distributed knowledge fusion system:

- *Knowledge Retrieval:* here, users often simply want to find out everything the organisation knows about something. The knowledge fusion system extracts all relevant instances and associated constraints from all available resources, and delivers these in a common form to the user.

In the PC design domain, for example, the user might ask for all known PC OSes, including any "small print" constraints.

- *Problem-Solving:* here, users not only want the system to fuse knowledge, but also to use the fused knowledge to solve some problem. The system once again extracts the relevant instances and constraints, but now uses these as the basis of a dynamically-constructed constraint satisfaction problem.

  In the PC design domain, for example, the user might specify that they want a PC for real-time video editing; the system will need to extract candidate solution components with attached "small print" constraints, and solve these to construct a suitable PC configuration.

1.2   Services of a Knowledge Fusion System

From the above discussion, it is clear that a knowledge fusion system needs the following services:

- *Knowledge location services:* there must be mechanisms by which a user, and other components, can locate relevant knowledge on the network.

- *Knowledge transformation services:* there must be mechanisms to transform knowledge in individual resources into a common representation language and ontology.

- *Knowledge fusion services:* there must be mechanisms to combine knowledge, and process it — conjoining, simplifying, and finding solutions that satisfy constraints.

These services are the basic requirements of an architecture for building knowledge fusion systems. By implementing software components that provide these services, developers can:

- bring new knowledge sources on-line so that they announce their presence to the network, advertise their services, and commit to providing information in a common representation language and ontology;

- create new knowledge-processing facilities to filter, fuse, adapt, and otherwise add value to the knowledge in the on-line sources;

- construct querying interfaces for users that give them ready access to the rich services of the knowledge fusion system.

The KRAFT project (Knowledge Reuse And Fusion/Transformation) aims to provide such an architecture. The following section presents an overview of the KRAFT architecture; subsequent sections examine the operations of individual components of the architecture.

2 Overview of the KRAFT Architecture

The KRAFT system has an agent-based architecture, in which all knowledge processing components are realised as software agents. An agent-based architecture was chosen for KRAFT for the following reasons:

- Agent architectures are designed to allow software processes to communicate knowledge across networks, in high-level communication protocols; as constraints are a sub-type of knowledge, this was seen as an important feature for KRAFT.

- Agent architectures are highly dynamic and open, allowing agents to locate other agents at run-time, discover the capabilities of other agents, and form cooperative alliances; as KRAFT is concerned with the fusion of knowledge from available on-line sources, these features were seen as being of great value.

The design of KRAFT is consistent with several emerging agent standards, notably the de facto KQML standard [11] and the de jure FIPA standard [6]. Agents are peers; any agent can communicate with any other agent with which it is acquainted. Agents become acquainted by registering their identity, network location, and an advertisement of their knowledge-processing capabilities with a specific type of agent called a *facilitator* (essentially an intelligent yellow pages service).

When an agent needs to request a service from another agent, it asks a facilitator to recommend an agent that appears to provide that service. The facilitator attempts to match the requested service to the advertised knowledge-processing capabilities of agents with which it is acquainted. If a match is found, the facilitator can inform the service-requesting agent of the identity, network location, and advertised knowledge-processing capabilities of the service provider. The service-requesting agent and service-providing agent can now communicate directly.

It is worth emphasising that, while this model is superficially similar to that used in distributed object architectures such as CORBA and DCOM, the important difference is the semantic level at which interactions take place: In distributed object architectures, objects advertise their presence by registering method signatures with registry services, and communicate by remote method invocations. In agent-based systems, advertisements of capabilities are much richer, being expressed in a declarative knowledge representation language, and communication uses a high-level conversational protocol built from primitive conversational actions such as *ask*, *tell*, *advertise*, and *recommend*. Distributed object architectures are in fact highly suitable for implementing agent-based architectures (for example, the ADEPT system used CORBA [9]) but the converse is not true.

A conceptual view of the KRAFT architecture is shown in Figure 1. KRAFT agents are shown as ovals. There are three kinds of these: wrappers, mediators, and facilitators. All of these are in some way knowledge-processing entities.

Wrappers are agents that act as proxies for external knowledge sources, typically databases and knowledge-based systems. These are often legacy systems, so one task of a wrapper is to provide a bridge between the legacy system interface and the KRAFT agent interface. For example, the legacy interface of a relational database will

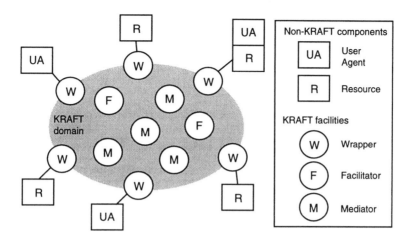

Figure 1: A conceptual view of the KRAFT architecture.

typically be SQL/ODBC; the KRAFT wrapper will accept incoming request messages from other agents in the KRAFT agent communication language, transform these into SQL queries, run them on the database, and transform the returned results to an outgoing message in the KRAFT agent communication language.

Wrappers also provide entry-points into the KRAFT system for *user agents*. User agents allow end-users access to a KRAFT knowledge processing system. A user agent will offer some kind of user interface, with which the user will present queries to the KRAFT network. The user agent will transform the users' queries into the internal knowledge representation language of the KRAFT system, and interact with other KRAFT agents to answer the queries. A user agent will typically also do some local processing on knowledge, at least to transform it for presentation.

Mediators are the internal knowledge-processing agents of the KRAFT system: every mediator adds value in some way to knowledge obtained from other agents. Typical mediator tasks include filtering, sorting, and fusing knowledge obtained from other agents.

Facilitators have already been mentioned above: these are the "matchmaker" agents that allow agents to become acquainted and thereby communicate. Facilitators are fully-fledged knowledge- processing entities: establishing that a service request "matches" a service advertisement requires reasoning with the declarative representations of request and advertisement.

KRAFT agents communicate via messages using a nested protocol stack. KRAFT messages are implemented as character strings transported by a suitable underlying protocol (for example, CORBA IIOP or TCP via sockets). A simple message protocol encapsulates each message with low-level header information including a timestamp and network information.

The body of the message consists of two nested protocols: the outer protocol is the agent communication language CCQL (*Constraint Command and Query Language*) which is a subset of the Knowledge Query and Manipulation Language (KQML) [11].

Nested within the CCQL message is its content, expressed in the CIF protocol (*Constraint Interchange Format*) — a superset of the CoLan constraint language shown in Section 1.

Syntactically, KRAFT messages are implemented as Prolog term structures. An example message is shown below. The outermost kraft_msg structure contains a context clause (low-level header information) and a ccql clause. The message is from an agent called os_vendor to an agent called pc_designer. The ccql structure contains, within its content field, an encoded CIF expression (here, we see a "pretty-printed" CoLan constraint; actually, CIF expressions are transmitted in a compiled internal format).

```
kraft_msg(
    context(1,id(19), pc_designer, os_vendor,
        time_stamp(date(21,5,1999), time(15,35,10)))),
    ccql(tell, [
        sender : os_vendor,
        receiver : pc_designer,
        reply_with : id(41),
        ontology : shared,
        language : cif,
        content : [
            constrain each o in pc_os
                such that name(o)="winNT"
                to have memory_requirement(o) >= 32
    ])
)
```

Use of Prolog term structures is chiefly for convenience, as most of the knowledge-processing components are written in Prolog. However, the Prolog term structures are easily parsed by non-Prolog KRAFT components; currently there are several components implemented in Java, for example.

As explained in Section 1, the terms used in the CIF part of the message are defined in the shared ontology. To support the representation, storage, and transmission of data instances, the ontology has schema-level information in addition to conceptual-level definitions.

The remainder of this paper is organised as follows: Section 3 explains how the KRAFT facilitator agents work; Section 4 decribes the role of wrapper agents and the common ontology; Section 5 descibes how mediators perform knowledge fusion and associated problem-solving operations; Section 6 discusses an example KRAFT system in a telecommunications design application domain; Section 7 concludes the paper.

3 Facilitator Agents

As introduced above, facilitators provide various routing services within a KRAFT network. As there are many different definitions of facilitators in the literature [1, 3, 4,

10, 14, 16], and the range of services provided by these facilitators varies considerably, this section looks in more detail at exactly how facilitators are used in KRAFT.

In the KRAFT project, the facilitator provides routing functionalities to agents' queries. These basic functions are:

Advertisement handling When the facilitator receives an advertisement from a resource, it is able to process and store this information for further use. An advertisement is a (set of) capabilities that a resource commits to provide. These capabilities are defined in a formalism common to the facilitator and the resources (see Section 3.2).

Facilitation For a given query, this is the action of finding a (set of) resources that comply with a satisfiability (or suitability) criterion. In other words, it is the action of finding a resource whose advertised capability matches the requirements derived from the query. This satisfiability criterion depends on the search strategy adopted for the resolution of the query but it is always somewhere in the spectrum bounded by "the most exact match" on one hand and by "the set of all approximate matches" on the other hand. In other words, the satisfiability criterion is a tradeoff between correctness and completeness in the set of solutions.

3.1 CCQL Facilitation Performatives

As stated in Section 2, CCQL is a subset of KQML [11]. The two main functionalities described in the previous section are supported by the following CCQL operations:

Advertisement Every resource willing to advertise its capabilities does so first by registering with a facilitator (by sending a `register` message containing the references and location of the resource), then by sending an `advertise` message containing the formal description of its capabilities (see Section 3.2). No replies are issued to the originators of these messages unless an error has occured.

Facilitation The protocol encapsulating the facilitation mechanism has two variants:

Forwarding: on receiving a query enclosed in a `recommend_one` (or `recommend_all`) message, the facilitator will reply to the agent at the origin of the query, a singleton (or a list) of matching advertisements (including the references to the corresponding resource). The replied advertisement(s) is contained in a `forward` message.

Brokerage: on receiving a query enclosed in a `broker_one` (or `broker_all`) message, the facilitator will send the enclosed query to the most (or all) relevant resource. The answer to the query is then brought back to the facilitator, which in turn forwards the reply to the originator of the query.

3.2 Expressing capabilities

A resource capability must be represented intentionally for compactness, but in a way that minimises imprecision. The abstract characteristics of a resource are:

- network information to locate and query the wrapper of the resource;

- the CCQL performatives that the wrapper can handle;

- the intentional content of the resource (or a subset of it);

- an abstract representation of the functionality of the resource.

Advertisements are the basic data structure used to communicate these characteristics. The terms used in the body of advertisments are defined in the shared ontology. The possible components of an advertisement are:

- list of allowed CCQL *performatives*;

- list of available *services*, where each service is defined in the shared ontology;

- list of *domains* that the database can deal with, where each domain is defined in the shared ontology;

- specification of a subset of the CIF language, delimiting the expressiveness of the resource query language within CIF as a whole.

The facilitator encapsulates a database of received advertisements with the above components; the CCQL facilitation operations (forwarding and brokerage) are implemented as queries on this advertisement database.

An example CCQL advertisement message follows (the KRAFT message header is not shown). This advertisement is from the wrapper of a PC software vendor called os_vendor, sent to a facilitator called yellow_pages. The content says that the advertiser can handle CCQL ask_one and ask_all messages, expressed in a subset of CIF corresponding to SQL queries (from the service description, defined in the shared ontology), about ontology concepts pc_os (PC operating systems) and pc_util (PC utility software).

```
ccql(advertise, [
    sender : os_vendor,
    receiver : yellow_pages,
    reply_with : id(66),
    ontology : advertise_ontology,
    language : cif,
    content : [
        advertisement.performativeList =
            [ ask_one, ask_all ],
        advertisement.serviceList = [ <database, sql> ],
        advertisement.domainList = [ pc_os, pc_util ] ]
])
```

4   Wrapper Agents and the Shared Ontology

There are three levels of heterogeneity that inhibit the re-use of information stored in resources that we wish to connect to a KRAFT network:

1. *interaction:* different knowledge sources can be interacted with in different ways, e g. some systems only allow the user to pose queries whereas other systems will ask the user for information;

2. *syntactic:* knowledge sources use different representation formats;

3. *semantic:* variations in terminology across knowledge sources.

As outlined in Section 2, interaction and syntactic heterogeneity are addressed by the use of the CCQL and CIF protocols within the KRAFT network and by providing wrapper agents that translate all messages into and out of these protocols. Here we focus on the third of these levels.

To overcome the problem of semantic heterogeneity, a *shared ontology* is specified, which formally defines the terminology of the problem domain. The content of messages within a KRAFT network must be expressed using terms that are defined in the shared ontology. For each knowledge source, a local ontology is specified. For example, where the knowledge source is a database, the local ontology defines the terms that are used in the database schema. Between a local ontology and the shared ontology, there will be a number of *ontology mismatches*, which are instances of semantic heterogeneity [15]. These include the use of different terms to refer to the same concept (i.e. synonyms) and the use of the same term to refer to different concepts (i.e. homonyms). To overcome these mismatches, for each knowledge source an *ontology mapping* is defined. An ontology mapping is a partial function that specifies mappings between terms and expressions defined in a source ontology to terms and expressions defined in a target ontology. To enable bidirectional translation between a KRAFT network and a knowledge source, two such ontology mappings must be defined. We will now describe the format that we use to specify ontology mappings.

In defining an ontology mapping, we begin by specifying a set of ordered pairs or *ontological correspondences*. An ontological correspondence specifies the term or expression in the target ontology that represents as closely as possible the meaning of the source ontology term or expression. For each term in the source ontology, we try to identify a corresponding term in the target ontology. It may not be possible to directly map all of the source ontology terms to a corresponding target ontology term. For some of the terms in the source ontology that cannot be mapped in this way, it may be possible to include them in the ontology mapping by defining correspondences between compound expressions. This leads us to the following classification of ontological correspondences:

1. *class-to-class:* maps a source ontology class name to a target ontology class name;

2. *attribute-type-to-attribute-type:* maps the set of values of a source ontology attribute to a set of values of a target ontology attribute;

3. *attribute-to-attribute:* maps a source ontology attribute name to a target onto-logy attribute name;

4. *relation-to-relation:* maps a source ontology relation name to a target ontology relation name;

5. *compound-expression-to-compound-expression:* maps compound source onto-logy expressions to compound target ontology expressions.

As the local and shared ontologies are not represented in the same format that is used for the CIF, the semantic transformation of CIF expressions by wrappers is not based directly on ontology mappings. The relevant ontology mappings are used as part of the specification of a wrapper rather than directly by the wrapper. Consequently, developers have complete autonomy in the implementation of wrappers. In the current KRAFT prototype described in Section 6, we have implemented the transformation of CIF expressions using rewrite rules [8].

A pair of terms and/or expressions in an ontological correspondence are not ne-cessarily semantically equivalent. However, when a wrapper translates a CIF expres-sion, we need to ensure that the target CIF expression is semantically equivalent to the source CIF expression. If this were not the case, constraints passed to a mediator using terms defined in the shared ontology could express very different knowledge than the original constraints expressed in terms defined in the local ontology. We ensure that the semantics of CIF expressions are maintained by defining *pre-* and *post-conditions* for each ontological correspondence. A wrapper that implements an ontology map-ping must ensure that these conditions are satisfied when translating the terms in CIF expressions from the source to the target ontology.

5 Mediator Agents and Constraint Fusion

5.1 Constraint Fusion

An application problem in KRAFT is specified by constraint fragments distributed in different resources. Each constraint is part of a conjunctive statement describing the application problem as a constraint satisfaction problem (CSP).

Consider the PC hardware configuration domain: Problem solving knowledge comes from the user requirements, restrictions attached to hardware components from different vendors, and generic design knowledge governing a workable configuration. The following example constraint from the user agent specifies that the PC must use a "pentium2" processor but not the "win95" OS:

```
constrain each p in pc
    to have cpu(p)="pentium2"
    and name(has_os(p)) <> "win95"
```

For the components to fit together, they must satisfy certain constraints. For ex-ample, the size of the OS must be smaller or equal to the hard disk space for a proper installation:

```
constrain each p in pc
    to have size(has_os(p)) =< size(has_disk(p))
```

Now the candidate components from different vendors may have instructions attached to them as constraints. In the vendor database of operating systems, "winNT" requires a memory of at least 32 megabytes:

```
constrain each p in pc such that name(has_os(p))="winNT"
    to have memory(p) >= 32
```

The KRAFT approach to this task employs a constraint-fusing mediator which extracts and combines constraints from distributed sources for problem solving purposes. Constraints as abstract mobile objects are transported and transformed to compose a constraint satisfaction problem (CSP), which is then analysed and solved by a combination of distributed database queries and constraint logic programs. With the help of a facilitator, this approach allows tailoring of an execution plan in a dynamic environment, depending on the capability and availability of active online resources.

Our sample constraints give the following fused constraint, which describes the overall requirement on the variables involved:

```
constrain each p in pc
    to have cpu(p)="pentium2"
    and name(has_os(p)) <> "win95"
    and size(has_os(p)) =< size(has_disk(p))
    and if name(has_os(p))="winNT"
        then memory(p)) >= 32
        else true
```

The reason for fusing the constraint fragments is to provide the basis for exploring how the CSP can best be divided into sub-problems of distributed database queries and sub-CSPs. When a single piece of constraint is insufficient to solve a CSP effectively, we hope to combine information from multiple constraint fragments to arrive at a more solvable solution. It is from the fusion process that useful information can be inferred and captured for problem solving purposes.

5.2 CSP Solving

The constraint fusion process composes a concrete description of the overall CSP in a declarative form. To solve a composed CSP efficiently, a mediator feeds it into a problem decomposer which extracts selection information from the CSP description to generate distributed database queries, with the remaining constraints forming a smaller sub-CSP. The mediator then sends these database queries in multiple messages to different database wrappers to retrieve candidate data values.

Database query generation constitutes an important phase of pre-processing. It shifts part of the problem solving process into the distributed databases by composing data filters as database queries. This prevents unnecessary transportation of irrelevant data into the KRAFT domain and relieves network traffic in a distributed system. Data filtering by database query generation, however, is not sufficient to resolve all constraints. The amount of selection information which can be represented as database queries depends on the expressiveness of the database query language. The remaining sub-CSP has to be resolved by a more powerful constraint solver in the next stage. The final stage of the problem solving process is to feed data and constraints into a constraint solver so that solutions to the CSP can be obtained. In the current proto-type, described in Section 6, we use the finite domain constraint solver in the ECLiPSe constraint logic programming (CLP) system.

To form the initial value domains of variables in a CLP program, candidate data retrieved in the previous stage are compiled into CLP data structures. The sub-CSP which is formed by the problem decomposer is then compiled into CLP program codes to impose constraints on these variables. Finally, the mediator sends the CLP program and data to the constraint solver and waits for the result to be returned.

6   An Example KRAFT Application

The KRAFT architecture is being tested on a realistic application in the domain of tele-communications network data services design; this application has been provided by BT. The network data services design problem considered by KRAFT is in the phase of network configuration from the viewpoint of a customer at a single site, allowing a BT network designer to select to meet the customers' requirements: (1) a suitable Point of Presence (POP) at which to connect to the BT network and (2) suitable Customer Premises Equipment (CPE) with which to service the connection (types of CPE include routers, bridges, and FRADs, though it was decided to focus initially solely on router products).

A conceptual view of the application architecture is shown in Figure 2(a). Note that a more detailed description of the network data services design application appears in [7]. In the current implementation, all KRAFT agents (mediators, facilitators, and wrappers) are implemented in Prolog. The user interfaces (user agent and message monitor) are Java applications. The database resources are managed by independent instances of the P/FDM DBMS[1], each with its own local schema. The constraint solver is ECLiPSe. Inter-agent communication is implemented by asynchronous message passing using the Linda model [5].

The prototype application employs three sources of knowledge:

- a database of POP information;

- two databases of CPE information: one for each of two competing router vendors.

These information sources are considered to be pre-existing legacy databases. For the purposes of the prototype, simplified versions of these databases were created; however, care was taken to ensure that the databases of CPE information were created independently, so as to ensure realistic heterogeneity. Each of the databases was populated with data and constraints; for example, a vendor database was populated with data on the vendor's CPE products, and constraints defining the valid usage of each product. The main aim of creating the three resources was to test the feasibility of creating wrapper agents to transform between the internal knowledge representation (data and constraints) and the KRAFT CIF language.

In the prototype, the tasks of identifying potential POPs and CPEs are the responsibility of mediators. As the two tasks are independent in practice (it is possible

---

[1]http://www.csd.abdn.ac.uk/~pfdm

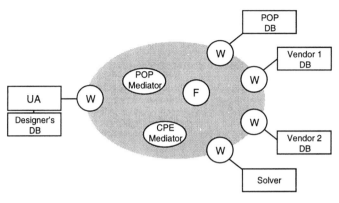

(a) The Network Services Scenario conceptual architecture

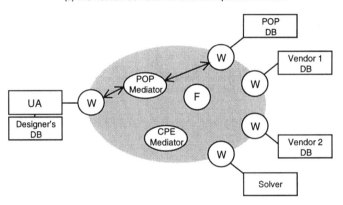

(b) Network Services Scenario interaction 1: locate a POP

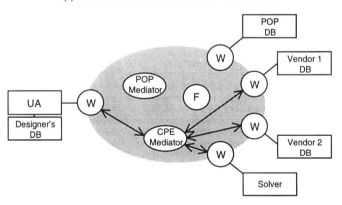

(c) Network Services Scenario interaction 2: locate a CPE

Figure 2: A conceptual view of the KRAFT architecture.

to select a CPE on the basis of a customer's LAN and WAN requirements, without knowing which POP will be used, and vice versa), it was decided to provide a separate mediator for each task.

A user agent serves as the front-end to the test system, with a graphical user interface allowing a BT network designer to enter the customer's requirements, and launch two kinds of query into the KRAFT system:

1. For a POP query, the user specifies the location of the customers' site, and the customers' required wide-area network (WAN) services (for example, Frame Relay and ISDN). The user agent formulates the POP query as a KRAFT message, and attempts to locate an agent that can answer the query. It does this by contacting a facilitator, which in turn puts it in contact with the POP Mediator. Upon receipt of the user agent's query, the POP mediator obtains a list of POPs from the POP DB, and filters these according to the user's requirements. It then sends a reply to the user agent. If one or more suitable POPs were found these will be displayed to the user, ranked in order of proximity to the customers' site. These interactions are shown in Figure 2(b).

2. For a CPE query, the user specifies additional constraints on the type of equipment needed, including support for various LAN protocols used within the customer's site (TCP/IP, AppleTalk, 10 base T Ethernet, etc) and support for the required WAN services that determined the choice of POP (Frame Relay, ISDN, etc). Having acquired these constraints, the user agent issues a query to the KRAFT network as above. This time, the CPE Mediator interacts with vendors to select apparently-suitable products, together with any "small print" constraints on these. Fusing these constraints with those from the customer's requirements, the CPE Mediator then calls upon a constraint solver to identify actually-suitable CPE products. These it relays back to the user agent. These interactions are shown in Figure 2(c).

The prototype application has been constructed and is currently under evaluation. Further details on the prototype are available in [7].

7   Conclusion

This paper has described the KRAFT architecture for knowledge fusion and transformation. The generic framework of the architecture is reusable across a wide range of knowledge fusion systems. In addition to the network data services design application described in the previous section, the framework of the KRAFT architecture has been tested in prototype systems for advising students on options to transfer between universities, and advising health care practitioners on drug therapies [13]. Specific software components of the KRAFT system are also reusable, including the CCQL messaging system, facilitators, wrapper shells, and several mediator and solving-related components. Evaluation of the KRAFT architecture is ongoing, and refinements will continue to be made.

Acknowledgements   KRAFT is a collaborative research project between the Universities of Aberdeen, Cardiff and Liverpool, and BT. The project is funded by EPSRC and BT. We would like to thank Mike Shave and Jean-Christophe Pazzaglia for their comments on an earlier draft of this paper.

References

[1] Y. Arens, R. Hull, R. King, and M. Siegel, Reference architecture for the intelligent integration of information, Technical report, DARPA — Defense Advanced Research project Agency, August 1995.

[2] N. Bassiliades and P. M. D. Gray, CoLan: A functional constraint language and its implementation, *Data and Knowledge Engineering*, 14:203–249, 1994.

[3] W. P. Birmingham,   An agent-based architecture for digital libraries. *D-Lib Magazine*, July 1995.

[4] U. M. Borghoff, R. Pareschi, H. Karch, M. Nöhmeier, and J. H. Schlichter, Constraint-based information gathering for a network publication system,   In *Proc. 1st Int. Conf. on the Practical Application of Intelligent Agents and Multi-Agent Technology*, pages 45–59, April 1996.

[5] N. Carriero and D. Gelernter, Linda in Context, *Communications of the ACM*, 32:444–458, 1989.

[6] L. Chiariglione, FIPA — agent technologies achieve maturity, *AgentLink Newsletter*, 1:2–4, 1998.

[7] N. J. Fiddian, P. Marti, J-C. Pazzaglia, K. Hui, A. Preece, D. M. Jones, and Z. Cui, Application of KRAFT in data service network design, *BT Technical Journal*, in press.

[8] P. M. D. Gray, S. M. Embury, K. Y. Hui, and G. Kemp, The evolving role of constraints in the functional data model, *Journal of Intelligent Information Systems*, 1–27, 1999.

[9] N. Jennings, P. Faratin, M. Johnson, T. Norman, P. O'Brien, and M. Wiegand, Agent-based business process management, *International Journal of Cooperative Information Systems*, 5:105-130, 1996.

[10] D. R. Kuokka, J. G. McGuire, J. C. Weber, J. M. Tenenbaum, T. R. Gruber, and G. R. Olsen, Shade: Technology for knowledge-based collaborative engineering, *Journal of Concurrent Engineering: Applications and Research*, 1(2), 1993.

[11] Y. Labrou, *Semantics for an Agent Communication Language*, PhD Thesis, University of Maryland, Baltimore MD, USA, 1996.

[12] R. Neches, R. Fikes, T. Finin, T. Gruber, R. Patil, T. Senator, and W. Swartout, Enabling technology for knowledge sharing, *AI Magazine*, 12:36–56, 1991.

[13] A. Preece, A. Borrowman, and T. Francis, Reusable components for KB and DB integration, in *ECAI'98 Workshop on Intelligent Information Integration*, 157–168, 1998.

[14] N. Singh, M. Genesereth, and M. A. Syed, A distributed and anonymous knowledge sharing approach to software interoperation, *International Journal of Cooperative Information Systems*, 4(4):339–367, 1995.

[15] P. R. S. Visser, D. M. Jones, T. J. M. Bench-Capon, and M. J. R. Shave, Assessing heterogeneity by classifying ontology mismatches, in *Proc. International Conference on Formal Ontology in Information Systems (FOIS'98)*, IOS Press, 148–162, 1998.

[16] G. Wiederhold, Mediators in the architecture of future information systems, *IEEE Computer*, 38–49, March 1992.

SESSION 1
LEARNING

Sequencing Training Examples for Iterative Knowledge Refinement

Nirmalie Wiratunga and Susan Craw

School of Computer and Mathematical Sciences

The Robert Gordon University,

St Andrew Street, Aberdeen AB25 1HG, Scotland, UK

Email: nw|smc@scms.rgu.ac.uk

Abstract

Refinement tools seek to correct faulty knowledge based systems (KBSs) by identifying and repairing faults that are indicated by training examples for which the KBS gives an incorrect solution. Refinement tools typically use a hill-climbing search to identify suitable repairs. Backtracking search algorithms, developed for constraint satisfaction problems, have been incorporated with an iterative knowledge refinement tool, to solve local maxima problems. This paper investigates how the efficiency of such a tool can be improved and introduces new and general heuristics for ordering training examples. Experimental results reveal that these heuristics applied to static and dynamic ordering of training examples can significantly improve the efficiency of the iterative refinement tool, without increasing the error-rate of the final refined KBS.

1   Introduction

Refinement tools support the knowledge acquisition and development of knowledge based systems (KBSs) by assisting the debugging of incorrect systems and the adaptive maintenance of KBSs whose problem-solving environment changes [3]. Refinement tools are presented with examples that indicate there are one or more faults in the KBS; these are often examples of problem-solving where the expert's solution is inconsistent with the KBS's solution. The tool also benefits from knowing some correctly solved examples as well, so that repairs are not too closely fitted to wrongly-solved examples only, to the detriment of the KBS's more general problem solving. Therefore the training set for the refinement tool's learning contains a selection of wrongly and correctly solved examples, each consisting of the facts that describe the problem-solving task, together with the expert's solution.

Refinement tools adopt an incremental approach where each cycle attempts to fix one or more, but typically not all, of the wrongly-solved examples in the training set, and to reduce the error-rate on the training set with a view to reducing the error-rate more generally. The refinement task is sufficiently complex that the space of possible repairs demands a heuristic search, typically hill-climbing. EITHER [12] and FORTE [14] try to repair the outstanding fault that is indicated by the *largest* number of examples, and choose the repair with the *fewest* changes to rules which are *nearest* the observables. KRUSTTools are KBS specific refinement tools, assembled from our KRUSTWorks generic refinement toolkit and the refinement algorithm central to this family also applies a hill-climbing search. Although it generates many refined KBSs designed to fix each incorrect example, it then chooses the refined KBS with the *lowest* error-rate on the training examples as the input KBS for the next iteration. The result is that refinement tools are dogged by the standard hill-climbing problem of getting caught in local maxima, so the performance of the KBS must be reduced before an overall improvement can be gained.

In previous work we described how informed backtracking search algorithms from Constraint Satisfaction Problems (CSPs) can be incorporated within knowledge refinement so that KRUSTTools may exploit previously abandoned repairs when the refinement process comes to a halt [18]. In this paper we investigate how the efficiency of such search algorithms can be improved. Section 2 illustrates situations when KRUSTTools fail to generate refined KBSs and indicates how backtracking search is applied. We introduce concepts from CSPs and outline the search algorithm that proved best for knowledge refinement in Section 3. Heuristics to improve efficiency are discussed in Section 4 and experimental results are presented in Section 5. We conclude with directions for future work in Section 6.

2 Refinement with a KRUSTTool

A faulty KBS is incrementally refined by a KRUSTTool based on the fault evidence provided by examples $e_1, \ldots, e_n$ (Figure 1). This process is iterative with examples utilized one at a time. The input KBS for each iteration is the best refined KBS from the previous iteration, or the original faulty KBS in the first iteration. The *training examples buffer* contains all examples that are yet to be used by the KRUSTTool, and the top most example in this buffer at each iteration is chosen as the *refinement example* and drives that refinement cycle. If the refinement example is correctly solved then refinement is not required, otherwise the fault evidence is employed to allocate blame, generate refinements and implement them as refined KBSs. The refinement example is then transfered into the *constraint examples buffer*, containing all previously solved examples. The constraint examples buffer helps filter the potential refined KBSs, by rejecting those that incorrectly answer any of the constraint examples. The filtered refined KBSs are then ranked by their error-rate on the training examples buffer. Consequently, the refined KBS with the lowest error-rate is the best refined KBS for this iteration.

The KRUSTTool algorithm is unusual in generating many refined KBSs in each iteration, and the hill-climbing selection of the *one* best refined KBS for the next iteration occurs at the *end* of each cycle. This offers the possibility of backtracking to alternative refined KBSs thereby achieving a best-first search. Figure 2 illustrates the start of a potential backtracking scenario; the updates to the training examples buffer (tebuf) and the constraint examples buffer (cebuf)

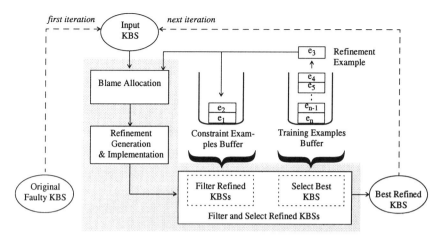

Figure 1: The KRUSTTool Process.

are shown on the right. Refinement example e_2 generates 3 refined KBSs and R_{21} is selected as best. Refinement examples e_3 and e_4 generate several refined KBSs and again the best is selected. But now suppose R_{41} cannot be refined by e_5 because although 4 refinements are generated, all are rejected by cebuf; this is shown by a darkly shaded node for e_5.

So what should the refinement algorithm do now: continue with e_6 and ignore the fact that e_5 is not corrected, and is unlikely to be by future refinements? A better alternative backtracks through the solution space of refined KBSs and restarts the refinement process from an earlier node. Simple backtracking undoes each step one at a time, and so refinement is restarted with R_{42} and e_5. In the next section we look at a more informed backtracking that helps restart refinement from earlier points when appropriate, say R_{22} with e_3.

3 Informed Backtracking

We borrow an approach developed to direct the backtracking search for solutions to constraint satisfaction problems (CSPs). We outline the CSP method and then draw an analogy between CSPs and knowledge refinement so that we can adapt the method for knowledge refinement.

3.1 Heuristic Searches Solve CSPs

CSPs consist of a set of ordered variables $\{v_1, \ldots, v_n\}$, a specified domain for each variable v_i and a set of constraints. A constraint is a relation defined on a subset of variables, specifying all simultaneous value assignments within this subset that are forbidden by this constraint. A CSP solution is an instantiation of each variable with a value from its respective domain such that none of the

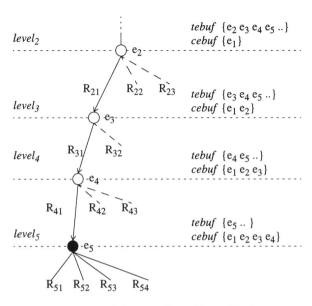

Figure 2: A Backtracking KRUSTTool.

constraints is violated [17]. CSPs are often solved by constructive algorithms where each variable is instantiated in turn, so that the constraints are satisfied for this and the previous variable instantiations.

However, this hill-climbing approach may also fail: the next variable v_i may not be instantiated without violating the constraints involving v_i and the previous variables $v_1, \ldots, v_{i-1}$. Various backtracking searches have been proposed that partially undo the instantiation and resume the constructive process from a previous variable instantiation. We shall re-use chronological backtracking (BT) [1] and backjumping (BJ) [7]. Unlike BT, BJ does not step back to the previous variable v_{i-1} but instead jumps back to the latest variable v_j whose instantiation conflicts with any of the instantiations for v_i. If there are no new instantiations available for v_j then BJ reverts to backtracking from v_j. With binary CSPs, where all constraints contain at most 2 variables BJ will still find all solutions [10].

3.2 A Backjumping KRUSTTool

In refinement, we incrementally refine the KBS to correctly answer the current and previous refinement examples. So, the most natural analogy between CSPs and refinement links variables with training examples, the current variable with the refinement example, and instantiated variables with correctly solved constraint examples in cebuf. CSP constraints correspond to achieving consistency with the constraint examples. Finally the domain for a variable is the repairs triggered by fault evidence provided by the refinement example.

The KRUSTTool algorithm must backjump when the refinement example e_i and the input KBS R fail to create any refined KBSs (i.e. the generated KBSs $Generated_{Ri}$ is empty) or those generated are rejected by the constraint examples (i.e. the filtered KBSs $Filtered_{Ri}$ is empty). If $Filtered_{Ri} = \{\}$ then we must determine the most recent constraint example that caused the removal of each generated KBS, and backjump there. If $Generated_{Ri} = \{\}$ then BT is the only option; no conflicting constraint examples can be identified since there are no KBSs to test!

Let us revisit the scenario in Figure 2. $Generated_{R_415} = \{R_{51}, R_{52}, R_{53}, R_{54}\}$ and so refinement can backjump, but since $Filtered_{R_415} = \{\}$, each KBS in $Generated_{R_415}$ must have been rejected by at least one constraint example in cebuf. Suppose R_{51}, R_{52} wrongly solve e_2, and R_{53}, R_{54} wrongly solve e_3. Then refinement will continue from e_3, because it is the most recent on the path. The next available refined KBS R_{32} is selected with e_4 as the refinement example. Finally, e_5 is moved back into tebuf to be a future refinement example. If no more KBSs were available from e_3 then BJ backtracks to node e_2.

There are two obvious differences between CSPs and refinement. Firstly, the domain of potential repairs is not known in advance, instead it is constructed incrementally during refinement generation and filtering. This is handled by associating refined KBSs with refinement examples that generate them, and reasoning about backjumping using constraint examples rather than KBSs. Secondly, the behaviour of constraint examples can change – they can become uncorrected and so provide new fault evidence generating further refined KBSs. The algorithm identifies and reinstates these examples in tebuf.

4 Improving Backjumping for Refinement

Backjumping was introduced as a way to reduce the search of backtracking. Contrary to expectation we found that BJ often increases the number of iterations but that these extra iterations were used profitably and the BJ KRUST-Tool on average provided refined KBSs with lower error-rates than the BT KRUSTTool [18]. Therefore our next concern is to improve efficiency of the BJ KRUSTTool by reducing the number of refinement cycles without increasing the error-rate. We investigated techniques that improve CSP search efficiency [15].

- Value ordering heuristics select those values that conflict least with variables that are yet to be instantiated;

- Variable ordering heuristics deal with most constrained variables first.

CSP value ordering is analogous to ordering the refined KBSs; KRUSTTools already does this when the accuracy filter orders the refined KBSs in increasing order of error-rate on tebuf. In fact the general KRUSTTool approach is closely related to the repair-based approach to solving CSPs and its greedy min-conflict heuristic for repair selection [11]; and the refined KBS ordering itself is similar to the look-ahead value ordering min-conflicts heuristic that ranks the values of a variable in increasing order based on the number of incompatibilities with values of future variables [6].

For the rest of this paper, we concentrate on how variable ordering can be applied to a KRUSTTool. A CSP variable is generally constrained in two ways, firstly by the constraints it is involved in and secondly by its domain size. Most common variable ordering heuristics exploit these 2 properties [5, 8]. Heuristics for static ordering exploit relationships among variables identified from the topology of the constraint graph [17]. Dynamic variable ordering addresses the fact that invariably the best variable order is different in different branches of the search tree, by taking advantage of the information available after each variable instantiation to move the search to branches that are more likely to contain a solution [9]. Various look-ahead strategies select the variable that most constrains the remainder of the search [16]. The motivation behind all such heuristics is to deal with difficult variables first.

We now turn to how this is applied to knowledge refinement. CSP variables involved in the most or tightest constraints correspond to training examples whose repairs put the highest consistency demands on other training examples; current work investigates clustering training examples as a way to address this. CSP variables with the smallest domain correspond to refinement examples that generate the smallest set of refined KBSs in a refinement cycle. But, going as far as refinement generation can be computationally expensive. In this paper we establish heuristics that predict how constrained the refinement cycle for each training example will be, and use these to order the training examples.

4.1 Evidence From the Recent Refinement Cycle

Simple constrainedness information comes from the newly completed refinement cycle; where the final step executed all the refined KBSs generated in that cycle on the remaining training examples in tebuf. Although this was done to calculate the error-rate of each of these refined KBSs, it also determines an estimate of how faulty each training example is; i.e. how many of these refined KBSs got the training example wrong. Remember, all these refined KBSs are related since they were all derived from the previous best refined KBS.

Table 1 demonstrates how fault evidence from the most recent refinement cycle can be employed to select the next refinement example from tebuf. Let us assume that m refined KBSs $R_{i1}, R_{i2}, \ldots, R_{im}$ were generated with e_i as the refinement example and that tebuf now contains training examples e_{i+1}, $e_{i+2}, \ldots, e_n$. The table entry for e_j and R_{ik} has value 1 if R_{ik} **incorrectly** answers e_j, and 0 otherwise. Therefore, the *error-rate* of R_{ik} on tebuf, $err_{R_{ik}}$ is the column total (divided by n). The row total f_j is the level of *faultiness* of e_j as judged by $R_{i1}, R_{i2}, \ldots, R_{im}$. The refined KBS with the lowest error-rate, $\min(err_{R_{ik}})$, is selected as the best refined KBS. We now use, the training example with the highest level of faultiness, $\max(f_j)$, as the next refinement example. All ties are broken randomly.

Generated Refined KBSs

		R_{i1}	R_{i2}	$\ldots$	R_{im}	*faultiness*
tebuf	e_{i+1}	1	0	$\ldots$	0	$f_{e_{i+1}}$
	e_{i+2}	0	1	$\ldots$	0	$f_{e_{i+2}}$
	$\vdots$	$\vdots$	$\vdots$	$\ldots$	$\vdots$	$\vdots$
	e_n	1	1	$\ldots$	0	f_{e_n}
	error-rate	$err_{R_{i1}}$	$err_{R_{i2}}$	$\ldots$	$err_{R_{im}}$	

Table 1: Faultiness of remaining examples.

This heuristic is reminiscent of the best known CSP dynamic ordering heuristic, dynamic search rearrangement (DSR), which selects the next variable having the minimal number of values that are consistent with the current partial solution [5]. Of course the difference is that with knowledge refinement the set of potential refined KBSs is not known in advance and so we use fault evidence from the most recent potential refined KBSs as the basis for selecting the most constrained training example for the next iteration.

4.2 Evidence From How the Problem was Solved

A more direct estimate of how many refinements will be generated for a particular training example is the number of places where the problem solving behaviour for that training example can be changed. The KRUSTTool algorithm already creates a data structure containing precisely this information. The *problem graph* captures the problem-solving for the refinement example and allows the KRUSTTool to reason about the fault that is being demonstrated [4]. Essentially, the problem graph records what happened, and also shows all possible rule activation routes to the required goal, of which only one is actually used. Problem graphs can become quite complex with long chains and complicated branching. Figure 3 shows some simple problem graphs with which we illustrate their function. Training example A is a problem described by a set of observables including $T_{A1} - T_{A4}$, which the expert solves as $goal_A$. However the KBS currently reasons from the observables by applying leaf rules $R7$ and $R4$, which together allow a middle rule $R13$ to fire, and finally the end rule $R11$ concludes S_A the faulty solution. The darkened area of the problem graph is the *positive problem graph* and corresponds to the problem solving that has been undertaken by the faulty KBS. Therefore it contains the solution subgraph for the training example but also contains other partial proofs; e.g. T_{A1} allows $R7$ to fire, but this only partially satisfies $R12$. The positive problem graphs for the other 2 training examples are similar but notice neither provides a solution since each partial solution subgraph terminates with an intermediate result.

Repairs correspond to preventing faulty rule chains from being activated and so the number of rule activations in the positive problem graph is a sim-

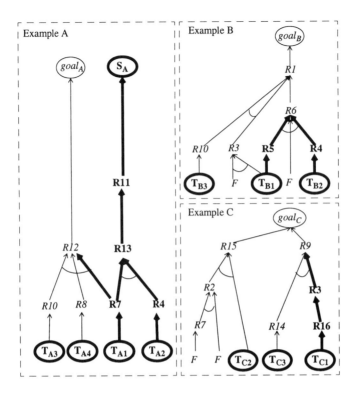

Figure 3: Problem Graph for training examples, A, B and C.

ple measure to predict the number of potential refined KBSs, and hence how constrained the refinement cycle for that training example will be. Activation counts for training examples A, B and C in Figure 3 return 4, 2 and 2 respectively, indicating that B and C are the most (and equally) constrained and so will be selected over A. All ties are broken randomly.

4.3   Evidence From How the Problem Should be Solved

The problem graph captures more about the problem-solving than simply recording what happened. It also contains a *negative problem graph* that shows all possible rule activation routes to the required goal. Thus in Figure 3 the expert's solution for training example A ($goal_A$) has not been proved because, $R10$, $R8$ and $R12$ are only partially satisfied, and are unable to fire. We have not darkened the arrows leading from T_{A3} and T_{A4} to indicate that the conditions in $R10$ and $R8$ do not match observables T_{A3} and T_{A4}, and must be weakened before they are satisfied. In contrast conditions in $R4$, $R13$ or $R11$ must be strengthened in order to stop S_A being asserted. Similar explanations hold for training examples B and C, but now in addition some rule conditions (e.g. the first condition of $R3$ for training example B), cannot be weakened to match any observable or rule conclusion and so are not linked to any rule or observable but instead these "non-observables" are labelled F.

The negative problem graph provides additional information on how constrained the refinement cycle will be. Counting all the rule "activations" in both the positive and negative parts of the problem graph provides a second measure of constrainedness. This measure promises to be more informative since it adds the locations of possible repairs in the negative problem graph to those from the positive part.

In practice we found it was better to distinguish between rules in the negative problem graph whose conditions could be weakened to match observables from those that could never match. We amended the heuristic so that it ignored any negative rule activation whose conditions are *all* linked to (or derived from) "non-observables" (F's in the diagram); e.g. rules $R7$ and $R2$ will be omitted from C's count. Without this modification the heuristic can estimate a training example like C to be less constrained than it actually is. Such an amendment requires the assumption that training examples are noise free and that leaf rules are correct, however this seems acceptable given our need simply to estimate constrainedness.

Table 2 lists all the refinement places for the 3 training examples at the left. The count of rule activations in the complete problem graph, with and without the non-observables correction, appears at the right. Therefore, example C with the lowest improved rule activation count is selected over A and B. We note that although the improved heuristic is a good predictor of the number of refinements here, more complex problem graphs may need a more sophisticated way to combine rule activation counts from the positive and negative parts of the problem graph.

Training	Refinements				Rule Activations	
Example	Strengthen	Weaken	None	Count	All	Improved
A	$R4$ $R13$ $R11$	$R10$ $R8$ $R12$	$R7$	6	7	7
B		$R1$ $R3$ $R10$ $R6$	$R5$ $R4$	4	6	6
C		$R9$ $R14$ $R15$	$R3$ $R16$ $R7$ $R2$	3	7	5

Table 2: Refinements and rule activations from the complete problem graph.

5 Results

We evaluate backjumping KRUSTTools that apply static and/or dynamic ordering of the training examples using the heuristics we have developed in Section 4. The problem graph heuristics define a static ordering of the training examples before the iterative refinement cycles are started. They can also be used for dynamic ordering where the measures are recalculated on the best refined KBS output from a cycle and applied to re-order the remaining training examples. The emphasis of the evaluation is to compare the number of iterations, error-rate and finally the resource usage.

Our testbed is a corrupted student loans KBS, created by introducing 5 faults to the 20 rules in the original KBS [13]: an extra rule, a changed comparison operator in 2 rules and an extra condition in 2 other rules. Although this is not a highly realistic scenario, the faults are sufficiently interacting that it allows experimentation in carefully controlled conditions.

Since our experiments involve an assessment of the effectiveness of backjumping with various orderings of training examples, we had to ensure that backtracking is triggered. We chose 8 specific "difficult" examples from the standard student loans dataset that are correctly answered by the uncorrupted KBS, but whose repairs for the corrupted KBS are particularly conflicting. In fact there are 9 ways to pair these 8 examples so that the refined KBSs triggered by one training example tightly interacts with the other's refined KBSs. We then randomly selected a further 22 "normal" examples to make a 30 example dataset for our experiments.

For each run we randomly select n conflicting pairs, duplicates are removed and further examples are randomly selected (from the "normal" examples) until the training set contained 15 examples. The remaining 15 examples become the independent test set. The dataset was partitioned this way 20 times, with 8 conflicting pairs in the first 10 runs, and 9 conflicting pairs in the next 10 runs. The results of each experiment refer to these 20 training/test splits. Significance results are based on a 95% confidence level and apply the Wilcoxen signed-rank test (2 data sets) or the Kruskal Wallis test (3 or more data sets), since our data is not normally distributed.

5.1 Static Ordering

Static ordering provides a sequence of training examples prior to the iterative refinement cycles. We compare two orderings using the problem graph heuristics[1] with a random ordering.

- RANDOM: move all correctly solved training examples into cebuf then randomly order tebuf.

- PGRAPH+: move all correctly solved training examples into cebuf, then

---

[1]The other heuristic (Section 4.1) can only be applied as a dynamic ordering since it exploits information from all the refined KBSs from the previous cycle.

sort the remaining training examples in decreasing order of the number of rule activations in the positive problem graph only.

- PGRAPH±: as for PGRAPH+ but use the number of rule activations in the complete problem graph (positive and negative) including the modification for "non-observables".

Error-rate for the final refined KBS was not impaired by PGRAPH+ and PGRAPH±, and they both reduced the error compared to RANDOM in 4 test runs. More pertinent to this evaluation is the number of iterations for these three algorithms listed in Table 3. PGRAPH+ required significantly (p-value = 0.028) fewer iterations compared to RANDOM; 10 test runs had fewer iterations and only 2 test runs had more iterations and this was at most 2 iterations longer. PGRAPH± improved on PGRAPH+ by reducing the number of iterations in 4 test runs, however despite the added information acquired from the negative problem graph this reduction is not statistically significant. Any improvements in PGRAPH± over PGRAPH+ is due to the added information causing fewer ties, which essentially mean fewer randomly resolved tie-breaks. This may be explained by observing that refinement generation explores both the positive and negative problem graphs and that refinements can include changes to both parts of the reasoning. Therefore a more complex combination of the rule activation counts may be required so that it takes account of those activations that contribute towards the required goal and are also part of the positive problem graph, by not counting them as individual activations.

Static ordering	Mean	Median	95% Confidence
RANDOM	9.05	8.0	±1.420
PGRAPH+	7.65	7.0	±0.717
PGRAPH±	7.65	7.5	±0.410

Table 3: Number of iterations for static ordering.

The test results clearly indicate that the order in which training examples are processed by the KRUSTTool affects the number of backjumps and iterations. It also confirms that the number of rule activations is an indicator of the level of constraint of a training example.

5.2 Dynamic Ordering

The original backjumping KRUSTTool already employs one form of dynamic ordering by reinstating latent examples; these are constraint examples that did not require refinement at the time, and so contributed no fault evidence as refinement examples, but are now incorrectly solved by the current KBS and so are moved back into tebuf. This reordering is applicable only when backjumping occurs. We now extend training example ordering by applying each of the three heuristics from Section 4 to also reorder before every refinement cycle, where

---

1. Current best refined KBS is the input faulty KBS.

2. Apply static ordering on tebuf.

3. Loop until tebuf is empty:
   (a) Execute the refinement cycle with the current best refined KBS and the top most example in tebuf to generate and filter the refined KBSs.
   (b) Apply dynamic ordering on tebuf.
   (c) If the set of filtered refined KBSs is not empty then choose the current best refined KBS.
   (d) If the set of filtered refined KBSs is empty:
       i. If there are latent examples then these are pushed into tebuf, after all correctly solved training examples are moved into cebuf.
       ii. Otherwise, employ BJ to identify the conflict example and its next best refined KBS to backtrack to, and all constraint examples on the way are moved back into tebuf.

Figure 4: Algorithm combining static and dynamic ordering.

again ties are ranked randomly. This more general reordering is employed first, to ensure that reordering enforced by backjumping is not undone.

Figure 4 outlines the basic algorithm combining static and dynamic ordering in a BJ KRUSTTool algorithm. Any of the three static orderings RANDOM, PGRAPH+, PGRAPH± from Section 5.1 can be used in step 2 and influences the selection of the first refinement example only. Dynamic ordering occurs in step 3b, where any of the following can be applied:

- FAULTBASED: re-order tebuf in decreasing order according to evidence from KBSs from the recent refinement cycle (Section 4.1), after moving all correctly solved training examples from tebuf into cebuf; or

- DYNPGRAPH+: apply PGRAPH+'s heuristic (now in every cycle); or

- DYNPGRAPH±: apply PGRAPH±'s heuristic (now in every cycle).

5.3 Static and Dynamic Combinations

Our experiments looked at seven (of the nine possible) static-dynamic combinations; we used the same problem graph heuristic in the static and dynamic orderings. Once again the error-rate of the final KBS was unaffected. Comparing the results in Table 4 with the static ordering results in Table 3, we see that all combinations have reduced the number of iterations by at least two iterations. All heuristics employing the complete problem graph resulted in lower average number of iterations but FAULTBASED results are very close. However the differences among all the static + dynamic combinations are not significant; PGRAPH± + DYNPGRAPH± has the fewest iterations but this is not significant (p = 0.932 > 0.05). These results show that using static + dynamic ordering gives significant gain over using static ordering only but that none of the combinations is better than any other.

Static	+	Dynamic	Mean	Median	95% Confidence
RANDOM	+	FAULTBASED	5.15	5	±0.532
RANDOM	+	DYNPGRAPH+	5.40	5	±0.765
RANDOM	+	DYNPGRAPH±	5.15	5	±0.613
PGRAPH+	+	FAULTBASED	5.60	5	±0.864
PGRAPH+	+	DYNPGRAPH+	5.80	5	±0.893
PGRAPH±	+	FAULTBASED	5.10	5	±0.524
PGRAPH±	+	DYNPGRAPH±	5.05	5	±0.557

Table 4: Number of iterations for static+dynamic ordering combinations.

We have succeeded in reducing the number of iterations but at what computational cost? Table 5 shows the number of cpu cycles for our seven heuristic combinations; the figures for static ordering only have been included for reference. FAULTBASED has proved to be very effective for dynamic ordering since the overhead of applying it with any static ordering is not significant. The orderings based on problem graphs have not been so effective; any gain in reducing the iterations has been overwhelmed by the expense of each iteration. We hope that with more complex KBSs, the richness of the information in the problem graph will result in sufficient quality gains in the refined KBS that the expensive computation is worthwhile.

		Static		
		RANDOM	PGRAPH+	PGRAPH±
Dynamic	None	286480	453030	384910
	FAULTBASED	246060	454590	398670
	DYNPGRAPH+	477760	564810	
	DYNPGRAPH±	581020		798910

Table 5: Cpu cycles for static + dynamic combinations.

The reduction in the number of iterations may actually be worthwhile, even at the expense of some increase in the total effort. Many iterations to achieve consistency with a training set may be regarded as many tinkering repairs; while fewer more fundamental repairs may create a higher quality KBS.

6 Conclusions

The emphasis of this paper is improving the search efficiency of backtracking KRUSTTools, and in particular BJ KRUSTTools, however this approach is applicable more generally. Refinement algorithms tend to use a hill-climbing approach, and so to avoid suboptimal refined KBSs, they should introduce some form of backtracking, and thus could benefit from backjumping.

BJ KRUSTTools produce final refined KBSs with lower error-rates than BT KRUSTTools since the repairs for potentially conflicting training examples are often handled in consecutive cycles, leading to repairs that are better for new problems. However, despite the fact that backjumping had been introduced as a more informed search than chronological backtracking, BJ KRUSTTools result in more iterations. This paper explored methods to reorder training examples with the goal of improving BJ KRUSTTools by reducing the number of iterations whilst maintaining the accuracy of the final refined KBS.

Two static orderings were defined from two heuristics based on counting rule activations. Both maintained the reduced error-rates of backjumping with no example ordering as reported in [18] but achieved this in fewer iterations. The information from the negative problem graph allowed PGRAPH± to cause fewer tie-breaks. Further work could investigate how the heuristics can be extended to resolve tie-breaks strategically as opposed to randomly as at present. We also believe that the overlapping rule activations from the positive and negative problem subgraphs should be exploited to give a more informed heuristic for PGRAPH± and DYNPGRAPH±.

Three dynamic orderings were defined by these two heuristics and a simpler fault evidence heuristic. Algorithms combining static and dynamic ordering further reduced the number of refinement cycles, without increasing the error-rate of the final refined KBS. An important issue with dynamic ordering is the additional computational effort introduced by the reordering at each cycle. FAULTBASED very effectively guided the search without adding much computation and for one combination actually lowered the total effort, but the problem graph heuristics were computationally very expensive. However, we are currently reordering the complete set of remaining training examples from scratch every cycle. Future work will investigate whether knowledge about the repair from the previous cycle will allow less frequent calculation of the problem graph heuristics, or a more targetted application to examples that are most likely to be highly constrained. The calculation for the previous cycle or knowledge of the repair may provide a suitable estimate or an incremental update of the value for this cycle. More experience of the effect of re-ordering may limit the number of training examples that need to be considered. Current work on clustering training examples may also focus the reordering effort.

We must bear in mind that our search space is extremely dynamic with sequences of refinement examples altering the refined KBSs being considered. As with CSPs, our goal is to reduce the search effort and still find a good sequence of repairs rather than simply hill-climb through the repair space without backtracking. But unlike CSPs, where an instantiation for one variable can only restrict the domain of another, in knowledge refinement the repair for one training example may also lead to a totally different set of proposed refinements for a later training example.

Acknowledgments

The KRUSTWorks project is supported by EPSRC grant GR/L38387 awarded to Susan Craw. Nirmalie Wiratunga is partially funded by ORS grant 98131005.

References

[1] J. R. Bitner and E. Reingold. Backtrack programming techniques. *Communications of the ACM*, 18:651–656, 1975.

[2] C. Blake and E. Keogh and C.J. Merz. UCI Repository of Machine Learning Databases. In University of California, Irvine, Dept. of Information and Computer Sciences, 1998. www.ics.uci.edu/~mlearn/MLRepository.html.

[3] Robin Boswell, Susan Craw, and Ray Rowe. Knowledge refinement for a design system. In Enric Plaza and Richard Benjamins, editors, *Proceedings of the Tenth European Knowledge Acquisition Workshop*, pages 49–64, Sant Feliu de Guixols, Spain, 1997. Springer.

[4] Susan Craw and Robin Boswell. Representing problem-solving for knowledge refinement. In *Proceedings of the Sixteenth National Conference on Artificial Intelligence*, pages 227–234, Menlo Park, California, 1999. AAAI Press.

[5] Rina Dechter and Itay Meiri. Experimental evaluation of preprocessing algorithms for constraint satisfaction problems. *Artificial Intelligence*, 68:211–341, 1994.

[6] Daniel Frost and Rina Dechter. Look-ahead value ordering for constraint satisfaction problems. In *Proceedings of the Fourteenth IJCAI Conference*, pages 572–578, 1995.

[7] J. Gaschnig. Performance measurements and analysis of certain search algorithms. Technical Report CMU-CS-79-124, Carnegie-Mellon University, PA, 1979.

[8] Ian Gent, Ewan MacIntyre, Patrick Prosser, Barbara Smith, and Toby Walsh. An empirical study of dynamic variable ordering heuristics for the constraint satisfaction problem. In *in Principles and Practice of Constraint Programming*, pages 179–193. Springer-Verlag, 1996.

[9] R.M. Haralick and G.L. Elliott. Increasing tree-search efficiency for constraint satisfaction problems. *Artificial Intelligence*, 14:263–313, 1980.

[10] Grzegorz Kondrak and Peter van Beek. A theoretical evaluation of selected backtracking algorithms. *Artificial Intelligence*, 89:365–387, 1997.

[11] Steven Minton, Mark D. Johnston, Andrew B. Philips, and Philip Laird. Minimizing conflicts: A heuristic repair method for constraint satisfaction and scheduling problems. *Artificial Intelligence*, 58:161–205, 1992.

[12] D. Ourston and R. Mooney. Theory refinement combining analytical and empirical methods. *Artificial Intelligence*, 66:273–309, 1994.

[13] Michael J. Pazzani. Student loan relational domain. In UCI Repository of Machine Learning Databases [2], 1993.

[14] B. Richards and R. Mooney. Automated refinement of first-order horn-clause domain theories. *Machine Learning*, 19:95–131, 1995.

[15] Norman M. Sadeh and Mark S. Fox. Variable and value ordering heuristics for the job shop scheduling constraint satisfaction problem. In *Proceedings of the Fourth International Conference on Expert Systems in Production and Operations Management*, pages 134–144, 1990.

[16] Barbara Smith and Stuart Grant. Trying harder to fail first. In *Proceedings of the ECAI98 Conference*, pages 249–253, Brighton, UK, 1998. John Wiley and Sons Ltd.

[17] Edward Tsang. *Foundations of Constraint Satisfaction*. Academic Press, San Diego, 1993.

[18] Nirmalie Wiratunga and Susan Craw. Incorporating backtracking search with knowledge refinement. In Anca Vermesan and Frans Coenen, editors, *Proceedings of the Sixth European Symposium on the Validation and Verification of Knowledge Based Systems*, Oslo, Norway, 1999. Kluwer Academic Publishers.

Multistrategy Relational Learning of Heuristics for Problem Solving

Daniel Borrajo
Universidad Carlos III de Madrid
Avda. de la Universidad, 30
28911 Leganés (Madrid). Spain

David Camacho
Universidad Carlos III de Madrid
Avda. de la Universidad, 30
28911 Leganés (Madrid). Spain

Andrés Silva
Universidad Politécnica de Madrid
Campus de Montegancedo s/n
28660 Boadilla del Monte (Madrid). Spain

Abstract

Knowledge-based tools and applications gradually require more automatic acquisition of knowledge, which continues to be the bottleneck of systems development. This need is even stronger for the acquisition of control knowledge (heuristics) that transform an application in an efficient application. Inductive Logic Programming (ILP) has proven successful in a wide variety of domains, ranging from drugs design to logic programs synthesis. The majority of these domains are highly declarative and usually lack procedural-oriented knowledge. Also, most of the systems have been devoted to acquire rules that represent domain knowledge. However, very few have concentrated on the problem of learning control knowledge, which we believe is a type of task for which ILP can be very appropriate, since most representations of heuristics in many knowledge-based systems (KBS) are based on predicate logic. Here, we present a relational learning system, HAMLET, that combines an analytical learning strategy, with an inductive strategy for incremental refinement of learned knowledge. We provide experimental results that show the effectiveness of such automatic acquisition approach. We compare its performance to the performance of other ILP systems, and we also discuss why we believe our approach outperforms the others on this learning task.

1 Introduction

Modern industrial processes require advanced computer tools that should adapt to the user requirements and to the tasks being solved. In particular, KBS should be the ones that first incorporate the adaptation, given that they are usually build with the bias that knowledge changes over time. Almost all KBS involve some kind of heuristic search. Therefore, methods for automatically acquiring the necessary control knowledge to adequately prune the search have been a main issue in the field [5, 6, 7, 17, 15]. Strategy learning consists of automating the acquisition of patterns of actions used while solving particular tasks.

Currently, the ILP community is one of the most active ones in the field of Machine Learning applied to symbolic tasks. However, most of the applications of ILP techniques have been in the field of concept learning (closer to *data mining*). We believe that there are many opportunities to apply these techniques or a generalization of them also for acquiring other types of knowledge, such as control knowledge for problem solving. The few exceptions have been systems applied to linear problem solving [17], or systems that learn domain knowledge [14]. With respect to the strategies used in linear problem solving (independence of goals), they are hard to generalize in the case of nonlinear problem solving, and, in particular, planning, where it is difficult to capture correct explanations of the interactions among goals, multiple planning operator choices, and situational data [2]. With respect to the learning task, we preferred exploring the learning of control knowledge instead of domain knowledge.

In this paper, we use HAMLET, a relational system that learns control knowledge for a non linear planner.[1] HAMLET uses a lazy multistrategy approach, combination of analytical and inductive techniques [2]. As most relational learning systems, it learns by generalizing and specializing a set of rules/clauses using an "ad-hoc" definition of subsumption. The terms ILP and relational learning have sometimes been used indistinctly. We will use ILP as a subclass of systems that perform relational learning. On the one hand, ILP is a set of techniques that learn in the context of Logic Programming, and whose output, is normally used as a PROLOG program. On the other hand, relational learning techniques can use any representation formalism equivalent to predicate logic, and whose output do not have to be strictly used in the sense of a PROLOG program.

In order to evaluate the performance of the system, we compared it with two ILP systems, FOIL [11], and PROGOL [8], and we failed to compare it with another ILP system, CLINT [12] for reasons later explained. Section 2 describes the nonlinear planner used for the experiments, PRODIGY4.0, and the learning system HAMLET[2]. Section 3 explains the representation changes done to translate between PRODIGY's output into/from the inputs and outputs of the ILP systems. Section 4 shows the experimental results in which it is shown how HAMLET outperforms the rest of ILP systems. Section 5 presents the related work, and Section 6 draws some conclusions.

2 PRODIGY and HAMLET

HAMLET is a learning system integrated in the planning and learning architecture PRODIGY [16]. In the following subsections, we will briefly describe PRODIGY's planner, the architecture of HAMLET, and the refinement of learned knowledge.

---

[1]The authors are currently defining an incremental inductive learning technique, using the same ideas to be applied in *data mining* applications.

[2]We denoted some space to the description of HAMLET as an ILP system given that it provides a new insight on how it works.

2.1 PRODIGY's problem solver

The current nonlinear problem solver in PRODIGY, PRODIGY4.0, follows a means-ends analysis backward chaining search procedure reasoning about multiple goals and multiple alternative operators relevant to the goals [16]. The inputs to the problem solver algorithm are: a domain theory, $\mathcal{D}$, that includes a set of generalized operators (similar concept to rules in KBS) and an object hierarchy; a problem to be solved specified in terms of an initial state (starting knowledge) and a set of goals; and control knowledge (heuristics), described as a set of control rules, that guide the search process.

In PRODIGY, the decision cycle first encounters the steps of selecting a goal (from the set of open goals at a given moment), operator (transformation to the state that can make the goal true), and bindings (values to be assigned to variables of the operator that would make it appropriately achieve the goals), followed by the same set of steps, or by applying an operator (when its preconditions are true in the current state). From the point of view of understanding what follows, the main issue is that it has several decision points, and all of them are controlled by default by PRODIGY, though these choices can be directed by explicit control knowledge. Each control rule has an *if*-part and a *then*-part. The *if*-part are the conditions that have to be met in a given search node in order to fire that control rule. These conditions refer to the current state of the search and to some aspects of the search process, such as what is the goal in which PRODIGY is working on, or what operators can achieve a given goal. The *then*-part describes what decision should be made and how.

Figure 1 shows a simplified example of a control rule for the blocksworld domain. `current-goal`, and `true-in-state` are meta-predicates. The control rule says that if PRODIGY is working on trying to hold an object, `<object1>`, and this object is on top of another, `<object2>`, in the current state, then PRODIGY should select the operator `UNSTACK` and reject the rest of operators that could achieve the same goal.

```
(control-rule select-operators-unstack
  (if (and (current-goal (holding <object1>))
           (true-in-state (on <object1> <object2>))))
  (then select operator unstack))
```

Figure 1: Example of a control rule for making the decision of what operator to use.

2.2 HAMLET's architecture

Although PRODIGY uses powerful domain-independent heuristics that guide the decision making process, it is still difficult and costly to characterize when these heuristics are going to succeed or fail. Characterizing the heuristics by interviewing experts is one of the most difficult issues in the knowledge acquisition phase of building knowledge based systems. And this is true for all search processes without strong heuristics, as, for instance, in standard PRO-LOG. Therefore, learning has been used for automatically acquiring control knowledge to override the default behavior, so that it guides the planner more efficiently to solutions of good quality.

HAMLET is integrated with the PRODIGY planner. The inputs to HAMLET are a task domain ($\mathcal{D}$), and a set of training problems ($\mathcal{P}$). The output is a set of control rules ($\mathcal{C}$). HAMLET has two main modules: the Bounded Explanation module, and the Refinement module. The Bounded Explanation module extracts positive examples of the decisions made from the search trees created by PRODIGY when solving the training problems, and generates control rules from those examples. These rules might be overly specific or overly general.

The Refinement module solves the problem of being overly specific by generalizing rules with more positive examples. It also finds negative examples for the wrong decisions made by the planner or by the learned rules. Those negative examples help to replace overly general rules with more specific ones. In order to specialize or generalize, the Refinement module uses a set of *knowledge intensive* generalization and specialization operators. They intersect preconditions of control rules of the same target concept by carefully choosing what preconditions can be combined. These generalization biases can be easily used in learning modules of other searching systems.

2.3 Representation language

HAMLET learns five kinds of control rules, corresponding to PRODIGY's decisions. These are the generalized target concepts:[3] decide to apply an *operator* for achieving a *goal*; decide to subgoal on an unachieved *goal*; select an unachieved *goal*; select an *operator* to achieve some *goal*; and select bindings for an *operator* when trying to achieve a *goal*. Each of the five kinds of generalized target concepts has a template for describing its *if*-part. Figure 2 shows the template for the `select-operator` target concepts. They use a planning-dependent representation language with conditions, called meta-predicates, that refer to the search process. The arguments of those meta-predicates can be literals, as in the case of the meta-predicate `true-in-state` that tests whether a given literal is true in the state of the search, lists of literals, or atoms. Positive examples are created by instantiating those templates according to past successful problem solving episodes, and generalizing the constants of the specific training problem into variables.

With respect to HAMLET's representation bias:

- The strongest language bias that HAMLET has is that target concepts (correct control rules) have to be defined in terms of the defined language. We believe that this bias is the one that differentiate the performance of HAMLET and the rest of generic systems; efficient learning in problem solving needs to have an specific language bias for inducing concepts.

- There are no negated meta-predicates.

---

[3]HAMLET does not yet learn rules to control the choice of which operator to apply.

```
(control-rule name
  (if (current-goal goal-name)
     [(prior-goals (literal*))]
     (true-in-state literal)*
     (other-goals (literal*))
     (type-of-object object type)*)
  (then select operators operator-name))
```

Figure 2: Template of the operator decisions target concepts.

- There should be at least s conditions referring to the state in the *if*-part of control rules ($s = 1$ by default).
- There is no restriction with respect to other ILP parameters, such as determination, depth or relation of variables in the meta-predicates.

2.4 Generalization of control knowledge

In order to generalize control rules, as soon as HAMLET finds multiple examples of the same target concept, the generalization component of HAMLET tries to apply the following set of operators relative to the representation aspects of each control rule:

- *Intersection of preconditions*: From two rules, R_1 and R_2, of the same target concept, it creates a new rule with what we call θ-intersection of the preconditions of R_1 and R_2. HAMLET applies the following definition of θ-intersection.

$$\text{preconds}(R) \ \theta\text{-intersect} \ \text{preconds}(R') \ \text{if}$$
$$\texttt{target-concept}(R)\texttt{=target-concept}(R') \ \text{AND}$$
$$\exists \theta \ \text{such that} \ |\textit{true-in-state}(R)\theta \cap \ \textit{true-in-state}(R')| \geq s$$

where *true-in-state*(R_x) is the set of all conditions of rule R_x that refer to the state, $|S|$ is the number of elements in set S, and s is the parameter for the minimum number of conditions from the state that a control rule should have (see Section 2.3). When there is more than one substitution that makes them θ-intersect, the generalization operator uses the one that has less number of variables to substitute and stores the rest for the specialization operators.

- *Delete rules that are $\theta-subsumed$ by others*: if, after generalizing a rule, HAMLET finds that the rule is subsumed by another, it deletes it. If it finds that the rule subsumes another rule, then it deletes the second rule. HAMLET needs a special definition for $\theta-$subsumption instead of the usual one employed by most ILP systems [10], and applies the following definition:

R θ-**subsumes** R' if
target-concept(R)=target-concept(R') AND
$\exists$ θ such that:
$other\text{-}goals(R)\theta \subseteq other\text{-}goals(R')\wedge$
$prior\text{-}goals(R)\theta \subseteq prior\text{-}goals(R')\wedge$
$rest\text{-}of\text{-}preconds(R)\theta \subseteq rest\text{-}of\text{-}preconds(R')\wedge$
$effects(R)\theta = effects(R')$

HAMLET always tries to keep, for each target concept, the set of most general control rules (according to the previous definition of subsumption) that do not cover negative examples.

- *Refinement of subgoaling dependencies*: If there are two rules, R_1 and R_2, sharing all their preconditions but not their prior-goals, they are merged into a new rule with the union of the prior-goals of the two rules.

- *Refinement of goals dependencies*: The same as the above, but with the *other-goals* meta-predicate.

- *Relaxing the subgoaling dependency*: If there is no evidence that the prior goal is needed, it is deleted until needed. Currently, we are always applying this operator by default.

- *Find common superclass*: When two rules can be unified by two variables that belong to subtypes of a common type (except for the root type), this operator generalizes the variables to the common type.

Upon generating a new control rule for a target concept, HAMLET tries to generalize it with previously learned control rules of the same target concept. If there were none, then the rule is stored as the only one of its target concept. If there were rules, it tries to apply the generalization operators to combine it with all existing rules of the same target concept (deleting subsumed rules). If it succeeds, it will create a new generalized rule and delete the old ones. Also, it will recursively call itself with the new induced rule and the rest of rules in its target concept. If it fails to generalize the rule with any other rule, the rule is simply added to the set of rules of the target concept.

For generalizing two control rules, the generalization algorithm tries first to find an intersection of the state part of them (first operator). If it finds a substitution that will make them intersect, it will try to apply the rest of the generalization operators over the *if*-part generated by applying the substitution over the *if*-part of the first rule.

In general, we can look at the generalization process within a target concept as it is shown in Figure 3. "WSP_i" stands for *Whole Set of Preconditions* for rule R_i and refers to the complete description of the current state and all available information about the meta-level decision on a certain search node. It searches in the state space of hypothesis with the relations of $\theta-$subsumption and θ-intersection. Step (a) shows the Bounded-Explanation step in which the WSP_1 is generalized to R_1 by *goal regression* and parameterization. Step (b) shows a generalization from two bounded rules, R_1 and R_2. Step (c) shows another generalization, from I_1 and R_3, generating a new rule I_2.

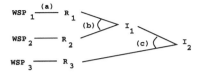

Figure 3: Three learning episodes of HAMLET within the same target concept.

2.5   Example of generalization

In a logistics transportation domain, objects must be delivered to some destinations by airplanes or by trucks (trucks cannot move between cities, while airplanes can) [15]. Now, suppose that trying to achieve the goal of having an object in an airport, being the object inside an airplane that is located in that airport, the operator that leads to the solution is the unload-airplane operator. This positive example is transformed by the Bounded Explanation module of HAMLET in the control rule of Figure 4(a).

```
(control-rule select-operator-unload-airplane-1
   (if (current-goal (at-obj <ob3> <a2>))
       (true-in-state (at-airplane <pl0> <a2>))
       (true-in-state (inside-airplane <ob3> <pl0>))
       (other-goals nil)
       (type-of-object <ob3> object)
       (type-of-object <a2> airport)
       (type-of-object <pl0> airplane))
   (then select operator unload-airplane))
                        (a)
(control-rule select-operator-unload-airplane-2
   (if (current-goal (at-obj <ob3> <a2>))
       (true-in-state (at-airplane <pl0> <a1>))
       (true-in-state (inside-airplane <ob3> <pl0>))
       (other-goals nil)
       (type-of-object <ob3> object)
       (type-of-object <a1> airport)
       (type-of-object <a2> airport)
       (type-of-object <pl0> airplane))
   (then select operator unload-airplane))
                        (b)
(control-rule select-operator-unload-airplane-3
   (if (current-goal (at-obj <ob3> <a2>))
       (true-in-state (inside-airplane <ob3> <pl0>))
       (other-goals nil)
       (type-of-object <ob3> object)
       (type-of-object <a2> airport)
       (type-of-object <pl0> airplane))
   (then select operator unload-airplane))
                        (c)
```

Figure 4: Example of three control rules generated by HAMLET from the solution of two different problems by PRODIGY and applying generalization.

This rule is overly specific, since the condition that requires the airplane <pl0> to be at the same airport, <a2>, than the object, is not needed; the airplane can be in any other airport, and it would still be valid the decision of using the airplane instead of any truck. From the solution of another problem in which the airplane is, initially, in another airport as the destination airport, HAMLET would extract a new positive example of the same target concept, shown in Figure 4(b). Using this new control rule, HAMLET would apply the generalization operators, and would generate the control rule in Figure 4(c), which is the correct one.

2.6 Specialization of control knowledge

HAMLET may generate overly general rules, either by doing *goal regression* when generating the rules or by applying the generalization operators. The overly general rules are specialized through the analysis of negative examples. A negative example for HAMLET is a situation in which a control rule was applied, and the resulting decision led to either a failure (instead of the expected success), or a worse solution than the best one for that decision. The *most general* negative examples are stored in their corresponding target concept. When a new negative example is found, HAMLET checks whether it θ-subsumes any prior negative example or if any prior negative example θ-subsumes it. If so, it keeps the more general negative example. Negative examples serve two purposes: refine an overly general rule, and establish an upper limit of generalization for future applications of the generalization operators. Every time a rule is generated by either the Bounded-Explanation or by the application of a generalization operator, it is checked against the negative examples of its target concept to know if the rule covers any one of them. In order to test the coverage, the previous definition of θ-subsumption is used. If the rule θ-subsumes any negative example, the rule is deleted.

When a new negative example of a control rule is found, HAMLET recovers from this over generalization by refining the rule, using a set of specialization operators. The specialization algorithm tries these operators one by one until any returns a specialization of the control rule that does not subsume a negative example. The operators are:

- *Use different substitution*: from the ones generated by the generalization operator *Intersection of preconditions*.

- *Add one literal from the state*: This is the most simple operator, present in almost all ILP systems: adding a literal to a clause. In our case, the literal is selected from the ones referring to the state.

- *Add one prior-goal*: The same as above, but using the prior-goals metapredicate.

- *Add two preconditions*: They can be either literals from the state or prior-goals. There is no refinement operator that adds more than two preconditions.

- *Specialize the type constraints*: It changes the types of the objects involved in the rule from general types to more specific ones.

- *Delete control rule*: it deletes a control rule, so that the whole set of control rules is more specific.

Figure 5 shows the case in which, while refining an overly general rule I_2,[4] one of its generating rules, I_1, was also overly general. In this case, it backtracks, and refines I_1 and I_2 with the rules that generated them, R_1, R_2, and R_3. R_1 was also overly general, so it had to backtrack to consider WSP_1, generating a refined version of R_1, RF_1. It generates RF_1 by using the specialization operators, using $\{preconds(WSP_1) - preconds(R_1)\}$ as the set of possible literals to add. Then, HAMLET deletes R_1. R_2 was not overly general, so it created a rule RF_2 from R_2 and I_1, then deleted I_1. Finally, R_3 was not overly general, so it generated a new rule RF_3, and deleted I_2. The dotted lines represent deleted links, the dotted boxes deleted rules, and the solid boxes the active rules after refinement.

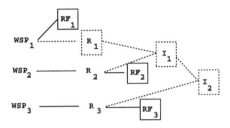

Figure 5: Refinement process of an overly general control rule I_2.

3 From HAMLET to ILP

In order to use any ILP system for learning control knowledge, we first had to devise a way to give it examples to learn from. The strategy we followed was giving the same examples that HAMLET extracted from the search trees. However, since the languages used by PRODIGY, HAMLET and the ILP systems are different, a translation had to be done. While HAMLET examples are in the form of rules, the examples for ILP systems are sets of instantiated predicates (FOIL), or Horn clauses (PROGOL). The following is the method we used to translate from one representation to another, also shown in Figure 6:[5] We run HAMLET/PRODIGY in a set of planning problems and extract a description of the examples that were used to learn control rules. All the meta-level information about the search of each example is given to the ILP system as background knowledge. The decisions made in each node are the target concepts given to the ILP system. The Horn clauses that the ILP system obtains are translated back to control rules in the PRODIGY language.

For instance, suppose HAMLET generated the example partially shown in Figure 7(a) from an analysis of a search tree, when PRODIGY solved a problem

---

[4] R_i means a directly learned rule, I_i a generalized rule, and RF_i a specialized rule.

[5] The translation was suggested by Ivan Bratko in a personal communication and by some anonymous reviewers.

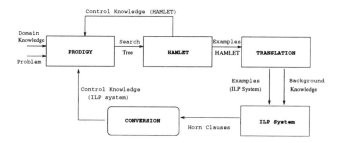

Figure 6: Relations between PRODIGY, HAMLET, and the ILP systems.

in the logistics transportation domain. Each example has four elements: an identifier; the type of example, `positive` or `negative`; a set of preconditions describing the search situation; and the decision made in that search node. Figure 4(a) showed the control rule that HAMLET would generate from the example of Figure 7(a).

FOIL needs as input all the examples at once in a *flatten* format. Therefore, the given example is translated into the set of tuples partly specified in Figure 7(b). The predicates marked with an asterisk define the background knowledge and those not marked are the target concepts, whose description the ILP system will learn. For each metapredicate, the translator generates an ILP system predicate for each possible argument that it might have. Also, in order to relate the examples for the ILP system (decisions made), and its corresponding background knowledge, the translator defines a first argument for each ILP system predicate that is called `EXAMPLE`. This represents the identifier that appears in HAMLET examples. For the experiments, we used firstly the same *flatten* input for PROGOL. We will refer to it as F-PROGOL. However, PROGOL also accepts more structured input, so the translation is more straightforward, as shown in Figure 7(c). We will refer to it as S-PROGOL.

Then, the ILP systems run on the generated tuples, and the clausal descriptions learned by the ILP systems are translated back into PRODIGY's format. So, if the ILP system learns the clause of Figure 8(a) it will be translated into the control rule expressed in Figure 8(b). In the process of the translation from the ILP system output to PRODIGY, some literals must be added to the left hand side of the control rule. These are the literals in lower case. The reason is that the problem solver would fail without those literals when trying to evaluate the rule. In the example, for the rule being able to force the bindings, a `current-operator` is needed, and a `current-goal` must be the goal the operator is trying to reduce. Otherwise, the control rule would fire for each possible goal, when the operator chosen is `load-truck`. Also, the type of the variable <c> must be specified, for it is a variable appearing in the *then*-part of the rule, but not in the *if*-part.

```
(365 + ((current-goal (at-obj ob3 a2))
        (current-operator unload-truck)
        (true-in-state (same-city a2 po2))
        (true-in-state (same-city po2 a2))
        . . .
        (true-in-state (at-truck tr1 po2))
        (other-goals nil)
        . . .)
        (select bindings ((<obj> . ob3) (<truck> . tr1)
                          (<loc> . a2))))
```
(a)

```
*current-goal-at-obj(example,obj,loc)
365,ob3,a2
. . .
*true-in-state-same-city(example,loc,loc)
365,a2,po2
365,a1,po1
. . .
*true-in-state-at-truck(example,truck,loc)
365,tr1,po2
. . .
*other-goals-nil(example)
365
. . .
select-bind-unload-truck(example,obj,truck,loc)
365,ob3,tr1,a2
. . .
```
(b)

```
select-bindings-unload-truck(ob3,tr1,a2) :-
    current-goal(at-obj(ob3,a2)),
    current-operator(unload-truck())
    true-in-state(same-city(a2,po2)),
    true-in-state(same-city(po2,a2)),
    . . .
    true-in-state(at-truck(tr1,po2)),
    other-goals(nil),
    . . .
```
(c)

Figure 7: Example of decision extracted by HAMLET after PRODIGY solved a problem (a), tuples generated by the translator from HAMLET examples into FOIL's input language (b) and PROGOL's input language (c).

4   Experimental results

For the experiments, we used FOIL6 and PROGOL4.2. We considered using CLINT,[6] given that it is incremental, but since it is also interactive, it was totally impractical to enter by hand the amount of data that we gave as input to the learning systems. The experiments were carried out in two domains: blocksworld and logistics. Tables 1 and 2 summarize the results on two different domains: blocksworld and logistics. HAMLET was given 400 training problems of one and two goals. It generated a set of control rules for each domain, shown in the row "Control rules" from a set of examples, which were translated and used as input for FOIL and PROGOL (7659 in the blocksworld and 5462 in the logistics). A problem we found is that we could not give as input the whole

---

[6] As previous reviewers suggested.

```
                                    (control-rule select-bindings-unload-truck-3
                                      (if (current-goal (at-obj <b> <d>))
  select-bindings-unload-truck(a,b,c,d) :-   (current-operator unload-truck)
    true-in-state-at-obj(a,b,e),            (TRUE-IN-STATE (AT-OBJ <b> <e>))
    true-in-state-at-truck(a,f,e),          (TRUE-IN-STATE (AT-TRUCK <f> <e>))
    true-in-state-inside-truck(a,g,f).      (TRUE-IN-STATE (INSIDE-TRUCK <g> <f>))
                                            (type-of-object <c> truck))
                                      (then SELECT BINDINGS
                                        ((<obj> . <b>) (<truck> . <c>) (<loc> . <d>))))
              (a)                                         (b)
```

Figure 8: Horn clause output from an ILP system (a) and its translation into its corresponding PRODIGY control rule (b).

set of examples to FOIL and to F-PROGOL, since they could not handle such amount of data. So, we randomly splitted the input files of examples in m files with n examples, where n was the maximum number of examples we found that each system could handle for each domain. This number is represented in the table by the row "Size of input files". Then, we run the two systems (PROGOL in its two versions) with the m files and collected the generated Horn clauses in a single file (row "Horn clauses"), that was translated into control rules in the PRODIGY language (row "Control rules"). We deleted some Horn Clauses, since some of them were $\theta-$subsumed by others.[7]

Then, we compared the different sets of control rules obtained by each system with test examples of increasing complexity: 375 problems in the blocksworld (1 to 10 goals); and 525 problems in the logistics domain(1 to 50 goals). 50 goals problems are very hard problems. The results are shown in the last two rows, where the number and percentage of solved problems are represented.[8]

	PRODIGY	FOIL	PROGOL		HAMLET
			F-	S-	
Size of input files		546	4000		
Horn clauses		133	20	9	
Control rules		57	16	9	12
Solved problems	196	4	87	262	312
% of solved problems	52%	1%	23%	70%	80%

Table 1: Comparison between PRODIGY, FOIL6, PROGOL4.2 with the flatten format (F-PROGOL) and with the structured format (S-PROGOL), and HAMLET in the blocksworld domain.

As it can be seen, representation of input examples for the ILP systems make a big difference in the case of the blocksworld (compare the results of F-PROGOL with those of S-PROGOL). However, it does not improve much the performance in the case of a more complex domain, such as the logistics. In

---

[7]Every time that a specific (deleted) rule would fire, its decision would still be made, because the more general one would also fire. Therefore, there is no need to keep the more specific ones, and they would make the output of the ILP systems less efficient.

[8]A problem is solved if, given a time bound, the planner is able to produce a solution. We have extensively experimented with different time bounds, and the results are usually equivalent, unless time is incremented exponentially.

	PRODIGY	FOIL	PROGOL		HAMLET
			F-	S-	
Size of input files		82	546		
Horn clauses		68	129	32	56
Control rules		33	48	23	
Solved problems	282	21	3	21	319
% of solved problems	54%	3.6%	0.5%	3.6%	61%

Table 2: Comparison between PRODIGY, FOIL6, PROGOL4.2 with the flatten format (F-PROGOL) and with the structured format (S-PROGOL), and HAMLET in the logistics domain.

both domains HAMLET outperforms the performance of the other selected ILP systems. In Section 6 we analyze why we believe this is so.

5 Related Work

Most of previous approaches to relational learning have concentrated on concept learning. There has been very little work on learning control knowledge. Estlin and Mooney [4] describe an approach that uses FOIL to learn control knowledge for a partial-order planner, UCPOP [9]. As in the case of HAMLET, in order to improve the behavior of FOIL, they bounded the set of literals to add to a clause by using the information from the search trees. It is difficult to compare the results with their work, since they used a different kind of planner with very different search techniques and approach. For instance, they used a different representation of the domains, and presented results on simpler problems than the ones we report. Also, Zelle and Mooney use a combination of ILP and EBG to speed-up logic programs, but they used a linear problem solver [17]. In [14], the authors present an application of iterative version spaces in the ILP framework for an event calculus planner, but their goal is to learn domain knowledge instead of control knowledge.

6 Discussion and conclusions

Hypothesis construction in ILP is usually done in an eager oriented basis, trying to explain correctly all positive examples at once. Instead, HAMLET's process of learning search control heuristics achieves its goal in a local, lazy oriented basis, building one hypothesis (control rule) for each positive example, and then incrementally refining the hypothesis that are overly general or overly specific, as new problems are solved and more positive or negative examples are found. This approach seems to be more adequate than standard ILP when facing more complex domains, such as the problem of search control learning, for the following reasons:

- When learning search control knowledge, specialization and generalization operators have to be biased towards the kind of knowledge that the search algorithm is using. The idea of having an unique type of generalization operators for any kind of domain, as standard ILP does, is not always adequate. On the other side, having such a strong language bias makes HAMLET less general and autonomous. A solution to this problem consists on allowing the learning system to receive as input a grammar that defines the language in which control knowledge (or learned knowledge in general) has to be represented. This approach was followed in [1] by using Genetic Programming in combination with HAMLET.

- The generation of a control rule, by means of a lazy explanation, must follow a template for each target concept. This restriction can be seen as a kind of "language bias" for control rules imposed by HAMLET, and it is very difficult to translate such bias into the first-order language used by other ILP systems. This might be solved by using more declarative systems such as Claudien [13] or Grendel [3], to which we will compare in the future.

- Some important issues in nonlinear planning, such as goal interactions or goal regression, are easily handled by an analytical learner. Again, all that knowledge is difficult to translate into first-order relations, as an input for an inductive system. Even if it is translated it is difficult to understand how that would make it easier the task of learning control knowledge for the ILP systems.

- HAMLET is an incremental, non interactive system that learns multiple predicates. We believe that these features are needed for learning control knowledge in problem solving.

Acknowledgements

The authors would like to thank Manuela Veloso for all the ideas that led to the implementation of the HAMLET system.

References

[1] Ricardo Aler, Daniel Borrajo, and Pedro Isasi. Genetic programming and deductive-inductive learning: A multistrategy approach. In Jude Shavlik, editor, *Proceedings of the Fifteenth International Conference on Machine Learning, ICML'98*, pages 10–18, Madison, Wisconsin, July 1998.

[2] Daniel Borrajo and Manuela Veloso. Lazy incremental learning of control knowledge for efficiently obtaining quality plans. *AI Review Journal. Special Issue on Lazy Learning*, 11(1-5):371–405, February 1997.

[3] William W. Cohen. Grammatically biased learning: learning logic programs using an explicit antecedent description language. *Artificial Intelligence*, 68(2):303–366, 1994.

[4] Tara A. Estlin and Raymond J. Mooney. Multi-strategy learning of search control for partial-order planning. In *Proceedings of the Thirteenth National Conference*

on Artificial Intelligence, volume I, pages 843–848, Portland, Oregon, August 1996. AAAI Press/MIT Press.

[5] Richard E. Fikes, P. E. Hart, and Nils J. Nilsson. Learning and executing generalized robot plans. *Artificial Intelligence*, 3:251–288, 1972.

[6] John E. Laird, Paul S. Rosenbloom, and Allen Newell. Chunking in SOAR: The anatomy of a general learning mechanism. *Machine Learning*, 1:11–46, 1986.

[7] Steven Minton. *Learning Effective Search Control Knowledge: An Explanation-Based Approach*. Kluwer Academic Publishers, Boston, MA, 1988.

[8] Stephen Muggleton. Inverse entailment and Progol. *New Generation Computing, Special issue on Inductive Logic Programming*, 13(3-4):245–286, 1995.

[9] J. S. Penberthy and D. S. Weld. UCPOP: A sound, complete, partial order planner for ADL. In *Proceedings of KR-92*, pages 103–114, 1992.

[10] G. D. Plotkin. A note on inductive generalisation. In B. Meltzer and D. Michie, editors, *Machine Intelligence*, volume 5, pages 153–163. Elsevier. North Holland, New York, 1970.

[11] J. Ross Quinlan. Learning logical definitions from relations. *Machine Learning*, 5(3):239–266, August 1990.

[12] Luc De Raedt. *Interactive Theory Revision: An Inductive Logic Programming Approach*. Academic Press, 1992.

[13] Luc De Raedt. Clausal discovery. *Machine Learning*, 26:99, 1997.

[14] Gunther Sablon, Luc De Raedt, and Maurice Bruynooghe. Iterative version-spaces. *Artificial Intelligence*, 69:393–409, 1994.

[15] Manuela Veloso. *Planning and Learning by Analogical Reasoning*. Springer Verlag, December 1994.

[16] Manuela Veloso, Jaime Carbonell, Alicia Pérez, Daniel Borrajo, Eugene Fink, and Jim Blythe. Integrating planning and learning: The PRODIGY architecture. *Journal of Experimental and Theoretical AI*, 7:81–120, 1995.

[17] J. Zelle and R. Mooney. Combining FOIL and EBG to speed-up logic programs. In *Proceedings of the Thirteenth International Joint Conference on Artificial Intelligence*, pages 1106–1113, Chambery, France, 1993. Morgan Kaufmann.

Learning Perceptual Schemas to Avoid the Utility Problem

Peter C.R. Lane, Peter C-H. Cheng and Fernand Gobet
ESRC Centre for Research in Development, Instruction and Training,
School of Psychology, University of Nottingham,
University Park, NOTTINGHAM NG7 2RD, UK
{pcl,pcc,frg}@psychology.nottingham.ac.uk
www.psychology.nottingham.ac.uk/research/credit

Abstract: This paper describes principles for representing and organising planning knowledge in a machine learning architecture. One of the difficulties with learning about tasks requiring planning is the utility problem: as more knowledge is acquired by the learner, the utilisation of that knowledge takes on a complexity which overwhelms the mechanisms of the original task. This problem does not, however, occur with human learners: on the contrary, it is usually the case that, the more knowledgeable the learner, the greater the efficiency and accuracy in locating a solution. The reason for this lies in the types of knowledge acquired by the human learner and its organisation. We describe the basic representations which underlie the superior abilities of human experts, and describe algorithms for using equivalent representations in a machine learning architecture.

1. Introduction

As computers are applied to increasingly complex tasks, the extent and organisation of knowledge required for success becomes an additional complex task in its own right. For this reason, an important branch in the study of Artificial Intelligence deals with algorithms which learn and organise their own knowledge directly from experience. In this paper, we are interested in those domains where a system must find a solution path between some start and some goal state. The task of "speed-up" learning refers to the acquisition of information which improves the efficiency of finding solution paths. Examples of tasks where such learning is beneficial include: board games, controlling a mobile robot, various scheduling and planning problems, and the construction of proofs of mathematical theorems. Two of the more successful speed-up learning systems are PRODIGY [1] and SOAR [2]. These systems learn rules by generalising an example start state to as wide a class of potential start states as possible; future problems from within this class may have the same solution path applied to them without incurring the cost of its rediscovery. However, as shown by Minton [1], such systems can suffer from the "utility problem", where system efficiency is degraded by the cost of managing the collection of learnt rules.

Such considerations do not seem to apply to human learners, in which increasing knowledge is typically accompanied by increasing accuracy and efficiency. We therefore consider whether machine learning algorithms can be improved by including what is known about human expert representations. Research on skill acquisition in humans shows that expert representations differ from those of novices in two ways. First, experts have a large number of *perceptual chunks*, which enables them to rapidly identify and categorise a sample problem [3]. Second, they associate these perceptual chunks with possible operator sequences in knowledge structures known as *schemas* [4]. These schemas encode domain-specific knowledge based on the expert's experience, and it is the propagation of knowledge through schemas which distinguishes expert behaviour from that of the novice; the expert can use information perceived in the problem statement to retrieve a suitable schema, which then guides the formation of a solution, whereas the novice often resorts to search strategies. However, earlier work on human expertise does not provide a computational model for learning such schemas directly from experience. In this paper, we address this problem with a set of principles and computational algorithms for learning these representations.

This paper is organised as follows. In Section 2, an example domain requiring the computation of unknown quantities within electric circuits is used to illustrate the way in which humans acquire a skill. Section 3 describes the main findings on expert representations, i.e. perceptual chunks and schemas. Section 4 shows how machine learning algorithms can be designed to learn and work with such representations. Finally, Section 5 returns to the utility problem, and discusses how the model for expert representations can be used to provide efficient indexing into domain-specific knowledge for problem solving.

2. Computing Unknowns in Electric Circuits

In this section we describe a typical task in which speed-up learning may be observed. We discuss two representations for solving problems, the more conventional algebraic method and a diagrammatic representation. The purpose of this section is not to argue for the benefits of the latter, which has been done elsewhere [5,6,7,8,9]; instead this section provides an example of the kind of representation which humans find easiest to master. This permits us to draw some conclusions about the mechanisms underlying the human learning process, which may then be implemented in a machine learning algorithm.

2.1 Algebraic and Diagrammatic Circuit Representations

We consider a problem solving domain in which subjects are given circuit diagrams consisting of a battery and a number of resistors. Various numerical quantities will be supplied, such as the voltage of the battery and the resistance of some of the resistors. Then some unknown quantity will be asked for, such as the total current drawn from the battery.

Consider the three resistor circuit in Figure 1(a). The battery provides a voltage of 12V, and the resistors have the indicated resistances. In order to compute the total current drawn from the battery, one of several approaches may be taken: the individual currents drawn by the different resistors may be calculated, and the total worked out, or the total resistance of the three resistors may be computed, exploiting the property that complex networks may be replaced with equivalent sub-networks. In the given case, it is easiest to compute the total resistance of the circuit. This requires the following recognition: two of the resistors form a parallel

74

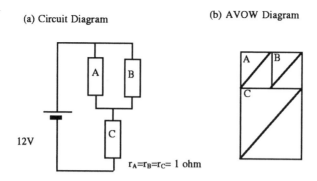

(a) Circuit Diagram

(b) AVOW Diagram

12V

$r_A = r_B = r_C = 1$ ohm

Figure 1 : Equivalent circuit and AVOW diagrams.

network, which is in series with the third resistor. The resistance of the parallel network can be computed as 0.5 ohm from the rule $1/r_P = 1/r_A + 1/r_B$. Then this can be combined with the resistance of the third resistor using the rule that, for resistors in series, $r_T = r_P + r_C$; thus the total circuit resistance is 1.5 ohm and the total current drawn will be $I_T = V_T/r_T = 8A$.

This is an example of the standard algebraic approach for solving such problems. Note that the solver must remember rules for resistors in parallel and series, as well as recognise circuit decompositions which enable these rules to be applied in sequence. Also, the entire procedure would be different if numerical quantities had been supplied for different parameters. In contrast, we describe a diagrammatic representation for electric circuits, known as AVOW diagrams [6].

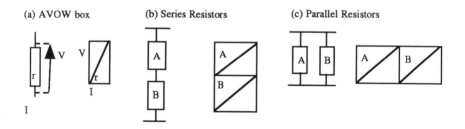

(a) AVOW box

(b) Series Resistors

(c) Parallel Resistors

Figure 2 : An AVOW box (a), and rules for their composition:
(b) series and (c) parallel resistors.

An AVOW diagram is composed of AVOW boxes, each AVOW box being a diagrammatic representation of a resistor (or load) within an electric circuit, as shown in Figure 2(a). A resistor has the properties of voltage (V), current (I) and resistance (r). These properties are represented in the AVOW box by scaling the indicated dimension, voltage being the height, current the width, and resistance the gradient of the box's diagonal. It can be seen that the relation of the gradient to the box's height and width encapsulates Ohm's law (r=V/I), and also that the area of the box represents the power expended in the resistor (P=I*V).

The AVOW boxes are combined into an AVOW diagram for an entire circuit using simple rules of composition. In order to represent two series resistors, two AVOW boxes are aligned vertically, as shown in Figure 2(b). Similarly, two parallel resistors are represented by aligning the boxes horizontally, as shown in Figure 2(c). The alignment rules encapsulate Kirchhoff's Laws which govern the flow of current and distribution of potential differences in electric circuits. For the completed AVOW diagram to be a well-formed representation of the circuit, it must be a rectangle completely filled with AVOW boxes with no overlap or gaps. This requirement captures an important abstraction used in circuit analysis: a collection of resistors in a circuit can be regarded as equivalent to a single resistor. In the same way, the composite AVOW diagram is also an AVOW box, containing all the information for this equivalent single resistor. Just as with the single AVOW box, the resistance of the total AVOW diagram can be found by measuring the gradient of the total rectangle's diagonal. The geometrical nature of this constraint on the final AVOW diagram and the rules for composing separate AVOW boxes mean that it is very natural for humans to work within this representation, a fact which has important pedagogical implications.

As an example of their use, we return to the example problem in Figure 1(a). In order to construct an equivalent AVOW diagram for this circuit, three AVOW boxes must be drawn, each requiring its dimensions (height, width, gradient) and position in the diagram to be determined: the final diagram is shown in Figure 1(b). Human subjects typically proceed as follows. Beginning with resistor A, the only known quantity is its resistance, which determines the gradient of the diagonal of its AVOW box. In this instance the resistance is 1, so a square box is drawn. Similarly, for resistor B a further square AVOW box is required, and it is drawn alongside that of resistor A with the same height because the two resistors are in parallel. Resistor C is also represented by a square AVOW box, but this time, because it is in series with resistors A and B, it is drawn below these two boxes but with their combined width. Finally, the *scale* of the diagram is found by recognising that the height of the final diagram represents the voltage across the entire circuit, i.e. the 12V supplied by the battery. Hence, by measuring the width of the combined box and scaling, the current drawn from the battery is determined.

2.2   Comparison

It is evident that the steps followed by a solver using the diagrammatic representation are qualitatively different from those followed by the solver using algebra. The major difference being the immediate goal: with the AVOW diagrams, the goal is to correctly draw an equivalent representation of the circuit. That this is sufficient for then providing a solution to the given problem is a property of the AVOW diagram representation, specifically, its encoding of domain laws in the geometry of the representation. Cheng [5,6] discusses this topic in more depth.

From studies on human subjects [7], it is clear that learners using AVOW diagrams generalise the perceptual information in the diagrams more than the numerical information. For instance, circuits with the same structure are considered similar, and not circuits requiring the same sequences of algebraic manipulations, i.e. learners rely on the perceptual properties of the diagrams. It is only whilst in the process of producing a scaled diagram that the learner will incorporate the numerical quantities in the given circuit. The studies show that the improvement in ability of subjects is based, to a large extent, on the acquisition and retrieval of perceptual information relating to circuit topologies and AVOW diagrams. Similar studies with subjects using algebraic solution techniques have not shown such a strong improvement. Hence the claim that perceptual processes are an important source of the power in speed-up learning observed in humans.

3.   Expert Representations: Chunks and Schemas

Research on skill acquisition in humans has shown that experts have a large number of *perceptual chunks*, which enables them to rapidly identify and categorise a sample problem [3]. Second, they associate these perceptual chunks with possible operator sequences in knowledge structures known as *schemas* [4]. In this section we briefly describe the acquisition of perceptual chunks and their association with information in schemas.

3.1   Perceptual Chunking Theory

The use by experts of perceptual chunks to discriminate between examples from their domain of expertise was first described in the seminal work of de Groot [3]. He found that one of the most effective tests (beyond playing ability) which distinguished expert from novice chess players was the recall of chess positions presented for short periods of time; the expert could recall typical game positions almost exactly after only a few seconds presentation, whereas the novice could recall only a few pieces. This ability of the expert was not due simply to a better recall of visual phenomena, as experts were only marginally better than novices with board positions with random placements of pieces [10]. These results have been replicated and extended upon in work by Gobet and Simon [11], work which also provides a computational model of this ability. The model, CHREST, learns a discrimination network of chunks relating to typical configurations of pieces. These configurations may be rapidly identified in novel board positions, and enable the whole board to be retained as a relatively small number of chunks, each chunk containing several pieces. Tests show that CHREST conforms very closely to the performance of human subjects, with different abilities of chess player corresponding to differing numbers of acquired perceptual chunks.

Although most of the detailed modelling work has been confined to work on chess, the basic hypothesis that experts possess a large number of perceptual chunks has been validated in many domains, e.g. ice hockey, football and electric circuits. Estimates for the number of chunks acquired by an expert are typically of the order of 50,000 chunks [12]. The large number of chunks enable the expert to do two things. First, the expert can use the chunks as an efficient indexing mechanism into knowledge relevant for problem solving. Second, the chunks help the expert to 'zero-in' on unique features of the current problem. For example, in the chess domain, a piece in an unusual position will not have an associated chunk, priming the expert to consider the consequences of his position compared with the more familiar situation.

Template for parallel resistors   *Possible rules and actions:*

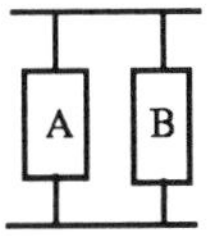

If r_A and r_B known, then $1/r_{Total} = 1/r_A + 1/r_B$

If I_A and I_B known, then $I_{Total} = I_A + I_B$

If V_{Total} known, then $V_A = V_B = V_{Total}$

Figure 3 : An example of a schema.

3.2   Knowledge for Problem Solving

According to Sweller [13], a *schema* is simply a "structure which allows problem solvers to recognize a problem state as belonging to a particular category of problem states that normally require particular moves". This implies that "certain problem states can be grouped, at least in part, by their similarity and the similarity of the moves that can be made from those states." Analysis of the performance of subjects and their protocols [6,4] has provided considerable evidence of the kinds of information contained in schemas; it is the nature of this information and its propagation which largely distinguishes expert behaviour from the novice. An example of a schema is given in Figure 3. The template provides the perceptual pre-conditions for determining whether this schema applies in the current situation. Various slots determine different behaviours depending on different constraints found in the problem. Such schemas have been shown to support flexible problem solving strategies and explain how experts can employ a direct forward-inferencing strategy when solving relatively simple problems [4]. The collection together of domain knowledge in schemas is similar to that achieved by frames [14]. The difference here is the emphasis on perceptual knowledge for forming the template.

However, in spite of such work on the content of schemas, and even their use in intelligent tutoring systems [15], no substantive computational model has been proposed for learning such representations. We address this question in the next section.

4.   Learning Perceptual Schemas: CHREST+

The previous two sections have outlined the principles which underlie an efficient representation for supporting skill acquisition, and also the mechanisms thought to explain the superior performance of human experts. There are two central underlying mechanisms: the acquisition of perceptual chunks and the acquisition of knowledge for problem solving. This section considers these in turn, illustrating how they may be implemented and combined in a machine learning architecture.

4.1   Learning Perceptual Chunks

The heart of the expert's representation is an efficient indexing mechanism to a large number of perceptual chunks. Here we describe an effective algorithm for learning and indexing this knowledge. The algorithm, CHREST [16,11], builds up a discrimination network from the presented examples. It functions in a similar manner to EPAM [17], but has some important differences. The discrimination network is learnt as follows.

The network consists of a collection of chunks, with each chunk representing a meaningful group of basic elements. For example, in the circuit domain, the basic elements are the resistors and connections; the chunks are the collections of resistors which comprise circuits and sub-circuits. The chunks are developed as the discrimination network grows through the processes of discrimination and familiarisation. Essentially, each node of the network holds a chunk of information about an object in the world. The nodes are interconnected by links into a network, with each link representing the result of applying a test to the object. When trying to recognise an object, the tests are applied beginning from the root node, and the links are followed until no further test can be applied. The information held in the stored chunk is then compared with that in the current object: the object matches the stored chunk if the chunk is a more general description than that of the object. At the node reached during sorting, if the stored chunk matches that of the object then familiarisation occurs, in which the chunk is specialised by adding more details of the features in that object. If the current object and the chunk at the node reached differ in some feature, then discrimination occurs, which adds a new node and a new link based on the mis-matched feature. Therefore, with discrimination, new nodes are added to the discrimination network; with familiarisation, the resolution of chunks at those nodes is increased.

There are two distinguishing features of CHREST which are important to its efficiency. First, information is not confined to the leaf nodes of the discrimination network (which is similar to the organisation in UNIMEM [18]). Hence, each node will contain information describing one perceptual chunk, and its descendant nodes will contain information about closely related chunks. The second feature is that CHREST uses perceptual chunks as tests. Thus, when discrimination occurs, instead of simply taking a single feature from the current object for use as a test, CHREST will search the network for a node which represents the mismatched sub-chunk; the information at that node can then be used as a test on the new link.

These two features have an important consequence for the use of CHREST to rapidly discriminate perceptual information: the node in the discrimination network relating to the currently perceived chunk will suggest, via its links, where the next piece of perceptual information should be looked for. Also, because the tests are themselves acquired perceptual chunks, the information looked for will not be at the lowest level of resolution, but instead reflect the amount of knowledge of the system. It is usual for experts to require far fewer pieces of perceptual information to acquire a far greater amount of conceptual information, and this behaviour is captured quite effectively in CHREST [11].

4.2 Learning Knowledge for Problem Solving

The previous section described an algorithm which learns perceptual chunks. As suggested by previous researchers, e.g. [3,17,4], we assume that these chunks are the right information to be problem templates in a schema, as discussed in Section 3.2. What we require is a learning mechanism to associate with each template information relevant for solving the problems which it matches. As an example, we

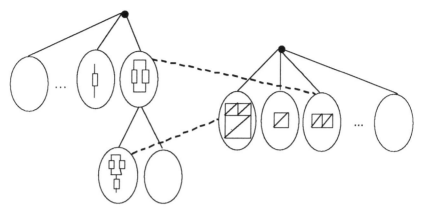

Figure 4 : Multiple discrimination networks, showing two equivalence links and the inheritance structure. Chunks are illustrated at some of the nodes.

consider the learner attempting to acquire schemas for the circuit domain from Section 2, and we will assume that the learner is working with AVOW diagrams.

We consider a learner in a supervised situation provided with a sample circuit and its equivalent AVOW diagram. The discrimination process for perceptually distinguishing instances from each of these representations will tend to build up separate networks, one for the circuits and one for the AVOW diagrams. This process can be performed by CHREST. We now use the methods for combining multiple networks described in [19] to provide CHREST with the ability to associate the node for the circuit diagram with the node for the AVOW diagram. This link between two equivalent representations is known as an *equivalence link*, and we call the extended model CHREST+. The result of this process is illustrated in Figure 4, where some equivalent nodes in discrimination networks for the two representations are shown.

If the learner sees the same circuit in a later setting, either on its own or as part of a larger circuit, then that circuit's chunk will be retrieved from the discrimination network. The equivalence link enables the learner to retrieve a representation for the final form of the AVOW diagram. This mechanism means the learner can decompose complex circuits into sub-circuits which have been encountered previously. As was shown in Section 2.1, the visual pattern of an AVOW diagram works as a template, as it applies to a variety of possible quantities in the circuit. This means that each schema generalises to a wide range of possible problems, thus supporting rapid speed-up learning. However, other representations for solution paths may be used. For instance, if the learner is using algebra, the sequence of algebraic manipulations may be encoded as an ordered list and, through variabilisation, the particular equations may be generalised to a wider class of circuits. This ordered list may be discriminated by CHREST in the same way as the AVOW diagrams, and equivalence links added between the circuit and algebraic nodes. However, because the algebra does not generalise across instances as well as the AVOW diagrams, the complete system will not learn as rapidly, just as is the case with human subjects.

Given quantities	Solution path for the unknown V_A
I_A r_A	Compute $V_A = I_A r_A$
I_B r_B	Compute $V_B = I_B r_B$, then infer $V_A = V_B$
I_B I_C r_A	Infer $I_A = I_C - I_B$, then compute $V_A = I_A r_A$
V_{TOT} V_C	Infer $V_A = V_{TOT} - V_C$
V_{TOT} I_C r_C	Compute $V_C = I_C r_C$, then infer $V_A = V_{TOT} - V_C$

Table 1: Some possible problems from the circuit in Figure 1(a).

5. Avoiding the Utility Problem?

This paper is concerned with the organisation of knowledge for efficient speed-up learning. Earlier work has shown that systems such as PRODIGY [1] and SOAR [2] suffer from the utility problem, in which system efficiency is degraded by the cost of managing the collection of learnt rules. As Minton [1] explains: "To be useful, the cumulative benefits of applying the knowledge must outweigh the cumulative costs of testing whether the knowledge is applicable." In Section 3 we argued that experts use chunks of perceptual information to index domain-specific information stored within schemas. In this section we discuss the efficiency of retrieving the relevant schema based on perceptual information.

As an example, let us consider the circuit in Figure 1(a). Restricting consideration to voltage (V), current (I) and resistance (r), this circuit contains at least 12 quantities: those for the individual resistors and values for the whole circuit. Any one of these may be used as the target unknown for a given problem. For example, assuming the unknown is the voltage across resistor A, V_A, Table 1 lists some possible problems and their solution path. One such table would be required for each of the other 11 quantities.

Imagine now a learning system confronted with a sequence of circuit problems and solution paths such as in the table. The question is how to store this information for later recall. Note that each solution path must be accompanied by its preconditions: in the second example in the table, the resistors A and B must be in parallel. As can be seen, the amount of information which even a simple circuit structure may generate is large. The utility problem now arises because of the cost of locating, within all this information, the piece which relates to a novel situation. Such a system is described by Kieras [20], where explanations for solution paths are used to build up knowledge such as that in Table 1. Kieras notes that "in terms of CPU time, the pattern matching required to instantiate [these rules] can overwhelm the savings from the faster processing of explanations". In other words, the utility problem arises. The assumption in many psychological models using production-rules is that all the productions are matched in parallel, but this condition is not met by designers of practical systems which usually possess a single or restricted number of processors.

In contrast, Section 3 has argued that experts do not directly store information relating to solution paths. Instead, they use easily indexed chunks of perceptual information as a means of referencing information about the kind of problems which arise from similar circuits. Thus, a schema for the circuit in Figure 1(a) will contain a perceptual chunk for the circuit as a whole, and then pointers to the possible solution paths contained in Table 1. The expert therefore does not immediately attempt to recognise a possible solution path out of all those theoretically possible, but instead locates a similar looking circuit: a task of much reduced complexity.

It should also be noted that this method facilitates reuse of previously learnt information. For instance, in recognising the example circuit, the expert, in passing, will identify the top two resistors as a parallel circuit. Any schema for that parallel circuit will thus also be indexed. This means that the information in the second line of Table 1 may be inferred from the parallel circuit schema and not require relearning for more complex examples.

There is still the question of matching the possible solution paths in the schema to the specific circuit quantities; for large circuits the number of possible paths can become large. It is at this point that the advantage of a diagrammatic representation may be seen. The AVOW diagrams discussed in Section 2.1 provide a unified representation for all the possible solution paths given in Table 1: independent of the target unknown and the given quantities, the problem solver must draw a correctly scaled AVOW diagram for the circuit. In every case, a similar series of operations must be carried out, and obtaining the quantity of the unknown is reduced to a simple measurement of the relevant dimension. This unification of solution paths into a diagram means that separate algebraic and inference techniques need not be learnt for every possible solution path. It also means that sequences of operators are automatically fitted to the values provided in the problem. This enables the solver to skip unnecessary steps [4,15].

Further, the separation of the solution template from the sequence of solution steps means the system may readily incorporate information about the problem from different sources. Therefore CHREST+ may be used as an additional mechanism to established problem solving techniques; the proposed solution template may enter a further module which considers its sequence of actions based on the template, other sources of planning information and formal look-ahead.

6. Conclusion

The primary conclusion from this paper is that the avoidance by human experts of the utility problem may be explained through efficient computational mechanisms for learning perceptual schemas. These mechanisms can be incorporated into standard machine learning systems, and also provide guidelines for knowledge representation to maximise the effects of learning.

However, this paper does not claim that the use of expert representations will entirely solve the problems of acquiring and using large volumes of information. This paper is instead intended as a contribution towards designing computers which emulate the ability of humans to learn effective and efficient rules for problem solving. As such, it has proposed a method for using expert representations in learning knowledge for problem solving, and also described principles and computational justifications underlying representations which support efficient problem solving.

References

[1]   Minton, S. (1990). Quantitative results concerning the utility of explanation-based learning. *Artificial Intelligence*, 42, 363-391.

[2]   Laird, J. E., Rosenbloom, P. S., and Newell, A., (1986). Chunking in SOAR: The anatomy of a general learning mechanism. *Machine Learning*, 1, 11-46.

[3]   de Groot, A. N. (1946). *Het denken van den schaker* [Thought and choice in chess]. Amsterdam: North-Holland.

[4]   Koedinger, K. R., & Anderson, J. R. (1990). Abstract planning and perceptual chunks: Elements of expertise in geometry. *Cognitive Science*, 14, 511-550.

[5]   Cheng, P. C-H. (1996). Scientific discovery with law-encoding diagrams. *Creativity Research Journal*, 9, 145-162.

[6]   Cheng, P. C-H. (1998). A framework for scientific reasoning with law encoding diagrams: Analysing protocols to assess its utility. In M. A. Gernsbacher & S. J. Derry (Eds.) *Proceedings of the Twentieth Annual Conference of the Cognitive Science Society* (pp. 232-235). Mahwah, NJ: Erlbaum.

[7]   Cheng, P. C-H. (submitted). Electrifying representations for learning: An evaluation of AVOW diagrams for electricity.

[8]   Larkin, J. H. & Simon, H. A. (1987). Why a diagram is (sometimes) worth ten thousand words. *Cognitive Science*, 11, 65-99.

[9]   Tabachneck-Schijf, H. J. M., Leonardo, A. M., & Simon, H. A. (1997). CaMeRa: A computational model of multiple representations. *Cognitive Science*, 21, 305-350.

[10] Chase, W. G., & Simon, H. A. (1973). Perception in chess. *Cognitive Psychology*, 4, 55-81.

[11] Gobet, F. & Simon, H. A. (in press). Five seconds or sixty? Presentation time in expert memory. *Cognitive Science*.

[12] Simon, H. A. & Gilmartin, K. J. (1973). A simulation of memory for chess positions. *Cognitive Psychology*, 5, 29-46.

[13] Sweller, J. (1988). Cognitive load during problem solving: Effects on learning. *Cognitive Science*, 12, 257-285.

[14] Minsky, M. (1975). A framework for representing knowledge. In P. H. Winston (Ed.), *The psychology of computer vision*. McGraw-Hill, New York.

[15] Koedinger, K. R., & Anderson, J. R. (1993). Reifying implicit planning in geometry: Guidelines for model-based intelligent tutoring system design. In S. P. Lajoie & S. J. Derry (Eds.), *Computers as Cognitive Tools*, Lawrence Erlbaum, New Jersey.

[16] Gobet, F. (1998). Memory for the meaningless: How chunks help. In M. A. Gernsbacher & S. J. Derry (Eds.) *Proceedings of the Twentieth Annual Conference of the Cognitive Science Society* (pp. 398-403). Mahwah, NJ: Erlbaum.

[17] Feigenbaum, E. A., & Simon, H. A. (1984). EPAM-like models of recognition and learning. *Cognitive Science*, 8, 305-336.

[18] Lebowitz, M. (1987). Experiments with incremental concept formation: UNIMEM. *Machine Learning*, 2, 103-138.

[19] Gobet, F. (1996). Discrimination nets, production systems and semantic networks: Elements of a unified framework. *Proceedings of the Second International Conference of the Learning Sciences* (pp. 398-403). Evanston, III: Northwestern University.

[20] Kieras, D. A. (1993). Learning schemas from explanations in practical electronics. In S. Chipman & A. L. Meyrowitz (Eds.) *Foundations of Knowledge Acquisition: Cognitive Models of Complex Learning*, Kluwer Academic Publishers.

Extracting Constraint Knowledge from Code: A Case-Based Reasoning Approach

Andrew Broad[1] and Nick Filer
Department of Computer Science, University of Manchester,
Manchester, England
{broada/nfiler}@cs.man.ac.uk
http://www.cs.man.ac.uk/~broada/

Abstract

The underlying motivation for the authors' research on constraint understanding is *comparative constraint understanding*. The same constraint can be expressed in different ways in different models, and a comparative constraint-understanding system would be able to assess the extent to which two models have equivalent constraint semantics. Understanding constraint semantics can be used to support tasks such as mediation and mapping.

This paper presents a prototype method for understanding constraints in code. In particular, it focuses on understanding the constraints in EXPRESS information models, for which an experimental computerised system has been implemented. A case-based reasoning approach is taken, in which cases suggest so-called *higher-level constraints* to extract from matching fragments of EXPRESS code.

1 Introduction

This paper is about *code understanding*. This means extracting knowledge from code written in a formal language. In particular, this paper focuses on extracting knowledge about *constraints* from code. Constraints are conditions that must not be violated, and can feature, in various guises, in all kinds of code.

The literature on code understanding has tended to focus on program code,

---

1. This work was supported by the Engineering and Physical Sciences Research Council (EPSRC).

calling it *program understanding* [1] or *reverse engineering* [2]. Figure 1 shows a fragment of program code which searches an array for a given goal element. The conditional expressions in the `while` and `if` statements can be thought of as constraints on when the bodies of these constructs can be executed.

```
int index= 0;
while ((index < length) && (array[index] != goal)) {
    index= index + 1;
}
if (index < length) {
    System.out.println(goal + " found at array[" + index
    + "]");
} else {
    System.out.println(goal + " not found");
}
```

Figure 1. Some program code written in Java^2 [3].

Code understanding need not be limited to program code, however. It can be generalised to code written in *any* formal language. For example, Figure 2 shows excerpts from two formal specifications of a stack: a model-based specification, and an algebraic specification.

- The *model-based specification* (Figure 2(a)) specifies two operations on a stack, push and pop. It gives their *signatures* and *preconditions* (constraints on the acceptable inputs to these operations), and *postconditions* (constraints on the output).
- The *algebraic specification* (Figure 2(b)) specifies these two operations in a different way. Two axioms specify their behaviour in relation to each other (as opposed to specifying the operations themselves), and to a third operation, Create (which returns an empty stack).

```
push (s : stack, x : int)                Pop(Create) = Create
    pre true                             Pop(Push(s,i)) = s
    post s' = x::s
pop (s : stack)
    pre length(s) > 0
    post s' = tail(s)
```

| (a) The push and pop operations from a model-oriented specification (adapted from Figure 11.6 in [4]). | (b) Two axioms from an algebraic specification (adapted from Figure 11.5 in [4]). |

Figure 2. Some code from two formal specifications of a stack.

---

2. *Java* is a trademark of Sun Microsystems, Inc.

Figures 2(a) and 2(b) both specify the same behavioural constraints on push and pop in different ways. The constraints are semantically equivalent - implicitly, at an abstract level - in both specifications (except that Figure 2(a) implies that an empty stack cannot be popped, whereas Figure 2(b) *does* sanction popping an empty stack). The authors are particularly interested in *comparative* code understanding, where the same semantics can be expressed in different ways, and in assessing the extent to which the semantics are equivalent.

Information models and *database schemata* are two other kinds of code. They specify integrity constraints on the entities that they model, and so are particularly appropriate to the study of understanding constraints in code. Section 2 of this paper will focus on understanding the constraints in EXPRESS[3] information models. A simple example of an EXPRESS information model is given in Figure 3.

```
SCHEMA simple_people_model;
   ENTITY person;
      name : STRING;
      age : INTEGER;
   WHERE
      age_must_be_sensible:
         (age >= 0) AND (age < 130);
   END_ENTITY;
END_SCHEMA;
```

Figure 3. A simple EXPRESS information model.

The model in Figure 3 defines an entity person (which represents a living person):

- The entity has two *attributes*, name and age. They are not specified to be optional, so every instance of this entity must have values for these attributes, which must be a string and an integer respectively. These can be thought of as constraints imposed by the structure of the model.
- The entity has a *domain rule* called age_must_be_sensible. It constrains the age of a person to be at least zero, and less than 130 years.

Other types of code which can contain constraints include:

- *Database queries* can be thought of as constraints on the records that they retrieve;
- In *rule-based systems*, the antecedents of rules are constraints on when the rules can be fired.
- *Constraint languages* encode networks of constraints (such as adders and multipliers), through which information can propagate (these constraints are tight enough to be able to derive new information from existing information);
- Even languages themselves can be thought of as constraints, which legal strings must satisfy.

---

3. EXPRESS [5] is an international standard (ISO 10303-11) information modelling language.

2 Understanding Constraints in Information Models

The authors' research has focused on understanding the constraints in information models written in EXPRESS. An *information model* is a precise formal specification of the entities in a domain, the relationships between those entities, and the constraints on those entities and relationships [6]. The purpose of an information model is to communicate the semantics of a domain, often with no particular regard for the implementation of applications in that domain.

A *constraint* in an information model is any condition that must not be violated by instances of entities in a repository that conforms to the model. This includes both *explicit conditions* (e.g. domain rules) and *implicit conditions* (e.g. an entity instance must have a value for each of its mandatory attributes, and the value for an attribute must be of the type of that attribute).

```
SCHEMA complicated_people_model;
   ENTITY person ABSTRACT SUPERTYPE OF (ONEOF (man,woman));
      name : STRING;
      age : INTEGER;
      father : OPTIONAL man;
      mother : OPTIONAL woman;
   DERIVE
      orphaned : BOOLEAN
         := NOT EXISTS(father) AND NOT EXISTS(mother);
   UNIQUE
      name;
   WHERE
      age_must_be_sensible:
         (age >= 0) AND (age < 130);
      parents_must_be_older_than_self:
         (father.age > age) AND (mother.age > age);
   END_ENTITY;

   ENTITY man SUBTYPE OF (person);
      wife : OPTIONAL woman;
   END_ENTITY;

   ENTITY woman SUBTYPE OF (person);
   INVERSE
      husband : SET [0 : 1] OF man FOR wife;
   END_ENTITY;
END_SCHEMA;
```

Figure 4. A more complicated EXPRESS information model.

Section 1 has already given an example of an EXPRESS information model and discussed some of the constraints in it. Figure 4 gives a more complicated toy example to illustrate a broader range of constraints in EXPRESS. The constraints, other than the kinds that were covered in the previous example, are:

- The entity `person` is an *abstract supertype* of one of man and woman. This means that every person must be either a man or a woman. The fact that `person` is abstract rules out the possibility of a person being neither a man nor a woman. The `ONEOF` expression rules out the possibility of a person being both a man and a woman.
- The entities man and woman are *subtypes* of `person`. This means that every instance of man or woman must be linked in the subtype-supertype relationship to an instance of `person`. The subtypes man and woman can be thought of as *inheriting* the attributes and constraints from their supertype, `person`.
- The attributes `person:father`, `person:mother` and `man:wife` are *optional attributes*, which means that they are not constrained to have values (they can be 'indeterminate' instead), but if an optional attribute does have a value, that value must be of the type of that attribute. The types of these attributes happen to be entities, which means that their values will be references to entity instances - this establishes association relationships between entities. The model is implicitly restricted to people who are alive at a particular moment in time, so if `father` or `mother` is indeterminate, this could be taken to mean that that parent is dead.
- The entity `person` has a *derived attribute*, `orphaned`. The type of this attribute is `BOOLEAN`, which means its value will be either `TRUE` or `FALSE`. A person is orphaned if both of his/her parents are dead, i.e. if both `father` and `mother` are indeterminate (`EXISTS` is a built-in predicate which returns `true` if an attribute has a value and `false` if it is indeterminate).
- The attribute `person:name` is constrained to be *unique*. That is to say, no two instances of `person` may have the same value for name in this simplified model.
- The entity woman has an *inverse attribute*, `husband`. The type of husband is a set of at least zero and at most one instances of man. That is to say, a woman can either have no husbands or one husband. The inverse attribute constrains the woman's husband (if she has one) to have that woman as his wife. The attributes `man:wife` and `woman:husband` together establish a one-to-one relationship between the entities man and woman.

3 Higher-Level Constraints

The first author has implemented a *constraint-understanding system (CUS)* for EXPRESS models. This work is described in detail in [7].

The CUS 'understands' the constraints in the input model by extracting *higher-level constraints (HLCs)*. Each HLC makes explicit some aspect of the model's constraint semantics, representing this knowledge at a higher level of abstraction than the EXPRESS code itself.

For example, the CUS extracts two instances of the bound HLC class from the domain rule `age_must_be_sensible` in Figure 3. One HLC, extracted from (age >= 0), encodes the fact that there is a lower bound of zero on age, and that the bound is inclusive and discrete. The other HLC, extracted from (age < 130), encodes the upper bound of 130 on age, which is exclusive and discrete.

Having extracted the two bounds, the CUS then extracts an instance of the range HLC class to encode the fact that there is a numeric range constraint on age. So the CUS can extract HLCs directly from the input EXPRESS model, and then more. It can build up a hierarchy of HLCs at increasing levels of abstraction.

Figure 5 shows what these HLCs actually look like when represented formally. They are represented as frames in a language called FIL.[4] Figure 5 is part of a much larger network of frames representing the input model and the HLCs extracted therefrom. Thus, the input model is represented as data which the extraction engine operates on. Figure 5 is annotated with comments to indicate what the other frames referred to represent.

```
INSTANCE bound#19;
   extracted_from = {binary_operation#23}; (* age >= 0 *)
   kind = lower;
   inclusive = true;
   discrete = true;
   variable = explicit_attribute#110; (* age *)
   limit = 0;
END_INSTANCE;

INSTANCE bound#20;
   extracted_from = {binary_operation#24}; (* age < 130 *)
   kind = upper;
   inclusive = false;
   discrete = true;
   variable = explicit_attribute#110; (* age *)
   limit = 130;
END_INSTANCE;

INSTANCE range#2;
   extracted_from = {bound#19, bound#20};
   lower_bound = bound#19;
   upper_bound = bound#20;
   variable = explicit_attribute#110; (* age *)
END_INSTANCE;
```

Figure 5. Three HLCs extracted from the model in Figure 3.

---

4. *FIL* [7] stands for *Frame Instance Language*. Frames are actually instances of entities in EXPRESS models - EXPRESS is used as the frame class language. Any formal language can be represented by an EXPRESS model, and any code in that language can be represented in FIL as an 'abstract syntax tree' of frames that conform to the EXPRESS model.

The underlying motivation for the authors' research on constraint understanding is *comparative constraint understanding*. Whereas the current CUS just extracts HLCs from a single input model, a long-term aim is to be able to compare the semantics of the constraints in two models. The same constraint can be expressed in different ways in different models, and a comparative constraint-understanding system would be able to assess the extent to which two models have equivalent constraint semantics (and the idea generalises to all kinds of code, not just EXPRESS models). The purpose of comparative constraint understanding has driven the invention of HLC types to capture the common semantics of different ways of expressing constraints.

For example, compare Figure 4 with the alternative model of people given in Figure 6. This model represents gender by an enumeration type, rather than by subtypes of person. However, it still has the abstract constraint that an instance of person must have one of two properties to encode his or her gender. This abstract constraint is represented by a HLC called exactly_one, which the CUS can extract from the models in both Figure 4 and Figure 6.

```
SCHEMA flat_people_model;
   ENTITY person;
      name : STRING;
      age : INTEGER;
      gender : gender_type;
   END_ENTITY;

   TYPE gender_type = ENUMERATION OF (male, female);
   END_TYPE;
END_SCHEMA;
```

Figure 6. An alternative model of people.

Some of the other simple HLC classes recognised by the CUS are:

- at_most_one: This is like exactly_one except that it encodes the fact that instances of an entity are constrained to have at most one, rather than exactly one, of a set of properties. This HLC would be extracted from Figure 4 if the supertype were not abstract, and from Figure 6 if gender were an optional attribute.

- non_null: This HLC represents the fact that an attribute is constrained not to be indeterminate. It is extracted from all non-optional attributes (such as name and age in Figure 3), and also when an attribute is constrained by the EXISTS predicate to have a value.

- equation: This HLC encodes the fact that two (or more) expressions are constrained to be equal. It can be extracted from '=' operations in domain rules, and from derived attributes (such as orphaned in Figure 4).

- `adder` and `multiplier`: These HLCs encode the fact that three expressions x, y and z are constrained by the equations $(x + y = z)$ or $(x * y = z)$ respectively. They are extracted from an `equation`, one of whose expressions is a '+' or '*' operation respectively. These two HLCs are other examples of further HLCs (`adder`, `multiplier`) being extracted from HLCs already extracted (`equation`).

4 A Case-Based Reasoning Approach

The CUS takes a *case-based reasoning (CBR)* approach to understanding constraints.

CBR [8] is the enterprise of solving new problems by analogy with old ones, rather than solving all problems from first principles. Essentially, a *case* consists of an old problem and its solution. Cases are stored in a *case library*. To solve a new problem, a case-based reasoner *retrieves* a case in which the old problem is usefully similar to the new problem, so that the old solution can be *adapted* to solve the new problem. The new problem and its solution may then be stored in memory as a case, which can be used in turn to solve future problems.

4.1 The Applicability of CBR to Code Understanding

This section justifies the application of CBR to constraint understanding by justifying its application to the more general topic of code understanding.

One of the main advantages of CBR is that cases can suggest solutions to problems in weak-theory domains [8]. Domains such as medicine and law cannot be completely formalised by a hard-wired algorithm, a set of rules, or a general model. However, there are many *cases* of solving problems in such domains - experiences that are useful for solving similar problems in the future. Code understanding is also a weak-theory domain, in that the link between code and higher-level knowledge - or implementation and specification - is often ill-defined. However, there are plenty of cases of code from the history of computer science, for which a human understanding exists.

A key feature of CBR is that cases cover not just *normative* situations, but also *idiosyncratic* situations [8]. For example, a CBR system might be able to recognise a piece of code as being an implementation of a standard algorithm that differed in some way from the norm. The code might match a case only partially, and the CBR system might have to adapt the 'solution' accordingly. It might even record the experience as a case in memory, to help it to recognise similar situations in the future. Whereas a non-CBR system that relied on exact matching might fail to understand the code at all.

The most obvious advantage of CBR is that it should be more efficient to solve problems by adapting old solutions, rather than trying to solve all new problems from first principles [8]. A case can be thought of as several inferences chunked together, which can be used to solve a new problem in one step rather than many small inference steps. The case holds these inferences together so that the system does not have to search the space of possible inferences, which could lead to combinatorial explosion (code understanding is an NP-complete problem [9]).

Above all, case-based reasoners can learn from experience (by acquiring new cases), which occurs as a natural by-product of reasoning [8]. This enables a CBR system to become more efficient and more competent as it gains in experience, as opposed to traditional expert systems which are brittle because they cannot improve beyond their particular plateaux of expertise [10].

Further advantages of CBR are that it alleviates the *knowledge-elicitation bottleneck* [11] - it is often easier, in complex domains, to elicit cases than a complete set of rules. A CBR system is often easier to build and maintain than the equivalent rule-based system [8], which suggests that CBR is good for prototyping if not for final implementations as well (a case library could be compiled into a hard-wired algorithm for efficiency, at the expense of CBR's ability to learn from experience, and of the flexibility and comprehensibility of a data-driven system).

4.2 A Simple Application of CBR to Constraint Understanding

For code understanding, a case associates a fragment of code (the 'problem' part) with some higher-level knowledge about that code (the 'solution' part). Specifically, in our task of understanding constraints in information models, a case associates a fragment of EXPRESS code with a HLC (or more than one) that expresses the abstract constraint semantics of that fragment. Figure 7 shows a case for extracting an inclusive lower bound from an expression of the form (`attribute` `>=` `limit`).

This is the case that would be used to extract `bound#19` in Figure 5. The CUS retrieves this case whenever it encounters a `binary_operation` frame in (the internal representation of) the input model. It then proceeds to match that frame to the top-level problem frame (`binary_operation#1`) in the case. For the case to match the input model, every slot in `binary_operation#1` must match the corresponding slot in the `binary_operation` frame from the input model. When a slot filler is a reference to another frame in the case, that frame is matched recursively to the corresponding frame in the input model. Variables (such as `?limit`) are matched by unification.

If the 'problem' part of the case (i.e. all frames in the transitive closure of the `case_frame`'s `problem` slot) successfully matches the input model, then the frame(s) in the 'solution' part is reinstantiated for, and attached to, the input model. Any references the solution makes to frames in the case are replaced with the frames they matched in the input model, and variables are replaced with the values they were bound to during matching.

The CUS's cases are all stored in a case library. Cases encode how to extract HLCs of particular classes (such as those listed in Section 3) from an EXPRESS model. There is usually more than one case for each HLC class, either because the semantics of that HLC can be expressed in different ways in EXPRESS, or because of combinatorial variations in its parameters (there are 16 cases to extract bounds, which can be either lower or upper, either inclusive or exclusive, either discrete or continuous, and the relational operation can be written either way round, e.g. a > b is equivalent to b < a).

Cases can include HLCs, as well as EXPRESS code, in their problem parts. These cases are used to extract further HLCs from HLCs already extracted, such as a range from two bounds, or an adder from an equation.

```
INSTANCE case_frame#1;
   problem = binary_operation#1;
   solution = bound#1;
END_INSTANCE;

(***********)
(* Problem *)
(***********)

INSTANCE binary_operation#1;
   operator = greater_than_or_equals;
   first_expression = explicit_attribute#1;
   second_expression = literal_expression#1;
END_INSTANCE;

INSTANCE explicit_attribute#1;
   tipe¹ = simple_type(integer_type);
END_INSTANCE;

INSTANCE literal_expression#1;
   literal_value = integer_literal(?limit);
END_INSTANCE;

(************)
(* Solution *)
(************)

INSTANCE bound#1;
   kind = lower;
   variable = explicit_attribute#1;
   limit = ?limit;
   inclusive = true;
   discrete = true;
   extracted_from = {binary_operation#1};
END_INSTANCE;
```

---

1. type is a reserved word in EXPRESS.

Figure 7. A case (written in FIL) for extracting a bound HLC.

The case in Figure 7 is actually very rule-like, in that it associates a tiny fragment of EXPRESS code with a single HLC, and entails no partial matching and adaptation other than frame substitution and variable binding. However, there could be more 'case-like' cases, which are larger and do require partial matching and adaptation. An example might be interpreting whether an instance of a given entity actually represents an individual object or a class of individual objects (e.g. whether an instance of an entity book represents a book or a copy of a book). There is no hard-and-fast rule for deciding this; there might be clues in the model, but any general rule is likely to have exceptions.

5 Related Work

Code understanding, as reported in the literature, has tended to focus on program code. The motivations for program understanding usually relate to *software maintenance*. It is necessary to understand existing code in order to modify it to meet new requirements (e.g. for extra functionality, improved performance, improved user interface, or debugging).

A common problem mentioned in the literature is that of legacy systems. A *legacy system* is an old piece of software, typically written in an archaic language such as COBOL to run on a long-since outdated platform. Legacy systems often need to be reimplemented in more modern languages, to run on more modern platforms. Also, it is not uncommon for vital knowledge to be embedded in legacy code without having been satisfactorily documented elsewhere.

The process of *reengineering* consists of a reverse engineering (code understanding) step, followed by a forward engineering (code generation) step [2]. Reengineering can be used for such tasks as reimplementing legacy systems, restructuring existing code to make it more readable, efficient or reusable, and translating code from one language to another. Such tasks may not be achievable by direct transformation of the code; rather, they may need to take higher-level knowledge of the source code (as extracted by code understanding techniques) into account.

An important class of code understanding techniques is based on *clichés* [12]. Clichés are commonly-used computational structures. There are *data-structure clichés* such as stacks, queues and hash tables, and *algorithmic clichés* such as sorting or binary search. A system that uses clichés for code understanding has a *cliché library*, which contains *overlays*. Each overlay associates an *implementation cliché* with a *specification cliché*, and encodes the correspondences between the two. Implementation clichés can comprise both fragments of concrete code and intermediate clichés (from which further, more abstract clichés may be extracted). Cliché-based code understanding algorithms work by matching actual fragments of code (and clichés already extracted) to the implementation clichés of overlays, and extracting an instance of the specification cliché of each matching overlay. In this way, a hierarchy of clichés representing the design of the code is built up.

Cliché-based code understanding algorithms can work bottom-up or top-down. Bottom-up approaches start from the code and extract clichés, and can be prone to combinatorial explosion. Top-down approaches start with hypothesised clichés and try to extract them from the code. Quilici [1] uses a hybrid approach which is predominantly bottom-up, but uses top-down recognition for clichés whose presence is implied by others. The CUS presented in this paper works in a wholly bottom-up manner, but will incorporate some top-down extraction for comparative constraint understanding in the future (see Section 6).

There is an analogy between cliché-based and case-based approaches to code understanding. Overlays correspond to cases, and clichés correspond to higher-level knowledge (e.g. HLCs) extracted from code. However, overlays do not admit of any partial matching and adaptation, they correspond to single-step inferences, and they are not learned automatically.

6 Conclusions and Future Work

This paper has presented a system for understanding constraints in EXPRESS information models. The CUS extracts HLCs from EXPRESS code, which embody an understanding of the constraints at an abstract level.

The CUS has been tested on 'toy' EXPRESS models such as Figure 4, and on 'real' EXPRESS models, namely AP212 [13] and the EDIF 4 0 0 Level 0 model [14]. Table 1 shows the number of HLCs, of each class described in Section 3, extracted from each of these models.

	Figure 4	AP212	EDIF 4 0 0 Level 0
bound*	2	0	0
range	1	0	0
exactly_one	1	35	249
at_most_one	0	10	76
non_null	2	415	911
equation	1	241	274
adder	0	3	8
multiplier	0	3	4

*.   The cases for extracting bounds are currently too inflexible
to match in all situations.

Table 1. Table to show the numbers of higher-level constraints of each kind
extracted from three sample models (adapted from Figure 7-1 of [7]).

There are several ways that the CUS could be extended in the future. A short-term goal is to extend it to understand code in languages other than EXPRESS (as discussed in Section 1). The range of HLCs will be extended to cover more of EXPRESS as well as the other languages.

The current version of the CUS is a first step towards case-based code understanding, which is itself useful. However, to reap the full benefits of CBR, it needs to be able to learn its own cases, have cases that it can use to make inferential leaps such as extracting several HLCs at once, and it needs partial matching and adaptation beyond variable unification and frame substitution.

A major area for future research is *comparative constraint understanding* (and, more generally, *comparative code understanding*). This will entail understanding the comparative semantics of the HLCs on two (related) models, assessing to what extent they are semantically equivalent. We will investigate when one constraint *semantically implies* another, in the sense that if the first constraint is satisfied then the second constraint will be satisfied. This would have applications in, for example, transference of constraints for schema-to-schema mapping (see [7]). Comparative code understanding need not be limited to constraints in. EXPRESS models, of course, but may involve comparing other kinds of code (which may or may not be written in the same language as each other).

An issue which arises when code is being understood for a specific purpose (such as *comparative code understanding*) is the *discriminate* extraction of higher-level knowledge. That is to say, some of the higher-level knowledge which the code understanding system knows how to extract might not be useful for the purpose at hand. It will be desirable, in terms of time and space efficiency, to avoid extracting unnecessary knowledge from code. This is likely to entail *meta-level reasoning* about which pieces of knowledge are worth extracting. Meta-level reasoning could also be used to ensure termination within a reasonable length of time (although the current CUS always does so by design).

Finally, the inverse of code understanding, *code generation*, is of interest to the authors. This could range from generating constraints for information models to a CBR approach to the total goal of automatic programming. A *bidirectional* CBR approach may be considered, in which the cases used for code understanding would be used the other way round, for code generation. As well as comparative code understanding, we may also consider *comparative code generation* - generating code to bridge the semantic gap between two pieces of code.

References

1. Quilici A. A memory-based approach to recognizing programming plans. *Communications of the ACM* 1994; 37(5):84-93
2. Chikofsky EJ, Cross JH II. Reverse engineering and design recovery: A taxonomy. *IEEE Software* 1990; 7(1):13-17
3. Grand M. *Java language reference*. O'Reilly & Associates, Sebastopol, 1997
4. van Vliet JC. *Software engineering: Principles and perspective*. John Wiley & Sons, Chichester, 1993

5. ISO TC184/SC4. Industrial automation systems and integration - Product data representation and exchange - Part 11: Description methods: The EXPRESS language reference manual. ISO standard, reference no. ISO 10303-11. ISO, Switzerland, 1994

6. Kasadha FS. An approach to the application of information models. MSc thesis, University of Manchester, Manchester, 1996

7. Broad AP. The application of case-based reasoning to the understanding of constraints on information models. MPhil thesis, University of Manchester, Manchester, 1999. Internet: `http://www.cs.man.ac.uk/~broada/cs/mphil/thesis/`

8. Kolodner JL. *Case-based reasoning*. Morgan Kaufmann Publishers, San Mateo, 1993

9. Woods S, Yang Q. The program understanding problem: Analysis and a heuristic approach. In: Proceedings of the 18th International Conference on Software Engineering (ICSE-96), Berlin, Germany, 1996, pp 6-15

10. Brown MG. A memory model for case retrieval by activation passing. PhD thesis, University of Manchester, Manchester, 1993. Technical report UMCS-94-2-1. Internet: `ftp://ftp.cs.man.ac.uk/pub/TR/UMCS-94-2-1.ps.Z`

11. Watson ID. *Applying case-based reasoning: Techniques for enterprise systems*. Morgan Kaufmann Publishers, San Francisco, 1997

12. Rich C, Wills LM. Recognizing a program's design: A graph-parsing approach. *IEEE Software* 1990; 7(1):82-89

13. ISO TC184/SC4. Industrial automation systems and integration - Product data representation and exchange - Part 212: Application protocol: Electrotechnical design and installation. ISO committee draft, reference no. ISO 10303-212. ISO, Switzerland, 1996. Internet: `http://www.nist.gov/sc4/step/parts/part212/current/part212.exp`

14. Lau RYW. EDIF: Electronic Design Interchange Format version 4 0 0 level 0 information model. Electronic Industries Association, EDIF Steering Committee, 1996

SESSION 2
KNOWLEDGE DISCOVERY

Automatic Induction of Classification Rules from Examples Using N-Prism

Max Bramer

Faculty of Technology, University of Portsmouth, Portsmouth, UK

Max.Bramer@port.ac.uk

www.dis.port.ac.uk/~bramerma

Abstract

One of the key technologies of data mining is the automatic induction of rules from examples, particularly the induction of classification rules. Most work in this field has concentrated on the generation of such rules in the intermediate form of decision trees. An alternative approach is to generate modular classification rules directly from the examples. This paper seeks to establish a revised form of the rule generation algorithm *Prism* as a credible candidate for use in the automatic induction of classification rules from examples in practical domains where noise may be present and where predicting the classification for previously unseen instances is the primary focus of attention.

1 Introduction

In recent years the considerable commercial potential of the sub-field of Machine Learning known as *Data Mining* has increasingly become recognised.

One of the key technologies of data mining is the automatic induction of rules from examples, particularly the induction of classification rules. Many practical questions can be formulated as classification problems, e.g. hospital patients who need an urgent operation, a non-urgent operation or no operation at all, shares which should be sold or bought, those who are likely to respond or not respond to mailshots.

Most work in this field has concentrated on the generation of classification rules in the intermediate form of decision trees, although problems with this approach were identified over a decade ago by Cendrowska [1,2].

In work supervised by the present author, Cendrowska proposed a method of generating modular classification rules directly from examples.

This paper seeks to bring this work up to date and to establish Prism, in a revised form known as N-Prism, as a credible candidate for use in the automatic induction of classification rules from examples in practical domains where noise may be present and where predicting the classification for previously unseen instances (rather than finding the most compact representation of a training set) is the primary focus of attention.

2 Automatic Induction of Classification Rules

2.1 Basic Terminology

It is assumed that there is a universe of *objects*, each of which belongs to one of a set of mutually exclusive *classes* and is described by the values of a collection of its *attributes*. The attributes may either be *categorical*, i.e. take one of a set of discrete values, or *continuous*. Descriptions of a number of objects are held in tabular form in a *training set*, each row of the table comprising an *instance*, i.e. the attribute values and the classification corresponding to one object.

The aim is to develop *classification rules* from the data in the training set in order to enable the classification of previously unseen data in a *test set* to be determined on the basis of its attribute values.

As an example, Table 1 below is a fragment of a training set containing the examination results for a set of university students, linking the results for five final-year subjects (coded as SoftEng, ARIN, HCI, CSA and Project), with their degree classifications (First, Second or Third).

SoftEng	ARIN	HCI	CSA	Project	Class
A	B	A	B	B	Second
A	B	B	B	B	Second
B	A	A	B	A	Second
B	A	A	B	B	Third
A	A	B	B	A	First
B	A	A	B	B	Third
....	....	....	....	....	....
A	A	B	A	B	First

Table 1. Example Training Set: Degree Classifications

The aim is to derive a set of classification rules from the training set which will enable the degree classification to be correctly estimated for students who are not included in the training set. For the above example some possible rules might be:

IF SoftEng = A AND ARIN = A AND Project = A THEN Class = First
IF SoftEng = A AND ARIN = A AND CSA = A THEN Class = First
IF SoftEng = B AND Project = B THEN Class = Third

2.2 Top-Down Induction of Decision Trees

Many systems have been developed to derive classification rules from a training set such as the above. Most do so via the intermediate form of a decision tree constructed using a variant of the basic TDIDT (top-down induction of decision trees) algorithm which can be described informally as follows:

IF all cases in the training set belong to the same class

THEN return the value of the class
ELSE
    (a) select an attribute A to *split* on *
    (b) sort the instances in the training set into non-empty subsets, one for each value of attribute A
    (c) return a tree with one branch for each subset, each branch having a descendant subtree or a class value produced by applying the algorithm recursively for each subset in turn.

* When selecting attributes at step (a) the same attribute must not be selected more than once in any branch.

The induced decision tree can be regarded as a set of *classification rules*, one corresponding to each branch (i.e. each path through the tree from the root node to a leaf node).

Provided that no two instances have the same values of all the attributes but belong to different classes, any method of choosing attributes at step (a) will suffice to produce a decision tree, providing that the same attribute is not chosen twice in the same branch. As the number of attributes is finite, the algorithm is certain to terminate however the attributes are chosen. The most widely used attribute selection criterion is probably *Information Gain*, which uses the information-theoretic measure *entropy* to choose at each stage the attribute which maximises the expected gain of information from applying the additional test. This is the approach adopted in well-known systems such as ID3 [3, 4] and C4.5 [5]. Further details about automatic induction of classification rules are given in [6] and [7].

2.3. Problems with Decision Trees

In a PhD project at the Open University, supervised by the present author, Cendrowska [1, 2] strongly criticised the principle of generating decision trees which can then be converted to decision rules, compared with the alternative of generating decision rules directly from the training set. She comments as follows [the original notation has been changed to be consistent with that used in this paper]:

"[The] decision tree representation of rules has a number of disadvantages. Firstly, decision trees are extremely difficult to manipulate - to extract information about any single classification it is necessary to examine the complete tree, a problem which is only partially resolved by trivially converting the tree into a set of individual rules, as the amount of information contained in some of these will often be more than can easily be assimilated. More importantly, there are rules that cannot easily be represented by trees.

Consider, for example, the following rule set:

Rule 1: IF a = 1 AND b = 1 THEN Class = 1

Rule 2: IF c = 1 AND d = 1 THEN Class =1

Suppose that Rules 1 and 2 cover all instances of Class 1 and all other instances are of Class 2. These two rules cannot be represented by a single decision tree as the root node of the tree must split on a single attribute, and there is no attribute which is common to both rules. The simplest decision tree representation of the set of instances covered by these rules would necessarily add an extra term to one of the rules, which in turn would require at least one extra rule to cover instances excluded by the addition of that extra term. The complexity of the tree would depend on the number of possible values of the attributes selected for partitioning. For example, let the four attributes a, b, c and d each have three possible values 1, 2 and 3, and let attribute a be selected for partitioning at the root node. The simplest decision tree representation of Rules 1 and 2 is shown [below].

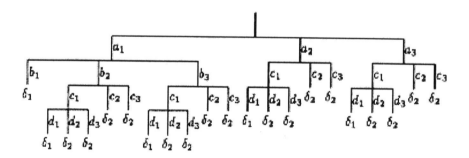

[NOTE: In the figure, notation such as a_1 is used to denote that the value of attribute a is 1 and $\square_1$ to denote that the class value is 1]

The paths relating to Class 1 can be listed as follows:

IF a = 1 AND b = 1 THEN Class = 1
IF a = 1 AND b = 2 AND c = 1 AND d = 1 THEN Class = 1
IF a = 1 AND b = 3 AND c = 1 AND d = 1 THEN Class = 1
IF a = 2 AND c = 1 AND d = 1 THEN Class = 1
IF a = 3 AND c = 1 AND d = 1 THEN Class = 1

Clearly, the consequence of forcing a simple rule set into a decision tree representation is that the individual rules, when extracted from the tree, are often too specific (i.e. they reference attributes which are irrelevant). This makes them highly unsuitable for use in many domains."

The phenomenon of unnecessarily large and confusing decision trees described by Cendrowska is far from being merely a rare hypothetical possibility. It will occur whenever there are two (underlying) rules with no attribute in common, a situation that is likely to occur frequently in practice.

All the rules corresponding to the branches of a decision tree must begin in the same way, i.e. with a test on the value of the attribute selected at the top level. This effect will inevitably lead to the introduction of terms in rules (branches) which are unnecessary except for the sole purpose of enabling a tree structure to be constructed. Considerable practical problems can arise when the value of the attribute which all the derived rules have in common is unknown at problem-solving time or can only be obtained by means of a test that carries an unusually high cost or risk to health.

Systems which generate classification *rules* e.g. C4.5Rule [5] generally do so by *post-pruning*, i.e. first generating a classification tree, converting this to a set of equivalent classification rules (one rule per branch of the tree) and then generalising the rules by removing redundant terms. Although reasonably successful this seems an unnecessarily indirect way of generating a set of rules.

2.4 The Prism Algorithm

The approach adopted by Cendrowska in her Prism system was to induce classification rules directly from the training set, by selecting a combination of attribute-value pairs to maximise the probability of each target outcome class in turn.

In its basic form, the Prism algorithm for induction of classification rules is as follows, assuming that there are n (>1) possible classes:

For each class i from 1 to n inclusive:

(1) Calculate the probability that class = i for each attribute-value pair

(2) Select the attribute-value pair with the maximum probability and create a subset of the training set comprising all instances with the selected combination (for all classes)

(3) Repeat 1 and 2 for this subset until it contains only instances of class i. The induced rule is then the conjunction of all the attribute-value pairs selected in creating this subset

(4) Remove all instances covered by this rule from the training set

Repeat 1-4 until all instances of class i have been removed

Note that the training set is restored to its original state for each new class.

A detailed example showing the above algorithm applied to a small example dataset is given in the Appendix.

Although successful in terms of its original objectives, as determined by measurements against ID3, an algorithm widely used for decision tree induction [4], Cendrowska's project focussed on the problem of inducing a complete and correct set of 'maximally general' rules from a complete set of examples rather than the problem of predicting the classification of other instances (previously unseen). It is this latter problem which is currently of primary interest.

3 N-Prism and Inducer

N-Prism is a reimplementation of the basic form of the Prism algorithm in Java, incorporating a number of revised features, some of which are described in the following sections.

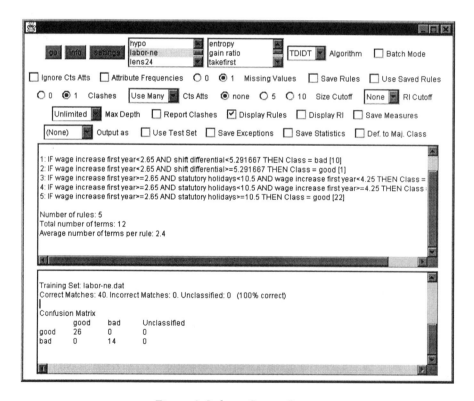

Figure 1. Inducer Screen Image

The algorithm is implemented in Java version 1.1 as part of the **Inducer** classification tree and classification rule induction package [8]. The package is available both as a standalone application and as an applet. Inducer also incorporates the TDIDT algorithm with the entropy attribute selection criterion (as well as a range of alternative criteria).

Figure 1 shows a screen image of Inducer running the 'labor negotiations' dataset from the UCI repository [9].

The package, which was originally developed for teaching purposes, includes a wide range of features to aid the user, including facilities to save rule sets and other information, to apply a variety of cut-offs during tree/rule generation and to adopt different strategies for handling missing data values.

In the following sections a number of experiments are described which compare the two principal approaches to classification rule generation implemented in Inducer, i.e. TDIDT with entropy as the attribute selection criterion and Prism in its revised form as N-Prism. The algorithms will generally be referred to simply as TDIDT and Prism where there is no likelihood of confusion arising. Classification trees generated by TDIDT are treated throughout as equivalent to collections of rules, one corresponding to each branch of the tree.

The approach adopted here, i.e. comparing two algorithms on a common platform (Inducer) is preferred in the interest of fair comparison to the near-traditional one of making comparison with Quinlan's well-known program C4.5. The latter contains many additional features developed over a period of years that might potentially be applied to a wide range of other tree/rule generation algorithms as well as the ones included, and therefore might make a fair comparison of basic algorithms difficult to achieve.

4 Rule Set Complexity

The complexity of a rule set can be measured in terms of (at least) three parameters:

(a) the number of rules
(b) the average number of terms per rule
(c) the total number of terms in all rules combined

the third value being simply the product of the first two.

To compare TDIDT and N-Prism against these three criteria, classification rules were generated using both algorithms for eight selected datasets (training sets). The datasets used are summarised in Table 2.

The *contact_lenses* dataset is a reconstruction of data given in [2]. The *chess* dataset is a reconstruction of chess endgame data used for experiments described in [10]. The other six datasets have been taken from the well-known UCI repository of machine learning datasets [9], which is widely used for experiments of this kind. Where necessary, they have been converted to the data format used by *Inducer*. Further information about the datasets used here and in subsequent experiments is generally provided with the datasets themselves in the UCI repository.

Dataset	Description	Number of Classes	Number of Attributes	No. of Instances *
agaricus_ lepiota +	Mushroom Records	2	22	5000 (74)
chess	Chess Endgame	2	7	647
contact_ lenses	Contact Lenses	3	5	108
genetics	Gene Sequences	19	35	3190
monk1	Monk's Problem 1	2	6	124
monk2	Monk's Problem 2	2	6	169
monk3	Monk's Problem 3	2	6	122
soybean	Soybean Disease Diagnosis	19	35	683 (121)

Table 2. Datasets used in Rule Set Complexity Experiment

* Figures in parentheses denote the number of instances with missing values included in the previous value. Only non-zero values are shown. Missing values can be handled in a variety of ways. For the purposes of the experiments described in this paper, missing values of an attribute have been replaced by the most commonly occurring value of that attribute in every case.

+ Only the first 5000 instances in the dataset were used.

The table shows the number of attributes used for classification in each of the given datasets. The principal criterion for selecting the datasets was that all the attributes should be *categorical*, i.e. have a finite number of discrete values. In its present implementation, N-Prism does not accept continuous attributes. In practice this limitation can be overcome if necessary by prior discretization of any continuous attributes using an algorithm such as *ChiMerge* [11]. A version of N-Prism that includes the processing of continuous attributes is currently under development.

4.1 Experimental Results

Table 3 summarises the number of rules, the average number of terms per rule and the total number of terms for all rules combined for both algorithms for each of the eight datasets.

The results are displayed graphically in Figures 2, 3 and 4. In the first two, the number of rules and terms generated by Prism for each dataset have been expressed as a percentage of the figure for TDIDT (given as 100 in each case).

	No. of Instances	Number of Rules		Av. No. of Terms		Total No. of Terms	
		TDIDT	Prism	TDIDT	Prism	TDIDT	Prism
agaricus_ lepiota	5000	17	22	2.18	1.23	37	27
chess	647	20	15	5.25	3.20	105	48
contact_ lenses	108	16	15	3.88	3.27	62	49
genetics	3190	389	244	5.71	3.95	2221	963
monk1	124	46	25	4.04	3.00	186	75
monk2	169	87	73	4.74	4.00	412	292
monk3	122	28	26	3.36	2.81	94	73
soybean	683	109	107	5.45	3.57	594	382

Table 3. Comparison of Rule Set Complexity: TDIDT v Prism

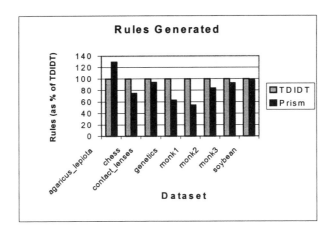

Figure 2. Comparison of Rule Set Complexity: Rules Generated

With the (partial) exception of *agaricus_lepiota*, the results uniformly show that Prism produces fewer rules than TDIDT and that on average each rule includes fewer terms. The combined effect of these results can be a very substantial reduction in the total number of terms generated for all rules combined (down from 2221 to 963 in the case of *genetics*).

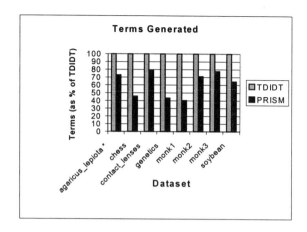

Figure 3. Comparison of Rule Set Complexity: Terms Generated

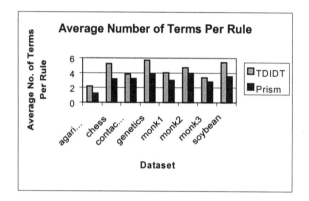

Figure 4. Comparison of Rule Set Complexity: Average Number of Terms per Rule

The above results strongly indicate that Prism produces a more compact set of classification rules than TDIDT. This is in line with Cendrowska's original findings. In the following sections further experiments are described, first to compare the classification accuracy of the two algorithms on previously unseen data, followed by experiments with less 'well-behaved' datasets than those examined so far.

5 Classification Accuracy

The same eight datasets were used for this experiment as for the experiment on rule set complexity. In each case the complete dataset was divided randomly into two parts, a training set and a test set, in the approximate ratio 70% to 30%. Each algorithm was then used to construct a set of classification rules from the training set. The rules were then used to classify the instances in the previously unseen test set.

5.1 Experimental Results

Table 4 below summarises the results.

The numbers of unseen instances correctly classified by the two algorithms are similar, with a small advantage to TDIDT. The number of incorrectly classified instances is generally smaller in the case of Prism, with a particularly substantial improvement over TDIDT in the case of the *genetics* dataset.

	No. of Instances in Test Set	Correct		Incorrect		Unclassified	
		TDIDT	Prism	TDIDT	Prism	TDIDT	Prism
agaricus_ lepiota	1478	1474	1474	1	1	3	3
chess	182	181	178	1	2	0	2
contact_ lenses	33	30	28	3	3	0	2
genetics	950	839	825	90	58	21	67
monk1	36	26	25	9	8	1	3
monk2	52	22	27	28	24	2	1
monk3	36	33	28	3	5	0	3
soybean	204	174	169	22	20	8	15

Table 4. Comparison of Classification Accuracy: TDIDT v. Prism

The main difference between the two algorithms is that Prism generally produces more unclassified instances than TDIDT does. In most cases this corresponds principally to a reduction in the number of misclassified instances. This result is in line with those obtained from other datasets (not reported here).

In some task domains, there may be no significant difference between wrongly classified and unclassified instances. In others, it may be of crucial importance to avoid classification errors wherever possible, in which case using Prism would seem to be preferable to using TDIDT. In some domains, unclassified instances may not be acceptable or the principal objective may be to maximise the number of correct classifications. In this case, a method is needed to assign unclassified instances to one of the available categories. There are several ways in which this may be done.

A simple technique, which is implemented in Inducer for both TDIDT and Prism, is to assign any unclassified instances in the test set to the largest category in the training set. Table 5 shows the effect of adjusting the results in Table 4 by assigning unclassified instances to the majority class in each case.

	No. of Instances in Test Set	Correct		Incorrect	
		TDIDT	Prism	TDIDT	Prism
agaricus_lepiota	1478	1477	1477	1	1
chess	182	181	180	1	2
contact_lenses	33	30	29	3	4
genetics	950	849	847	101	103
monk1	36	27	28	9	8
monk2	52	24	28	28	24
monk3	36	33	30	3	6
soybean	204	175	173	29	31

Table 5. Comparison of Classification Accuracy:
Unclassified Assigned to Majority Class

With this change the results for TDIDT and Prism are virtually identical, although marginally in favour of TDIDT. More sophisticated methods of dealing with unclassified instances might well swing the balance in favour of Prism.

6 Dealing with Clashes

Clashes occur during the classification tree/rule generation process whenever an algorithm is presented with a subset of the training set which contains instances with more than one classification, but which cannot be broken down further. Such a subset is known as a 'clash set'.

The principal cause of clashes is the presence of inconsistent data in the training set, where two or more instances have the same attribute values but different classifications. In such cases, a situation will inevitably occur during tree/rule generation where a subset with mixed classifications is reached, with no further attributes available for selection.

The simplest way to deal with clashes is to treat all the instances in the clash set as if they belong to the class of the majority of them and generate a rule (or branch of a classification tree) accordingly. This 'assign all to majority class' method is the default method used in *Inducer*.

In its original form Prism had no provision for dealing with clashes. This is in line with the aim of finding compact representations of a complete training set (i.e. a training set containing all possible combinations of attribute values). However, for practical applications it is imperative to be able to handle clashes.

Step (3) of the basic Prism algorithm states:

'Repeat 1 and 2 for this subset until it contains only instances of class i'.

To this needs to be added 'or a subset is reached which contains instances of more than one class, although all the attributes have already been selected in creating the subset'.

The simple approach of assigning all instances in the subset to the majority class does not fit directly into the Prism framework. A number of approaches to doing so have been investigated, the most effective of which would appear to be as follows.

If a clash occurs while generating the rules for class i:

(a) Determine the majority class for the subset of instances in the clash set.
(b) If this majority class is class i, then complete the induced rule for classification i. If not, discard the rule.

6.1 Clashes in Training Sets

The next experiment is a comparison between TDIDT and Prism in the case of datasets where there is a substantial total number of 'clash instances'.

To generate such datasets, five standard datasets were selected from the UCI repository, each with both categorical and continuous attributes. In each case the continuous attributes were effectively discarded, using the 'ignore continuous attributes' facility of *Inducer*. This results in training sets with a high level of inconsistency, from which a significant number of misclassifications of unseen test data would be expected.

Table 6 summarises the five datasets used in this experiment. The comparative classification accuracy of the two algorithms is summarised in Table 7, with unclassified instances assigned to the majority class as before. (In the case of TDIDT, clashes encountered during tree generation are handled by the default method described previously.)

Although the two algorithms again produce very similar results, in this case Prism outperforms TDIDT for four datasets out of the five tested.

Dataset	Description	No of Classes	Number of Attributes		No. of Instances *	Clash Instances **
			Categ.	Contin.		
australian_credit	Credit Approval	2	8	6	690	164
crx	Credit Card Applications	2	9	6	690 (37)	170
hepatitis	Medical	2	13	6	155	20
hypo	Hypothyroid Data	5	22	7	2514 (2514)	1843
sick-euthyroid	Medical	2	18	7	3163	2264

Table 6. Datasets used in Clash Experiment

* Figures in parentheses denote the number of instances with missing values included in the previous value. Only non-zero values are shown.
** Following deletion of the continuous attributes.

	No. of Instances in Test Set *	Correct		Incorrect	
		TDIDT	Prism	TDIDT	Prism
australian_credit	202	164	158	38	44
crx	200 (12)	181	188	19	12
hepatitis	48	35	36	33	12
hypo	1258 (1258)	1158	1159	100	99
sick-euthyroid	943	855	857	88	86

Table 7. Comparison of Classification Accuracy:
Unclassified Assigned to Majority Class

* Number of instances with missing values in parentheses (if non-zero)

7 Noise in Datasets

The presence of noise in data is an unavoidable problem in many domains and it is important that any algorithm intended for practical use copes well when it is present.

The effect of noise on a classification algorithm can be examined by taking a dataset which is known (or believed) to be free of noise in both the training set and the test set and then progressively introducing noise into both. The dataset chosen for this final experiment was the Vote dataset from the UCI repository, which contains information taken from the 1984 United States congressional voting records. The dataset has 16 attributes (all categorical), 2 classes (Republican and Democrat), with 300 instances in the training set and 135 instances in the test set.

As a preliminary to the experiment, a number of versions of both the training set and the test set were generated by introducing noise into the values of all the attributes (including the classification). If the noise level were 20% say, then for each instance in the training or test set every attribute (including the classification) was randomly assigned either a noise value or its own original value on a random basis in proportion 20% to 80%. A 'noise value' here denotes any of the valid values for the attribute (or classification), including its original value, chosen with equal probability.

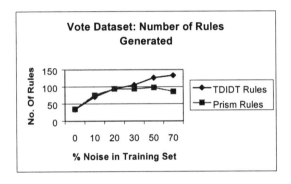

Figure 5. Number of Rules Generated for Varying Levels of Noise in the 'Vote' Training Set

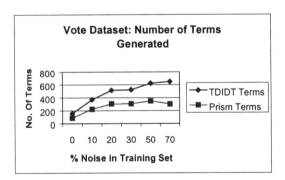

Figure 6. Number of Terms Generated for Varying Levels of Noise in the 'Vote' Training Set

For each of a range of levels of noise in the training set (0%, 10%, 20%, 30%, 50% and 70%) a set of classification rules was generated for each algorithm and then used to classify different versions of the test data with noise levels from 0%, 10%, 20% up to 80%. The results of the experiments are summarised in Figures 5-7.

114

From Figures 5 and 6 it can be seen that TDIDT almost invariably produced more rules and more total terms compared with Prism. As the level of noise in the training set increases, Prism's advantage also increases until with 70% noise in the training set, the number of rules and terms produced by TDIDT are as much as 55% and 113% greater respectively than those produced by Prism (133 v 86 rules, 649 v 304 terms).

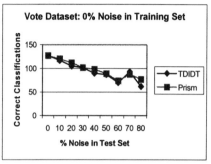
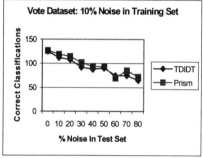
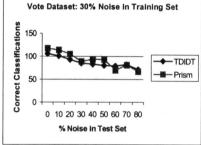
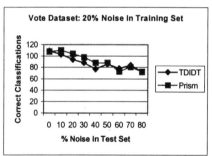
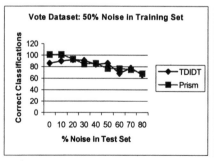
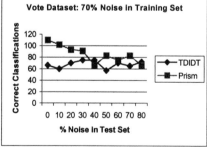

Figure 7. Effects of Introducing Noise into the 'Vote' Training and Test Sets

Figure 7 shows the comparative levels of classification accuracy of the two algorithms for varying levels of noise in the training set. Again Prism outperforms TDIDT in almost all the trials, the advantage increasing as the level of noise increases.

8 Conclusions

The experiments presented here suggest that the Prism algorithm for generating modular rules gives classification rules which are at least as good as those obtained from the widely used TDIDT algorithm. There are generally fewer rules with fewer terms per rule, which is likely to aid their comprehensibility to domain experts and users. This result would seem to apply even more strongly when there is noise in the training set.

As far as classification accuracy on unseen test data is concerned, there appears to be little to choose between the two algorithms for 'normal' (noise-free) datasets, including ones with a significant proportion of clash instances in the training set. The main difference is that Prism generally has a preference for leaving a test instance as 'unclassified' rather than giving it a wrong classification. In some domains this may be an important feature. When it is not, a simple strategy such as assigning unclassified instances to the majority class would seem to suffice.

When noise is present, Prism would seem to give consistently better classification accuracy than TDIDT, even when there is a high level of noise in the training set. In view of the likelihood of most 'real world' datasets containing noise, possibly in a high proportion, these results strongly support the value of using the Prism modular rule approach over the decision trees produced by the TDIDT algorithm. The reasons why Prism should be more tolerant to noise than TDIDT are not entirely clear, but may be related to the presence of fewer terms per rule in most cases.

The computational effort involved in generating rules using Prism, at least in its standard form, is greater than for TDIDT. However, Prism would seem to have considerable potential for efficiency improvement by parallelisation.

Future investigations will use the *Inducer* framework to compare Prism, in its revised form as N-Prism, with other less widely used algorithms such as ITRULE [12].

References

1. Cendrowska, J. PRISM: an Algorithm for Inducing Modular Rules. International Journal of Man-Machine Studies, 1987; 27: 349-370

2. Cendrowska, J. Knowledge Acquisition for Expert Systems: Inducing Modular Rules from Examples. PhD Thesis, The Open University, 1990

3. Quinlan, J.R. Learning Efficient Classification Procedures and their Application to Chess Endgames. In: Michalski, R.S., Carbonell, J.G. and Mitchell, T.M. (eds.), Machine Learning: An Artificial Intelligence Approach. Tioga Publishing Company, 1983

4. Quinlan, J.R. Induction of Decision Trees. Machine Learning, 1986; 1: 81-106

5. Quinlan, J. R. C4.5: Programs for Machine Learning. Morgan Kaufmann, 1993

6. Bramer, M. A. Rule Induction in Data Mining: Concepts and Pitfalls (Part 1). Data Warehouse Report. Summer 1997; 10: 11-17

7. Bramer, M. A. Rule Induction in Data Mining: Concepts and Pitfalls (Part 2). Data Warehouse Report. Autumn 1997; 11: 22-27

8. Bramer, M. A. The Inducer User Guide and Reference Manual. Technical Report: University of Portsmouth, Faculty of Technology, 1999

9. Blake, C.L. and Merz, C.J. UCI Repository of Machine Learning Databases [http://www.ics.uci.edu/~mlearn/MLRepository.html]. Irvine, CA: University of California, Department of Information and Computer Science, 1998

10. Quinlan, J.R. Discovering Rules by Induction from Large Collections of Examples. In: Michie, D. (ed.), Expert Systems in the Micro-electronic Age. Edinburgh University Press, 1979, pp 168-201

11. Kerber, R. ChiMerge: Discretization of Numeric Attributes. In: Proceedings of the 10th National Conference on Artificial Intelligence. AAAI, 1992, pp 123-128

12. Smyth, P. and Goodman, R.M. Rule Induction Using Information Theory. In: Piatetsky-Shapiro, G. and Frawley, W.J. (eds.), Knowledge Discovery in Databases. AAAI Press, 1991, pp 159-176

13. McSherry, D. Strategic Induction of Decision Trees. In: Miles, R., Moulton, M. and Bramer, M. (eds.), Research and Development in Expert Systems XV. Springer-Verlag, 1999, pp 15-26

Appendix. Prism: A Worked Example

The following example shows in detail the operation of the basic Prism algorithm when applied to the training set *lens24*, which has 24 instances.

This dataset was introduced by Cendrowska [1,2] and has been widely used subsequently (see for example [13]). It is a subset of Cendrowska's 108-instance *contact_lenses* dataset referred to in Table 2.

The attributes *age*, *specRx*, *astig* and *tears* correspond to the age of the patient, the spectacle prescription, whether or not the patient is astigmatic and his or her tear production rate, respectively. The three possible classifications are that the patient should be fitted with (1) hard contact lenses, (2) soft contact lenses or (3) is not suitable for wearing contact lenses.

In this example, Prism is used to generate the classification rules corresponding to class 1 only. It does so by repeatedly making use of the probability of attribute-value pairs.

age	specRx	astig	tears	class
1	1	1	1	3
1	1	1	2	2
1	1	2	1	3
1	1	2	2	1
1	2	1	1	3
1	2	1	2	2
1	2	2	1	3
1	2	2	2	1
2	1	1	1	3
2	1	1	2	2
2	1	2	1	3
2	1	2	2	1
2	2	1	1	3
2	2	1	2	2
2	2	2	1	3
2	2	2	2	3
3	1	1	1	3
3	1	1	2	3
3	1	2	1	3
3	1	2	2	1
3	2	1	1	3
3	2	1	2	2
3	2	2	1	3
3	2	2	2	3

Table 8. The lens24 Training Set

Class 1: First Rule

The table below shows the probability of each attribute-value pair occurring for the whole training set (24 instances).

Attribute-value pair	Frequency for class = 1	Total Frequency (24 instances)	Probability
age = 1	2	8	0.25
age = 2	1	8	0.125
age = 3	1	8	0.125
specRx = 1	3	12	0.25
specRx = 2	1	12	0.083
astig = 1	0	12	0
astig = 2	4	12	0.33
tears = 1	0	12	0
tears = 2	4	12	0.33

The attribute-value pairs that maximise the probability of Class 1 are *astig = 2* and *tears = 2*. Choose *astig = 2* arbitrarily.

The (incomplete) rule induced so far is: **IF astig = 2 THEN class = ?**

The subset of the training set covered by this rule is:

age	specRx	astig	tears	class
1	1	2	1	3
1	1	2	2	1
1	2	2	1	3
1	2	2	2	1
2	1	2	1	3
2	1	2	2	1
2	2	2	1	3
2	2	2	2	3
3	1	2	1	3
3	1	2	2	1
3	2	2	1	3
3	2	2	2	3

The next table shows the probability of each attribute-value pair (not involving attribute *astig*) occurring for this subset

Attribute-value pair	Frequency for class = 1	Total Frequency (12 instances)	Probability
age = 1	2	4	0.5
age = 2	1	4	0.25
age = 3	1	4	0.25
specRx = 1	3	6	0.5
specRx = 2	1	6	0.17
tears = 1	0	6	0
tears = 2	4	6	0.67

The maximum probability occurs when *tears* = 2

Rule induced so far: **IF astig = 2 and tears = 2 THEN class = ?**

The subset of the training set covered by this rule is now

age	specRx	astig	tears	class
1	1	2	2	1
1	2	2	2	1
2	1	2	2	1
2	2	2	2	3
3	1	2	2	1
3	2	2	2	3

The next table shows the probability of each attribute-value pair occurring for this subset

Attribute-value pair	Frequency for class = 1	Total Frequency (6 instances)	Probability
age = 1	2	2	1.0
age = 2	1	2	0.5
age = 3	1	2	0.5
specRx = 1	3	3	1.0
specRx = 2	1	3	0.33

The maximum probability occurs when *age* = 1 or *specRx* = *1*. Choose (arbitrarily) *age* = 1

Rule induced so far: **IF astig = 2 and tears = 2 and age = 1 THEN Class = ?**

The subset of the training set covered by this rule is:

age	specRx	astig	tears	class
1	1	2	2	1
1	2	2	2	1

This subset contains only instances of class 1.

The final induced rule is therefore
IF astig = 2 and tears = 2 and age = 1 THEN Class = 1

Class 1: Second Rule

Removing all instances covered by this rule from the training set gives a new training set (22 instances)

age	specRx	astig	tears	class
1	1	1	1	3
1	1	1	2	2
1	1	2	1	3
1	2	1	1	3
1	2	1	2	2
1	2	2	1	3
2	1	1	1	3
2	1	1	2	2
2	1	2	1	3
2	1	2	2	1
2	2	1	1	3
2	2	1	2	2
2	2	2	1	3
2	2	2	2	3
3	1	1	1	3
3	1	1	2	3
3	1	2	1	3
3	1	2	2	1
3	2	1	1	3
3	2	1	2	2
3	2	2	1	3
3	2	2	2	3

The table of frequencies for attribute-value pairs corresponding to *class* = *1* is now as follows

Attribute-value pair	Frequency for class = 1	Total Frequency (22 instances)	Probability
age = 1	0	6	0
age = 2	1	8	0.125
age = 3	1	8	0.125
specRx = 1	2	11	0.18
specRx = 2	0	11	0
astig = 1	0	12	0
astig = 2	2	10	0.2
tears = 1	0	12	0
tears = 2	2	10	0.2

The maximum probability occurs when *astig* = *2* or *tears* = *2*.
Choose *astig=2* arbitrarily.

Rule induced so far: **IF astig=2 THEN Class= ?**

The subset of the training set covered by this rule is:

age	specRx	astig	tears	class
1	1	2	1	3
1	2	2	1	3
2	1	2	1	3
2	1	2	2	1
2	2	2	1	3
2	2	2	2	3
3	1	2	1	3
3	1	2	2	1
3	2	2	1	3
3	2	2	2	3

Giving the following frequency table

Attribute-value pair	Frequency for class = 1	Total Frequency (10 instances)	Probability
age = 1	0	2	0
age = 2	1	4	0.25
age = 3	1	4	0.25
specRx = 1	0	5	0
specRx = 2	2	5	0.4
tears = 1	0	6	0
tears = 2	2	4	0.5

The maximum probability occurs when *tears* = *2*.

Rule induced so far: **IF astig = 2 and tears = 2 then class = ?**

The subset of the training set covered by this rule is:

age	specRx	astig	tears	class
2	1	2	2	1
2	2	2	2	3
3	1	2	2	1
3	2	2	2	3

Giving the following frequency table

Attribute-value pair	Frequency for class = 1	Total Frequency (4 instances)	Probability
age = 1	0	0	
age = 2	1	2	0.5
age = 3	1	2	0.5
specRx = 1	2	2	1.0
specRx = 2	0	2	0

The maximum probability occurs when *specRx = 1*

Rule induced so far: **IF astig = 2 and tears = 2 and specRx = 1 THEN class = ?**

The subset of the training set covered by this rule is:

age	specRx	astig	tears	class
2	1	2	2	1
3	1	2	2	1

This subset contains only instances of class 1.

So the final induced rule is:
IF astig = 2 and tears = 2 and specRx = 1 THEN class = 1

Removing all instances covered by this rule from the training set (i.e. the version with 22 instances) gives a training set of 20 instances from which all instances of class 1 have now been removed. So the Prism algorithm terminates (for class 1).

The two rules induced by Prism for Class 1 are therefore:

IF astig = 2 and tears = 2 and age = 1 THEN class = 1
IF astig = 2 and tears = 2 and specRx = 1 THEN class = 1

Learning Lazy Rules to Improve the Performance of Classifiers

Kai Ming Ting, Zijian Zheng & Geoffrey Webb

School of Computing and Mathematics,

Deakin Univeristy, Australia.

{kmting,zijian,webb}@deakin.edu.au

Abstract

Based on an earlier study on lazy Bayesian rule learning, this paper introduces a general lazy learning framework, called LAZYRULE, that begins to learn a rule only when classifying a test case. The objective of the framework is to improve the performance of a base learning algorithm. It has the potential to be used for different types of base learning algorithms. LAZYRULE performs attribute elimination and training case selection using cross-validation to generate the most appropriate rule for each test case. At the consequent of the rule, it applies the base learning algorithm on the selected training subset and the remaining attributes to construct a classifier to make a prediction. This combined action seeks to build a better performing classifier for each test case than the classifier trained using all attributes and all training cases. We show empirically that LAZYRULE improves the performances of naive Bayesian classifiers and majority vote.

1 Introduction

Lazy learning [2] is a class of learning techniques that spend little or no effort during training and delay the computation to the classification time. No concise models, such as decision trees or rules, are created at training time. When classifying a test case, a lazy learning algorithm performs its computation in two stages. First, it selects a subset of the training cases that are relevant to classifying the case in question. Then, a classifier is constructed using this training subset; and the classifier is ultimately employed to classify the test case. The case selection process in the first stage is a crucial part in lazy learning that ultimately influences the classifier to be constructed in the second stage.

The archetypal example of a lazy learning algorithm is the k-nearest neighbor algorithm or instance-based learning algorithm [1, 8, 10]. In its basic form, the k-nearest neighbor algorithm stores all training cases. At classification time, it computes a distance measure between the test case and each of the training cases, and selects the nearest k training cases from the first stage. A simple majority vote is used in the second stage—the majority class of the k nearest training cases is predicted to be the class for the test case. Another example is LAZYDT [12], which creates decision rules at classification time to select a subset of training cases, and then performs majority vote to make a prediction.

LBR [20] uses a lazy learning technique developed to improve the performance of naive Bayesian classification. For each test case, it generates a most appropriate rule with a conjunction of attribute-value pairs as its antecedent and a local naive Bayesian classifier as its consequent. The local naive Bayesian classifier is built using the subset of training cases that satisfy the antecedent of the rule, and is used to classify the test case. The main objective of creating rules is to alleviate the attribute inter-dependence problem of naive Bayesian classification.

There are several variations, especially on the method to select a training subset. For example, the Optimized Set Reduction (OSR) algorithm [5] first identifies a set of plausible rules R, based on an entropy measure, that cover the case X to be classified. The set of training cases S is then formed, containing all training cases covered by any rule in R. X is then classified using Bayesian classification with probability estimates derived from the distributions of attribute values in S. Fulton et al. [13] describe a variation of the k-nearest neighbor algorithm that selects more than one subset. For a given test case, a sequence of k decision trees is induced using 1,2,...,k nearest cases. Then a weighted voting scheme is employed to make the final prediction. Fulton et al. [13] also explore two other alternative techniques to select a single training subset. One or more decision trees are generated in all these techniques. Because all of these three techniques always produce the same training subset for a test case no matter what base learning algorithm is used in the second stage, they are unlikely to be amenable for different types of base learning algorithm. The Learning All Rules approach [19] performs lazy learning of decision rules.

The lazy learning algorithms described so far are meant to be used as a stand-alone classifier. There is a lack of a general framework of lazy learning that can be used to improve the performance of a chosen learning algorithm which is to be employed to produced a classifier in the second stage of the lazy classification process. In the crucial stage of training subset selection, the criteria, usually heuristics, used by these lazy learning algorithms except LBR are not directly relevant to the base classifiers employed in the second stage. This paper introduces a lazy learning framework, as a generalization of LBR [20], that performs both attribute elimination and training case selection. When doing these, the chosen learning algorithm, which is to be employed in the second stage, is utilized in the evaluation process. This framework is intended to improve the performance of the chosen base learning algorithm.

The following section describes the LAZYRULE framework. Section 3 contains the empirical evaluation to investigate whether the framework can be used to improve the performance of two types of base learning algorithms. Section 4 discusses the advantages and limitations of LAZYRULE. The final section summarizes our findings and describes possible future work.

2 The Lazy Rule Learning Framework

This section describes the lazy learning framework, called LAZYRULE. Like most of the other lazy learning algorithms, LAZYRULE stores all training cases, and begins to compute only when a classification is required.

To classify a test case, LAZYRULE generates a rule that is most appropriate to the test case. The antecedent of a lazy rule is a conjunction of attribute-value pairs or conditions, and each condition is in the form of 'attribute=value'. The current version of LAZYRULE can only directly deal with nominal attributes. Numeric attributes are discretized as a pre-process. The consequent of a lazy rule is a local classifier created from those training cases (called *local training cases*) that satisfy the antecedent of the rule. The local classifier is induced using only those attributes that do not appear in the antecedent of the rule.

During the generation of a lazy rule, the test case to be classified is used to guide the selection of attributes for creating attribute-value pairs—only values that appear in the test case are being considered in the selection process. The objective is to grow the antecedent of a rule that ultimately decreases the errors of the local classifier in the consequent of the rule. The antecedent of the rule defines a sub-space of the instance space to which the test case belongs, and selects a subset of the available training instances. For all instances in the instance sub-space, each of the attributes occurring in the antecedent has an identical value which is the same as the one in the antecedent, thus not affecting the behavior of the local classifier. These attributes are removed from the local classifier for computational efficiency. Finally, the local classifier of the rule classifies the test case, since this case satisfies the antecedent of the rule. Table 1 outlines the LAZYRULE framework. One must choose a base learning algorithm for inducing local classifiers before using this framework.

For each test case, LAZYRULE uses a greedy search to generate a rule of which the antecedent matches the test case. The growth of the rule starts from a special rule whose antecedent is *true*. The local classifier in its consequent part is trained on the entire training set using all attributes. At each step of the greedy search, LAZYRULE tries to add, to the current rule, each attribute that has not already been in the antecedent of the rule, so long as its value on the test case is not missing. The objective is to determine whether including this attribute-value pair on the test case into the rule can significantly improve the estimated accuracy.

The utility of every possible attribute-value pair to be added to the antecedent of a rule is evaluated in the following manner. A subset of examples D_{subset} that satisfies the attribute-value pair is identified from the current local training set $D_{training}$, and is used to train a temporary classifier using all attributes that do not occur in the antecedent of the current rule and are not the attribute being examined. Cross-validation (CV) is performed to obtain the estimated errors of both the local and temporary classifiers.[1] Estimated errors of the temporary classifier on D_{subset} together with estimated errors of the local

---

[1] We choose cross-validation as the evaluation method because cross-validated errors are more reliable estimates of true errors than re-substitution errors [4].

Table 1: The LAZYRULE Framework

Given a base learning algorithm **Alg**.

LazyRule($Att, D_{training}, E_{test}$)
    $INPUT$: Att: a set of attributes,
                $D_{training}$: a set of training cases described using Att and classes,
                E_{test}: a test case described using Att.
    $OUTPUT$: a predicted class for E_{test}.
$LocalClr$ = a classifier induced by **Alg** using Att on $D_{training}$
$Errors$ = errors of $LocalClr$ estimated using CV on $D_{training}$
$Cond = true$
$REPEAT$
    $TempErrors_{best}$ = the number of cases in $D_{training}$ + 1
    FOR each attribute A in Att whose value v_A on E_{test} is not missing DO
        D_{subset} = cases in $D_{training}$ with $A = v_A$
        $TempClr$ = a classifier induced by **Alg** using $Att - \{A\}$ on D_{subset}
        $TempErrors$ = errors of $TempClr$ estimated using CV on D_{subset} +
                      the portion of $Errors$ in $D_{training} - D_{subset}$
        IF (($TempErrors < TempErrors_{best}$) AND
          ($TempErrors$ is significantly lower than $Errors$))
        $THEN$
            $TempClr_{best} = TempClr$
            $TempErrors_{best} = TempErrors$
            $A_{best} = A$
    IF (an A_{best} is found)
    $THEN$
        $Cond = Cond \wedge (A_{best} = v_{Abest})$
        $LocalClr = TempClr_{best}$
        $D_{training} = D_{subset}$ corresponding to A_{best}
        $Att = Att - \{A_{best}\}$
        $Errors$ = errors of $LocalClr$ estimated using CV on $D_{training}$
    $ELSE$
        $EXIT$ from the $REPEAT$ loop
classify E_{test} using $LocalClr$
$RETURN$ the class

classifier of the current rule on $D_{training} - D_{subset}$ are used as the evaluation measure of the attribute-value pair for growing the current rule. If this measure is lower than the estimated errors of the local classifier on $D_{training}$ at a significance level better than 0.05 using a one-tailed pairwise sign-test [7], this attribute-value pair becomes a candidate condition to be added to the current rule. The sign-test is used to control the likelihood of adding conditions that reduce error by chance. After evaluating all possible conditions, the candidate condition with the lowest measure (errors) is added to the antecedent of the current rule.

Training cases that do not satisfy the antecedent of the rule are then discarded, and the above process repeated. This continues until no more candidate conditions are found. This happens, when no better local classifier can be formed, or the local training set is too small (i.e., ≤ 30 examples) to further reduce the instance sub-space by specializing the antecedent of the rule. In such cases, further growing the rule would not significantly reduce its errors. Finally, the local classifier of this rule is used to classify the test case under consideration.

LAZYRULE is a generalization of LBR [20]. In principle, the general framework can be used with any base classifier learning algorithms.

3 Does LAZYRULE improve the performance of classifiers?

In this section, we evaluate whether the LAZYRULE framework can be used to improve the performance of a base learning algorithm. In order to show the generality of the framework, two different types of base learning algorithm are used in the following experiments. They are majority vote (MV) and the naive Bayesian classifier (NB). MV classifies all the test cases as belonging to the most common class of the training cases.

NB [16, 17, 18] is an implementation of Bayes' rule:

$$P(C_i|V) = P(C_i)P(V|C_i)/P(V)$$

for classification, where P denotes probability, C_i is class i and V is a vector of attribute values describing a case. By assuming all attributes are mutually independent within each class, $P(V|C_i) = \prod_j P(v_j|C_i)$ simplifies the estimation of the required conditional probabilities. NB is simple and computationally efficient. It has been shown that it is competitive to more complex learning algorithms such as decision tree and rule learning algorithms on many datasets [9, 6].

Because the current version of LAZYRULE only accepts nominal attribute inputs, continuous-valued attributes are discretized as a pre-process in the experiments. The discretization method is based on an entropy-based method [11]. For each pair of training set and test set, both the training set and the test set are discretized by using cut points found from the training set alone.

LAZYRULE with MV or NB uses the N-fold cross-validation method (also called leave-one-out estimation) [4] in the attribute evaluation process because both MV and NB are amenable to efficiently adding and subtracting one case. We denote LR-NB as the LAZYRULE framework that incorporates NB as its base learning algorithm; likewise for LR-MV. Note that LR-NB is exactly the same as LBR [20].

Ten commonly used natural datasets from the UCI repository of machine learning databases [3] are employed in our investigation. Table 2 gives a brief summary of these domains, including the dataset size, the number of classes, the number of numeric and nominal attributes. Two stratified 10-fold cross-validations [15] are conducted on each dataset to estimate the performance of each algorithm.

Table 3 reports the average test classification error rate for each of the experimental datasets. To summarize the performance comparison between an

Table 2: Description of learning tasks

Domain	Size	No. of Classes	No. of Attributes	
			Numeric	Nominal
Annealing	898	6	6	32
Breast cancer (Wisconsin)	699	2	9	0
Chess (King-rook-vs-king-pawn)	3196	2	0	36
Credit screening (Australia)	690	2	6	9
House votes 84	435	2	0	16
Hypothyroid diagnosis	3163	2	7	18
Pima Indians diabetes	768	2	8	0
Solar flare	1389	2	0	10
Soybean large	683	19	0	35
Splice junction gene sequences	3177	3	0	60

Table 3: Average error rates (%) of LAZYRULE and its base learning algorithms.

Datasets	NB	LR-NB	MV	LR-MV
Annealing	2.8	2.7	23.8	8.2
Breast(W)	2.7	2.7	34.5	10.3
Chess(KR-KP)	12.2	2.0	47.8	4.5
Credit(Aust)	14.0	14.0	44.5	15.0
House-votes-84	9.8	5.6	38.6	4.5
Hypothyroid	1.7	1.6	4.7	2.3
Pima	25.2	25.4	34.9	26.4
Solar-flare	19.4	16.4	15.7	15.7
Soybean	9.2	5.9	86.6	23.2
Splice-junction	4.4	4.0	48.1	14.7
mean	10.1	8.0	37.9	14.5
ratio		.73		.32
w/t/l		7/2/1		9/1/0
p. of wtl		.0352		.0020

algorithm and LAZYRULE with it, Table 3 also shows the geometric mean of error rate ratios, the number of wins/ties/losses, and the result of a two-tailed pairwise sign-test. An error rate ratio for LR-NB versus NB, for example, is calculated using a result for LR-NB divided by the corresponding result for NB. A value less than one indicates an improvement due to LR-NB. The result of the sign test indicates the significance level of the test on the win/tie/loss record.

We summarize our findings as follows. LAZYRULE improves the predictive accuracy of NB and MV. The framework achieves a 68% relative reduction in error rate for MV, and 27% relative reduction for NB. The improvement is significant at a level better than 0.05 for both MV and NB. LAZYRULE improves the performance of MV on all datasets. It improves the performance of NB on

Table 4: Average rule lengths of LAZYRULE.

Dataset	LR-NB	LR-MV
Annealing	0.20	1.90
Breast(W)	0.00	1.63
Chess(KR-KP)	4.10	4.00
Credit(Aust)	0.10	2.55
House-votes-84	0.90	2.23
Hypothyroid	0.40	4.21
Pima	0.10	2.13
Solar-flare	1.10	2.65
Soybean	0.90	2.35
Splice-junction	0.70	2.14
mean	0.85	2.58

7 datasets, and keeps the same performance on 2 datasets. Only on the Pima dataset does LR-NB slightly increase the error rate of NB.

Table 4 shows the average length of all rules produced by LR-NB and LR-MV. The average rule length is the ratio of the total of conditions produced for all test cases and the total number of test cases, averaged over all runs.

The mean values across all datasets are 0.85 and 2.58 for LR-NB and LR-MV, respectively. Examining the figures on each dataset indicates that LAZYRULE only produces rules when it is possible to improve the performance of the classifier trained using all training cases and all attributes. On average, LR-MV produces a rule with more than 1.5 conditions for each test case on each of the experimental datasets. This is an indication that LAZYRULE could improve the performance of MV on all of these datasets. Small values of average rule length indicate either no or minor improvement. This is shown by LR-NB on the Annealing, Breast(W), Credit(Aust), Hypothyroid and Pima datasets, which have average rule lengths less than 0.5.

LAZYRULE is expected to require more compute time than the base learning algorithm. For example, in the Breast(W) dataset in which LR-NB produces no rule, the execution time is 0.241 seconds as compared to .005 seconds for NB. In the Chess dataset in which LR-NB produces the longest rule, LR-NB requires 213.13 seconds whereas NB requires only 0.034 seconds. The time is recorded from a 300MHz Sun UltraSPARC machine.

Being a lazy learner, another important factor that affects LAZYRULE's execution time is the test set size. The execution time of LAZYRULE is proportional to the size of the test set. For example, in the Chess dataset, the test size used in the current experiment is 319. When we change the experiment from ten-fold cross-validation to three-fold cross-validation (the test set size is increased to 1066), the execution time of LR-NB increases from 213 seconds to 299 seconds.

4 The Advantages and Limitations of LAZYRULE

LAZYRULE's primary action is to eliminate attributes and select training cases that are most relevant to classifying the current test case. This builds a better performing classifier for the test case than the classifier trained using all attributes and all training cases. This flexible nature of LAZYRULE stretches the base learning algorithm to its best potential under these two variables: attribute elimination and training case selection.

The key advantage of LAZYRULE over a previous system LAZYDT [12] is the use of the cross-validation method for attribute elimination and training case selection. The use of this technique allows different types of learning algorithm to be incorporated into the LAZYRULE framework. LAZYDT uses an entropy measure for attribute elimination which leads to selecting cases with the same class. As a result, only majority vote can be used to form the local classifier.

The idea of using cross-validation and the learning algorithm, which is to be used to induce the final classifier, in the evaluation process is called the wrapper method [14]. This method was initially proposed solely for the purpose of attribute selection/elimination. LAZYRULE uses the method for both attribute elimination and training case selection.

The major computational overhead in LAZYRULE is the cross-validation process used in the evaluation of an attribute. The nature of the lazy learning mechanism requires that the same process is repeated for each test case. This computational overhead can be substantially reduced by caching the useful information. In the current implementation of LAZYRULE, the evaluation function values of attribute-value pairs that have been examined are retained from one test case to the next. This avoids re-calculation of the evaluation function values of the same attribute-value pairs when classifying unseen cases that appear later, thus reducing the entire execution time. Our experiment shows that caching this information reduces the execution time of LAZYRULE with the naive Bayesian classifier by 93% on average on the 10 datasets used in the experiment. This happens, because the evaluation of attribute-value pairs for different test cases are often repeated, including repeated generation of identical rules for different test cases. LAZYRULE could be made even more efficient by caching further information such as local classifiers and indices for training cases in different stages of the growth of rules. Of course, this would increase memory requirements.

Caching the local classifiers has an added advantage apart from computational efficiency. Now, the number of different rules together with local classifiers induced thus far are ready to be presented to the user in any stage during the classification time.

In theory, decision tree learning algorithm is a candidate to be used in the LAZYRULE framework. There are reasons why we did not include it in our experiments. First, given a test case, only one path is needed, not the entire tree. Second, the process of growing a lazy rule is similar to the process of growing a tree. Only the criterion for attribute selection is different. Lastly, building a tree/path at the consequent of the rule would actually use different criteria for two similar processes. This seems undesirable.

5 Conclusions and Future Work

We introduce the LAZYRULE framework based on an earlier work for learning lazy Bayesian rules, and show that it can be used to improve the performance of a base classifier learning algorithm. The combined action of attribute elimination and training case selection of LAZYRULE, tailored for the test case to be classified, enables it to build a better performing classifier for the test case than the classifier trained using all attributes and all training cases. We show empirically that LAZYRULE improves the performance of two base learning algorithms, the naive Bayesian classifier and majority vote.

Our future work includes extending LAZYRULE to accept continuous-valued attribute input, and experimenting with other types of learning algorithm such as k-nearest neighbors. It is interesting to see how it will perform when a lazy learning algorithm such as k-nearest neighbors is incorporated in this lazy learning framework. The current implementation of LAZYRULE only considers attribute-value pairs each in the form of 'attribute = value'. Alternatives to this form are worth exploring. Applying this framework to regression tasks is also another interesting avenue for future investigation.

References

[1] Aha, D.W., Kibler, D., & Albert, M.K. Instance-based learning algorithms. *Machine Learning, 6*, 37-66, 1991.

[2] Aha, D.W. (ed.). *Lazy Learning.* Dordrecht: Kluwer Academic, 1997.

[3] Blake, C., Keogh, E. & Merz, C.J. UCI Repository of Machine Learning Databases [http://www.ics.uci.edu/~mlearn/MLRepository.html]. Irvine, CA: University of California, Department of Information and Computer Science, 1998.

[4] Breiman, L., Friedman, J.H., Olshen, R.A., & Stone, C.J. *Classification And Regression Trees*, Belmont, CA: Wadsworth, 1984.

[5] Briand, L.C. & Thomas, W.M. A pattern recognition approach for software engineering data analysis. *IEEE Transactions on Software Engineering, 18*, 931-942, 1992.

[6] Cestnik, B. Estimating probabilities: A crucial task in machine learning. *Proceedings of the European Conference on Artificial Intelligence*, pages 147-149, 1990.

[7] Chatfield, C. *Statistics for Technology: A Course in Applied Statistics.* London: Chapman and Hall, 1978.

[8] Cover, T.M. & Hart, P.E. Nearest neighbor pattern classification. *IEEE Transactions on Information Theory, 13*, 21-27, 1967.

[9] Domingos, P. & Pazzani, M. Beyond independence: Conditions for the optimality of the simple Bayesian classifier. *Proceedings of the Thirteenth International Conference on Machine Learning*, pages 105-112, 1996. San Francisco, CA: Morgan Kaufmann.

[10] Duda, R.O. & Hart, P.E. *Pattern Classification and Scene Analysis*. New York: John Wiley, 1973.

[11] Fayyad, U.M. & Irani, K.B. Multi-interval discretization of continuous-valued attributes for classification learning. *Proceedings of the Thirteenth International Joint Conference on Artificial Intelligence*, pages 1022-1027, 1993. San Mateo, CA: Morgan Kaufmann.

[12] Friedman, J., Kohavi, R., & Yun, Y. Lazy decision trees. *Proceedings of the Thirteenth National Conference on Artificial Intelligence*, pages 717-724, 1996. Menlo Park, CA: The AAAI Press.

[13] Fulton, T., Kasif, S., Salzberg, S., and Waltz, D. Local induction of decision trees: Towards interactive data mining. *Proceedings of the Second International Conference on Knowledge Discovery and Data Mining*, pages 14-19, 1996. Menlo Park, CA: AAAI Press.

[14] John, G.H., Kohavi, R., & Pfleger, K. Irrelevant features and the subset selection problem. *Proceedings of the Eleventh International Conference on Machine Learning*, pages 121-129, 1994. San Francisco, CA: Morgan Kaufmann.

[15] Kohavi, R. A study of cross-validation and bootstrap for accuracy estimation and model selection. *Proceedings of the Fourteenth International Joint Conference on Artificial Intelligence*, pages 1137-1143, 1995. San Mateo, CA: Morgan Kaufmann.

[16] Kononenko, I. Comparison of inductive and naive Bayesian learning approaches to automatic knowledge acquisition. In B. Wielinga *et al.* (eds.), *Current Trends in Knowledge Acquisition*, 1990. Amsterdam: IOS Press.

[17] Langley, P., Iba, W.F., & Thompson, K. An analysis of Bayesian classifiers. *Proceedings of the Tenth National Conference on Artificial Intelligence*, pages 223-228, 1992. Menlo Park, CA: The AAAI Press.

[18] Langley, P. & Sage, S. Induction of selective Bayesian classifiers. *Proceedings of the Tenth Conference on Uncertainty in Artificial Intelligence*, pages 339-406, 1994. Seattle, WA: Morgan Kaufmann.

[19] Viswanathan, M. & Webb, G.I. Classification learning using all rules. *Proceedings of the Tenth European Conference on Machine Learning*, pages 149-159, 1998. Berlin: Springer-Verlag.

[20] Zheng, Z. & Webb, G.I. Lazy Learning of Bayesian rules. To appear in *Machine Learning*.

[21] Zheng, Z., Webb, G.I. & Ting, K.M. Lazy Bayesian rules: A lazy semi-naive Bayesian learning technique competitive to boosting decision trees. *Proceedings of the Sixteenth International Conference on Machine Learning*, pages 493-502, 1999. Morgan Kaufmann.

ALGORITHMS FOR COMPUTING ASSOCIATION RULES USING A PARTIAL-SUPPORT TREE

Graham Goulbourne, Frans Coenen and Paul Leng
Department of Computer Science,
University of Liverpool, UK
graham_g, frans, phl@csc.liv.ac.uk

Abstract

This paper presents new algorithms for the extraction of association rules from binary databases. Most existing methods operate by generating "candidate" sets, representing combinations of attributes which may be associated, and then testing the database to establish the degree of association. This may involve multiple database passes, and is also likely to encounter problems when dealing with "dense" data due to the increase in the number of sets under consideration. Our methods uses a single pass of the database to perform a partial computation of support for all sets encountered in the database, storing this in the form of a set enumeration tree. We describe algorithms for generating this tree and for using it to generate association rules.

KEYWORDS: Association Rules, Partial Support, Set Enumeration

1 INTRODUCTION

Modern businesses have the capacity to store huge amounts of data regarding all aspects of their operations. Deriving *association rules* [1] from this data can lead to previously unknown and interesting information being made available, which may provide the basis for some commercial "edge" to be gained over competitors. This paper describes a new method for the extraction of such rules from binary data. An association rule R is of the form $A{\rightarrow}B$, where A and B are disjoint subsets of a set I of binary attributes. The *support* for the rule R is the number of database records which contain $A \cup B$ (often expressed as a proportion of the total number of records). The *confidence* in the rule R is the ratio:

$$\frac{support\ for\ R}{support\ for\ A}$$

These two properties, support and confidence, provide the basis for the inference expressed in the rule. The support for a rule expresses the number of records within which the association may be observed, while the confidence expresses this as a proportion of the instances of the antecedent of the rule. In practical investigations, it is usual to regard these rules as "interesting" only if the support and confidence exceed some threshold values. Hence the problem may be formulated as a search for all association rules within the database for which the required support and confidence levels are attained. Note that the confidence in a rule can be determined immediately once the relevant support values for the rule and its antecedent are computed. Thus the problem essentially resolves to a search for all subsets of I for which the support exceeds the required threshold. Such subsets are referred to as "large", "frequent", or "interesting" sets.

In this paper we present a method which, in a single database pass, reorganises an $m \times n$ database table into a simple tree structure while at the same time, performing a partial computation of support-counts for sets of attributes found in the table. We describe an algorithm for generating this tree, using a conservative storage regime which often requires significantly less space than the original database, we present experimental results to demonstrate its performance. We also describe an algorithm which computes final support totals from the partial supports stored in the tree and a mode of operation whereby all interesting sets can be generated given a partial support tree and using the summation algorithm described.

The paper is organised as follows. Section 2 provides a review of work within the field of association rule mining. Section 3 describes the theory of the partial support notion and explains its advantages. Section 4 describes our algorithm for generating a partial-support tree, and presents experimental results for the performance of the method. Section 5 presents an algorithm for computing final support-count totals using this tree, and Section 6 describes the generation of interesting sets from this data. Finally Section 7 outlines some directions for future research which we think will improve still further the algorithms outlined in this paper and some concluding remarks.

2 ALGORITHMS FOR COMPUTING SUPPORT

For a database of n attributes, to compute support counts for all 2^n subsets of I is likely to be infeasible, so practicable algorithms proceed in general by computing support-counts only for those sets which are identified as potentially interesting. To assist in identifying these candidate sets, observe that the subsets of the attribute set may be represented as a lattice. One form of this is shown as Figure 1, for a set of four attributes, $\{A, B, C, D\}$.

The best-known algorithm, "Apriori" [2], proceeds essentially by breadth-first traversal of this lattice, starting with the single attributes in I. Repeated passes of the database are performed, on each of which a candidate set C_k of attribute sets is examined. The members of C_k are all those sets of k attributes which remain in the search space. Initially, the set C_1 consists of the individual attributes in I. The kth cycle of the algorithm then first performs a pass over the database to compute the support for all members of C_k, and from this, produces the set L_k of interesting sets of size k. This is then used to derive the candidate sets C_{k+1}, using the "downward closure" property, that all the subsets of any member of C_{k+1} must be members of L_k. Other algorithms, AIS [1] and SETM [3], have the same general form but differ in the way the candidate sets are derived.

Two aspects of the performance of these algorithms are of concern: the number of passes of the database that are required, which will in general be one greater than the number of attributes in the largest interesting set, and the size of the candidate sets which may be generated, especially in the early cycles of the algorithm. The number of database passes can be reduced by strategies which begin by examining subsets of the database. The Partition algorithm [6] divides the database into a number of non-overlapping partitions of equal size, and proceeds in two passes. In the first pass, each partition is taken in turn, and all the *locally* frequent sets, for which the support exceeds the required (proportional) threshold within at least one partition, are computed. The set L of locally frequent sets is a superset of the set of all (globally) frequent sets, and becomes the search space in a second full pass of the database, in which the support-counts of all its members are computed.

An alternative approach, also using a subset of the database, is described by Toivonen [7]. In this method, a single sample of the database is taken from which is derived a candidate set for the full database search. To ensure (with high probability) that this candidate set contains all the actual frequent sets, two devices are used. First, the support threshold is lowered when the database sample is processed, leading to a candidate set S which is a superset of the actual (locally) frequent set. Secondly, the set is further extended by adding its *negative border*, i.e. those sets that are not members of S, but all of whose subsets are included in S. This extended set is used as the candidate set for a full database pass, which, if no members of the negative border are found to be frequent, completes the search.

The drawback of these methods is that the candidate set derived is necessarily a superset of the actual set of frequent sets, so again the search space may become very large, especially with densely packed database records. This has led researchers to look for methods which seek to identify *maximal* interesting sets without first examining all their smaller subsets, i.e. a depth-first search of the lattice of Figure 1. An exhaustive depth-first traversal is, of course, computationally infeasible for large n. Zaki et al [4] address this issue by partitioning the lattice, using *clusters* of associated attributes. Each cluster generates a subset of the lattice, for which a number of traversal methods are described. However, the approach depends critically on the ability to partition the attributes into relatively small clusters. Also, the clustering algorithms generally begin by computing L_2, which in itself involves a pass of the database and significant

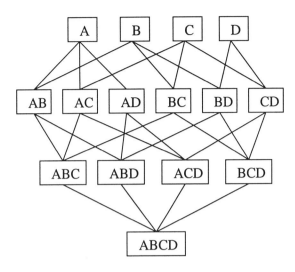

Figure 1: Lattice of subsets of $\{A, B, C, D\}$

computation.

Bayardo's [5] Max-Miner algorithm also searches for maximal sets, using Rymon's set enumeration framework [8] to order the search space as a tree. Max-Miner reduces the search space by pruning the tree to eliminate both supersets of infrequent sets and subsets of frequent sets. Max-Miner improves on the performance of the previously descrbed algorithms when dealing with dense datasets, but at the cost of multiple database passes.

3 PARTIAL SUPPORT

The algorithms described above all depend to some degree on a reduction of the search space of candidates for support to a number which can be retained in memory and counted feasibly. In most cases, each pass of the database proceeds by examining each record to identify all the members of the candidate set that are subsets of the record. This can be computationally expensive, especially when records are densely populated, i.e. when the average number of attributes present in a record is high. In principle, however, it is possible to reduce this cost by exploiting the relationships between sets of attributes illustrated in the lattice. For example, in the simplest case, a record containing the attribute set ABD will cause incrementation of the support-counts for each of the sets ABD, AB, AD, BD, A, B and D. Strictly, however, only the first of these is necessary, since a level of support for all the subsets of ABD can be inferred from the support-count of ABD.

Let i be a subset of the set I (where I is the set of n attributes represented by the database). We define P_i, the *partial support* for the set i, to be the number of records whose contents are identical with the set i. Then T_i, the *total support* for the set i, can be determined as:

$$T_i = \sum P_j \qquad (\forall j, j \supseteq i)$$

This allows us to postulate an exhaustive algorithm for computing all (total) supports:

Algorithm A:

        Stage 1: for all records j in database do
                begin add 1 to $P(j)$
                end;
        Stage 2: for all distinct j found in database do
                begin for all $i \subset j$ do
                        begin add $P(j)$ to $T(i)$
                        end
                end

For a database of m records, the algorithm performs m support-count incrementations in a single pass (stage 1), to compute a total of m' partial supports, for some $m' \leq m$. Stage 2 involves, for each of these, a further 2^i additions, where i is the number of attributes present in the set being considered. If the database contains no duplicate records, then the method will be less efficient than an exhaustive computation which enumerates subsets of each record as it is examined. Computing via summation of partial supports will be superior, however, in two cases. Firstly, when n is small ($2^n \ll m$), then stage 2 involves the summation of a set of counts which is significantly smaller than a summation over the whole database, especially if the database records are densely-populated. Secondly, even for large n, if the database contains a high degree of duplication ($m' \ll m$) then the stage 2 summation will be significantly faster than a full database pass.

Computing partial supports as described above allows us, in one pass of the database, to capture all the relevant information in a form which enables efficient computation of the totals we need, exploiting the structural relationships inherent in the lattice of partial supports, and taking advantage of the duplication of records which we expect to be a significant feature of many databases. For effective implementation of the method, however, we require a method of storing the partial supports in a form which facilitates the stage 2 computation. For this purpose, we make use of Rymon's [8] set enumeration framework. Figure 2 shows the sets of subsets of I, for $I = \{A, B, C, D\}$, in this form. In this structure, each subtree contains all the supersets of the root node which follow the root node in lexicographic order.

Using this tree as a storage structure for support-counts in stage 1 of the algorithm is straightforward and computationally efficient: locating the required position on the tree for any set of attributes requires at most n steps. We may

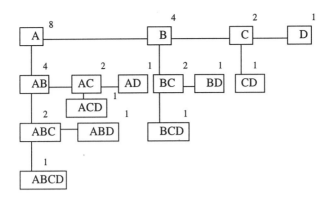

Figure 2: Tree storage of subsets of $\{A, B, C, D\}$ (interim support counts shown above each node)

go further, however, and begin to take advantage of the structural relationships implied by the tree to begin the computation of total supports. This is because, in locating a node on the tree, the traversal will pass through a number of nodes which are subsets of the target node. In doing so, it is inexpensive to accumulate *interim* support-counts at these nodes. A (stage 1) algorithm for this has the following form:

Algorithm B:

        for all records j in database do
            starting at root node of tree:
                begin if $j \supseteq$ node then increment $Q(\text{node})$;
                    if $j =$ node then exit
                      else if $j \supseteq$ node then recurse to child node
                      else recurse to next sibling;
            end

This algorithm will, in stage 1, compute interim support-counts Q_i for each subset i of I, where Q_i is defined thus:

$$Q_i = \sum P_j \qquad (\forall j, j \supseteq i, j \; follows \; i \; in \; lexicographic \; order)$$

It then becomes possible to compute total support using the equation:

$$T_i = Q_i + \sum P_j \qquad (\forall j, j \supset i, j \; precedes \; i \; in \; lexicographic \; order)$$

Storage of the complete tree of subsets of I, of course, has a requirement of order 2^n, which will in general be infeasible. We can avoid this, however, by observing that for large n it is likely that most of the subsets i will be unrepresented in the database and will therefore not contribute to the partial-count summation. A version of algorithm B to exploit this builds the tree dynamically as records are processed, storing partial totals only for records which appear in the database. Nodes are created only when a new subset i is encountered in the database, or when two siblings i and j share a leading subset which is not already represented. The latter provision is necessary to maintain the structure of the tree as it grows. The formulae for computing total supports still apply, and we need only to sum interim supports that are present in the tree. Building the tree dynamically implies a storage requirement of order m rather than 2^n. This will be reduced further, perhaps substantially, if the database contains a high incidence of duplicates. In the following sections we describe implementations of algorithms for building the partial support tree in this way, and then for completing the support-count computation using the tree.

4 ALGORITHM FOR GENERATING PARTIAL SUPPORT TREE

In this section we present an algorithm to produce a partial support tree with dummy nodes. The nodes in the tree represent either unique rows in the table, or dummy nodes inserted to prevent the tree from degenerating into a "linked list". The nodes are arranged so that parent nodes are subsets of their descendent nodes. Sibling nodes are ordered lexicographically, consequently we conceive of "elder" and "younger" siblings. Examples are given later in the text. The algorithm operates by passing through the database row by row in an iterative manner. On each iteration if the row under consideration is already represented by a node in the tree the support associated with this node is incremented by one. Otherwise a new node is created for the row and inserted in the appropriate location in the tree. This requires a search through the tree as a consequence of which the new node is inserted as a parent, child, elder sibling or younger sibling of some existing node. On route supports associated with existing nodes may be incremented. Where necessary an additional (dummy) node may also be created to preserve the desired tree structure. Alternatively, when inserting a new node it may be necessary to break certain portions of the tree and reconnect them so as to conform to the defined structure of the tree. To achieve this the tree is traversed in an iterative manner also. On each iteration the nature of the search is defined by a set of five basic rules. These rules are described in detail below (where R represents the bit pattern of the table row currently under consideration, and B a bit pattern attached to an existing tree node under consideration). The search commences at the root of the tree and may progress down either the sibling branch or child branch of this node. So that knowledge of the nature of the current branch is maintained a flag is set with the values 0 (root), 1 (child) or 2 (sibling). Note; the $<$ and $>$ operators are used to define lexicographic not numeric ordering.

Rule 1($R = B$, an identical node is found) : Simply increment the support associated with B and return.

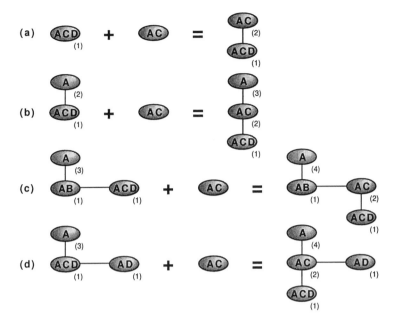

Figure 3: Application of Rule 2

Rule 2($R < B$ and $R \subset B$, new row is a parent of currentnode) :

1. Create a new node for R and place the node associated with B on the new node's child branch.

2. Place the new node either as a new root node, or add it to the child or sibling branch of the previously investigated node (as indicated by the flag). This is illustrated in Figure 3(a), (b) and (c). In Figure 3 (a) the new node is added as a new root node, in (b) as a child of the previously investigated node and in (c) as a elder sibling.

3. If necessary move one or more of the younger siblings of the previously existent node up to become younger siblings of the newly created node. This is illustrated in Figure 3(d) where the node AD, which was an elder sibling of ACD is moved up to become an elder sibling of the newly created node AC.

Rule 3($R < B$ and $R \not\subset B$, new row is an elder sibling of existing node) :

1. If R and B have a leading sub string S and S is not equal to the code associated with the parent node of the node representing B then:

   • Create a dummy node for S with support equivalent to that associated with the node for B.

   • Place the new dummy node either as a new root node, or add it to the child or sibling branch of the previously investigated node

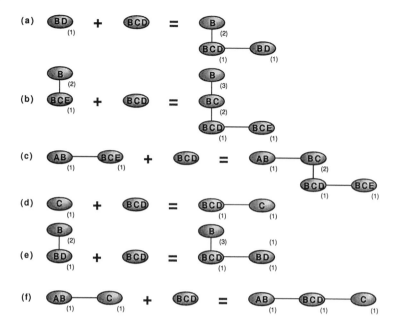

Figure 4: Application of Rule 3

(as indicated by the flag). A number of examples illustrating this are given in Figure 4. In Figure 4(a) we create a dummy node (B) as a new root node, in 4(b) we create a dummy node (BC) as child node of node B, and in Figure 4(c) we create a dummy node (BC) as an elder sibling node of AB.

- Then create a new node for R and place this so that it is a child of the newly created dummy node.
- Finally place the previously existent node for B as a younger sibling of the node for R.

2. Else create a new node for R and place the node associated with B on the new node's sibling branch. The new node is then placed either as a new root node, or is added to the child or sibling branch of the previously investigated node (as indicated by the flag). Examples are given in Figure 4 (d), (e) and (f).

Rule 4($R > B$ and $R \supset B$, new row child of current node) : Increment the support for the current node (B) by one and:

1. If node associated with B has no child node create a new node for R and add this to the existing node's child branch.

2. Otherwise proceed down child branch (with flag set appropriately) and apply the rules to the next node encountered.

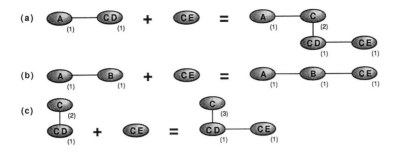

Figure 5: Application of Rule 5

Rule 5 ($R > B$ and $R \not\supset B$, **new row is a younger sibling of current node)**
:

1. If node associated with B has no sibling node, and:
   - If current node (node for B) does not have a parent node and R and B have a leading sub string S then:
     - Create a dummy node for S with support equivalent to that associated with the node for B.
     - Place the new dummy node either as a new root node, or add it to the child or sibling branch of the previously investigated node (as indicated by the appropriately set flag). This is illustrated in Figure 5(a) where the dummy node C is created.
     - Create a new node for R and place this so that it is a younger sibling of B.
     - Place B as the child of the dummy node S.
   - Otherwise create a new node for R and add this to the existing node's sibling branch (Figure 5(b) and (c)).

2. Otherwise proceed down sibling branch and (with flag set appropriately) and apply the rules to the next node encountered.

Thus given a bit Pattern R and a bit pattern B associated with an existing node there are five broad possible outcomes; each with a number of variations according to the nature of the tree so far, and the relationship between R and B.

4.1 ANALYSIS

To determine the performance of the algorithm it was tested with a series of randomly generated tables each with 20,000 rows ($m = 20,000$) and varying numbers of columns from $n = 10$ to $n = 100$ with each element having 0.5 probability of having a value of 1. For each test the storage required by the resulting tree (in bytes) and the number of *comparison tests* required to generate

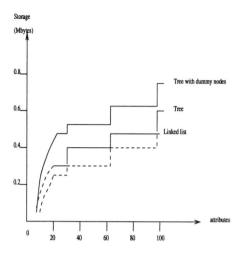

Figure 6: Comparison of storage requirements for linked list and partial support tree algorithms ($m = 20000$)

the tree was recorded. Similar tests were run using a *bench-mark* algorithm ([9]) where the partial supports were stored in a linked list structure; and using a precursor of the current algorithm ([10]) which did not incorporate the dummy node concept.

A graph indicating the storage requirements for the three algorithms derived from the test data is given in Figure 6. It should be noted that substrings of 32 table attributes are stored as 32 bit integers. An entire attribute set is thus stored in the form of a k element array where k is calculated as follows:

$$k = \frac{n}{32} (rounded\ up\ to\ the\ nearest\ integer)$$

As a consequence of the above the "staircase" effect which is a feature of the graph presented in Figure 6 is produced where a new "step" occurs at intervals of 32. From the graph it can be seen that the tree algorithm with no dummy nodes requires more storage than the linked list algorithm. While the algorithm with dummy nodes requires more than that without dummy nodes. This is not surprising because each linked list node has one branch, while each tree node has two branches. From the graph in Figure 6 it can also be seen that, in each case, the slope levels off where n is equivalent to about 17. This change occurs because at this point 2^n overtakes m, i.e. to the left of $n = 17$ duplicates are guaranteed while to the right this is not the case. Inspection of the test data shows that for $n > 22$ the number of duplicates is such that storage can be calculated using:

$$m \times (k + s)$$

where s represents the storage requirements for an individual node. Thus when

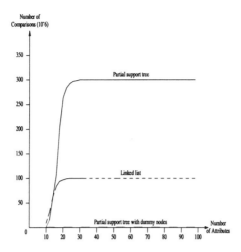

Figure 7: Comparison of number of "tests" (comparisons) for linked list and partial support tree algorithms ($m = 20000$)

2^n is greater than m (which in practice is likely to be the case) storage will be a function of m rather than n.

A second graph is presented in Figure 7 which compares the number of "tests" associated with each of the algorithms. Considering only the linked list and (non-dummy node) partial support tree algorithms first, it can be seen that the partial support tree works better than the linked list algorithm to the left of $n = 15$ (i.e. where the likelihood of subsets and duplicates is high), but as n increases beyond 15 this advantage is lost. For both the linked list and partial support graphs the gradient of the slope again decreases at $n = 17$, the point beyond which duplicates are no longer guaranteed. Consequently, in both cases the number of comparisons becomes a function of m rather than n. In the case of the partial support tree the tree in fact becomes "flat", i.e. it degenerates into what is effectively a linked list due to the lack of subsets in the test data. However, for each row, checks are still made for the possibility of adding child branches, corresponding to only one check in the linked list algorithm. This makes the tree algorithm extremely "expensive". If we now consider the partial support tree with dummy nodes this does not degenerate into a "linked list", but maintains a genuine tree structure, and the amount of work to generate the tree is significantly less. For example where $n = 20$, the number of comparisons required to produce the linked list structure is approximately 98×10^6, for the non-dummy node tree 264×10^6 and with dummy nodes 0.8×10^6. The efficiency gains can thus be said to be "significant". There is still a gradient change at $n = 17$; however, the scale of the graph in Figure 7 is such that this is not perceptible.

The overall advantages offered by the tree algorithm is, of course, also dependent on the "added value" offered by the tree organisation when determining supports — an algorithm whereby this may be achieved is described in the following section.

5 SUMMATION OF PARTIAL SUPPORTS

The tree structure now contains an image of the database together with the partially supported sets. To enable rule generation the total support for particular sets must be determined.

The proposed summation algorithm operates in a depth first manner by proceeding down child branches first and then exploring elder sibling branches. When considering a child node we proceed according to the rules presented below where: R is a set of attributes for which we wish to determine the support, B is a node in the tree (which will be the root node at commencement of the calculation), and N is the support calculated so far (0 at the start). The *flag* variable indicates whether an exact match (*flag* = 0) has been found or not (*flag* = 1). Where an exact match has been found, or when all possibilities have been exhausted, the search is terminated.

Child summation rules:

Rule 1(a): If there is no node B set *flag* to 1 and return (and possibly continue the search down a sibling branch).

Rule 1(b): If the code associated with B is identical to R, add the support for B to N, set *flag* to 0 and return (terminate search).

Rule 1(c): If the code associated with B is a superset of R, add the support for B to N, set *flag* to 1 and return (to possibly continue the search down a sibling branch).

Rule 1(d): Proceed down child branch emanating from B and reapply these rules. If as a result of this exploration *flag* is set to 0 (i.e. an identical match has been found) return. Otherwise go on to explore the sibling branch emanating from B (see below).

Investigation of a sibling branch proceeds in a similar manner:

Sibling summation rules:

Rule 2(a): If there is no sibling node B set *flag* to 1 and return (to possibly continue the search down another sibling branch).

Rule 2(b): If the code associated with B is identical to R, add the support for B to N, set *flag* to 0 and return (thus terminating the search).

Rule 2(c): If the code associated with B is a superset of R, add the support for B to N, set *flag* to 1 and return (to possibly continue the search elsewhere).

Rule 2(d): If the code associated with B is (lexicographically) after R no occurrences of R will exist in any of the child/sibling branches emanating from S, set $flag$ to 1 and return (and possibly continue the search down another sibling branch).

Rule 2(e): Proceed down child branch emanating from current sibling node B and apply the rules presented above for investigating child nodes. If as a result of this exploration $flag$ is set to 0 simply return (i.e. an identical match has been found therefore terminate the search). Otherwise go on to explore the immediate sibling emanating from B by reapplying these rules.

For example considering the tree presented in Figure 2 and if $R = \{AD\}$, the search would be restricted to the A sub-tree, and would proceed as follows. We commence with the root node A and apply the child summation rules. Repeated application of rule 1(d) will bring us to node $ABCD$ as a result of which $N = 1$ and $flag = 1$ (rule 1(c)). We will now back track to ABC and (rule 1(d) proceed down the sibling branch. Using the sibling summation rules, rule 2(c) will apply as a result of which $N = N + 1 = 2$ and $flag = 1$. Backtracking again will return us to AB and we will then (rule 1(d)) then continue down the sibling branch of this node to AC. Application of rule 2(e) will then lead us down the child branch emanating from AC to ACD and (as a result of rule 1(c)) branch emanating from AC to ACD and (as a result of rule 1(c)) $N = N + 1 = 3$ and $flag = 1$. We will then again backtrack, to AC, and proceed down the sibling branch of this node to investigate AD using the sibling summation rules. Rule 2(b) will be applicable, $N = N + 1 = 4$ and $flag = 0$ hence the search will be terminated

6   INTERESTING SET GENERATION

To determine all the interesting sets in a database presented in the form of a tree generated using the algorithm presented in Section 4 we proceed in an "apriori" manner, using the summation algorithm presented in Section 5, as follows:

1. Generate the set K_1 of all elements with adequate support. If K_1 is empty return (there are no interesting sets), otherwise continue.

2. From the set K_1 generate a candidate set C_2 of two element sets.

3. Prune the set C_2, using the summation algorithm, to produce the set K_2 — the sets of two element sets which are appropriately supported. If K_2 is empty return (there are no interesting sets with more than one element), otherwise continue.

4. From the set K_2 generate a candidate set C_3 of three element sets.

5. Prune the set C_3, using the summation algorithm, to produce the set K_3 — the sets of two element sets which are appropriately supported.

6. Continue in this manner until the set K_n has been produced (n is the number of columns in the database) or a particular set K is empty.

In this manner all interesting sets will be discovered, and consequently appropriate association rules can be generated.

7   CONCLUSION AND FUTURE WORK

In this paper we have presented an algorithm to produce a partial support tree. From this tree it is possible to generate support for interesting sets in a database table. The work presented addresses two of the fundamental issues within association rule mining;

- The reduction of the number of database passes required to generate rules. The above can be categorised as 1+ pass. In one full pass of the database, computation of the partial support for the attributes is completed; at the same time the database is reorganised into a structure that can be efficiently summed.

- The ability to cope with dense data without encountering an exponential increase in the size of the search space.

As can be seen from the results presented in Figures 6 and 7 generating the partial support tree with dummy nodes is extremely efficient. The higher the level of duplication within the database the more the algorithm improves.

Future work will concentrate on both the data structure and the summation algorithm. The possibility of partitioning the data structure into distinct trees, groups of trees or trees mixed with other structures is to be examined. This restructuring may lead to the possibility of various "lazy" techniques for the summation algorithm. This would reduce even further the "restricted" exhaustive search outlined above.

References

[1] Agrawal, R. Imielinski, T. Swami, A. Mining Association Rules Between Sets of Items in Larg e Databases. SIGMOD-93, 207-216. May 1993.

[2] Agrawal, R. and Srikant, R. Fast Algorithms for Mining Association Rules. Proc 20th VLDB Conference, Santiago, 487-499. 1994

[3] Houtsma, M. and Swami, A. Set-oriented mining of association rules. Research Report RJ 9567, IBM Almaden Research Centre, San Jose, October 1993.

[4] Zaki, M.J., Parthasarathy, S. Ogihara, M. and Li, W. New Algorithms for fast discovery of association rules. Technical report 651, University of Rochester, Computer Science Department, New York. July 1997.

[5] Bayardo, R.J. Efficiently mining long patterns from databases. Proc ACM-SIGMOD Int Conf on Management of Data, 85-93, 1998.

[6] Savasere, A., Omiecinski, E. and Navathe, S. An efficient algorithm for mining association rules in large databases. Proc 21st VLDB Conference, Zurich, 432-444. 1995.

[7] Toivonen, H. Sampling large databases for association rules. Proc 22nd VLDB Conference, Bombay, 1996.

[8] Rymon, R. Search Through Systematic Set Enumeration. Proc. 3rd Int'l Conf. on Principles of Knowledge Represenation and Reasoning. 539-550.

[9] Coenen, F. (1999). Partial Support. Dept of Computer Science, University of Liverpool. Working Paper 4. http://www.csc.liv.ac.uk/~graham_g/kdfm.html.

[10] Coenen, F. (1999). Partial Support Using a "Partial Support Tree". Dept of Computer Science, University of Liverpool. Working Paper 5. http://www.csc.liv.ac.uk/~graham_g/kdfm.html.

Discovering Surprising Patterns by Detecting Occurrences of Simpson's Paradox

Carem C. Fabris
CEFET-PR
CPGEI
Av. Sete de Setembro, 3165
Curitiba-PR, 80230-901. Brazil
carem@dainf.cefetpr.br

Alex A. Freitas
PUC-PR
PPGIA-CCET
Rua Imaculada Conceicao, 1155
Curitiba-PR, 80215-901. Brazil
alex@ppgia.pucpr.br
http://ppgia.pucpr.br/~alex

Abstract

This paper addresses the discovery of surprising patterns. Recently, several authors have addressed the task of discovering surprising prediction rules. However, we do not focus on prediction rules, but rather on a quite different kind of pattern, namely the occurrence of Simpson's paradox. Intuitively, the fact that this is a paradox suggests that it has a great potential to be a surprising pattern for the user. With this motivation, we make the detection of Simpson's paradox the central goal of a data mining algorithm explicitly designed to discover surprising patterns. We present computational results showing surprising occurrences of the paradox in some public-domain data sets. In addition, we propose a method for ranking the discovered instances of the paradox in decreasing order of estimated degree of surprisingness.

1 Introduction.

Surveying the data mining literature, one can say that most algorithms focus on the discovery of accurate, comprehensible knowledge, even though comprehensibility is a kind of subjective concept which is rarely discussed in depth in the literature.

Ideally, however, a data mining algorithm should go beyond the discovery of accurate, comprehensible knowledge. The discovered knowledge should be also interesting, or surprising. The classic example to show the importance of surprisingness is the hypothetical discovery, in a medical database, of the pattern: "if the patient is pregnant, then the sex of the patient is female." Clearly, this pattern is highly accurate and highly comprehensible, but it is useless for the user, because it states the obvious.

Recently, several authors have focused on the important issue of discovering surprising/interesting patterns – see e.g. [8], [13], [2], [3], [1], [12], [6], [5], [9], [11]. The majority of this work focus on the discovery of surprising prediction rules.

This paper is one more stride towards the discovery of surprising patterns. However, we do not focus on prediction rules, but rather on a quite different kind of pattern, namely the occurrence of Simpson's paradox. Intuitively, the fact that this is a paradox suggests that it has a great potential to be a surprising pattern for the user.

Although some authors have flagged the pitfalls associated with Simpson's paradox in the context of data mining - see e.g. [4] - little research has been done on how to cope with occurrences of this paradox, or how to modify a data mining algorithm to cope with this paradox. This paper follows an intriguing direction, which consists of making the detection of Simpson's paradox the central goal of a data mining algorithm explicitly designed to discover surprising patterns.

This paper is organized as follows. Section 2 presents a review of Simpson's paradox. Section 3 describes our approach for detecting occurrences of Simpson's paradox and estimate their degree of surprisingness for the user. Section 4 presents computational results. Finally, section 5 summarizes and discusses the results reported in the paper.

2 A Review of Simpson's Paradox.

Let a population be partitioned into two mutually exclusive and exhaustive populations, denoted Pop_1 and Pop_2, according to the value of a given binary attribute, denoted 1stPartAtt (First Partitioning Attribute). Let G be a binary goal attribute, which takes on a value indicating whether or not a given situation of interest has occurred in a population, and let G_1 and G_2 be the value of the attribute G in each of the respective populations Pop_1 and Pop_2. Let $Pr(G_1)$ and $Pr(G_2)$ denote the probability that the situation of interest has occurred in Pop_1 and Pop_2, respectively. Assume that $Pr(G_1) > Pr(G_2)$.

Let us now consider the case where both the populations Pop_1 and Pop_2 are further partitioned, in parallel, according to the value of a given categorical attribute, denoted 2ndPartAtt. Let this attribute have m distinct categorical values. We can now compute the probability $Pr(G)$ in each population, for each of these m categories, which we denote by G_{ij}, where $i=1,2$ is the id of the population and $j=1,...,m$ is the id of the value of 2ndPartAtt. Let $Pr(G_{1j})$ and $Pr(G_{2j})$ denote the probability that the situation of interest has occurred in Pop_1 and Pop_2, in the j-th category of 2ndPartAtt, $j=1,...,m$.

Finally, Simpson's paradox occurs when, although the overall value of $Pr(G)$ is higher in Pop_1 than in Pop_2, i.e. $Pr(G_1) > Pr(G_2)$, in *each* of the categories produced by 2ndPartAtt the value of $Pr(G)$ in Pop_1 is lower than or equal to its value in Pop_2, i.e. $Pr(G_{1j}) \leq Pr(G_{2j})$, $j=1,...,m$. The paradox also occurs in the dual situation, i.e. when $Pr(G_1) < Pr(G_2)$ but $Pr(G_{1j}) \geq Pr(G_{2j})$, $j=1,...,m$ [10].

Some real-life examples of the occurrence of this paradox are mentioned in [14], [7]. For instance, the paradox occurred in a comparison of tuberculosis deaths in New York City and Richmond, Virginia, during the year 1910, as shown in Table 1. Overall, the tuberculosis mortality rate of New York was lower than Richmond's one. However, the opposite was observed when the data was further partitioned according to two racial categories: white and non-white. In both the white and non-white categories, Richmond had a lower mortality rate. In terms of the above notation, the 1stPartAtt was *city*; the situation of interest measured by attribute G was the *occurrence of death* in a tuberculosis case; and the 2ndPartAtt was *racial category*.

Table 1: Simpson's paradox in data about tuberculosis deaths.

	New York		Richmond	
Total Population	4766883		127682	
No. of deaths	8878		286	
Percentage	0.19%		0.22%	
	New York		**Richmond**	
	B	**NB**	**B**	**NB**
Total Population	4675174	91709	80895	46733
No. of deaths	8365	513	131	155
Percentage	0.18%	0.56%	0.16%	0.33%

3 Discovering occurrences of Simpson's paradox.

As mentioned in the introduction, some authors have alerted for the pitfalls associated with Simpson's paradox in the context of data mining - see e.g. [4]. In particular, the occurrence of this paradox in a given data set can easily fool a data mining algorithm, causing the algorithm to misinterpret a given relationship between some attributes.

For instance, decision-tree learners usually build a tree by selecting one attribute at a time. Hence, they can select an attribute that seems to have a certain relationship with a given class, when in reality the true relationship (taking into account attribute interactions) is the reverse of the apparent one.

Note that this monothetic nature (i.e. selecting one attribute at a time) is not unique to decision trees. Many other rule induction algorithms essentially work in this way, and so are also quite sensitive to the occurrence of Simpson's paradox.

Although data mining practitioners are starting to become more aware of the pitfalls associated with Simpson's paradox, little research has been done on how to cope with occurrences of this paradox, or how to modify a data mining algorithm to cope with this paradox.

This paper follows an intriguing research direction which, to the best of our knowledge, was first suggested in [2]. The basic idea is that, instead of trying to design an algorithm which avoids or mitigates the pitfalls associated with Simpson's paradox, we make the discovery of Simpson's paradox the central goal of the data mining algorithm.

The motivation can be summarized as follows. Simpson's paradox is, as the name implies, a paradox, and so it tends to be very surprising for the user.

The work described and empirically evaluated in this paper essentially consists of two parts. First, we discover occurrences of the paradox hidden in a data set. Second, we evaluate the "magnitude" (an estimate for the degree of surprisingness) of each discovered instance of the paradox, in order to report them to the user in decreasing order of magnitude (estimated degree of surprisingness). This approach gives the user flexibility to decide how many occurrences of the paradox (s)he will analyze, depending on her/his available time.

The rest of this section is divided into two parts. Section 3.1 describes an algorithm for discovering occurrences of Simpson's paradox. This algorithm is also described in our previous work [2], but it is included here to make the paper self-contained. Section 3.2 proposes a way to evaluate the "magnitude" of each discovered paradox - which was not addressed in our previous work - in an attempt to identify the most surprising instances of the paradox.

Finally, section 4 will present computational results reporting discovered occurrences of the paradox in several data sets - we note in passing that the above-mentioned previous work only proposed the algorithm, without reporting any computational results.

3.1 An algorithm for detecting occurrences of Simpson's paradox

The search for occurrences of Simpson's paradox can be performed by the Algorithm 1 below. The input for the algorithm is a list L_G of user-defined binary goal attributes, each of them indicating whether or not a given situation of interest has occurred.

INPUT: list of user-defined goal attributes, denoted L_G
BEGIN
    identify attributes that can be used as 1stPartAtt and put them in list L_1
    identify attributes that can be used as 2ndPartAtt and put them in list L_2
    FOR EACH goal attribute G in L_G
        FOR EACH attribute A_1 in L_1
            partition population into Pop_1 and Pop_2, according to values of A_1
            $Pr(G_1) = Pr(G="yes"|A_1=1)$
            $Pr(G_2) = Pr(G="yes"|A_1=2)$
            FOR EACH attribute A_2 in L_2 such that $A_2 \neq A_1$
                FOR i=1,2
                    partition Pop_i into m new populations Pop_{i1} ... Pop_{im},
                    according to the values of A_2
                    FOR j=1,...,m
                    $Pr(G_{ij}) = Pr(G="yes"|A_1=i,A_2=j)$
                IF ($Pr(G_1) > Pr(G_2)$ AND $Pr(G_{1j}) \leq Pr(G_{2j})$, j=1,...,m)
                OR ($Pr(G_1) < Pr(G_2)$ AND $Pr(G_{1j}) \geq Pr(G_{2j})$, j=1,...,m)
                report the occurrence of the paradox to the user
END

Algorithm 1: Search for occurrences of Simpson's paradox.

Algorithm 1 is specified in a high level of abstraction, so the two statements that identify the attributes to be put in lists L_1 and L_2 can be expanded in different procedures, using different criteria, as long as three conditions hold: (a) all attributes in L_1 are binary; (b) all attributes in L_2 are categorical; (c) any goal attribute contained in L_G does not appear in L_1 nor in L_2. Note that these conditions are not very strict, and in particular they allow the possibility that an attribute is contained in both L_1 and L_2 (since binary attributes are a particular case of categorical attributes). This possibility justifies the use of the condition $A_2 \neq A_1$ in the third FOR EACH statement of Algorithm 1. In practice, this and other more strict conditions may be directly implemented in the two statements that identify the attributes to be put in lists L_1 and L_2, when Algorithm 1 is refined to achieve a particular implementation.

3.2 Ranking the discovered occurrences of Simpson's paradox according to their degree of surprisingness.

The algorithm described in the previous subsection only discovers occurrences of Simpson's paradox in a black-and-white manner. For a given goal attribute and a given pair of partitioning attributes, either the paradox occurs or it does not. In practice, however, different instances of the paradox have different degrees of surprisingness for the user. Ideally, we would like to report the discovered instances of the paradox to the user in decreasing order of degree of surprisingness.

The problem is that surprisingness is, to a significant extent, a subjective (user-driven), domain-dependent concept. It is, however, both possible and desirable to develop an objective (data-driven), *domain-independent* measure of discovered-pattern surprisingness [2], [9]. In this spirit, we propose below a method to compute the "magnitude" of each instance of the paradox and use it as a measure of the degree of surprisingness of that instance of the paradox.

Once we have assigned to each discovered instance of the paradox a degree of surprisingness, we can report the discovered instances of the paradox to the user in decreasing order of degree of surprisingness, as mentioned earlier.

Intuitively, a reasonable measure of paradox magnitude would measure the degree to which the probability of the situation of interest was reversed when the second partition of the data was performed. Following the terminology and notation of section 2, this intuition can be better explained as follows.

If after the first partition of the data the probability of the situation of interest increases (decreases) very much from Pop_1 to Pop_2, and after the second partition of the data that probability decreases (increases) very much from Pop_1 to Pop_2 for each of the categories of 2ndPartAtt, then one can say that the paradox has a large magnitude. On the other hand, if after the first partition of the data the probability of the situation of interest increases (decreases) very little from Pop_1 to Pop_2, and after the second partition of the data that probability decreases (increases) very little from Pop_1 to Pop_2 for each of the categories of 2ndPartAtt, then one can say that the paradox has a small magnitude.

In other words, the larger the magnitude of the paradox, the more the probability of the situation of interest given the first partitioning attribute differs from the probability of the situation of interest given both the first and the second partitioning attributes. Therefore, the larger the magnitude, the larger the estimated degree of surprisingness for the user.

To formalize this intuition, the "magnitude" M of an instance of the paradox is given by the following formula:

$$M = (M1 + M2) / 2, \qquad (1)$$

where M1 measures by how much the probability of the situation of interest increases (decreases) from Pop_1 to Pop_2 after the first partition of the data and M2 measures by how much that probability decreases (increases) from Pop_1 to Pop_2 for each of the categories of 2ndPartAtt after the second partition of the data. We take the arithmetic average of M1 and M2, rather than simply taking the sum M1 + M2, mainly for the purpose of normalizing the magnitude M. Provided that both M1 and M2 vary in the range 0..100%, the value of M also varies in the range 0..100%.

The question is how to measure M1 and M2. At first glance, a sensible definition would be:

$$M1 = | Pr(G_1) - Pr(G_2) | \qquad (2)$$

$$M2 = (|Pr(G_{11}) - Pr(G_{21})| + |Pr(G_{12}) - Pr(G_{22})| + \ldots + |Pr(G_{1m}) - Pr(G_{2m})|) / m , \qquad (3)$$

where m is the number of values in the domain of 2ndPartAtt.

In formulas (2) and (3) M1 is the absolute value of difference between $Pr(G_1)$ and $Pr(G_2)$, the probability that the situation of interest has occurred respectively in Pop_1 and Pop_2 - the subpopulations created by splitting the data according to the first partitioning attribute. M2 is the average of the absolute values of the differences between $Pr(G_{1j})$ and $Pr(G_{2j})$, the probabilities that the situation of interest has occurred respectively in Pop_1 and Pop_2, in the j-th category of the second partitioning attribute, for j=1,...,m.

However, these definitions of M1 and M2 have a drawback. They take into account only the absolute values of differences between probabilities, and not the relative values of those differences. To see the problem, note that the absolute value of the difference between two probabilities of 5% and 10% is 5%, which is also the absolute value of the difference between two probabilities of 90% and 95%. Intuitively, however, an increase from 5% to 10% has a much larger relative magnitude than an increase from 90% to 95%. So, the former tends to be more surprising, and a good measure of magnitude ought to capture this notion.

Therefore, we propose a modification of formulas (2) and (3) to take into account the relative value of the differences between probabilities. The basic idea is to divide the difference between two probabilities x and y by the maximum value between x and y. (Alternatively, we could obtain a relative measure by using the minimum of x and y, but using the maximum value has the advantage of producing relative measures normalized in the range 0..1.)

The measures M1 and M2 used in this work are shown in formulas (4) and (5).

$$M1 = | Pr(G_1) - Pr(G_2) | / \max(Pr(G_1), Pr(G_2)) \qquad (4)$$

$$M2 = \sum_{k=1}^{m} (|Pr(G_{1k}) - Pr(G_{2k})| / \max(Pr(G_{1k}), Pr(G_{2k}))) / m \qquad (5)$$

Finally, there is a caveat in the implementation of formula (5). The denominator of any term in the summation can be 0. To avoid division by 0, if any of those terms is

0, the whole term is simply considered to be 0. For instance, if both $Pr(G_{11})$ and $Pr(G_{21})$ are 0, the whole term $|Pr(G_{11}) - Pr(G_{21})|/max(Pr(G_{11}),Pr(G_{21}))$ is considered to be 0. Note, however, that this term is still counted as one term (contributing for the value of m) for the purpose of taking the arithmetic average of all terms.

Note also that in principle both M1 and M2 can vary from 0 to 100%, so that the magnitude M can also vary from 0 to 100%. In practice values of M close to 100% are unlikely. (In all the experiments reported in this paper - described in section 4 - the highest value found for M was 46.76%.)

4 Computational Results.

We have implemented the algorithm described in section 3.1 and have applied it in seven public-domain data sets available from the UCI repository (URL: http://www.ics.uci.edu/AI/ML/Machine-Learning.html). These seven data sets are: Voting, Hepatitis, Australian Credit, Nursery, Heart, Car Evaluation, Adult.

We have not discovered any instance of Simpson's paradox in the Heart, Car Evaluation and Adult data sets. However, we have discovered in total 13 instances of the paradox in the other data sets, namely seven instances in Voting Records, two instances in Hepatitis, two instances in Australian Credit, and two instances in Nursery. Due to space limitation, we report here only seven discovered instances of the paradox, namely four instances in Voting Records, two instances in Hepatitis, and one instance in Australian Credit. The instances reported here are the ones with largest magnitude - our estimate for degree of surprisingness – for each data set. (The two instances of the paradox in the Nursery data set had very low – less than 1% - magnitude, that is why no instance is reported for this data set.)

The results are presented in the next three subsections. For the sake of uniformity and compactness, all the tables of results presented in this section have a title with the following format:

Table N: Dataset: D, Goal: G = v, 1stPartAtt: A1, 2ndPartAtt: A2,
Magnitude: X   (M1 = Y; M2 = Z)

where N is the number of the table, D is the name of the data set, G is the name of the goal attribute and v is the target value of G (i.e. the condition "G = v" defines the situation of interest), A1 and A2 are the names of the first and second partitioning attributes, X is the magnitude of the paradox – computed by formula (1) – and Y and Z are the values of the terms M1 and M2 used to compute magnitude, as defined in formulas (4) and (5).

Several of the data sets used in the experiments had missing attribute values. We coped with this problem as follows. When computing the probabilities of the situation of interest, an example was ignored – i.e. it was not counted for probability-computation purposes - if either the first partitioning attribute or the second partitioning attribute of that example had a missing value.

4.1 Results for the Voting Records data set.

This data set contains 435 examples and 16 binary attributes. The goal attribute predicts whether the Congressman is democrat or republican. The situation of interest used in our experiments was class = democrat. The four largest-magnitude instances of the paradox for this data set are reported in Tables 2 through 5.

The first two instances of the paradox, reported in Tables 2 and 3, have a large value of magnitude, so we estimate they are very surprising for the user. For instance, the upper part of Table 2 shows that the probability of a Congressman being a democrat given that (s)he voted "yea" (Yes) for export-administration-act-south-africa is much greater than the probability of a Congressman being a democrat given that (s)he voted "Nay" (No) for the same issue. However, the lower part of this Table shows that this is a deceptive relationship, once it is reversed when we take into account the interaction between the votes for export-administration-act-south-africa and for physician-fee-freeze.

Table 2: Dataset: Voting, Interest: class = democrat,
1stPartAtt: Export-administration-act-south-africa,
2ndPartAtt: Physician-fee-freeze
Magnitude: 46.76%   (M1 = 71.67%; M2 = 21.85%)

	Export-administration-act-south-africa=Yes		Export-administration-act-south-africa=No	
Total Populat.	264		61	
No. of Democr.	168		11	
Percentage	63.64%		18.03%	
	Phys-fee-frz=yes	**Phys-fee-frz=no**	**Phys-fee-frz=yes**	**Phys-fee-frz=no**
Total Populat.	98	166	55	6
No. of Democr.	4	164	5	6
Percentage	5.13%	98.98%	8.95%	100.00%

Table 3: Dataset: Voting, Interest: class = democrat,
1stPartAtt: Anti-satellite-test-ban, 2ndPartAtt: Physician-fee-freeze
Magnitude: 42.32%   (M1 = 62.78%; M2 = 21.85%)

	Anti-satellite-test-ban=Yes		Anti-satellite-test-ban=No	
Total Populat.	236		177	
No. of Democr.	197		55	
Percentage	83.47%		31.07%	
	Phys-fee-frz=yes	**Phys-fee-frz=no**	**Phys-fee-frz=yes**	**Phys-fee-frz=no**
Total Populat.	39	197	134	43
No. of Democr.	2	195	12	43
Percentage	5.13%	98.98%	8.95%	100.00%

Table 4: Dataset: Voting, Interest: class = democrat,
1stPartAtt: Water-project-cost-sharing, 2ndPartAtt: Mx-missile
Magnitude: 13.87%   (M1 = 1.98%; M2 = 25.76%)

	Water-project-cost-sharing=Yes		Water-project-cost-sharing=No	
Total Populat.	185		183	
No. of Democr.	110		111	
Percentage	59.46%		60.66%	
	Mx-miss.=yes	Mx-miss.=no	Mx-miss.=yes	Mx-miss.=no
Total Population	73	112	110	73
No. of Democr.	69	41	96	15
Percentage	94.52%	36.60%	87.27%	20.55%

Table 5: Dataset: Voting, Interest: class = democrat,
1stPartAtt: Water-project-cost-sharing, 2ndPartAtt: El-Salvador-Aid
Magnitude: 11.84%   (M1 = 1.53%; M2 = 22.14%)

	Water-project-cost-sharing=Yes		Water-project-cost-sharing=No	
Total Populat.	188		190	
No. of Democr.	114		117	
Percentage	60.64%		61.58%	
	El-Salv.-Aid=yes	El-Salv.-Aid=no	El-Salv.-Aid=yes	El-Salv.-Aid=no
Total Populat.	110	78	84	106
No. of Democr.	37	77	17	100
Percentage	33.64%	98.72%	20.24%	94.34%

4.2 Results for the Hepatitis data set.

This data set contains 155 examples and 19 attributes (most of them categorical). The goal attribute predicts whether the patient will die or live. The situation of interest used in our experiments was class = die.

We have found two instances of Simpson's paradox, reported in Tables 6 and 7. These two instances have a reasonable value of magnitude, namely 20.40% and 15.15%. Hence, they are estimated to be fairly surprising for the user.

For instance, the upper part of Table 6 shows that the probability of a patient dying given that (s)he has anorexia is significantly smaller than the probability of the patient dying given that (s)he does not have anorexia. However, the lower part of this Table shows that this is a deceptive relationship, once it is reversed when we take into account the interaction between the attributes anorexia and spiders.

Table 6: Dataset: Hepatitis, Interest: class = die,
1stPartAtt: Anorexia, 2ndPartAtt: Spiders
Magnitude: 20.40%   (M1 = 38.9%; M2 = 1.89%)

	Anorexia=no		Anorexia=yes	
Total Popul.		30		120
No. of deaths		9		22
Percentage		30.00%		18.33%
	Spid=no	Spid=yes	Spid=no	Spid=yes
Total Popul.	19	11	32	88
No. of deaths	8	1	14	8
Percentage	42.10%	9.09%	43.75%	9.09%

Table 7: Dataset: Hepatitis, Interest: class = die,
1stPartAtt: Liver Firm, 2ndPartAtt: Varices
Magnitude: 15.15%   (M1 = 22.15%; M2 = 8.14%)

	Liver Firm=no		Liver Firm=yes	
Total Popul.		60		83
No. of deaths		13		14
Percentage		21.67%		16.87%
	Varic=no	Varic=yes	Varic=no	Varices=yes
Total Popul.	12	48	6	77
No. of deaths	7	6	4	10
Percentage	58.33%	12.50%	66.67%	12.99%

4.3 Results for the Australian Credit data set.

This data set contains 690 examples and 14 attributes (6 continuous, 8 categorical). The original goal attribute can take on two values, class 1 and class 2 – the classes and all attribute names and values were changed to meaningless symbols, to protect the confidentiality of the data. The situation of interest used in our experiments was class = 2.

The largest-magnitude instance of the paradox is reported in Table 8. This instance has a magnitude of 7.15%. Hence, it is estimated to be little surprising for the user.

Table 8: Dataset: Australian Credit, Interest: class = 2,
1stPartAtt: A11, 2ndPartAtt: A8
Magnitude: 7.15%   (M1 = 6.82%; M2 = 7.47%)

	A11=0		A11=1	
Total Popul.		374		316
No. of class 2		161		146
Percentage		43.05%		46.20%
	A8=0	**A8=1**	**A8=0**	**A8=1**
Total Popul.	194	180	135	181
No. of class 2	14	147	9	137
Percentage	7.22%	81.67%	6.67%	75.69%

5 Summary and Discussion.

To the best of our knowledge, [2] was the first work to propose the idea of making the detection of Simpson's paradox the central goal of a data mining algorithm explicitly designed to discover surprising patterns.

As mentioned in section 3, this paper extends that previous work in two ways. First, we have reported computational results for the algorithm proposed in that previous work (where no computational results were reported). Second, we have proposed a new way to evaluate the "magnitude" of each discovered paradox in an attempt to identify the most surprising instances of the paradox. Discovered instances of the paradox can then be reported to the user in decreasing order of magnitude (estimated surprisingness). This approach gives the user flexibility to decide how many occurrences of the paradox (s)he will analyze, depending on her/his available time.

We have applied our algorithm to detect occurrences of Simpson's paradox in seven UCI data sets. In three of the data sets (Heart, Car Evaluation, Adult) we have found no occurrence of the paradox. In the other four data sets we have found 13 instances of Simpson's paradox with different degrees of magnitude. More precisely, we have found instances of the paradox with a large magnitude in the Voting Records data set, instances with a reasonably large magnitude in the Hepatitis data set, and instances with small magnitudes in the Australian Credit and Nursery data sets. Therefore, some of the instances of the paradox found in the Voting Records and the Hepatitis data sets are estimated to be truly surprising for the user.

It should be noted that, out of the seven data sets mined in this paper, the Voting Records has led not only to the discovery of the most surprising instances of the paradox but also to the largest number of detected instances of the paradox. This result can be at least partially explained by the facts that: (a) in this data set all attributes are binary; (b) the algorithm described in this paper requires that the first partitioning attribute be binary and the second partitioning attribute be categorical. Therefore, in this data set there is a larger number of attributes that can be used as the first-partitioning attribute, in comparison with other mined data sets. In addition, since binary attributes are a special case of categorical attributes, there is also a large number of attributes that can be used as the second-partitioning attribute.

Note also that the patterns discovered by the algorithm described in this paper do not have the same predictive power as other "stronger" kinds of patterns, such as prediction and classification rules. However, the patterns discovered in this paper satisfy not only the requirement of comprehensibility but also the requirement of surprisingness.

Concerning comprehensibility, the discovered patterns allow the user to understand better the interaction between a pair of predicting attributes (with respect to the prediction of a user-specified goal attribute) by using essentially the simple notion of a probability being greater than or smaller than another probability. This seems quite comprehensible, at least in the conventional sense of the term comprehensibility in the data mining literature, which is associated with syntactical simplicity and the use of simple comparison operators.

Concerning surprisingness, the discovered patterns directly represent instances of a paradox, which is, almost by definition, a kind of surprising knowledge. We also emphasize that the algorithm described in this paper was designed from scratch to discover surprising patterns. Actually, we believe that, in some sense, the algorithm described here is a stride towards the desirable goal of performing a true knowledge *discovery* task. In contrast, several data mining algorithms described in the literature are essentially variations of conventional machine *learning* algorithms designed to discover accurate, comprehensible (but not necessarily *surprising*) knowledge.

References.

[1] G. Dong & J. Li. Interestingness of discovered association rules in terms of neighborhood-based unexpectedness. *Research and Development in Knowledge Discovery & Data Mining (Proc. 2nd Pacific-Asian Conf., PAKDD-98). LNAI 1394*, 72-86. Springer-Verlag, 1998.

[2] A.A. Freitas. On objective measures of rule surprisingness. *Principles of Data Mining and Knowledge Discovery: Proc. 2nd European Symp. (PKDD'98). LNAI 1510*, 1-9. Nantes, France, Sep. 1998.

[3] A.A. Freitas. On rule interestingness measures. *To appear in Knowledge-Based Systems journal*, 1999.

[4]. C. Glymour, D. Madigan, D. Pregibon and P. Smyth. Statistical themes and lessons for data mining. *Data Mining and Knowl. Discov.* 1(1), 11-28. 1997.

[5] B. Liu & W. Hsu. Post-analysis of learned rules. *Proc. 1996 Nat. Conf. American Assoc. for Artificial Intelligence (AAAI-96)*, 828-834. AAAI Press, 1996.

[6] B. Liu, W. Hsu and S. Chen. Using general impressions to analyze discovered classification rules. *Proc. 3rd Int. Conf. Knowledge Discovery & Data Mining*, 31-36. AAAI, 1997.

[7] G. Newson. Simpson's paradox revisited. *The Mathematical Gazette 75(473)*, 290-293. Oct. 1991.

[8] B. Padmanabhan and A. Tuzhilin. A belief-driven method for discovering unexpected patterns. *Proc. 4th Int. Conf. Knowledge Discovery & Data Mining (KDD-98)*, 94-100. AAAI Press, 1998.

[9] A. Silberschatz & A. Tuzhilin. What makes patterns interesting in knowledge discovery systems. *IEEE Trans. Knowledge & Data Engineering*, 8(6), 970-974, Dec./1996.

[10] E.H. Simpson. The interpretation of interaction in contingency tables. *Journal of the Royal Statistical Society, Series B, 13*, 238-241. 1951.

[11] R. Subramonian. Defining *diff* as a data mining primitive. *Proc. 4th Int. Conf. Knowledge Discovery & Data Mining*, 334-338. AAAI, 1998.

[12] E. Suzuki. Autonomous discovery of reliable exception rules. *Proc. 3rd Int. Conf. Knowledge Discovery & Data Mining*, 259-262. AAAI Press, 1997.

[13] E. Suzuki & Y. Kodratoff. Discovery of surprising exception rules based on intensity of implication. *Proc. 2nd European Symp. Principles of Data Mining and Knowledge Discovery (PKDD'98). LNAI 1510*, 10-18. Nantes, France, Sep. 1998.

[14] C.H. Wagner. Simpson's paradox in real life. *The American Statistician*, 36(1), Feb. 1982, 46-48.

SESSION 3
CASE-BASED REASONING

Automating Case Selection in the Construction of a Case Library

David McSherry

School of Information and Software Engineering, University of Ulster, Coleraine BT52 1SA, Northern Ireland

Abstract

An approach to case selection in the construction of a case library is presented in which the most useful case to be added to the library is identified by evaluation of the additional coverage provided by candidate cases. Cases that can be solved by the addition of a candidate case to the library are discovered in the approach by reversing the direction of case-based reasoning. The computational effort required in the evaluation of candidate cases can be reduced by focusing the search on a specified region of the problem space. The approach has been implemented in CaseMaker, an intelligent case-acquisition tool designed to support the authoring process in a case-based reasoner for estimation tasks.

1 Introduction

Case-base maintenance and case authoring are topics of increasing importance in case-based reasoning (CBR) [1-3]. Recently, the development of tools to provide intelligent support for these activities has attracted significant research interest. Aha and Breslow [4] describe the use of machine learning techniques to refine case libraries to enhance their conformity with design guidelines and hence their performance. Zhu and Yang [5] propose a competence-preserving approach to maintenance in which cases from an existing case library are selected in order of usefulness for addition to a revised case library. Leake and Wilson [1] propose the use of maintenance rules to update existing cases at retrieval time as a solution to the maintenance problems presented by rapidly-changing domains. Racine and Yang [6] describe an agent-based approach to the detection of redundant and inconsistent cases. Another strategy for dealing with inconsistent cases is to prevent their admission to the case library [7].

Smyth and McKenna [2] have developed a model that enables the competence of a case library (the range of cases it can solve) to be predicted provided the case library is a representative sample of the target problem space. A case-authoring environment based on the model enables the competence of an evolving case library to be visualised, with regions of high and low competence highlighted so that authors can concentrate on areas of low competence. McSherry [8] describes an empirical approach to evaluation, rather than prediction, of problem-space coverage in which all cases that can be solved with a given case library are discovered by reversing the direction of case-based reasoning. This paper presents an approach to case selection in the construction of a case library in which evaluation of the coverage contributions of candidate cases is based on a similar strategy.

The approach has been implemented in an intelligent case-acquisition tool called CaseMaker which is designed to support the case-authoring process in CREST, a case-based reasoner for estimation tasks [7-9]. Selecting from a list of candidate cases ranked by CaseMaker in order of their coverage contributions, authors can focus on ensuring that practical constraints are observed and costs incurred in the acquisition of new cases are controlled. Alternatively, CaseMaker can be given greater autonomy in the construction of a case library, with the role of the author being simply to provide solutions for cases selected by the tool.

In Section 2, the problem of inferring by CBR the points scored by a football team from its wins, draws and losses is used to illustrate the case retrieval and adaptation strategies used in CREST. Section 3 examines the issues involved in case authoring and describes an algorithm for empirical evaluation of the problem-space coverage provided by a given case library. Section 4 describes the automation of case selection in CaseMaker and its use as a tool to support the authoring process. An empirical evaluation of the authoring support provided by the tool is also presented.

2 Case-Based Reasoning in CREST

CREST (Case-based Reasoning for ESTimation) is a case-based reasoner for estimation tasks in which there is no requirement for explicit adaptation knowledge. Instead, the solution of a target case is based on three existing cases, one retrieved for its similarity to the target case and the others to provide the knowledge required to adapt the similar case. This *demand-driven* approach to the discovery of adaptation knowledge has been shown to give good results in estimation tasks for which the value of a case is an additive or multiplicative function of its attributes [7,9]. Its application to the symbolic problem-solving task of differentiation [10] shows that the approach is not limited to estimation tasks.

The value of a case is assumed in CREST to be determined by an unknown function f of its attributes $x_1, x_2,..., x_n$, all of which are discrete. The task of the case-based reasoner is to evaluate a target case presented by the user; that is to infer or estimate its value from the values of existing cases in the case library. A problem space of dimensions $k_1 \times k_2 \times ... \times k_n$ is defined by the Cartesian product of the attribute domains $D_1, D_2,..., D_n$. A case is represented in CREST as a tuple $C = (a_1, a_2,..., a_n)$, where for $1 \le i \le n$, a_i is the value of the case attribute x_i for C.

The value of a case provided by the author of the case library, or inferred by the case-based reasoner, is denoted by $val(C)$.

2.1 Inferring Football Points as a CBR Problem

Inferring the points scored by a football team can be regarded as a CBR problem in which a case is a team, its attributes are its *wins*, *draws*, and *losses*, and the value of a case is the number of points scored by the team. Though unknown to the case-based reasoner, the value of a case is determined in this example by the function:

$$f(wins, draws, losses) = 3 \times wins + draws$$

That is, a team scores 3 points for winning a match, one point for a draw, and no points if it loses. An example library of 5 cases is shown in Table 1.

The team with two wins, no draws and one loss is represented in CREST by the tuple $C = (2,0,1)$ and the value of the case, that is the points scored by the team, is $val(C) = 6$. A target case that the case-based reasoner will be required to solve is $C_1 = (0,1,0)$, representing a team with no wins, one draw and no losses. It is worth noting that the problem is easily solved by an algebraic approach if a team's points total is assumed to be a linear function of its wins, draws and losses (which of course it is). However, the CBR approach described here relies on a weaker assumption that the value of a case is an additive function of its attributes and is therefore applicable to a wider range of problems.

Table 1. Example library of 5 cases.

Wins	Draws	Losses	Points
0	0	1	0
0	0	2	0
1	1	0	4
1	0	2	3
2	0	1	6

2.2 Case Retrieval and Adaptation

If an existing case matches a target case exactly, then the solution for the retrieved case can be applied without adaptation to the target case. In the absence of an exact match for a target case, the solution for a similar case must be adapted to fit the target case. An example of how this is achieved for the target case $C_1 = (0,1,0)$ is illustrated in Figure 1.

From Table 1, an existing case that differs from C_1 only in the number of wins is $C_2 = (1,1,0)$ and its value is known to be 4. On the usual CBR assumption that similar problems have similar solutions, we would expect the solution for C_1 to be similar to the solution for C_2. However, the solution for C_2 must be adapted to account for the difference between C_1 and C_2. To discover the knowledge required to adapt C_2, CREST searches the case library for a pair of existing cases C_3 and C_4 that also differ only in the number of wins and which are such that the number of wins is the same for C_1 and C_3 and the same for C_2 and C_4.

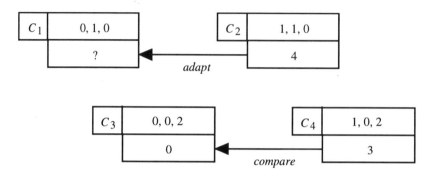

Figure 1. Adaptation in CREST.

Two such cases are $C_3 = (0,0,2)$ and $C_4 = (1,0,2)$ and their values are 0 and 3 respectively. Since both pairs of cases differ only in that one team has no wins and the other has one win, CREST assumes that the difference between the values of C_1 and C_2 will be the same as the difference between the values of C_3 and C_4. This assumption is the basis of the heuristic it uses to adapt the value of the similar case. For if $val(C_1) - val(C_2) = val(C_3) - val(C_4)$, it follows that:

$$val(C_1) = val(C_2) + val(C_3) - val(C_4)$$

The estimated value of the target case is therefore:

$$val(C_1) = 4 + 0 - 3 = 1$$

The triple C_2, C_3, C_4 of retrieved cases used in the adaptation is called an *adaptation triple* for C_1. The conditions that a triple of cases must satisfy to qualify as an adaptation triple for a target case are formally defined below.

Definition 1 Given a target case C_1, a triple C_2, C_3, C_4 of cases will be called an adaptation triple for C_1 if C_2 differs from C_1 only in the value of a single attribute, C_4 differs from C_3 only in the value of the same attribute, and the attribute whose values for C_1 and C_2 differ has the same value for C_1 and C_3 and the same value for C_2 and C_4.

The heuristic used to adapt the target case, according to which $val(C_1) = val(C_2) + val(C_3) - val(C_4)$ for any case C_1 and adaptation triple C_2, C_3, C_4 for C_1, is known as the *difference heuristic*. It always gives the correct value of a target case provided the value of a case is an additive function of its attributes and the values of existing cases in the case library are known without error [7]. An alternative heuristic called the *ratio heuristic* is available in CREST for use when the value of a case is suspected to be a multiplicative rather than an additive function of its attributes [9].

2.3 Recursive Adaptation

While the requirement for the adapted case to differ from the target case only in the value of a single attribute may seem a strong condition, problem-space coverage is significantly increased by recursive application [9]. The idea is that if one of the cases in an adaptation triple for a target case is unknown, it may be possible to solve the unknown case by CBR rather than discarding the adaptation triple. In the absence of a suitable adaptation triple for the unknown case, its solution may in turn rely on recursive adaptation. In problem spaces of dimension greater than three, coverage can be further increased by the use of *multi-dimensional* adaptation triples in which the adapted case is allowed to differ from the target case in more than one attribute [8]. Even when not essential for the solution of a target case, the alternative adaptation strategies admitted by the weaker similarity criteria may increase retrieval efficiency by reducing the need for recursive adaptation. In the present paper, however, adaptation is assumed to be based only on one-dimensional adaptation triples.

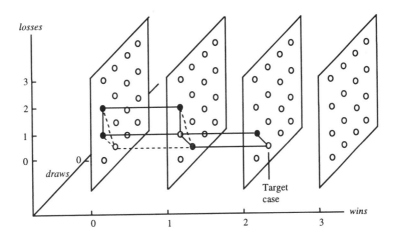

Figure 2. Recursive adaptation in CREST.

Recursive adaptation in the 4 x 4 x 4 problem space defined in the example CBR problem by restricting the values of the attributes *wins*, *draws* and *losses* to the integers from 0 to 3 is illustrated in Figure 2. The filled circles represent the cases in the example case library from Table 1 and the target case is $C_1 = (2,1,0)$. An adaptation triple for the target case is not available in the case library. However, an adaptation triple is provided for it by the known cases $C_2 = (1,1,0)$ and $C_3 = (2,0,1)$ and the unknown case $C_4 = (1,0,1)$. An adaptation triple for $(1,0,1)$ is in turn provided by the known cases $(1,0,2)$, $(0,0,1)$ and $(0,0,2)$. According to the difference heuristic, the value of the target case is therefore:

$$val(2,1,0) = val(1,1,0) + val(2,0,1) - val(1,0,1)$$

$$= 4 + 6 - val(1,0,2) - val(0,0,1) + val(0,0,2) = 4 + 6 - 3 - 0 + 0 = 7$$

The dashed lines in Figure 2 show an alternative solution path with evaluation of the unknown case $(0,1,0)$ as the recursive step.

As Figure 3 illustrates, the computational overhead associated with recursive adaptation is reduced in CREST by allowing only the use of adaptation triples in which at most one case is unknown. As confirmed by experimental results, good coverage of the target problem space is possible even with recursive adaptation restricted in this way.

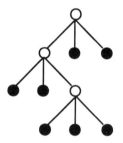

Figure 3. Recursive adaptation is restricted to adaptation triples in which at most one case is unknown.

3 The Case-Authoring Process

One objective in case authoring is to maximise coverage of the target problem space. It is also important to minimise redundancy in the case library so that retrieval times are maintained within acceptable levels [11]. Coverage of a target problem space provided by a given case library is defined here as the percentage of cases that are in the library or can be solved by adaptation. A library case is redundant if it can be solved by adaptation. The possible presence of redundant cases is one reason why the size of a case library may not be a reliable indicator of its coverage [2].

Rather than building a case library from scratch, the task of the case author may be to extend an existing case library to increase its coverage of the target problem space. Often in practice, existing library cases originate from legacy sources and the acquisition of additional cases is expensive. In these circumstances, maximising coverage and minimising redundancy may not be the only factors that need to be considered in the selection of new cases. Certain cases may be more difficult or expensive to acquire than others, and some may be impossible to acquire.

3.1 Problem-Space Coverage in CREST

Analysis of problem-space coverage in CREST shows that provided there are no constraints on case selection, full coverage of a target problem space can be achieved with a relatively small number of strategically selected cases [9]. In general, a problem space of dimensions $k_1 \times k_2 \times ... \times k_n$ can be fully covered by $\sum_{i=1}^{n}(k_i - 1) + 1$ cases. For example, the 4 x 4 x 4 problem space in the football points domain is fully covered by the 10 cases shown in Figure 4.

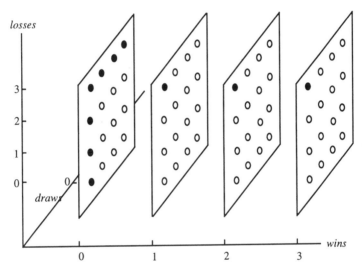

Figure 4. A 4 x 4 x 4 problem space can be fully covered
by 10 srategically selected cases.

However, strategic selection of all the cases in a case library is seldom possible. An example of practical constraints in the selection of library cases is provided by the football points domain. In Figure 5, the points enclosed by the pyramid correspond to possible team performances in a tournament such as the World Cup in which teams compete in groups of 4 teams for entry to a knockout stage. If the only source of library cases is a set of group tables for such a tournament, then the cases selected to populate the case library must satisfy the constraint:

$$wins + draws + losses \leq 3$$

Although full coverage of the target problem space by 10 cases that satisfy this constraint is still possible, as shown in Section 4, not any set of 10 cases will do. For example, the filled circles in Figure 5 are the points in the problem space that satisfy the stronger constraint:

$$wins + draws + losses = 3$$

These cases correspond to possible results for a team that has played all 3 of its group matches. In CREST, no additional case can be solved from these 10 cases. As no two of them differ only in *wins*, *draws* or *losses*, they cannot provide an adaptation triple for any case. Coverage of the target problem space provided by the 10 cases is therefore only $\frac{10}{64}$ or 16 per cent.

Coverage of the problem space provided by 10 cases randomly selected from the region of the problem space enclosed by the pyramid in Figure 5 therefore ranges from 16 to 100 per cent. The possibility of selecting 10 cases that provide no adaptive coverage illustrates the importance of intelligent support for case selection.

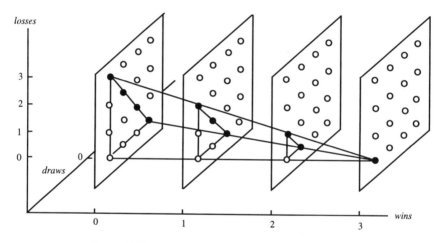

Figure 5. Ten cases that provide no adaptive coverage.

3.2 Empirical Evaluation of Coverage

The discovery of adaptation knowledge from case data is a promising application of data mining in CBR [9,12,13]. Interestingly, the evaluation (or prediction) of problem-space coverage in CBR also resembles data mining in several ways [8]. Both tasks may involve the analysis of large volumes of data, are necessarily performed off line, and may involve similar assumptions of *representativeness* of the available data [2,14]. An empirical approach to the evaluation of coverage in CREST has been implemented in an algorithm called disCover [8]. Cases that can be solved with a given case library are discovered in the algorithm by reversing the direction of case-based reasoning. Instead of reasoning backward from unknown cases to known cases which can be used to solve them, disCover reasons forward from known cases to unknown cases they can be used to solve.

The difference between these strategies is analogous to that between backward and forward chaining in an expert system. The analogy is strengthened by regarding an adaptation triple as a rule with 3 conditions and the target case as its conclusion. The discovery process takes advantage of the *reversibility* of adaptation triples. For example, if C_2, C_3, C_4 is an adaptation triple for C_1 then C_3, C_2, C_1 is an adaptation triple for C_4 [8].

In each cycle, disCover processes a list of *active* cases. In the first cycle, the active cases consist of all cases in a given case library L. For each active case C_1, and adaptation triple C_2, C_3, C_4 for C_1 such that C_2, $C_3 \in L$ and C_4 is an unknown case, disCover uses C_3, C_2, C_1 as an adaptation triple to solve C_4 and adds it to the list of discovered cases. Any adaptation triple for C_1 such that C_2, $C_4 \in L$ and C_3 is an unknown case, or C_3, $C_4 \in L$ and C_2 is an unknown case, similarly triggers the discovery of a new case. In each remaining cycle, the active cases are the cases that were discovered in the previous cycle.

As a by-product of the discovery process, disCover also provides useful maintenance information. Cases discovered in the first cycle are those that can be solved by non-recursive adaptation. Cases discovered in the second cycle are those that can be solved by recursive adaptation involving a sequence of two adaptation triples. In general, the number of the cycle in which a case is discovered is the minimum length of a sequence of adaptation triples required to solve the case.

When disCover was used to evaluate the coverage of the 4 x 4 x 4 problem space in Figure 2 provided by the 5 cases in the example case library, the discovered cases were (0,1,0), (1,0,1), (2,0,2) and (2,1,0), with recursive adaptation required only for (2,1,0). Coverage of the target problem space provided by the example case library is therefore $\frac{5+4}{64}$ or 14 per cent.

4 Case Authoring Support in CaseMaker

CaseMaker is an intelligent case-acquisition tool designed to guide the incremental construction of a case library in CREST by identifying the most useful case to be added to the case library at any stage of its evolution; that is, the case that provides maximum additional coverage. It can be used to support the construction of a case library from scratch or assist the author in extending an existing library to increase its coverage of a target problem space. The *closure* of a case library, defined below, is a useful concept for describing the case-selection process in CaseMaker.

Definition 2 The closure of a case library L, denoted by $\overline{L}$, is the set of cases that are in L or can be solved by adaptation.

4.1 Identifying the Most Useful Case

Given a problem space P and case library L, CaseMaker's task is to identify an additional case $C_a \in P - \overline{L}$ for which $card(\overline{L \cup \{C_a\}})$ is maximum. One way to achieve this, though likely to be prohibitively expensive, would be to apply disCover to the extended library $L \cup \{C_a\}$ for all $C_a \in P - \overline{L}$ and select the case that maximises the overall coverage. A more efficient strategy is to evaluate the *additional* coverage provided by each $C_a \in P - \overline{L}$ and select the case that offers maximum additional coverage. This is the strategy adopted in CaseMaker. Figure 6 illustrates how a previously covered case $C_1 \in \overline{L} - L$ triggers the discovery of a new case that will be covered if a candidate case C_a is added to the case library. An adaptation triple for C_1 is provided by C_2, C_3, C_4 where $C_2 \in L$, $C_3 = C_a$, and C_4 is a previously uncovered case. By the reversibility of adaptation triples, it follows that C_a, C_2, C_1 provides an adaptation triple which can be used to solve C_4.

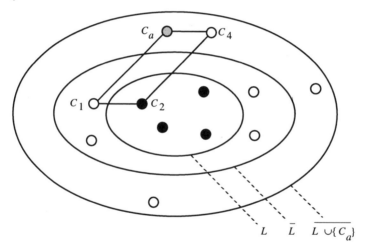

Figure 6. Evaluating the additional coverage provided by a candidate case
for insertion into the case library.

4.2 Focusing the Search for Useful Cases

By default, all uncovered cases are considered by CaseMaker as candidates for addition to the case library. Alternatively, the author of the case library can specify a region of the problem space from which the most useful case is to be selected. As well as reducing the computational overhead involved in the evaluation of candidate cases, this enables the author to eliminate cases that are known to be difficult or impossible to acquire. An example dialogue is shown below in which

CaseMaker's selection of cases for addition to the example case library in Table 1 is restricted to the region of the problem space enclosed by the pyramid in Figure 5; that is, those cases that satisfy the constraint:

$$wins + draws + losses \leq 3$$

The example case library already contains 5 and covers another 3 of the 20 cases in the specified region of the problem space. The remaining 12 cases in the specified region are the initial candidates for addition to the case library. Following the insertion of the selected case (2,0,0) into the library, only 6 eligible cases remain uncovered by the extended library. As only uncovered cases are considered for addition to the library, the author is left with only 6 cases from which to select the next case.

CaseMaker: Library now contains 5 cases and coverage is 14% (9 cases)
New total coverage (%) provided by candidate cases:

        [2, 0, 0]: 28
        [1, 1, 1]: 28
        [1, 0, 0]: 28
        [0, 1, 2]: 28
        [0, 1, 1]: 28
        [0, 0, 0]: 28
        [0, 2, 1]: 23
        [1, 2, 0]: 19
        [0, 3, 0]: 19
        [0, 2, 0]: 19
        [0, 0, 3]: 19
        [3, 0, 0]: 16

Which case do you wish to add to the library?
User: [2, 0, 0]
CaseMaker: Please enter the solution for [2, 0, 0]
User: 6
CaseMaker: Library now contains 6 cases and coverage is 28% (18 cases)
New total coverage (%) provided by candidate cases:

        [1, 2, 0]: 42
        [0, 3, 0]: 42
        [0, 2, 1]: 42
        [0, 2, 0]: 42
        [3, 0, 0]: 38
        [0, 0, 3]: 38

Which case do you wish to add to the library?
User: [1, 2, 0]
CaseMaker: Please enter the solution for [1, 2, 0]
User: 5
CaseMaker: Library now contains 7 cases and coverage is 42% (27 cases)
New total coverage (%) provided by candidate cases:

        [3, 0, 0]: 56
        [0, 3, 0]: 56
        [0, 0, 3]: 56

	Which case do you wish to add to the library?
User:	[3, 0, 0]
CaseMaker:	Please enter the solution for [3, 0, 0]
User:	9
CaseMaker:	Library now contains 8 cases and coverage is 56% (36 cases)

An interesting point to note is that in spite of their low coverage contributions at the outset, all three of the cases presented by CaseMaker on the third occasion are in fact essential for full coverage of the target problem space to be achieved by cases in the specified region of the problem space. For example, it is easily verified that if the library does not contain at least one case with *wins* = 3, then no such case can be solved.

As the following dialogue illustrates, CaseMaker can be given greater autonomy in the selection of library cases, with the role of the author being simply to provide solutions for the cases it selects. As in the first example dialogue, the starting point is the example case library in Table 1 and the author has restricted the selection of new cases to the region of the problem space enclosed by the pyramid in Figure 5.

CaseMaker:	Library now contains 5 cases and coverage is 14% (9 cases)
	Please enter the solution for [0, 0, 0]
User:	0
CaseMaker:	Library now contains 6 cases and coverage is 28% (18 cases)
	Please enter the solution for [0, 2, 0]
User:	2
CaseMaker:	Library now contains 7 cases and coverage is 42% (27 cases)
	Please enter the solution for [0, 0, 3]
User:	0
CaseMaker:	Library now contains 8 cases and coverage is 56% (36 cases)
	Please enter the solution for [0, 3, 0]
User:	3
CaseMaker:	Library now contains 9 cases and coverage is 75% (48 cases)
	Please enter the solution for [3, 0, 0]
User:	9
CaseMaker:	Library now contains 10 cases and coverage is 100% (64 cases)

In this example, an existing case library of 5 cases has been extended to achieve full coverage of the target problem space with 10 cases, equalling the efficiency of coverage known to be possible by strategic selection of all library cases [9].

4.3 Experimental Results

The results of an experiment to evaluate the case-authoring support provided by CaseMaker are presented in Figure 7. The experiment compared three different strategies in the selection of cases for addition to the example case library in Table 1. In the first strategy, the most useful case identified by CaseMaker, or one of the most useful cases in the event of a tie, was added to the case library at each stage. This is the strategy illustrated in the second example dialogue. In the second strategy, the case selected at each stage was one of those providing second-highest coverage according to CaseMaker. Finally, the selected case in the third strategy was the one of those identified by CaseMaker as providing least additional coverage.

In all three strategies, selection of new cases was restricted to the region of the problem space enclosed by the pyramid in Figure 5. Case selection continued until full coverage of the target problem space was achieved or no eligible cases remained; that is until all cases in the specified region of the problem space were in the case library or covered by it. Coverage of the problem space can be seen to have increased most rapidly when the case added to the case library at each stage was the one identified as most useful by CaseMaker. The other two strategies produced case libraries that provided much inferior coverage in the early stages of their construction. Interestingly, a dramatic recovery was observed in these strategies with the selection of the final case, though not sufficient to achieve full coverage of the problem space.

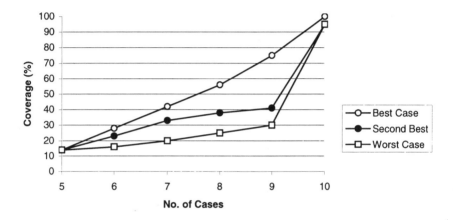

Figure 7. Comparison of three case-selection strategies.

While showing the benefits of coverage-guided case selection, the experimental results also illustrate the trade-off involved in considering only uncovered cases as candidates for admission to the case library. Although significantly reducing computational effort in case selection, and helping to avoid redundancy, this policy ignores the possibility that the addition of an already covered case to the case library may increase problem-space coverage. For example, in the third experimental strategy, one of the cases finally recommended by CaseMaker (in fact more than one) would increase coverage to 100 per cent. Instead, a case is selected which increases coverage only to 95 per cent. Although the recommended case would still increase coverage to 100 per cent, it is now covered by the extended case library and therefore no longer eligible for consideration by CaseMaker.

5 Discussion

An approach to automating the selection of cases in the construction of a case library has been presented. A key role in the approach is played by an algorithm called disCover which reverses the direction of CBR to discover all cases that can be solved with a given case library. Previously presented as a tool for evaluation of problem-space coverage in CREST [8], disCover has been adapted here as a tool for identifying the most useful uncovered case to be added to a case library at any stage of its evolution; that is the uncovered case that will provide maximum additional coverage. The result is an intelligent case-acquisition tool called CaseMaker in which the selection of cases to be added to a case library is guided by empirical evaluation of the coverage contributions provided by candidate cases.

Like exhaustive rule discovery in data mining, exhaustive evaluation of coverage in CBR is a computationally intensive process and is likely to be feasible only in problem spaces of small to medium size. In data mining, compromises are often necessary, such as mining only a sample of the data or limiting the number of conditions in a discovered rule [14,15]. In empirical evaluation of coverage, the estimation of a *lower bound* for coverage, based on the number of cases that can be solved in a reasonable time, may be an acceptable compromise [8]. While full evaluation of existing coverage is required for the selection of the most useful case to be added to a case library, computational effort in the evaluation of candidate cases can be reduced by focusing the search on a region of the problem space specified by the author.

Experimental results have been presented which show the potential benefits of coverage-guided case selection in case authoring. Further research will extend the capabilities of CaseMaker to provide more comprehensive support for case authoring, for example by automating the identification of cases that are essential to achieve full coverage of a target problem space.

References

1. Leake D, Wilson D. Categorizing case-base maintenance: dimensions and directions. In: Smyth B, Cunningham P (eds) Advances in Case-Based Reasoning, Springer-Verlag, Berlin-Heidelberg, 1998, pp 196-207 (Lecture notes in artificial intelligence no. 1488)

2. Smyth B, McKenna E. Modelling the competence of case-bases. In: Smyth B, Cunningham P (eds) Advances in Case-Based Reasoning, Springer-Verlag, Berlin-Heidelberg, 1998, pp 208-220 (Lecture notes in artificial intelligence no. 1488)

3. Watson I. Applying Case-Based Reasoning: Techniques for Enterprise Systems. Morgan Kaufmann, San Francisco, 1997

4. Aha D, Breslow L. Refining conversational case libraries. In: Leake D, Plaza E (eds) Case-Based Reasoning Research and Development. Springer-Verlag, Berlin-Heidelberg, 1997, pp 267-278 (Lecture notes in artificial intelligence no. 1266)

5. Zhu J, Yang Q. Remembering to add: competence-preserving case-addition policies for case-base maintenance. Proceedings of the Sixteenth International Joint Conference on Artificial Intelligence, Stockholm, 1999, pp 234-239

6. Racine K, Yang Q. Maintaining unstructured case bases. In: Leake D, Plaza E (eds) Case-Based Reasoning Research and Development. Springer-Verlag, Berlin-Heidelberg, 1997, pp 553-564 (Lecture notes in artificial intelligence no. 1266)

7. McSherry D. An adaptation heuristic for case-based estimation. In: Smyth B, Cunningham P (eds) Advances in Case-Based Reasoning, Springer-Verlag, Berlin-Heidelberg, 1998, pp 184-195 (Lecture notes in artificial intelligence no. 1488)

8. McSherry D. Relaxing the similarity criteria in adaptation knowledge discovery. Proceedings of the IJCAI-99 Workshop on Automating the Construction of Case-Based Reasoners, Stockholm, 1999, pp 56-61

9. McSherry D. Demand-driven discovery of adaptation knowledge. Proceedings of the Sixteenth International Joint Conference on Artificial Intelligence, Stockholm, 1999, pp 222-227

10. McSherry D. Differentiation by case-based reasoning. Pre-Proceedings of the Tenth Irish Conference on Artificial Intelligence and Cognitive Science, Cork, 1999, pp 150-156

11. Smyth B, Keane M. Remembering to forget: a competence-preserving case deletion policy for CBR systems. Proceedings of the Fourteenth International Joint Conference on Artificial Intelligence, Montreal, 1995, pp 377-382

12. Hanney K, Keane M. Learning adaptation rules from a case-base. In: Smith I, Faltings B (eds) Case-Based Reasoning Research and Development. Springer-Verlag, Berlin-Heidelberg, 1996, pp 178-192 (Lecture notes in artificial intelligence no. 1168)

13. Smyth B, Keane M. Adaptation-guided retrieval: questioning the similarity assumption in reasoning. Artif Intell 1998; 102:249-293

14. Frawley W, Piatetsky-Shapiro G, Matheus C. Knowledge discovery in databases: an overview. In: Piatetsky-Shapiro G, Frawley W (eds) Knowledge Discovery in Databases, AAAI Press, Menlo Park, 1991, pp 1-27

15. Smyth P, Goodman R. Rule induction using information theory. In: Piatetsky-Shapiro G, Frawley W (eds) Knowledge Discovery in Databases, AAAI Press, Menlo Park, 1991, pp 159-176

Improving a Distributed Case-Based Reasoning System Using Introspective Learning

Ian Watson
AI-CBR
University of Salford
Salford, M7 9NU
UK
ian@ai-cbr.org
www.ai-cbr.org

Dan Gardingen
Western Air Ltd.
McCabe Street, North Fremantle
Fremantle
Western Australia

Abstract

This paper describes the improvements to a fielded case-based reasoning (CBR) system. The system, called "Really Cool Air" is a distributed application that supports engineering sales staff. The application operates on the world wide web and uses the XML standard as a communications protocol between client and server side Java applets. The paper briefly describes the distributed architecture of the application, the two case retrieval techniques used, and improvements made in three areas: software infrastructure, retrieval algorithm and most crucially the automatic adjustments of query relaxation parameters by an incremental learning algorithm. The results of the incremental learning algorithm are quantified.

1 Introduction

A paper describing the design, implementation, testing, roll-out and benefits of the "*Really Cool Air*" system was presented to this conference in 1998 [Gardingen & Watson 1998] and subsequent improvements to the fielded system were briefly described in a paper presented at IJCAI-99 [Watson & Gardingen 1999]. However, the publication of the later paper came before detailed evaluation of the improvements could be reported. This paper is therefore able to present detailed quantitative results of experiments to test the efficiency of an introspective learning algorithm that automatically learns query relaxation parameters. For the benefit of readers who have not read the previous papers the systems purpose and architecture is briefly described before describing the improvements and evaluating the incremental learning strategy.

Thus, section 2 describes the background to the system, it's raison d'être, its implementation and architecture, case representation and retrieval strategy and its interface design. Section 3 describes the improvements to the system's architecture including an evaluation of the efficiency gains obtained through the implementation of an introspective learning algorithm. Section 4 concludes the paper.

2 Background

Western Air is a distributor of HVAC (heating, ventilation and air conditioning systems in Australia with a turnover in 1997 of $25 million (US dollars). Based in Fremantle the company operates mainly in Western Australia, a geographic area of nearly two million square miles. The systems supported range from simple residential HVAC systems to complex installations in new build and existing factories and office buildings.

Western Air has a distributed sales force numbering about 100. The majority of staff do not operate from head office but are independent, working from home or a mobile base (typically their car). Until recently, sales staff in the field would gather the prospective customer's requirements using standard forms and proprietary software, take measurements of the property and fax the information to Western Air in Fremantle. A qualified engineer would then specify the HVAC system. Typically the engineer would have to phone the sales staff and ask for additional information and the sales staff would have to make several visits to the customer's building and pass additional information back to the head office engineer.

Western Air felt that basing a quote on the price of a previous similar installation gave a more accurate estimation than using prices based on proprietary software, catalogue equipment prices and standard labour To try to help engineers make use of all the past installations a database was created to let engineers search for past installations. The database contained approximately 10,000 records, each with 60 fields describing the key features of each installation and then a list of file names for the full specification. Initially the engineers liked the database and it increased the number of past installations they used as references. However, after the honeymoon ended, they started to complain that it was too hard to query across more than two or three fields at once. And that querying across ten or more fields was virtually impossible. In fact most of them admitted to using the database to laboriously browse through past installations until they found one that looked similar to their requirements.

2.1 Implementation

Western Air decided that merely improving the efficiency of the engineers in Fremantle would not solve the whole problem. Ideally they would like the sales staff to be able to give fast accurate estimates to prospective customers on the spot. However, they were aware that there was a danger that the less knowledgeable sales staff might give technically incorrect quotes.

The solution they envisaged was to set up a web site that sales staff could access from anywhere in the country. Through a forms interface the prospect's requirements could be input and would be passed to a CBR system that would search the library of past installations and retrieve similar installations. Details of the similar installations along with the ftp addresses of associated files would then be available to the sales staff by ftp. The sales staff could then download the files and use these to prepare an initial quote. All this information would then be automatically passed back to an engineer to authorise or change if necessary. Once an installation was completed its details would be added to the library and its associated files placed on the ftp server.

2.2 Implementation Plan

Web based CBR applications have been demonstrated for a few years now such as the FAQFinder and FindME systems [Hammond et al., 1996] and those at Broderbund and Lucas Arts [Watson, 1997]. The solution they envisaged was to set up a web site that sales staff could access from anywhere in the country. Through a forms interface the prospect's requirements could be input and would be passed to a CBR system that would search the library of past installations and retrieve similar installations. Details of the similar installations along with the FTP addresses of associated files would then be available to the sales staff by FTP. The sales staff could then download the files and use these to prepare an initial quote. All this information would then be automatically passed back to an engineer to authorise or change if necessary. Once an installation was completed its details would be added to the library and its associated files placed on the ftp server.

Since a simple nearest neighbour retrieval algorithm would suffice implementing our own system was a viable option. Java (Visual Café) was chosen as the implementation language for both the client and server side elements of the CBR system. XML (eXtensible Markup Language) [WWW Consortium, 1997] was used as the communication language between client and server-side applets. The World-Wide Web Consortium (W3C) finalised XML 1.0 in December 1997 as a potential successor to HTML [WWW Consortium].

2.3 System Architecture

On the sales staff (client) side a Java applet is used to gather the customer's requirements and send them as XML to the server. On the server side another Java applet (a *servlet*) uses this information to query the database to retrieve a set of relevant records. The Java servlet then converts these into XML and sends them to the client side applet that uses a nearest neighbour algorithm to rank the set of cases.

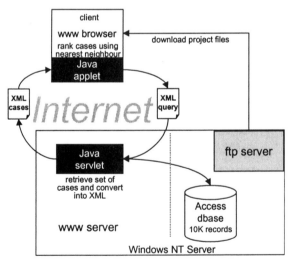

Figure 1. System Architecture

2.4 Case Representation

Cases are stored within a database. Each record (case) comprises 60 fields used for retrieval and many more used to describe the HVAC installations. In addition, links to other files on the FTP server are included to provide more detailed descriptions. Once retrieved from the database the records are ranked by a nearest neighbour algorithm and dynamically converted into XML for presentation to the client browser. An XML case representation is used by our system [Shimazu, 1998]. XML pages can contain any number of user defined tags defined in a document type definition (DTD) file. Tags are nested hierarchically from a single root tag that can contain any number of child tags. Any child tag in turn can contain any number of child tags. Each tag contains a begin statement (e.g. <Case>) and an end statement (e.g. </Case>). This is illustrated in Figure 4.

2.5 Case Retrieval

Case retrieval is a two stage process. In stage one the customer's requirements are relaxed through a process of *query relaxation*. This process takes the original query and relaxes terms in it to ensure that a useful number of records are retrieved from the database. This is similar to the technique used by Kitano & Shimazu [1996] in the SQUAD system at NEC, although as is discussed in section 3, we have improved it efficiency using an introspective learning heuristic.

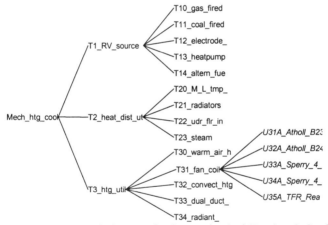

Figure 2. A Portion of a Symbol Hierarchy for Mechanical Heating & Cooling Systems

For example, assume we are trying to retrieve details of installations using Athol B25 equipment. An SQL query that just used "Athol_B25" as a search term might be too restrictive. Using an ordered symbol hierarchy (as in Figure 2) our system knows that "Athol B25" is a type of "Fan Coil" system so the query is relaxed to "Where (((EquipmentReference) = "T31_fan_coil"")..)). This query will include equipment from Athol, Sperry and TFR. An ordering of each set of symbols in the hierarchy is obtained through the reference number suffixes to each symbol (e.g. T10, T11, T12, T13, T14 as shown in Figure 2). The symbol hierarchies are stored in a table in the database.

Other specific criteria, elevations or temperatures that are numbers (integers or reals) can be relaxed by using simple ranges (e.g. a temperature of 65° F. could be relaxed to "Between 60 And 70"). Knowledge engineering was required to determine by what amounts numeric features should be relaxed. The relaxation is expressed as a term ± a percentage (e.g., "Relax_Temp = ± 10%"). These relaxation terms are stored in a table in the database.

In the second stage the small set of retrieved records are compared by the client-side applet with the original query and similarity is calculated using the simple nearest neighbour algorithm shown in Figure 3. The resulting similarity measure is normalised to give a percentage range of 0% (i.e. completely dissimilar) to 100% (i.e. completely similar). The weighting on the features by default is set to 1 (i.e., all features are by default considered of equal importance) However, the sales engineers can change the feature weightings to reflect client priorities or their own preferences.

$$Similarity(T,S) = \sum_{i=1}^{n} f(T_i, S_i) \times w_i$$

where:

T is the target case, S is the source case, n is the number of features in each case
i is an individual feature from 1 to n, f is a similarity function for feature i in cases T and S and w is the importance weighting of feature I

Figure 3 The Nearest Neighbour Algorithm

Once an HVAC installation is completed its details are added to the database and its associated files placed on the FTP server. Having a database management system for the case repository has proved essential since it makes it easier to generate management reports and ensure data integrity. It would be almost impossible to maintain a collection of 10,000 cases without a DBMS.

2.4   Interface Design

The interface to the system is a standard Java enabled web browser (Netscape or Internet Explorer). The forms within the Java applet were designed to look as similar to the original forms, HVAC specification tools and reports that the sales staff were already familiar with. Microsoft FrontPage 98 and Macromedia's DreamWeaver were the primary tools used to create the web site. A sample screen from the client side Java applet can be seen in Figure 6.

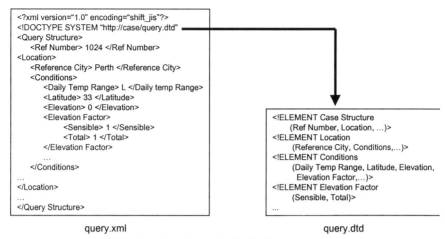

```
<?xml version="1.0" encoding="shift_jis"?>
<!DOCTYPE SYSTEM "http://case/query.dtd"
<Query Structure>
    <Ref Number> 1024 </Ref Number>
<Location>
    <Reference City> Perth </Reference City>
    <Conditions>
        <Daily Temp Range> L </Daily temp Range>
        <Latitude> 33 </Latitude>
        <Elevation> 0 </Elevation>
        <Elevation Factor>
            <Sensible> 1 </Sensible>
            <Total> 1 </Total>
        </Elevation Factor>
        ...
    </Conditions>
...
</Location>
...
</Query Structure>
```

```
<!ELEMENT Case Structure
    (Ref Number, Location, ...)>
<!ELEMENT Location
    (Reference City, Conditions,...)>
<!ELEMENT Conditions
    (Daily Temp Range, Latitude, Elevation,
    Elevation Factor,...)>
<!ELEMENT Elevation Factor
    (Sensible, Total)>
...
```

query.xml   query.dtd

Figure 4. A Sample of the XML Case Description

```
SELECT Location.ReferenceRegion, Location.DailyTempRange,
Location.Lattitude, Location.Elevation, Location.ElevationFactorS,
Location.ElevationFactorT, Location.DryBulbTempWin, Loca-
tion.DryBulbTempSum, Location.WetBulbTemp,
...
FROM Location
WHERE (((Location.ReferenceRegion)="SW") AND ((Loca-
tion.Elevation) Between 0 And 100) AND ((Loca-
tion.DryBulbTempWin) Between 50 And 60) AND ((Loca-
tion.DryBulbTempSum) Between 60 And 70))
...
```

Figure 5. Example of an SQL Query That Has Been Relaxed

3   System Enhancements

Although the initial testing and roll-out of the system was judged a success, not least in commercial terms the original implementation of the system experienced increasing load performance problems. The Java servlet approach suffered from poor performance because the web server loads, executes and terminates a new servlet program for each user access. Large data sets and complex queries especially burden the system because data querying takes place via the Java servlet program rather than directly via the database. This coupled with the fact that MS Access is not a particularly fast database caused time out problems as the server load increased. To rectify this problem the database was ported to mySQL (http://www.tcx.se) a freeware database with much better performance.

184

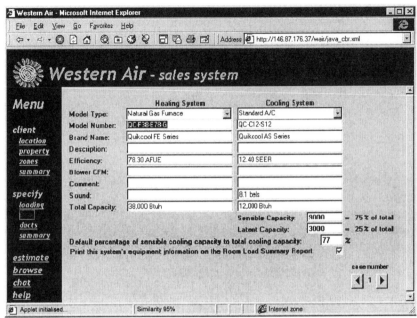

Figure 6. Client Side Java Applet Showing Retrieved HVAC Case

In addition Netscape's LiveWire database integration tool was used. This product has excellent database query functions, and importantly, because the LiveWire engine runs within the Netscape Web Server process it can share database connections across all Web accesses.

3.1 Introspective Learning

The initial query relaxation method of first performing a precise query and then relaxing the query through successive iterations until a sufficiently large set of cases was retrieved also compounded the performance problems. A suggestion was made to turn this process around – namely, why not relax the initial query far enough to ensure that a large set of cases would be retrieved (e.g. several hundred cases) and then refine the query to reduce the sub-set to around twenty cases). The obvious speed advantage in this approach is that only a small sub-set of the whole case-base is used in any subsequent iterations as opposed to the entire case-base in the original query relaxation approach.

However, deciding how much to relax the query was not straightforward so an introspective learning approach was taken. This is an approach in CBR where the reasoning system itself learns over time to modify its internal representation to improve its performance [Markovitch & Scott, 1993]. For example, CBR systems may learn to modify feature weights, adaptation rules [Leake, et al., 1995; Hanney & Keane, 1996], or even learn to forget redundant cases [Smyth & Cunningham, 1996].

A decision was made to log each time a feature was relaxed during the query relaxation process. When the same query term is encountered again the query is automatically relaxed by one of three methods:

1. by the precise amount it was relaxed the previous time,
2. by the average amount it was relaxed the previous N times it had been relaxed, and
3. by the mean amount it was relaxed the previous N times it had been relaxed.

Experiments were then conducted to see which, if any, of these simple heuristics most improved retrieval efficiency. This of course required that we decided what we meant by efficiency, was it:

*   Time efficiency, i.e. purely a measure of retrieval speed, or
*   Accuracy, i.e., a measure of the quality of the final suggested set of cases.

It was felt by the developers that both metrics were important so both were considered. Because of problems due to network and server loads and the way command stacks were executed it was difficult to directly measure retrieval speed accurately so the concept of *precision* was used as an analogue. That it how many cases were returned in the set of retrieved cases. The fewer the number the more precise. A smaller number of cases would always be processed faster by the system, hence retrieval time would be quicker (unless network traffic slowed down the exchange of XML information).

Therefore, if the query relaxation algorithm returned a single case that was a 100% match to the target case we would have an accuracy rating of a perfect 100% with a precision of 100%. It is worth remembering that this only tests the first stage of retrieval. In the second stage a nearest neighbour algorithm selects the most similar case from the retrieved set.

Testing

Test were conducted by partitioning the case-base. Approximately one fifth of the cases (2000) were removed at random from the case-base. These were then used in a random sequence as probes to query the case-base. Our hypothesis therefore was that if the introspective learning algorithm worked either the precision or accuracy or both of the system should improve over time.

Results

The results are presented as a series of graphs. three methods were used by the introspective learning algorithm to learn how to relax the query:

1. *precise relaxation* – i.e., relax query features by the precise amount they were relaxed the previous time.

2. *average relaxation* – i.e., relax query features by the average amount they were relaxed the previous n times they had been relaxed (where n is the total number of times it has been relaxed), and

3. *mean relaxation* – i.e., relax query features by the mean amount they had been relaxed the previous n times they had been relaxed.

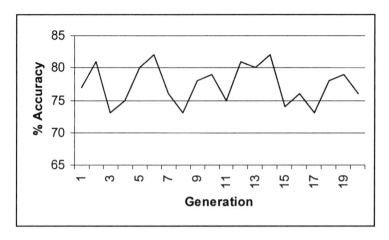

Figure 7 % Accuracy for Precise Relaxation
(Generation is in 100s)

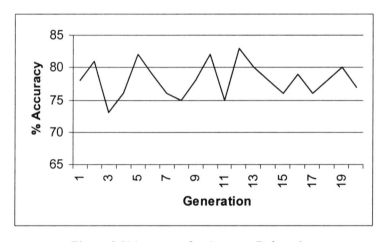

Figure 8 %Accuracy for Average Relaxation

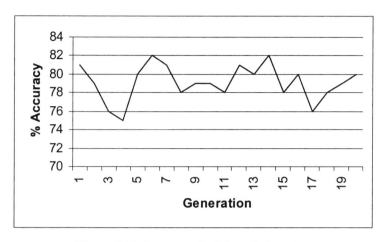

Figure 9 % Accuracy for Mean Relaxation

The results for percentage accuracy (Figures 7-9) were entirely inconclusive. % Accuracy did not improve using either of the three introspective learning algorithms. This is not surprising since the objective of the query relaxation method is not to retrieve the "best" matching case but rather to retrieve a set of good candidate cases upon which the nearest neighbour algorithm can work. However, conversely there was no evidence that introspective learning reduced the accuracy of the set of retrieved cases.

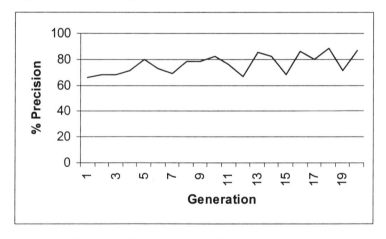

Figure 10 % Precision for Precise Relaxation

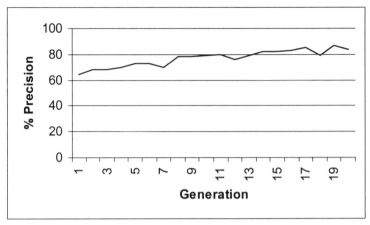

Figure 11 % Precision for Average Relaxation

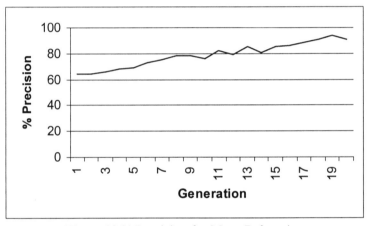

Figure 12 % Precision for Mean Relaxation

The results for precision were more encouraging (Figures 10-12), except for when the precise relaxation learning algorithm was used. It's results unsurprisingly showed wild fluctuations as each query relaxation was based purely on the previous query relaxation. Sometimes this worked and sometimes it didn't; in effect the learning algorithm had no long term memory. However, the average and mean relaxation results showed improvement with time. Precision for average relaxation improved from about 64% to 84%, whilst the mean relaxation improved from about 64% to 94%. In addition, mean relaxation showed smaller fluctuations. This shows that the system has been able to improve its precision (i.e., retrieve a smaller set of candidate cases) without harming its accuracy. This rescues the system's overall retrieval time.

4 Conclusions

This system has proved very effective. It was implemented quickly and made a positive return in investment in its first year [Gardingen & Watson, 98]. However, under increasing use its performance started to become an issue that was reducing its effectiveness. Several measures were taken to improve performance including using a faster database to store the cases, improving the way database access was managed on the server side and improving the way the query relaxation algorithm worked. This later improvement was significant because it involved the use of an introspective learning a accuracy of the algorithm that learns by how much to relax case features during the relaxation process. Our experimental findings show that although the learning algorithm does not improve the accuracy of the system it does improve its precision. For the future we would like to find a way to make the learning algorithm consider the interaction of case features. Currently features are considered in isolation which is obviously a weakness since there a re certainly both strong and weak dependencies between case features.

References

[Doyle, et al., 1998] Doyle, M., Ferrario, M.A, Hayes, C., Cunningham, P., Smyth, B. (1998). CBR Net: Smart Technology Over a Network, Internal Report Trinity College Dublin, TCD-CS-1998-07.
http://www.cs.tcd.ie/Padraig.Cunningham/publications.html

[Gardingen & Watson, 1998]. Gardingen, D. & Watson, I. (1998). A Web Based Case-Based Reasoning System for HVAC Sales Support. In, Applications & Innovations in Expert Systems VI. Milne, R., Macintosh, A. & Bramer, M. (Eds.), pp. 11- 23. Springer, London. ISBN 1-85233-087-2

[Hammond et al., 1996] Hammond, K.J., Burke, R., & Schmitt, K. (1996). A Case-Based Approach to Knowledge Navigation. In, Case-Based Reasoning: Experiences, Lessons, & Future Directions. Leake, D.B. (Ed.) pp.125-136. AAAI Press/The MIT Press Menlo Park, Calif., US.

[Hanney & Keane, 1996] Hanney, K. & Keane, M. (1996). Learning Adaptation Rules From a Case-Base. Advances in Case-Based Reasoning, Smith, I. & Faltings, B. (Eds.) Lecture Notes in AI # 1168 pp.179-192. Springer-Verlag, Berlin.

[Hayes, et al., 1998] Hayes, C., Doyle, M., Cunningham, P., (1998). Distributed CBR Using XML, Internal Report Trinity College Dublin, TCD--CS-1998-06.
http://www.cs.tcd.ie/Padraig.Cunningham/publications.html

[Kamp et al., 1998] Kamp, G. Lange, S. & Globig, C. (1998). Case-Based Reasoning Technology: Related Areas. In, Case-Based Reasoning Technology: From Foundations to Application. Lenz, M. et al (Eds.) LNAI # 1400 pp.325-351. Springer-Verlag, Berlin.

[Kitano & Shimazu, 1996] Kitano, H., & Shimazu, H. (1996). The Experience Sharing Architecture: A Case Study in Corporate-Wide Case-Based Software Quality Control. In, Case-Based Reasoning: Experiences, Lessons, & Future Directions. Leake, D.B. (Ed.) pp.235-268. AAAI Press/The MIT Press Menlo Park,Calif., US.

[Leake, et al., 1995] Leake, D.B., Kinley, A. & Wilson, D. (1995). Learning to Improve Case Adaptation by Introspective Reasoning and CBR. In, Case-Based Reasoning Research & Development, Veloso, M. & Aamodt, A. (Eds.), Lecture Notes in AI # 1010, pp.229-240. Springer-Verlag, Berlin.

[Markovitch & Scott, 1993] Markovitch, S. & Scott, P.D. (1993). Information Filtering. Selection mechanisms in Learning Systems. Machine Learning, 10, pp.113-151.

[Richter, 1998] Richter, M. (1998). Introduction - the basic concepts of CBR. In, Case-Based Reasoning Technology: from foundations to applications. Lenz, M., Bartsch-Sporl, B., Burkhard. H-D. & Wess, S. (Eds.). Lecture Notes In AI # 1400 Springer-Verlag, Berlin.

[Shimazu, 1998] Shimazu, H. (1998). Textual Case-Based Reasoning System using XML on the World-Wide Web. To appear in the Proc. Of the 4th European Workshop on CBR (EWCBR98), Springer Verlag LNAI.

[Smyth & Cunningham, 1996]. Smyth, B., & Cunningham,). (1996). The Utility Problem Analysed: A Case-Based Reasoning Perspective. Advances in Case-Based Reasoning, Smith, I. & Faltings, B. (Eds.) Lecture Notes in AI # 1168 pp.392-399. Springer-Verlag, Berlin.

[Watson, 1997] Watson, I. (1997). Applying Case-Based Reasoning: techniques for enterprise systems. Morgan Kaufmann Publishers Inc. San Francisco, CA.

[Watson, 1998] Watson, I. (1998). Case-Based Reasoning is a Methodology not a Technology. Research & Development in Expert Systems XV, Mile, R., Moulton, M. & Bramer, M. (Eds.), pp.213-223. Springer-Verlag, London.

[Watson & Gardingen, 1999] Watson, I. & Gardingen, D. (1999). A Distributed Case-Based Reasoning Application for Engineering Sales Support. IJCAI'99 31st. July - 6th August 1999, Vol. 1: pp. 600-605. Morgan Kaufmann Publishers Inc.

[Wilke, et al., 1998] Wilke, W. Lenz, M. Wess, S. (1998). Intelligent Sales Support with CBR. In, Case-Based Reasoning Technology: from foundations to applications. Lenz, M., Bartsch-Sporl, B., Burkhard. H-D. & Wess, S. (Eds.). Lecture Notes In AI # 1400 91-113. Springer-Verlag, Berlin.

[WWW Consortium 1997] World Wide Web Consortium, (1997). Extensible Markup Language 1.0, recommendation by W3C: www.w3.org/TR/PR-xml-971208

[WWW Consortium] World Wide Web Consortium home page: www.w3.org

further information on all aspect of case-based reasoning can be found at www.ai-cbr.org

Structured Cases in CBR – Re-using and Adapting Cases for Time-tabling Problems

E. K. Burke*, B. MacCarthy†, S. Petrovic*, R. Qu*
School of Computer Science and Information Technology*
Jubilee Campus, The University of Nottingham
Nottingham, NG8 1BB, U.K
Division of Manufacturing Engineering & Operations Management†
The University of Nottingham, University Park
Nottingham, NG7 2RD, U.K

Abstract

In this paper, we present a case-based reasoning (CBR) approach for solving educational time-tabling problems. Following the basic idea behind CBR, the timetables from previously solved problems are employed to aid in the generation of solutions for new time-tabling problems. A list of feature-value pairs is insufficient to represent all the necessary information. We show that attribute graphs can be used to represent information such as the relations between events and thus can help to retrieve re-usable cases that have similar structures to the new problems. The case base is organised as a decision tree that stores the attribute graphs of previously solved time-tabling problems hierarchically. A new problem is classified to a node in the tree and all the cases stored below that node are retrieved for re-use. An example is given to illustrate the retrieval, re-use and adaptation of structured cases. The results from our experiments show the effectiveness of the retrieval and adaptation in the proposed method.

1 Introduction

CBR [1] solves problems by retrieving the most similar previous cases in a case base (*source cases*) and by re-using the knowledge and experiences from previous good quality solutions. If necessary, the retrieved solutions are adapted by using domain knowledge so that they are applicable for the new problem. The case base is then updated by the new learned cases.

1.1 Traditional Case Representation in CBR

In traditional CBR, a list of feature-value pairs is typically employed to represent cases. The nearest-neighbour method is used extensively as a similarity measure that gives every feature a weight and results in a weighted sum to measure the similarity between two cases. Then the most similar case(s) retrieved from the case base are adapted for the new problem. In some domains, this representation and retrieval method is sufficient to find similar cases. However, some complex problems (such as time-tabling problems) consist of events that are heavily inter-connected with each other. A list of feature-value pairs by itself is not able to describe important information that could make differences in finding high quality solutions to this kind of problem. Thus the similarity measure cannot recognise the correspondence between the features in cases and characteristics of the solutions. It can be very difficult to adapt the retrieved cases for the new problems and the adaptation may take as much effort as scheduling from scratch. Smyth and Keane [2] questioned the similarity assumption in CBR and introduced a concept called "adaptation-guided retrieval". It is unwarranted to assume that the most similar case is also the most appropriate from the re-use perspective. Similarity must be augmented by a deeper knowledge about how easy it is to modify a case to fit a new problem. Traditional case representation does not enable this description of the deeper knowledge that is needed in cases such as heavily inter-connected time-tabling problem. A similarity measure such as the nearest-neighbour method is not sophisticated enough to reflect deeper similarities between these problems.

The aim of this paper is to present the possibilities and advantages of using attribute graphs to represent cases structurally in a CBR system which solves educational time-tabling problems. The attribute graphs are used to describe the relations between the events in a time-tabling problem more concisely and explicitly and thus can express deeper knowledge stored in the cases such as the correspondence between structures of events and characteristics of the solutions. The solutions of the retrieved cases are adaptable and can be reused for the new problem that has similar structure.

1.2 Structured Cases in CBR

Representing cases structurally has been discussed in the literature, but no general theory or methodology has been identified. Böner [3] proposed a CBR system that transformed a set of pre-selected candidate cases into a structural representation to find the common structure between the new problem and candidate cases. This approach was also used to represent the topological structure to support layout design [4]. Structural similarity is usually defined using maximum common sub-graphs, which are employed as prototypes to represent classes of cases thus reducing much of the memory retrieval effort.

Racci and Sender [5] used a tree to represent structured cases. The similarity measure takes into account both the structures and the labels in the cases. A set of algorithms was explored to solve subtree-isomorphism and it was shown that significant speed-up can be obtained on randomly generated case bases.

Two systems CHIRON and CAPER were used in [6] to show how the graph-structured representation implemented as semantic networks support Case-Based Planning in two domains. The benefits and cost associated with graph-structured representation were also discussed. In CAPER, the retrieval problem was solved by a massively parallel mechanism [7].

Jantke introduced "nonstandard concepts" [8] where cases are represented as structured cases. The similarity measure thus takes structural properties into account, with the aim of making the CBR approach more flexible and expressive.

The FABEL project [9] provides more details of some existing systems that employ structured cases. The case similarities described were classified into five groups: restricted geometric relationships; graphs; semantic nets; model-based similarities and hierarchically structured similarities.

1.3 CBR in Scheduling and Time-tabling Problems

1.3.1   CBR in Scheduling

As far as the authors are aware, there are few publications specifically on CBR for scheduling problems. MacCarthy proposed a general framework for CBR in general scheduling environments in [10] and the areas where CBR offered the most potential were justified. A review was also carried about CBR systems dealing with scheduling problems. Koton [11] proposed a system for the scheduling of a large-scale airlift management problem by abstracting and decomposing it, and afterwards the precedent cases were combined for the new problem. The CBR-1 project [12] used CBR in the dynamic job-shop scheduling problem. A pool of methods in the system provides rules dealing with a constrained environment but it requires a large amount of memory. Miyashita and Sycara [13] stored previous schedule repair tactics as cases in the CABIN system for job shop scheduling problems by incrementally revising a complete but sub-optimal schedule to produce a better schedule according to a set of optimisation criteria.

Hennessy and Hinkle [14] explored a new approach for retrieval and adaptation processes to solve the autoclave management and loading problem. Case adaptation finds the substitute by searching the case that has the correct context in the new environment for the unmatched parts. In [15] two approaches were explored that reuse the portions of good schedules to build new schedules. The experiment results were compared with other methods and showed that the approach worked efficiently for less-complex scheduling problems. Schmidt [16] proposed a problem solving system that used the theory of scheduling within CBR to solve production planning and control problems. Scheduling problems are organised by using "transformation graphs" to show similarities between problem characteristics in terms of polynomial transformation between cases. In [17] MacCarthy and Jou discussed the use of CBR in the development of a class of scheduling problems involving sequence dependent set up times. General problems about the application of CBR to scheduling problems were also addressed.

1.3.2 Time-tabling Problems

In this paper, structured cases are used in CBR to represent simple educational time-tabling problems. Time-tabling problems were defined by Wren [18] as: "the allocation, subject to constraints, of given resources to objects being placed in space-time, in such a way as to satisfy as nearly as possible a set of desirable objectives." Time-tabling problems are specific types of scheduling problems that can be highly constrained and difficult to solve. A general time-tabling problem consists of assigning a number of events (e.g. exams, courses, meetings, etc) into a limited number of timeslots (periods of time) so that no person is assigned to two or more events simultaneously. Constraints which should under no circumstances be violated are known as hard constraints. Other constraints which are desirable but not essential (such as that two events should be consecutive, etc) are known as soft constraints. The violations of the soft constraints should be minimised.

Various methods have been used to solve educational time-tabling problems [19, 20]. The graph theoretic approach was a widely employed technique in the early days of research on time-tabling problems.

Recent research has considered a variety of modern metaheuristic methods and approaches such as Tabu Search (e.g. see [21, 22]), Simulated Annealing (e.g. see [23, 24]), Genetic Algorithms (e.g. see [25, 26, 27]) and hybrid methods (such as Memetic Algorithms e.g. see [28, 29, 30, 31, 32]). A wide variety of research work on time-tabling can be found in [33, 34].

In this paper a simple course time-tabling problem is used as an example to interpret the retrieval and adaptation of structured cases. The representation of time-tabling problems by attribute graphs is given in Section 2. Section 3 describes the implementation of the proposed system organised as a tree and an example is shown in Section 4. A brief concluding discussion is presented in Section 5.

2 Attribute Graphs for Course Time-tabling Problems

In course time-tabling, a number of courses (events) have to be assigned to a limited number of timeslots. Two courses may have common students so they conflict with each other and cannot be assigned to the same timeslot.

Attribute graphs are used here to represent course time-tabling problems structurally. In attribute graphs, nodes indicate events and edges show the relation between any pair of events. Nodes and edges have attributes that represent the problem more precisely. Each attribute corresponds to a label assigned to nodes and edges. Table 1 and Table 2 show parts of the labels and attributes of nodes and edges that are used in our problems.

Label	Attribute	Value(s)	Notes
0	Ordinary course	N/A	Takes place once a week
1	Multiple course	N (No. of times)	Takes place N times a week
2	Pre-fixed course	S (Slot No.)	Assigned to timeslot S
3	Exclusive course	S (Slot No.)	Not assigned to timeslot S

Table 1. Some node attributes of course time-tabling problem

Label	Attribute	Values(s)	Notes
4	Before/after	1 or 0 (direction)	One before/after another course
5	Consecutive	N/A	Be consecutive with each other
6	Non-consecutive	N/A	Not consecutive with each other
7	Conflict	N/A	Conflict with each other

Table 2. Some edge attributes of course time-tabling problem

A simple example is shown in Figure 1 to illustrate a course time-tabling problem represented as an attribute graph. Nodes represent courses. Solid edges indicate hard constraints (labelled 7) which means that the adjacent courses cannot be held simultaneously. Dotted lines indicate soft constraints labelled 4, 5 or 6. The labels on the edges and inside the nodes correspond to the attributes shown in Table 1 and Table 2. For example, Maths, Physics and Chemistry are labelled with a 1 (to indicate that they are multiple courses) and with values 2, 3 and 2 that denote that they should be held 2, 3 and 2 times a week respectively. Other courses are labelled 0 (ordinary courses), which denote that they should be held just once a week. SpanishA should not be consecutive to Physics (because the edge between them is labelled by a 6) and Chemistry should be consecutive to SpanishB (labelled by a 5). The directed line between SpanishA and SpanishB has the label 4 (with value 1) which denotes that SpanishA should be held before SpanishB.

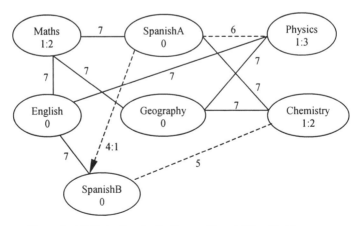

Figure 1. Attribute Graph of a Course Time-tabling Problem

Using this approach, the course time-tabling problems can be represented structurally. It enables us to describe the relations between events in the problem that is not possible by using feature-value pairs. Also the different cases of the problems can have different structures, unlike in traditional case representation using the list of feature-values pairs where all the cases have the same form of feature slots.

3 Implementation of the CBR System for Course Time-tabling Problems

3.1 The Graph Isomorphism Problem and Decision Tree Algorithm

Using attribute graphs to represent cases has many advantages. However, the matching problem between the structured cases is equivalent to that of the graph isomorphism or sub-graph isomorphism problem that is known to be NP-Complete [35]. A graph G is isomorphic to graph G' if there exists a one to one correspondence between nodes and edges of the two graphs. A graph G is sub-graph isomorphic to graph G' if G is isomorphic to a sub-graph of G'. Some methods have been attempted to solve this problem in CBR by detecting cliques of the graph [3]. The system being proposed here is based on Messmer's algorithm [36] where graphs are organised in a decision tree.

The attribute graph is represented by its adjacency matrix $M = m_{i,j}$, where $m_{i,j} \in L_e$ indicates the attribute of the edge between node i and node j and $m_{i,i} \in L_n$ indicates the attribute of node i. L_e and L_n are the sets of labels defined in Table 2 and Table 1. There are n! different adjacency matrices for an n-node attribute graph when the nodes are in different permutations. The basic idea of Messmer's algorithm is to pre-store all the adjacency matrices of some known graphs with their permutation matrices $P=p_{i,j}$ to the corresponding nodes in a decision tree. If graph G is isomorphic to graph G', then if $p_{i,j} = 1$, node i in graph G corresponds to node j in graph G'. If a new graph can be classified to a node in the decision tree at level k, then the permutation matrix(matrices) stored in this node indicate the matching between the k nodes of the new graph and that of previously stored graph(s). If the time spent on building up the decision tree is ignored, this algorithm guarantees that all the graph isomorphism(s) or sub-graph isomorphism(s) stored in the tree can be found in polynomial time (quadratic to the number of nodes of the new graph).

For example, in Figure 2, attribute graph G represents a 3-course time-tabling problem. Maths is labelled 1 with value 2 (multiple course, held twice a week). Physics and Spanish are labelled 0 (ordinary course, held once a week). Physics should be held before Maths. Spanish should not be scheduled simultaneously with Physics as Maths. There are 6 adjacency matrices M0~M5 representing graph G, X denotes that there is no edge between two nodes and the labels in the matrices are described in Table 1 and Table 2.

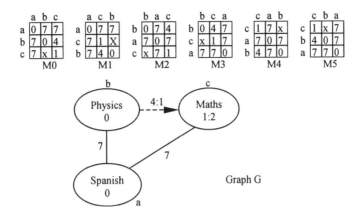

Figure 2. Matrices of Attribute Graph G of a Course Time-tabling Problem

These matrices are used to build the decision tree (see Figure 3). If a matrix M can be seen as consisting of an array of so-called row-column elements $a_i = (m_{1i}, m_{2i}, \ldots m_{ii}, m_{i(i-1)}, \ldots, m_{i1})$, then a 3 X 3 matrix consists of 3 elements: $a_1 = a_{11}$, $a_2 = a_{21}a_{22}a_{12}$ and $a_3 = a_{31}a_{32}a_{33}a_{23}a_{13}$. The first element of each of the matrices M0~M5 can be 1 or 0, and therefore there are two branches from the root node with label 0 and 1 on the first level. The second level under branch 1 can be 707 and 40x in M4 and M5, thus two branches below branch 1 are built. Then the following levels of the decision tree can be built by the same process, each branch on level i leads to a successor node that is associated with a specific value for the ith element of M0~M5. Each permutation matrix is stored in the corresponding node in the decision tree (not shown in the figure). Then all the other known attribute graphs can be added into the tree in the same way.

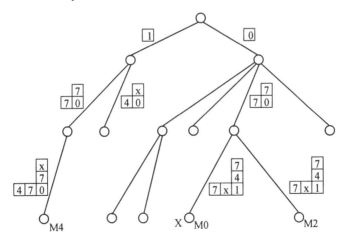

Figure 3. Part of a Decision Tree Storing Matrices of Attribute Graph G of a Course Time-tabling Problem. (M0, M2 and M4 are shown)

Let us suppose that we are presented with a new problem represented by matrix M for attribute graph G' (see Figure 4). The matrix M is inserted into the tree and can be classified to node X according to the values of each branch. The permutation stored to node X gives the isomorphism that tells us that Maths(c), Physics(b) and Spanish(a) in attribute graph G correspond to English(b), Chemistry(a) and Maths(c) in attribute graph G' respectively.

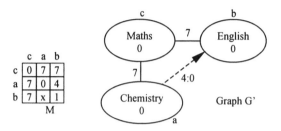

Figure 4. Matrices of Attribute Graph G' for a New Course Time-tabling Problem

3.2 Retrieving Structurally Similar Cases

Some course time-tabling problems are generated randomly and their attribute graphs are used to build up a decision tree in the proposed system. The solutions of these problems are obtained by using a heuristic graph colouring method described in [37].

A penalty is associated to each pair of labels described in Table 1 and Table 2 and used in the retrieval process. A threshold is also set to judge whether two labels are similar or not. When the system tries to match each pair of events in the new problem with source cases, the events can be seen as similar if the penalty between their labels is below the threshold. They are identified as similar and returned to be matched to each other.

If an event in the new problem has the same label and the same value as the source case, then they match with no penalty. Two events are considered not to be matching if the penalty between their labels exceeds the given threshold.

Two events that are labelled the same are further analysed to see if they have the same values. Penalties are given for the differences between the values and are taken into account in the similarity measure.

Every label is also given a weight using domain knowledge for the similarity measure. The similarity measure is thus given by formula (*):

$$S = 1 - \sum_{i,j=0}^{n} p_{ij} \times w_i / P \qquad (*)$$

where n is the total number of the labels, p_{ij} is the penalty between label i of node or edge in the new problem and label j of node or edge of source cases, w_i is the weight of label i in the new problem and P is the sum of the penalty for every pair of labels times the weight of every label.

Using the penalties assigned to each pair of labels in the course time-tabling problems, the retrieval is targeted at matching between every pair of events, not just a single judgement between the whole cases. The system can retrieve the case(s) suitable for adaptation for the new problem from the case base.

When a new problem is entered in the system, it is classified to a node in the decision tree and the system retrieves all the cases stored in and below that node as candidates. As the tree stores cases hierarchically, all the cases that have more events and/or more relations are stored below those having less events and/or relations. It is observed that solutions of more constrained cases can be adapted easily for less constrained problems. Thus all the cases in and below the node are retrieved.

Using the penalties for every pair of the labels of nodes and edges, the system calculates the similarity between the new problem and the candidate cases in and below the node. The most similar case(s) are selected for adaptation.

3.3 Reuse and Adaptation of the Solutions

After the system finds the most similar case(s), the solutions or part of the solutions of the retrieved case(s) can be reused. The system substitutes the events in the solution(s) of the retrieved case(s) with the matching events in the new problem according to the isomorphism(s) found. After the substitution, a partial solution for the new problem can be obtained although there may be some violations of constraints. If there is no violation of hard constraint in the retrieved solutions, there is also no violation of hard constraint in the solutions after substitution.

The graph heuristic method which tries to minimise the violations of constraints is used in the adaptation process. Events that violate the constraints are collected from the partial solution, and all the unscheduled events are ordered first by their degrees (number of conflicts of an event with other events) decreasingly and then are assigned one by one to the first available timeslot. If some events cannot be assigned to a timeslot without violation of constraints, they will be kept until all the other events have been scheduled. Then they are scheduled to the timeslots that lead to the fewest number of violations of constraints.

4 A Simple Illustrative Example

Let us suppose that the problem shown in Figure 1 is the new problem. All the cases and their isomorphisms are retrieved from the node that the new problem is classified to in the case base. Not only the case(s) that are graph isomorphic to the new problem can be adapted, but also the case(s) which the new problem is sub-graph isomorphic can be adapted, although they may not be "good" solutions for the new

200

problem. Two cases whose similarities pass a given threshold (a score we set) are considered to be the most similar to the new problem and are retrieved from the case base. The structures of these two cases are shown in Figure 4. It is possible to find more than one isomorphism between two graphs. Two isomorphisms were found for each of the retrieved cases in this example.

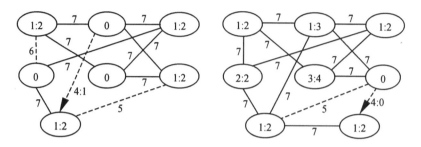

Figure 4. Two Retrieved Cases from Case Base

After substituting the events of the retrieved cases shown in Figure 4 by matching events indicated by the isomorphisms, four solutions can be obtained for the new problem (see Table 3).

	Timeslot1	Timeslot2	Timeslot3	Timeslot4	Timeslot5
Solution 1	Physics, Maths, Chemistry	English, Geography	SpanishA	SpanishB, Physics, Maths	Chemistry, Maths
Solution 2	Maths, Physics, Chemistry	English, Geography	SpanishA	SpanishB, Maths, Physics	SpanishB, Physics
Solution 3	Physics, Maths, Chemistry	English, Geography	SpanishA	SpanishB, Physics, Maths	Chemistry, Maths
Solution 4	Maths, Physics, Chemistry	English, Geography	SpanishA	SpanishB, Maths, Physics	Chemistry, Physics

Table 3. Solutions after Substitution by Using Isomorphism

It can be seen that there are 3 violations of soft constraints in solution 1: SpanishA is consecutive to Physics, Physics is held only 2 times and Maths is scheduled one more time. Using the graph heuristic method takes 2 adaptation steps: It deletes Maths from timeslot1 and adds another Physics to timeslot 5. It can also be seen that there are 1, 3 and 1 violation(s) of soft constraints in solution 2, 3 and 4 respectively. Using the graph heuristic method takes 1 and 2 adaptation step(s) respectively for solution 2 and 3. There is no adaptation for solution 4. After adaptation, there is only one violation of a soft constraint in each solution.

The simple example has demonstrated that only a few adaptations are needed to get solutions for the new problem on the basis of the solutions of the retrieved similar cases. Cases can explore deeper knowledge in course time-tabling problems by the structural representation. Retrieval that targets the adaptability of every pair of events between the new problem and the retrieved case(s) finds the most adaptable cases for the new problem, thus a corresponding relation between the events and adaptation requirements is built up. Employing the adaptation requirements in the definition of the similarity between every event pair gives a more elaborate description for the similarity measure. Thus the knowledge and experiences previously stored in the retrieved cases' solutions can be exploited for re-use for new similar problems. We note that the CBR can re-use the sub-solutions of previously solved problems within the case-base, a manner similar to that of experts in time-tabling.

5 Conclusions and Future Work

In this paper, a method is proposed to help solve course time-tabling problems using CBR in which attribute graphs are used to represent cases. To our knowledge, the CBR approach proposed in this paper is new in solving the timetabaling problems. *Retrieval targets every pair of nodes and edges between the new problem and source cases so that the retrieved case(s) are the most adaptable for the new problem.* The retrieved cases' solutions store good optimised or sub-optimised schedules for the previously solved problems. These schedules can be exploited and re-used for the new similar cases, after only limited adaptations for solutions which are then applicable for the new problem. The graph data structure gives a detailed description of the time-tabling problem. The relations between any events can be described clearly, and therefore the application of *this method to time-tabling problems is likely to find the similar cases adaptable for the new problem.*

In the current system, it is presumed that some pre-compiled cases exist so that the new problems can find isomorphic or sub-graph isomorphic cases from the case base. If only part of the structure of the new problem found correspondence to part of the structures of the source cases, the partial matching could also be reused for the new problem. Research work is being undertaken on searching and re-using the maximum-weighted common sub-graphs between source cases and the new problem. This work on the simple problem is a potential method and it provides promise. We believe it is applicable to large real world problems. Comparison with other methods will form a major part of our future work in this area.

References

1. Waston I, Marir F. Case-based reasoning: a review. The knowledge engineering review 1994; 9: 327-354

2. Smyth B, Keane ML. Adaptation-guided retrieval: questioning the similarity assumption in reasoning. Artificial Intelligence 1998; 102: 249-293
3. Börner K. Structural similarity as guidance in case-based design. In: Wess S, Althoff KD, Richter M (eds) Topics in case-based reasoning. Springer-Verlag, Kaiserslautern, 1993, pp 197-208 (EWCBR-93)
4. Börner K, Coulon CH, Pippig E, Tammer EC. Structural similarity and adaptation. In: Smith I, Faltings B (eds) Advances in case-based reasoning. Springer-Verlag, Switzerland, 1996, pp 58-75 (EWCBR-96)
5. Ricci F, Senter L. Structured cases, trees and efficient retrieval. To appear in proceedings of the fourth European workshop on case-based reasoning. Springer-Verlag, Dublin, 1998
6. Sanders KE, Kettler BP, Hendler JA. The case for graph-structured representations. To appear in Proceedings of the second international conference on case-based reasoning. Springer-Verlag, Berlin, 1997
7. Andersen WA, Evett MP, Kettler B, Hendler J. Massively parallel support for case-based planning. IEEE Expert 1994; 7: 8-14
8. Jantke KP. Nonstandard concepts of similarity in case-based reasoning. Proceedings of the 17th annual conference of the "Gesellllschaft für klassifikation e.V.". Springer-Verlag, Kaiderslautern, 1993
9. Gebhardt F. Methods and systems for case retrieval exploiting the case structure. FABEL-Report 39, GMD, Sankt Augustin, 1995
10. MacCarthy B, Jou P. Case-based reasoning in scheduling. In: Khan MK, Wright CS (eds) Proceedings of the symposium on advanced manufacturing processes, systems and techniques (AMPST96). MEP Publications Ltd, 1996, pp 211-218
11. Koton P. SMARTlan: A case-based resource allocation and scheduling system. In: Proceedings: workshop on case-based reasoning (DARPA) 1989, pp 285-289
12. Bezirgan A. A case-based approach to scheduling constraints. In: Dorn J, Froeschl KA (ed.) Scheduling of production processes, Ellis Horwood Limited, 1993, pp 48-60
13. Miyashita K, Sycara K. Adaptive case-based control of scheduling revision. In: Zweben M, Fox MS. (ed.) Intelligent Scheduling, 1994, Morgan Kaufmann, pp 291-308
14. Hennessy D, Hinkle D. Applying case-based reasoning to autoclave loading. IEEE Expert 1992; 7: 21-26
15. Cunningham P, Smyth B. Case-based reasoning in scheduling: reusing solution components. The International Journal of Production Research 1997; 35: 2947-2961
16. Schmidt G. Case-based reasoning for production scheduling. International journal of production economics 1998; 56-57: 537-546
17. MacCarthy B, Jou P. A case-based expert system for scheduling problems with sequence dependent set up times. In: Adey RA, Rzevski G (eds) Applications of Artificial Intelligence in Engineering X. Computational Machines Publications, 1995, Southampton, pp 89-96
18. Wren A. Scheduling timeatbling and rostering – a special relationship. In: [33] pp: 46-76
19. Carter MW, Laporte G. Recent developments in practical examination timetabling. In: [33] pp: 3-21
20. Carter MW, Laporte G. Recent developments in practical course timetabling. In: [34] pp: 3-19
21. Boufflet JP, Negre S. Three methods to solve an examination timetable problem. In: [33] pp: 327-344
22. Dowsland KA. Off-the-peg or made to measure? Timetabling and scheduling with SA and TS. In: [34] pp: 37-52
23. Thomson JM, Dowsland KA. General cooling schedules for a simulate annealing based timetabling system. In: [33] pp: 345-364

24. Elmohamed MAS, Coddington P, Fox G. A comparison of annealing techniques for academic course timetabling. In: [34] pp: 92-112

25. Rich DC. A smart genetic algorithm for university timetabling. In: [33] pp: 181-197

26. Erben W, Keppler J. A genetic algorithm solving a weekly course-timeatbling problem. [33] pp: 198-211

27. Ross P, Hart E, Corne D. Some observations about GA-based exam timetabling. In: [34] pp: 115-129

28. Burke EK, Newell JP, Weare RF. A memetic algorithm for university exam timetabling. In: [33] pp: 241-250

29. Burke EK, Newall JP. A multi-stage evolutionary algorithm for the timetable problem. IEEE transactions on evolutionary computation 1999; 3: pp 63-74

30. Burke EK, Newell JP, Weare RF. Initialisation strategies and diversity in evolutionary timetabling. Evolutionary computation journal (special issue on scheduling) 1998; 6: 81-103

31. Paechter B, Cumming A, Luchian H. The use of local search suggestion lists for improving the solution of timetable problems with evolutionary algorithms. In: Goos G, Hartmanis J, Leeuwen J (eds) AISB workshop, Springer-Verlag, Sheffield, U.K 1995, pp: 86-93 (Lecture notes in computer science 993)

32. Paechter B, Cumming A, Norman MG, Luchian H. Extensions to a memetic timetabing system. In: [33] pp: 251-265

33. Burke E, Ross P (ed.) The practice and theory of automated timetabling: Selected papers from the First international conference. Springer-Verlag, Berlin, 1996 (Lecture notes in computer science 1153)

34. Burke E, Carter M (ed.) The practice and theory of automated timetabling: Selected papers from the Second international conference. Springer-Verlag, Berlin, 1997 (Lecture notes in computer science 1408)

35. Garey MR, Johnson DS. Computers and intractability: A guide to the Theory of NP-Completeness. Freeman and Company. New York, 1979

36. Messmer BT. Efficient graph matching algorithms for preprocessed model graph. PhD thesis, University of Bern, Switzerland, 1995

37. Burke EK, Elliman DG, Weare RF. A university timetabling system based on graph colouring and constraint manipulation. Journal of research on computing in education 1994; 27: 1-18

Roget's Thesaurus: An additional knowledge source for Textual CBR?

Jeremy Ellman and John Tait
School of Computing, Engineering and Technology
University of Sunderland
St Peter's Basin
Sunderland SR6 0DD
UK

Jeremy.Ellman@sunderland.ac.uk

Abstract: Lenz, Hübner and Kunze have identified Textual CBR as a sub domain of case based reasoning that directly uses text documents. These are used to construct cases in a case base that is indexed using a manually identified vocabulary. A domain dependant similarity function is then required to recognise appropriate cases for a user's query. This paper describes a new similarity measure for Textual CBR that can be applied to any text. The measure is based upon the construction of a text representation based on the natural coherence of written texts. The Generic Document Profile (GDP) is an attribute-value vector that uses the categories of Roget's thesaurus as attributes, whose values are calculated algorithmically. This is done by looking for chains of related words whose degree of association can be calculated by reference to Roget's thesaurus as a general-purpose knowledge source. The GDP is theoretically motivated, and addresses the Ambiguity and Paraphrase problems identified by Lenz et. al. As common in Textual CBR. The paper will also report on the experimental evaluation of the GDP.

1. Introduction

Textual Case Based Reasoning (T-CBR) has been identified by Lenz and his colleagues [1, 31] as a sub domain of Case Based Reasoning that deals with text based knowledge sources. Lenz states that the construction of a similarity measure is especially crucial in Textual CBR. This paper describes a knowledge-based approach to the construction of such a similarity measure that uses Roget's thesaurus as a knowledge source.

A similarity measure for T-CBR has several requirements: Firstly, it needs to be applicable to any text, and secondly, it should take a set of texts and order them by similarity to a reference text. This would allow us to solve problems by identifying a previous successful solution, which is of course an important goal of CBR [3]

Complete machine understanding of natural language texts is an unsolved problem – largely due to the complexity and ambiguity of Natural Language. There are two extreme approaches to this: Ignore the complexity, and treat texts as unordered sets of terms, or try to determine its full structure and meaning. Typically, Information Retrieval (IR) has taken the former view [4,5] while Natural Language Processing (NLP) has taken the latter [6].

NLP and IR have come together within the context of Text REtrieval Conferences [7] whose objective is the comparative analysis of large volumes of text. Systems competing in TREC are given the same texts, data, and problems so that their performances may be comparatively compared. Statistical approaches to textual IR have consistently outperformed those that have used NLP [8]. Indeed, it is only in the most recent TREC competition that NLP systems could process the volumes of text [9] required.

IR systems have the advantage that they can process all text as they are only looking for terms. Thus, they satisfy the robustness criteria for CBR mentioned above. IR similarity metrics consider terms only, and their relative presence in a set of documents. They have been studied in detail, although Zobel and Moffat [10] found that no metric had superior performance in several different retrieval tasks.

Lenz [1] has identified two problems that apply to T-CBR when considering text as sets of keywords: The ambiguity problem, and the paraphrase problem. In the ambiguity problem identical words are used in different senses, and in the paraphrase problem the same meaning may be expressed using completely different words (e.g. printer failed" versus printer broke"). The same phenomenon is well known in IR, where it is known as the vocabulary" problem [11], and in NLP, the terms polysemy" and synonymy" are often used.

Any approach to representing a whole text needs to avoid over dependence on individual terms to alleviate the problems of polysemy and synonymy. One approach is to use a categorisation scheme, and thesaurus of related terms. Rada and Bicknell [12] found this successful in medical information retrieval. However, both their thesaurus and conceptual hierarchy were domain dependant. We propose using Roget's thesaurus, and argue in section two that its structure and organisation are especially suited to T-CBR.

The paper proceeds as follows. Firstly, we consider how to represent whole texts for T-CBR. Next, a program is described that generates this representation for any text, and permits several texts to be ordered in terms of their similarities. Evaluation is critical to support the claims for generality, and some initial experiments are described in section four. Finally, we conclude with a discussion of the limitations of the approach, and suggestions for future work.

2. Representing Texts for T-CBR

To represent texts for T-CBR we require

1. The selection of structure to represent a document's contents.
2. A method to derive this structure from texts.
3. A technique to compare the similarities of these structures.

These requirements are interdependent, since overly complex representations of different texts may not be directly comparable. If this representation is based on simple terms (i.e. words), the problem becomes hugely complex, since there are about 100,000 words in the English language. This would also be fragile, since semantically equivalent words would not count as equal.

We propose a middle way between treating documents as bags of words as in IR, and doing detailed linguistic analysis as in NLP. This will be based on textual cohesion -the property of text that causes it to be seen as one unit, rather than sequences of unrelated sentences. The linguists Halliday and Hasan [13] defined the term cohesive chain" as a set of terms that link the text into a coherent whole. They identified two types of cohesive chains: identity chains" where every member of the chain refers to the same thing (that is, they are co-referential), and similarity chains". In similarity chains, the terms are related by co-classification, or co-extension, that is, they refer to members of the same class of things or events.

The term Lexical Chain" is a simplification due to Morris and Hirst [14]. They used it to identify sequences of generally related words in a text, and particularly suggested that the relations between sequences could be identified using an external thesaurus.

Since Morris and Hirst [14] introduced the idea, lexical chains have been applied to several different areas of language processing. These include word sense disambiguation and text segmentation, [15], malapropism detection [16], detection of HyperText links in newspaper articles [17], lexical cohesion and Information Retrieval [18, 19], and text summarisation [30].

WordNet [20] has been used to implement all the English lexical chaining systems to date. It is large, freely available, and designed for computing. It contains 60,000 sets of synonyms (synsets") organised hierarchically in a database that is fully indexed. However WordNet's quality is variable", its hierarchy is uneven (varying from four ply to twelve ply deep), and there is no way to find an equivalence between the noun and verb components. Consequently, all the systems mentioned have used nouns only. As there are 60,000 synsets, WordNet is too large to be a tractable representation for T-CBR.

Roget's thesaurus has an implicit structured hierarchy that is evenly balanced, six ply deep, and contains approximately one thousand headwords. Consequently, it is computationally feasible to represent a document's meaning by strengths in these headword categories. Roget also has the advantage that each headword has noun, verb, adjective, and adverb divisions. This allows a simple mapping between concepts derived from different parts of speech.

Roget's thesaurus is also a knowledge source, since each entry contains sets of related words. These relationships correspond to association by use, and capture broader associations than the synonyms used in WordNet.

The following section describes a program that exploits Roget as a knowledge source to provide a document representation composed of thesaural categories. This attribute-value vector may then be used to calculate texts' similarities.

3. Hesperus: A System for comparing Text Similarity using Lexical Chains.

Hesperus is a system designed to compare how similar texts are by measuring their conceptual contents as determined by their thesaurally defined Lexical Chains. In outline the process as follows: Texts are processed to detect their lexical chains. Subsequently the lexical chains are analysed to calculate the strengths of the concepts they contain. This determines the text's generic document profile, which may then be stored in a Case Library. The profiles can then be clustered for similarity with an example text using a nearest neighbor" algorithm (e.g. [3, 21]). The architecture of the system is shown below in figure 1.

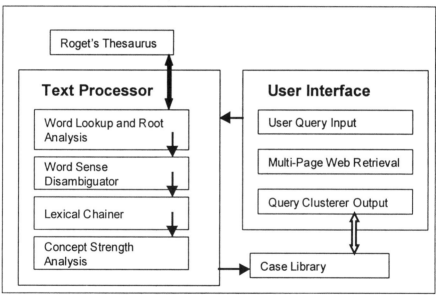

Figure 1: Hesperus System Architecture

3.1 A program to analyse Lexical Chains in a text using Roget's Thesaurus

This section describes a lexical chainer based on Roget. The techniques used are general, and depend on the organisation of the thesaurus as a structured resource.

Thus, they should be applicable to languages for which WordNet's have not been written, but for which texts like Roget are available.

The lexical chainer depends on the availability of an "Electronic Roget" -- a machine-readable version of Roget's thesaurus together with an indexing program. Details of how to create this are given in [22]. This makes it possible for a program to identify the Roget categories of which a word (or words) are members.

The index to the Electronic Roget is generated automatically. The editor of the 1967 (i.e. paper) Roget points out that the index was carefully created to not contain all possible terms. A fully automatic procedure will generate an index that contains infrequent associations that a lexicographer would eliminate. Consequently, an automatic approach is going to lead to a higher degree of lexical and term ambiguity.

The issue of word sense ambiguity inherent in an automatically created index is connected to an observation in [14] that of the visible connections between words in a text, only 80% (approximately) may be detected with Roget's thesaurus. Consequently, lexical chaining is an approximate procedure since it cannot detect all visible relationships, and it is error-prone. The objective for this work is to produce an implementation that is accurate enough to produce a usable Generic Document Profile. That is, sufficiently accurate as to offer an improvement over term-only similarity algorithms. It should also be suitable for real-time use (optimally with a runtime proportional to document length).

3.1.1 Chaining Algorithm

The implementation is a single-pass algorithm based on that given for WordNet in[16], who in turn followed [15] and [14]. That is, a linear pass is made through the text, and where words can be associated using relationships derived by reference to an external thesaurus a "link" is stored. If one member of the link was previously linked elsewhere in the text, the two links form a "chain", to which further links may be added.

Several relations between word pairs can be used to decide if they are members of the same lexical chain. These were first suggested by Morris and Hirst [14] (who give full descriptions). Some of their relations were not useful, as they were excessively prone to problems of word sense ambiguity.

The most important relation is term (or term stem) repetition, known as the ID or identical word relation. Simply, if two words are the same, they may be linked with high degree of certainty. Although there are an average of four thesaural entries per term, discourse topic acts to constrain sense usage. This means that a word used in one sense is frequently used in that sense throughout the same text. For example, "bond" has one common sense in financial journals, a second common usage in chemistry papers, and further widely accepted sense in Sociology books. This is an instance of "One Sense per Discourse"[23].

Next, we consider whether two words are members of the same thesaural category (CAT relation). Again, due to one sense per discourse, this is mostly successful. It is however more error prone than the ID method.

Since Roget's thesaurus contains groups of categories, we also consider whether word pairs are members of neighbouring thesaural categories. If so, and the two categories are members of the same thesaural group, the words may be linked with a GROUP relation.

Roget categories often refer to other categories. Words may therefore be related where a word's entry refers to an entry that contains the second word. This relationship is abbreviated as ONE, since there is one level of indirection from one thesaural category to the second.

All lexical chains are stored in common data structure called a ChainStore. Unlike StOnge's ChainStack, which ordered chains by recency of occurrence or Okumura and Honda [15] where chains were ordered by their length, Chains in the ChainStore are ordered by their value. This allows the concepts in a text to be differentially considered during the linear analysis while building up a picture of the text "context".

The ChainStore is linked to the application of a variable width window within which lexical links are considered. Furthermore, the type of link governs the region of text for which links are considered. Identical word links are considered then within a region of fifty non-stopwords, where a stopword is a common word that does not add to the information value of the text [5]. Other link types have this value reduced in proportion to their relative weights.

The variable width window is motivated by ambiguity considerations. The progressively weaker semantic relations consider increasing number of words. Consequently, they are proportionately more prone to forming spurious relations. The variable window size limits these.

3.2 An Example

Now we are going to briefly consider an example creation of a lexical chain using the "Hesperus". The following paragraph is from Einstein (1939, cited by StOnge1995). It is sufficiently brief to look at in some detail.

We suppose a very long train$_1$ traveling$_2$ along the rails$_1$ with the constant velocity$_2$t' and in the direction$_2$ indicated in Figure 1. People traveling$_2$ in this train$_1$ will with advantage use the train$_1$ as a rigid reference-body$_3$; they regard all events in reference$_3$ to the train$_1$. Then every event which takes place along the line$_1$ also takes place at a particular point$_i$ of the train$_1$. Also, the definition of simultaneity can be given relative to the train$_1$ in exactly the same way as with respect to the embankment$_1$. (Einstein, 1939)

StOnge [16] manually identified three lexical chains in this text.

1. {train, rails, train, train, train, line, point, train, train, embankment}
2. {traveling, velocity, direction, traveling}
3. {reference-body, reference}

It is important to remember that there is no absolute truth in the selection of any particular chain of words in a text. The relationships between words that form part of a coherent theme in the text may not be detectable by reference to an external thesaurus, and that the procedure is error prone due to problems of words sense ambiguity (section 2).

Hesperus finds the chains shown below in the text. Figure (2) illustrates their embedding.

> We suppose[4] a very long[6] train[0] travelling[3] along the rails with a constant velocity v and in the direction[1] indicated in figure . people travelling in this direction will with advantage[5] use the train as a rigid reference[2] - body ; they regard all events in reference-to to the train. Then every event which takes place along the line also takes place at a particular point[10] of the train. Also, the definition[8] of simultaneity[9] can be given relative-to to the train in exactly the same way as with respect to embankment

Figure 2: Example text with marked lexical chains.

The chains (numbered in importance from 0) are given below:

0. train, rails, train, train, line, train, train, embankment,
1. direction, people, direction,
2. reference, regard, relative-to, respect,
3. travelling, velocity, travelling, rigid
4. suppose, reference-to, place, place,
5. advantage, events, event
6. long, constant
7. figure, body

The remaining chains contain single words only (or are "atomic" using StOnge' terminology [16]).

The most important chain is given below in table 1. The word is shown, followed by its number in the text, and linking relationship in the chain. This is followed by the number of the word to which it is linked. The thesaural sense(s) possible those words in that chain are also given. Thus, in the following Word 6 (Train) at the head of the chain is not linked to anything (i.e. the link type is ???), whilst word 10 (rails) is linked to it by CAT. That is, they are members of the same thesaural category.

Table 1: A sample lexical chain from the "Einstein" example

Word	Word Number	Link Type	Linked to	Thesaural Category
train	6	???	0	railway_624_4011_n
rails	10	CAT	6	railway_624_4011_n
train	33	ID	6	railway_624_4011_n
train	47	ID	33	railway_624_4011_n
line	56	CAT	47	railway_624_4011_n
train	66	ID	47	railway_624_4011_n
train	78	ID	66	railway_624_4011_n
embankment	88	CAT	78	railway_624_4011_n

This lexical chain illustrates the reduction in possible word senses for "train" from twenty-three to one.

We also see that "direction" is mistakenly linked to "people", since both are members of the thesaural category "government". Nevertheless, the lexical chains produced by Hesperus overlap well with those manually identified by StOnge [1] above.

StOnge (Manual) Lexical Chains	Hesperus Chain number
1	0
2	3
3	2

3.3   The Generic Document Profile

The *Generic Document Profile"* is simply a set of semantic (Roget) categories with associated weights. These weights are based on chain length and strength attached to the thesaural categories. This profile can be matched against that derived from another text using a nearest neighbour algorithm (e.g. [3]).

We call this representation the *Generic Document Profile"*, since it is not word specific, and is derived from the whole text. Now we shall describe how a text may be analysed to calculate values in each particular category.

3.3.1 Creating the Generic Document Profile

The Generic Document Profile is created from the lexical chains identified in a text. The strength of every link in every chain is taken, and summed into the appropriate profile category. This gives the required attribute value representation.

Thus, the strength σ of any concept c where a text contains N lexical chains is:

$$\sigma_c = \sum_{n=0}^{n=N} C(n)$$

3.3.2 An Example Generic Document Profile

The following GDP is that derived from the example used above. For each thesaural category, the raw score is converted into a percentage of the total score. Using these percentages allows the conversion of documents of any length.

Table 2: The Document Profile for the "Einstein" example quote

Category name in Roget (name_group-no_category-no _part of speech)	Percent Value
railway_624_4011_n	31.97
government_733_4752_n	17.05
relation_9_54_n	15.00
put-in-front_64_442_v	9.29
chance_159_996_n	7.42
unconformable_84_561_a	6.48
lasting_113_699_a	5.29
motion_265_1743_n	3.58
person_371_2463_n	2.64
concerning_9_63_r	0.68
attribution_158_989_n	0.60

3.4 Summary

This section has described how to use Roget's thesaurus to identify the lexical chains in a text, and determine from them a description of the text's subject matter or Generic Document Profile (GDP). GDP's are stored in a case library. Identifying the similarity of texts involves applying a nearest neighbour algorithm to that. The case library is stored as a flat file and processed in memory, although for larger case bases better indexing and retrieval methods would be needed.

4. Evaluating the Generic Document Profile

4.1 Introduction

Lenz [1] has stated that evaluation is not well defined in T-CBR. Brüninghaus and Ashley [24] have argued the IR evaluation methods are not suitable for T-CBR. Consequently, we have chosen to evaluate Hesperus compared to human judgement of similarity. Since a generic technique is being proposed, it is important to use more than one subject domain. As there are few general-purpose text case bases available, it is necessary to find other forms of text – preferably that are authoritative, unbiased, and easily obtainable. Microsoft's Encarta"© CD-ROM encyclopaedia fulfils these criteria.

As there are multiple pages on almost every subject, the Internet is an ideal source of sample texts. It is also highly heterogeneous. Thus Internet derived sample data should show conceptual similarity better than data derived from a single subject source since it should be easier for the program to distinguish.

If the Internet is the source of sample texts, the subjects (i.e. topics) used in the experiment should correspond to Internet queries. These were chosen at random from real user queries that correspond to entries in MS-Encarta. The queries were: Rosetta, Ballot, Breakdance, Copyright, Socialism, and AI. The Encarta entries corresponding to these queries were used as the example texts. They were compared for similarity against (a subset of) the web pages retrieved.

There were two hypotheses to be tested:-

1. GDP Similarity matching will produce a ranking between an example text and several samples equivalent to those produced by human subjects.

2. GDP matching is not identical to a purely term based approach

The first of these hypotheses is most important. It raises the issue whether the GDP is sufficient for similarity matching. The second hypothesis follows from the first: We need to find out whether IR methods will give equivalent (or better) results than Hesperus.

Since judgements of similarity are dependent on particular subjects and the tasks they are involved in, we need to test this hypothesis in a realistic scenario. This should involve the type of task where people routinely use similarity judgements. We now go on to look at the experiment.

4.2   Method

The experiment was in three parts; human judgements of similarity, followed by comparable ranking using the GDP, and a statistical IR program (SWISH)

The human experiment[1] was constructed as a purpose built Internet WWW site. This ensured a high level of ecological validity [25], since the texts were being seen in the medium and by the means for which they were designed. The subjects were University of Sunderland students.

The major component of the Web site was a JavaScript program that guided interaction through the web site. This consisted of six component experiments that covered the selected topics. Both the topics and their contents were presented in random order.

After reading initial instructions, subjects were shown the Encarta entry as a Source text. This was shown in a Frame based layout with the text in the left of the screen (the right being initially blank). Four general statements about the text were shown in the lower part of the frame.

---

[1] I would like to acknowledge gratefully received advice on experimental design from Dr Sharon Macdonald, who recommended the use of Likert scale in conjunction with definitive statements.

Table 3: Statements for the Initial Topic Page

I1.	The Source Text is good explanation of the subject
I2.	I am very familiar with the topic of the Query
I3.	I would like to find the Source Text if I looked for this Query
I4.	The Source Text is a good definition of the subject

Subjects were required to indicate whether they agreed or disagreed with the statements using a five point Likert scale. When the responses had been completed, the sample texts were shown in random order in the right pane. Four further statements were made in the lower pane.

These statements also required agreement to be indicated on a 1-5 scale. Once all the replies had been completed, a further sample was shown. When all the samples had been seen on one subject, the experiment proceeded to the next topic, until all the topics had been covered.

Table 4: *Statements for the Example Comparison Pages*

The Example means the same as the Source Text
The Example is relevant to the Query
The Example more specific than the Query
The Example is a good definition of the subject

The responses to statements S1 to S4 were coded from one (disagree) to five (agree). The average score was then taken, giving a group measure of agreement to each statement. The replies made by the subjects were collected from the Web site log, and then analysed.

Similarity score were then calculated using Hesperus, and SWISH, and compared to the judgements of the subjects. The raw numeric values could not be compared directly however, since they are not derived from the same frequency distribution.

4.3   Results

The results were difficult to analyse as the experimental subjects produced approximately linear judgements, whilst Hesperus judgements followed a power law. That is, Hesperus' similarity judgements fall rapidly, and rarely exceed 40%, whereas 50% on the Likert scale is half way between "agree" and "disagree".

The order of similarity judgements can however be compared. That is, we can compare the most to least similar example ordering derived from the experiment, with that given by Hesperus, and that from the IR program (SWISH). Spearman's rank correlation for the six topic pairs is shown below.

Table 5: Experimental Rank Correlation

Topic	Hesperus Vs Subject Ordering Spearman Rank Correlation (Rs)		SWISH Vs Subject Ordering Spearman Rank Correlation (Rs)	
		Interpretation		Interpretation
Rosetta	.429	marginal	-0.029	poor
Ballot	.574	marginal	0.586	marginal
Breakdance	-.638	poor		
Copyright	.928**	good	0.643	marginal
Socialism	.314	poor	0.6	marginal
AI	.812*	good	0.186	poor

** Correlation is significant at the .01 level (1-tailed).
* Correlation is significant at the .05 level (1-tailed).

4.4 Discussion

Good correlation was found between the rank ordering given by human similarity judgements and Hesperus in one of the six topics, AI, and this was highly significant in another, Copyright. For two of the three remaining topics, Ballot, and Socialism, the two most similar texts as determined by the subjects were rated higher by Hesperus than the two least preferred. Consequently, there is some evidence that lexical chain based similarity matching will produce a ranking between an example text and several examples equivalent to those produced by human subjects. By contrast, none of the topics gave statistically significant results with the Information Retrieval program, SWISH.

5. Conclusion and Future Work

We have proposed that Roget's thesaurus would be a useful knowledge source for T-CBR. It provides categories to adequately represent a document, alongside with knowledge to help populate them. We have presented a program, Hesperus, which exploits lexical chaining to produce a Generic Document Representation based on these categories. Hesperus uses a nearest neighbour algorithm to rank these representations in terms of their similarities. We have shown this to be superior experimentally to a statistical term based approach.

We have deliberately avoided details of specific T-CBR Systems since the approach suggested is generic and did not require any specific text structure. However, many texts that may be used in T-CBR have structure that can be exploited. Kunze and Hübner [26] have used a combination of shallow NLP techniques and semi-structured documents in the FallQ project for document management in the ExperienceBook project that provided UNIX system administrators' support. Burke et. al. [27] exploit the question answer format in their FAQ Finder – system which finds FAQs on the Internet that correspond to a user's question. FAQ Finder uses a combination of statistical methods, and shallow WordNet based semantics.

The GDP procedure has several limitations that we are currently addressing. The similarity process is subject to problems of word sense ambiguity [28], which is still an unresolved problem [29]. Words not in the thesaurus cannot contribute to the text representation by definition. Consequently, our approach would need to be linked to a domain specific term bank in a real application. Finally, note that the nearest neighbour algorithm is currently unweighted, and takes no account of the prevalence or distinctiveness of terms in a particular area.

In the future, we intend to incorporate term frequency statistics as weights in the nearest neighbour algorithm as these have proved singularly effective in Information Retrieval. We also intend to apply our method to a practical T-CBR application in the pharmaceutical area.

In spite of the known limitations, Roget's thesaurus provides a useful knowledge source for an additional similarity measure for textual case based reasoning.

References

[1] Lenz M. 1998 "Textual CBR and Information Retrieval - A Comparison." In proc. 6th German Workshop on Case-Based Reasoning. Berlin, March 6-8, 1998

[2] Lenz Mario, Bartsch-Spörl Brigitte, Burkhard Hans-Dieter, Wess Stefan (Eds.) 1998: "Case-Based Reasoning Technology: From Foundations to Applications. "Lecture Notes in Artificial Intelligence 1400, Springer Verlag, 1998 ISBN 3-540-64572-1

[3] Aamodt A and Plaza E 1994 "Case Based Reasoning: Foundational Issues, Methodological Variations and System Approaches" AI Communication Vol. 7, 1 March 1994

[4] Salton, G. and McGill, M. (1983), Introduction to Modern Information Retrieval. McGraw-Hill.

[5] van Rijsbergen C. J. "Information Retrieval" London: Butterworths, 1979 (available on-line on 25th March 1999 at: http://www.dcs.gla.ac.uk/Keith/Preface.html

[6] Allen, J F., "Natural Language Understanding ", 2nd edition 1995 The Benjamin/Cummings Publishing Company, Menlo Park, California, ISBN 0-8053-0330-8.

[7] Vorhees, E. M., and Harman, D. K., "Overview of the sixth Text REtrieval Conference (TREC-6)", in Vorhees, E. M., and Karman, D. K. (eds.), Proceedings of the Sixth Text Retrieval Conference (TREC-6), 1998

[8] Sparck-Jones Karen, 1999 "What is the role of NLP in Text Retrieval" in Strzalkowski 1999

[9] Strzalkowski Tomek 1999 "Natural Language Informational Retrieval" Kluwer Academic, Dordrecht NL. ISBN 0-7923-5685-3

[10] Zobel J., and Moffat A. (1998) "Exploring the similarity space", SIGIR forum 32(1):18-34, Spring 1998

[11] Furnas, G.W., Landauer, T.K., Gomez, L.M., Dumais, S. T., "The vocabulary problem in human-system communication." Communications of the Association for Computing Machinery, 30 (11), Nov 1987, pp. 964-971.

[12] Rada R. & Bicknell E. "Ranking Documents with a Thesaurus" JASIS 40(5) pp304-310 1989

[13] Halliday, M.A.K. & Hasan, R.: 1989, "Language, context, and text". Oxford University Press, Oxford, UK.

[14] Morris, J. and Hirst, G. (1991). "Lexical Cohesion computed by thesaural relations as an indicator of the structure of text." Computational Linguistics, 17(1), pp21-48.

[15] Okumura M. and Honda T "Word Sense Disambiguation and text segmentation based on lexical cohesion" Proc. COLING 1994 vol. 2 pp 755-761

[16] St-Onge, D. (1995). Detecting and Correcting Malapropisms with Lexical Chains. MSc Thesis, University of Toronto. (Available via WWW).

[17] Green S 1997 "Automatically generating Hypertext by Computing Semantic Similarity" University of Toronto PhD Thesis. Computing Systems Research GroupTechnical Report 366

[18] Stairmand M and Black W J 1996 "Conceptual and Contextual Indexing using WordNet-derived Lexical Chains" in proc BCS IRSG

[19] Smeaton, Alan 1999 "Using NLP or NLP Resources for Information Retrieval Tasks" in Strzalkowski 1999

[20] Miller G., Beckwith R., Felbaum C., Gross D., and Miller K. 1990 "Introduction to WordNet: An on-line lexical database" J. Lexicography 3(4) pp235-244

[21] Watson I. "CBR Is A Methodology Not A Technology" in proc. ES98

[22] Ellman (forthcoming) "Using Roget's thesaurus to determine the similarity of text's" forthcoming PhD thesis University of Sunderland UK

[23] Krovetz R. and Croft W. B., "Lexical Ambiguity and Information Retrieval", ACM Transactions on Information Systems, Vol. 10(2), pp. 115-141, 1992.

[24] Brüninghaus Stefanie and Ashley Kevin D. (1998) Evaluation of Textual CBR Approaches. In: Proceedings of the AAAI-98 Workshop on Textual Case-Based Reasoning (AAAI Technical Report WS-98-12). Pages 30-34. Madison, WI.

[25] Hammond K. R. 1998. "Ecological Validity: Then and Now" The Brunswik Society:Web Essays #2 http://www.albany.edu/cpr/brunswik/essay2.html accessed 10th June 99.

[26] Kunze Mirjam and Hübner André 1998 "CBR on Semi-structured Documents: The ExperienceBook and the FAllQ Project" in proc 6th German Workshop On Case-Based Reasoning. http://www.informatik.hu-berlin.de/~cbr-ws/GWCBR98/program.html accessed 18/6/99

[27] Burke R., Hammond K., Kulyukin V., Lytinen S., Tomuro N., and Schoenberg S.. Question Answering from Frequently Asked Question Files. AI Magazine, pages 57--66, 1997.

[28] Ellman, J. Klincke I. & Tait J. 1999 "Word Sense Disambiguation by Information Filtering and Extraction" Computing in the Humanities. To appear.

[29] Ide Nancy, and Veronis Jean 1998 "Introduction to the Special Issue on Word Sense Disambiguation: The State of the Art" Computational Linguistics Vol24, No. 1 pp.1-41

[30] Barzilay R. and Elhadad M. 1997 "Using Lexical Chains for Text Summarization" ACL'97/EACL'97 Workshop on Intelligent Scalable Text Summarization

[31] Lenz Mario, Hübner Andre, Kunze Mirjam 1998 "Textual CBR" in Lenz, Bartsch-Spörl, Burkhard & Wess 1998.

SESSION 4
KNOWLEDGE ENGINEERING

Knowledge Management through Multi-Perspective Modelling: Representing and Distributing Organizational Memory

John Kingston
AIAI, Division of Informatics
The University of Edinburgh
80 South Bridge
Edinburgh EH1 1HN, Scotland
J.Kingston@ed.ac.uk
www.aiai.ed.ac.uk

Ann Macintosh
International Teledemocracy Centre
Napier University
10 Colinton Road
Edinburgh EH10 5DT, Scotland
A.Macintosh@napier.ac.uk
www.teledemocracy.org

Abstract: Full and accurate representation of an organization's knowledge assets, which together constitute "organizational memory", requires multi-perspective modelling at a number of levels of detail. We propose that the perspectives which need to be represented can be characterized as *who, what, how, when, where* and *why* knowledge; these perspectives, and necessary levels of abstraction, are captured by the Zachman framework for Information Systems Architecture We suggest modelling techniques that might be appropriate for different perspectives and levels of abstraction, and illustrate using examples from a medical domain. We also describe how an individual perspective can become the user interface of a knowledge distribution system, and illustrate this by describing the Protocol Assistant, a Web-based knowledge-based system capable of representing and reasoning with best practice guidelines ("protocols") in the medical domain.

1. Introduction

The management of knowledge within organizations has become a critical activity because many of the activities of organizations today, and of our economic and social life, are knowledge-driven. As Tom Stewart puts it:

"The quintessential raw materials of the Industrial Revolution were oil and steel. Now more than 50% of the cost of extracting petroleum from the earth is information gathering and information processing ... more and more of what we buy and sell is knowledge. Knowledge is now the principal raw material" [quoted in 1]

It is therefore critical to an organization's future success to manage this knowledge in a coherent manner, leading to the concept of **knowledge management**. Knowledge management is

"the identification and analysis of available and required knowledge assets and knowledge asset related processes, and the subsequent planning and control of

actions to develop both the assets and the processes so as to fulfill organizational objectives." [2]

The sum of all knowledge assets held by an organization can be considered to be its **organizational memory**.

The above definition of knowledge management implies that is necessary for organizations:

- to be able to **capture and represent** their knowledge assets;

- to share and re-use their knowledge for differing applications and differing users; this implies **making knowledge available** where it is needed within the organization;

- to **create a culture** that encourages knowledge sharing and re-use.

In this paper, we will focus on knowledge management through information technology – that is, the representation and distribution of knowledge assets using technologies such as knowledge based systems, ontology support systems, electronic documents, databases, and so on. Looking at the above three points from this viewpoint:

- The explosive growth in use and availability of the World Wide Web and of corporate intranets has provided an unparalleled opportunity to distribute knowledge assets throughout organizations, even multi-national organizations; if these knowledge assets can be represented in an accessible and comprehensible computer-based format, the problem of making knowledge assets widely available is therefore more or less solved. The choice of format is dependent on user requirements, knowledge form and organizational context; discussion of this is outside the scope of this paper.

- Developing a knowledge sharing culture must be preceded by making "knowledge distribution systems" accessible and comprehensible, for if knowledge re-use is difficult or frustrating, it is likely to be ignored in favour of knowledge re-invention – and a lack of observed knowledge re-use is a powerful disincentive to knowledge sharing.

- So the true challenge for technology-assisted knowledge management lies in accurate capture and accessible representation of knowledge assets. These are the areas to which the science of knowledge engineering has the most to contribute.

Previous work on structuring organizational memory has been carried out by van Heijst *et al.* [3] and Conklin [4]. Van Heijst *et al* suggest classifications of organizational memories according to active or passive collection and distribution of knowledge, and proposes that organizational memories should be indexed by hierarchies, attributes of knowledge items, and/or knowledge profiles of employees. While these suggestions are helpful, we believe that a broader framework is needed to represent not only knowledge assets, but also the context within which the assets are deployed. This is supported by Conklin, who asserts that:

> *"knowledge work ... requires tools and processes which preserve the context of the work as it evolves, and preserving merely the artifacts of the work (the formal documents) fails to do this. The preserved context [should] take the form of a web of information which includes facts, assumptions, constraints, decisions and their rationale, the meanings of key terms, and, of course, the formal documents themselves."*

2. Multi-Perspective Modelling

The thesis of this paper is that, for a knowledge asset to be represented in a manner which is accurate, complete, embedded in its context, and yet comprehensible, *multi-perspective modelling* is required. As the name implies, multi-perspective modelling requires that a knowledge asset should be represented using a collection of knowledge models, each of which takes a different viewpoint on that knowledge. The different viewpoints can be thought of as different managers' views on the organization: for example, an operations manager might view the organization as a user, consumer and producer of resources, while a personnel manager might view the organization as a network of interactions between agents. Knowledge models are often represented as diagrams, using nodes (boxes, circles, diamonds etc.) to represent items of knowledge and arcs (arrows, lines) to represent relationships between knowledge items. The diagram formats may (and probably should) differ between perspectives, but all knowledge items are drawn from a single underlying repository.

What perspectives are required in order to represent a knowledge asset comprehensively? As a starting point, we draw on the CommonKADS methodology [1] which is intended for supporting the development of knowledge based systems. CommonKADS proposes six models at successively deeper levels of detail: knowledge engineers are encouraged to model the **organization** in which the system will be introduced; the **task** (business process) which the KBS will support; the **agents** who are or will be involved in the process; required **communication** between agents during the process; the **expertise**[1] which is applied to performing the knowledge based process; and the **design** of the proposed KBS. Some of these models are subdivided further; for example, the Expertise model is divided into models of domain concepts and relationships, a model of the required inferences, and a model of the control required on the inferences. Despite these models being designed to solve different types of problem at different levels of abstraction, certain perspectives recur throughout the abstraction hierarchy.

---

[1] The recently published CommonKADS book [1] refers to this model as the "Knowledge model". However, to avoid confusion within this paper, we will continue to use the previous term of "Expertise model".

We propose that the various perspectives that are recommended by the CommonKADS methodology can be summarised under the following headings: *how* a process is carried out, *who* does it, *what* information is needed, *where* that information comes from, *when* each activity must be carried out, and (less explicitly) *why* the process is performed. Table 1 gives more detail on the expected contents of these perspectives.

Perspective	Description
What	Declarative knowledge about things as opposed to procedural knowledge about actions. "What" knowledge encompasses concepts, physical objects, and states. It also includes knowledge about classifications or categorisations of those states.
How	Knowledge about actions or events. It includes knowledge about which actions are required if certain events occur; which actions will achieve certain states; and the required or preferred ordering of actions.
When	When actions or events happen, or should happen; it is knowledge about the controls needed on timing and ordering of events.
Who	The agents (human or automated) who carry out each action, and their capabilities and authority to carry out particular actions.
Where	Where knowledge is needed and where its comes from -- communication and input/output knowledge.
Why	Rationale; reasons, arguments, empirical studies and justifications for things that are done and the way they are done.

Table 1: Descriptions of perspectives

A previous paper [5] demonstrated how these six perspectives, as well as the various levels of detail represented by the CommonKADS models, are represented in the Information Systems Architecture framework proposed by Sowa and Zachman [6]. The framework (also called the Zachman framework) has six columns representing *who, what, how, when, where* and *why* perspectives on knowledge, and six rows representing different levels of abstraction (see Table 2). Zachman illustrates the different levels of abstraction using examples from design and construction of a building, starting from the "scope" level (which takes a "ballpark" view on the building which is primarily the concern of the architect, and may represent the gross sizing, shape, and spatial relationships as well as the mutual understanding between the architect and owner), going through the "enterprise" level (primarily the concern of the owner, representing the final building as seen by the owner, and floor plans, based on architect's drawings) and on through three other levels (the "system" level, the "technology constrained" level and the "detailed representation" level, respectively the concerns of the designer, the builder and the subcontractor) before arriving at the "functioning enterprise" level (in this example, the actual building). Zachman describes this framework as *"a simple, logical structure of descriptive representations for identifying 'models' that are the basis for designing the enterprise and for building the enterprise's systems"* [7].

	Data "*what*"	Function "*how*"	Network "*where*"	People "*who*"	Time "*when*"	Motivation "*why*"
Objectives/ Scope "*contextual*"	List of things important to the business	List of processes the business performs	List of locations in which the business operates	List of Organiz- ations important to the business	List of Events significant to the business	List of Business goals/ strategies
Enterprise "*conceptual*"	e.g. Semantic Model	e.g. Business process Model	e.g. Business legacy systems	e.g. Work Flow model	e.g. Master Schedule	e.g. Business Plan
System "*logical*"	e.g. Logical data model	e.g. Application Architecture	e.g. Distributed Systems Architecture	e.g. Human Interface Architecture	e.g. Processing Structure	e.g. Business Rule Model
Technology constrained "*physical*"	e.g. Physical data model	e.g. System Design	e.g. System Architecture	e.g. Presentation Architecture	e.g. Control Structure	e.g. Rule design
Detailed represent- ations "*out- of-context*"	e.g. Data description	e.g. programs	e.g. Network architecture	e.g. Security Architecture	e.g. Timing Description	e.g. Rule Specific- ation
Functioning enterprise	e.g. Data	e.g. Function	e.g. Network	e.g. Organization	e.g. Schedule	e.g. Strategy

Table 2: The Zachman framework (from [7])

In practice, the models recommended by the Zachman framework provide "a basis for designing the enterprise" because the higher levels of abstraction (the top to rows) represent the organizational context in detail, and provide "a basis for building the enterprise's systems" because the lower level models act as a comprehensive design specification for enterprise systems. We argue that multi-perspective modelling is essential for accuracy, because it is much simpler to identify when all the knowledge for a single viewpoint has been captured, than to assess completeness of a complex artifact; it is useful for comprehensibility, because it is known that diagrams of organizational structures or business processes can be readily understood; and multi-perspective modelling at different levels of abstraction overcomes one of the main criticisms of knowledge modelling as an approach to knowledge management: that models are flawed because they eliminate contextual information which may be vital to devising an acceptable approach to leveraging a knowledge asset. Conklin [op.cit.] implied that organizational context should encompass "facts, assumptions, constraints, decisions and their rationale", and a set of models that cover all the perspectives of the Zachman framework should contain all this information.

Examples of multi-perspective models are given in Section 4.

3. Modelling Techniques

Which modelling techniques can or should be used in order to represent all these perspectives at appropriate levels of abstraction? We believe that a wide range of modelling techniques can be applied, from disciplines as diverse as business management, computer science, psychology and knowledge engineering. A "broad brush" distinction between techniques from different disciplines is that techniques from psychology and knowledge engineering which are designed for representing knowledge usually display a single perspective on knowledge, while many business management and computer science techniques are intended to represent two different perspectives in a single diagram, since this is helpful for analysis. Examples of techniques which are appropriate for particular perspectives (several of which are described in a survey of enterprise modelling techniques [8]) include:

- Business management techniques such as soft systems modelling [9] which has been used to represent *how* business processes are performed and *where* communication occurs between processes; role activity diagrams [10] which represent *who* performs particular activities and *where* they communicate with each other (see [5] for an example); and PERT charts, which emphasise *when* particular activities can be carried out, especially if critical path analysis is applied.

- Software engineering techniques such as flow charts, which represent *how* processes are carried out and *when* each step may be carried out; entity-relationship methods which represent *what* knowledge belongs to entities and *where* they obtain information from; and object-oriented analysis and design techniques which cover the same perspectives as entity-relationship methods but in more detail, and may also represent *how* objects process information.

- Representations drawn from research in cognitive psychology, such as clasification hierarchies which represent *what* knowledge is used and its categories; repertory grids [11] which gather information about *what* attributes and values are associated with a concept, and which concepts are similar; and decision trees, which represent *how* decisions are taken in a step-by-step manner.

- Knowledge engineering techniques, both those designed to cover many domains (such as VITAL [12] or CommonKADS) or those designed for specific domains (such as PRO*forma* [13], a method for representing protocols in the medical domain).

In addition, there are at least three families of methods that have been designed to provide a range of models that can provide a multi-perspective representation of knowledge: CommonKADS, UML and IDEF.

- CommonKADS covers most of the perspectives (as described above), and also most of the levels of abstraction: the Organizational model is suitable for addressing the "scoping" level, the Task and Agent models for the "enterprise" level, the Expertise and Communication models for the "system" level, and the Design model for the "technology" level.

- The Unified Modeling Language (UML) [14] recommends a range of diagrams, including use case diagrams (*who* knowledge), class diagrams (*what* knowledge), activity or state chart diagrams (*how* knowledge), sequence or collaboration diagrams (*where* knowledge) and component or deployment diagrams (the same types of knowledge already covered, but at lower levels of abstraction).

- The IDEF suite of methods [15] provide a range of modelling techniques for different tasks: IDEF0 is a "function modelling" method based on the Structured Analysis and Design Technique; IDEF1 is an entity-relationship modelling method; IDEF1X is a method for designing relational databases; IDEF3 is a process description capture method; the IDEF3 Object State Transition network shows the changes in state of objects are used by the processes; IDEF4 is an object-oriented design method; IDEF5 is an ontology description capture method, and so on. Like the CommonKADS models, different IDEF models are most useful at differing levels of abstraction.

To summarise: several modelling techniques are capable of representing each perspective, and it matters little which one(s) are used as long as every perspective is covered, the technique is appropriate for the desired level of abstraction, and the representation produced is sufficiently detailed for the problem being tackled.

4. Multi-Perspective Modelling Example: Clinical Procedures

For reasons of space, it is impossible to give a fully detailed example of multi-perspective models showing all six perspectives at all six levels of abstraction. Instead, we will look at all six perspectives at a single level of abstraction, using an example of following clinical procedures in an otolaryngological (ear, nose & throat) department. The example focuses on the treatment of a particular condition (parotid swellings – possibly malignant growths on the parotid gland, which is in the side of the neck). A model of a particular procedure within an organization is usually considered to be at the "enterprise" level of abstraction.

4.1. The *How* Perspective: Clinical Protocols

The expected contents of the "how" perspective, at higher levels of abstraction, are addressed by Melissa Cook in the context of building enterprise information architectures [16, pp.103-4]. She suggests that the "how" perspective should include functions at the scope level, primitive functions at the enterprise level, and processes at all lower levels. Functions are defined as "a high-level group of business activities ... that likely creates more than one entity", primitive functions are defined as "a high-level business activity ... that creates a single entity", and processes as "a business activity ... they create a single state of an entity and then move it forward into the next state".

Using this definition, the enterprise level of the "how" knowledge should create a single entity; in this case, the entity being created is a clinical diagnosis with a subsequent treatment plan. In this domain, the "how" knowledge can be represented by a clinical protocol. A clinical protocol gives a step by step guide to carrying out a certain specialized procedure, drawing on all (and only) the experiments and other knowledge relevant to that procedure. The motivation behind developing clinical protocols is to capture and represent "best practice".

In this example, the clinical protocol will be represented using PRO*forma*. PRO*forma* [13] is a simple but expressive technique for modelling best-practice guidelines in medicine. Its knowledge representation language supports four basic node types (Figure 1):

- A **Plan** is a sequence of sub-tasks, or components, which need to be carried out to achieve a clinical objective, such as a therapeutic objective. Plan components are usually ordered, to reflect temporal, logical, resource or other constraints.

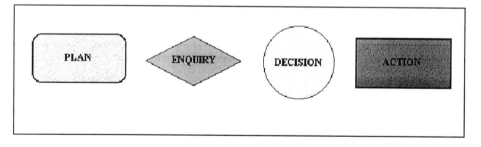

Figure 1: The four basic node types of PRO*forma*

- An **Enquiry** is a task whose objective is to obtain an item of information which is needed in order to complete a procedure or take a decision. The specification of an enquiry includes a description of the information required (e.g. a lab result) and a method for getting it (e.g. by query on a local patient record or a remote laboratory database).

- A **Decision** occurs at any point in a guideline or protocol at which some sort of choice has to be made, such as a diagnostic, therapeutic or investigative choice.

- An **Action** is a procedure that is to be enacted outside the computer system, typically by clinical staff, such as the administration of an injection.

Figure 2 shows a portion of the protocol that will be used throughout this example: it guides clinicians through the decision on how to treat a progressive lump (i.e. a lump that is growing progressively larger). See [17] for more details on this protocol.

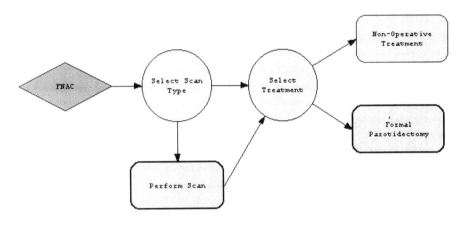

Figure 2: Protocol for diagnosing a progressive lump

FNAC stands for "fine needle aspiration cytology", which represents a clinical test that can be performed on fluid drawn from a parotid swelling. One of several types of scan may then be performed, and treatment choices include excising the lump (formal parotidectomy), chemo- or radio-therapy, or no treatment (because the risks of treatment outweigh the benefits).

4.2. The *Where* Perspective: Inter-Department Communication

The "where" perspective shows communication that is needed during a procedure. At the enterprise level of abstraction, communication is generally concerned with the transfer of information or artifacts between individuals or departments. In the example above, the clinician must communicate with the laboratory that performs the FNAC tests, with the radiology department that performs scans, and with the surgical unit that arranges operations.

This information can be represented in a Role Activity Diagram (RAD) [10], which shows which departments (or, more generally, which roles) perform which activities; by including the sequence of activities, the needs for communication become obvious. An example of a RAD can be seen in Figure 3.

4.3. The Who Perspective: Agent Modelling

In addition to the information captured in a Role Activity diagram, there is a need for the "who" perspective to represent the *capability* of agents, departments, or other role-players to perform certain actions and the *authority* that certain agents have to perform those actions or to use, consume or modify resources (Figure 4). At an enterprise level of abstraction, capability and authority may be expressed by defining the *rights* and *responsibilities* of an agent. For example, a doctor may have rights to add to a patient's medical record, implying both authority to change an artifact and the capability to do so, as well as responsibilities such as making sure a patient's medical record is kept up to date.

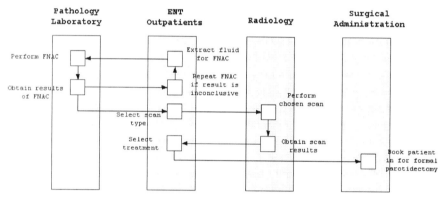

Figure 3: The "where" perspective -- Role Activity Diagram

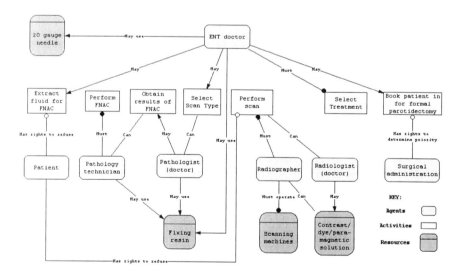

Figure 4: Capabilities, authorities, rights and responsibilities of agents

The modelling technique used here is loosely based on the ORDIT method for requirements definition [18] and the CommonKADS Agent Model [19]. Capability, authority, rights and responsibilities are represented by four different types of arc: these arcs are labeled "can", "may", "has rights to" and "must" respectively.

4.4. The What Perspective: Data, Information and Resources

The "what" perspective considers the *data* and *information* that are referred to and the *resources* that are used, consumed, modified, manipulated or otherwise involved in the overall process. Cook argues that

"the data architecture is more critical than the process architecture because most business processes exist to manage the assets, not the other way around" [16].

She proposes that the enterprise level of the "what" perspective should contain data classes, which are subclasses of global data classes; the relationships between classes can be defined using entity relationship diagrams. In practice, these data classes often subsume information (*"data with relevance and purpose ... data that makes a difference"* [20]) such as summations or categorizations as well as data. In this example, data classes might include clinical tests and patients; information represented in data classes might include results of tests; and resources include the machines required for scanning, the chemical solutions required as "markers" for scanning, and the needles required for extracting fluid for an FNAC. The resources may have associated constraints; for example, that use of a scanning machine requires several weeks notice, or that patients might be allergic to the iodine-based "contrast" that is injected as a marker for CT scans.

At the system level of abstraction, where resources, constraints, and information artifacts are identified individually, there are several ways in which resources might need to be modelled. If the resources can be grouped into classes, then a taxonomic hierarchy might be advantageous; for example, it might be helpful to know if scanning machines belong to a class of machines that uses computerized timing chips, and if so, whether they belong to the sub-class of machines that uses millennium-compatible chips. If a detailed representation of relationships between resources was needed, then a semantic network could be drawn. However, at the enterprise level of abstraction, a more general representation is more appropriate; an entity-relationship diagram could be used, but we have chosen to use a UML class diagram, to represent constraints more clearly. Figure 5 therefore shows a UML class diagram representing a simple hierarchy of resources and a simple hierarchy of test results.

4.5. The When Perspective: Schedules

Information about timing of activities and actions is very important in a planning problem; for other tasks, such as this diagnostic task, there is less need for such information. It is, nevertheless, advisable to draw a PERT chart, GANTT chart, or simple timeline of activities and any necessary inter-activity delay (such as the

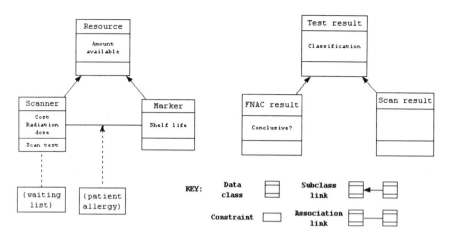

Figure 5: UML class diagram: resources and test results

waiting list for scanning appointments) in order to highlight any time-related issues (such as the fact that the chemicals used for marker solutions have a limited shelf life) or bottlenecks.

Figure 6 shows a PERT chart of activities and inter-activity delays; the durations (which appear at the bottom of the activity nodes) are in hours. It shows the two bottlenecks in the process (waiting lists for scanning and for operations) clearly. N.B. For illustrative purposes, it has been assumed that the "select scan type" activity can be carried out in parallel with awaiting the results of the FNAC.

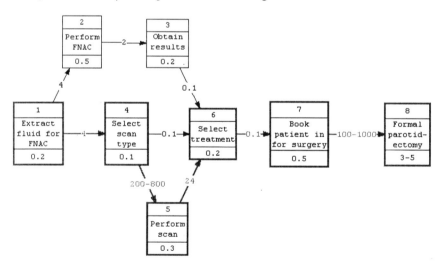

Figure 6: A timeline of activities in diagnosing progressive lumps

4.6. The Why Perspective: Published Clinical Evidence

The "why" knowledge for a clinical protocol consists of clinical evidence – published results of clinical trials, meta-studies, and expert opinions. The relative importance of different types of clinical evidence has been discussed in [21]. For the small part of the clinical process that we are considering, the "why" knowledge consists of all known articles published to date; at the time when this protocol was prepared, there were eight relevant published articles. Five of them argue for or against particular types of scan, the others argue for or (primarily) against formal parotidectomy.

These justifications can be represented in a rationale diagram; Figure 7 uses and extends the QOC (Questions, Options & Criteria) notation [22] to represent rationale for the "Select Scan Type" decision.

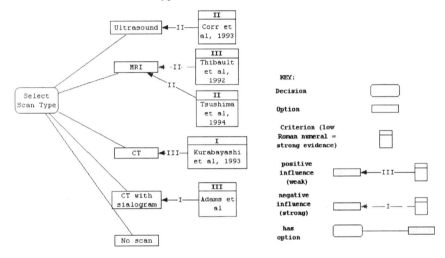

Figure 7: Extended QOC diagram showing the rationale for a decision

5. Knowledge Distribution Systems: Using Models as User Interfaces

We have shown how multi-perspective modelling uses different viewpoints to provide a complete yet comprehensible representation of knowledge; see [2] for a further discussion of the value of this approach in knowledge management. But however effectively organizational memory is represented, that representation is of little use unless it can be accessed and understood by members of the organization. In this section, we argue that a good user interface for a knowledge management system can be obtained by presenting the user with one of the graphical models representing a single knowledge perspective.

5.1. How a single perspective acts as a knowledge index

By using a single-perspective model as a user interface, a single coherent view on the entire knowledge asset is presented to the user, thus aiding comprehension. Since most knowledge items appear in more than one perspective, this model can also be used as an index to other perspectives, by linking information from other perspectives to appropriate knowledge items. This provides users with a structured way of navigating through knowledge from the various perspectives. By using a coherent (and hopefully validated) knowledge model as a user interface, users should be able to understand the structure of the knowledge better. In fact, a knowledge model user interface may not only assist comprehension but also concurrence and commitment to the knowledge. Conklin [4] proposes that knowledge development teams should use "knowledge display systems", arguing that:

> "a remarkable thing happens when knowledge teams use a display system to treat informal knowledge as if it were valuable ... there is less repetition in meetings, more rigor in decisions, and it is easier to bring others up to speed on the team's thinking and learning. In other words, when you take process-oriented knowledge seriously, the process itself immediately improves."

It seems possible, even likely, that giving a "display system" of organizational knowledge to the knowledge users will generate a similar effect of taking the knowledge seriously, and thus create process improvements over and above those expected.

The suggestion that a single-perspective model can act as an index to the other perspectives is an important one, because it is relatively easy to put into practice, since it is usually possible to identify knowledge that "belongs", or *should* belong to a knowledge item. In the "how" perspective, knowledge relevant to procedural steps may include justifications, case histories, organizational policies, descriptions of how to perform the step, or entire sub-procedures; in the "who" perspective, knowledge relevant to agents might include experience, authority, responsibilities, legal restrictions and appraisals; for the "what" perspective, knowledge relevant to classes might include ontological definitions, default attributes, class members, and key differentiators; and so on. Some of this knowledge is drawn from other perspectives (for example, justifications of decisions may be drawn from the "why" perspective), while other knowledge will be specific to a perspective (for example, instructions on how to carry out a procedure). If this knowledge can be linked directly to the relevant knowledge item in the model (via hypertext, pop-up menus, or whatever), then the user interface becomes an index to all knowledge relevant to particular knowledge items, thus providing the fundamentals for a good decision support system. In addition, knowing what knowledge is expected to "underlie" a particular component of a model greatly simplifies the identification of what knowledge **needs** to be captured in order to provide an adequate representation, which is a major stimulus to overcoming one of the biggest problems of knowledge management: the existence of large amounts of tacit knowledge, whose existence and contents are not only unrecorded, but may even be outside the conscious awareness of those who have and exercise the knowledge [23].

Choosing which perspective to use for the user interface depends on the purpose of the knowledge distribution system. If it is purely a "knowledge browser", then deciding which model to use as the user interface probably comes down to which model contains the most detail. For other purposes, however, particular perspectives may be more appropriate. Some suggestions are given below:

- The "how" perspective is useful for representing standard organizational procedures or regulated procedures;

- A taxonomy of classes and subclasses, representing the declarative ("what") perspective, can be used to distribute organizational ontologies, in order to support either structured addition to the organizational memory or structured searching for knowledge;

- An agent-based model (the "who" perspective) can go beyond organizational structure charts to indicate the roles, capabilities and responsibilities of different agents within the organization, thus providing a basis for project and resource management;

- The "when" perspective provides additional control information to the "how" perspective - such knowledge can be used for planning and scheduling applications;

- The "where" perspective can constitute a front end for real-life multi-agent tasks such as distributed collaborating project groups;

- The "why" perspective can be used as the front end of a justification system, such as a system for supporting legal argumentation, or a system which represents the justifications for regulations (e.g. PLINTH [24]).

5.2. A Knowledge Distribution System: the Protocol Assistant

The Protocol Assistant [17] is a system that illustrates these principles. It is a prototype expert decision support system for diagnosis and treatment of parotid swellings that can be run through an Internet browser; the many advantages of such a distribution method include ease of knowledge maintenance – if the evidence base should change through publication of new clinical studies, a single designated "protocol maintainer" can introduce the change into the knowledge base and make it immediately available to all users of the system. It was designed with four purposes in mind:

- to represent clinical protocols which describe specialized medical procedures in an accurate yet accessible format;

- to capture and represent the "evidence base" of clinical studies which provide evidence for or against particular steps in the protocol;

- to demonstrate how these protocols can be distributed over the Internet using HTML diagrams, and how abstracts of the relevant clinical studies can be made available to medical practitioners;

- to allow the system to reason with these clinical studies, according to the principles of "evidence-based medicine", thus allowing the entire protocol to be "run" as well as browsed.

A clinical protocol constitutes a standard organizational procedure, so the most appropriate perspective for the user interface is the "how" perspective. The Protocol Assistant used PRO*forma* models as its interface, and was able to function both as a decision support system (due to the hyperlinking of relevant underlying knowledge) and as an expert system.

In identifying which knowledge from other perspectives was relevant to each node, we were assisted by the PRO*forma* methodology, which specifies attributes that should be associated with each of its node types. Every node has attributes for preconditions, post-conditions and triggers (part of the "when" information); in addition:

- Decisions have attributes for argument rules for different candidate options ("why" knowledge) as well as rules for commitment to a candidate (more detailed "how" knowledge drawing on "what" knowledge) and information sources required ("where" knowledge);

- Plans have attributes for scheduling constraints, abort conditions and termination conditions (more "when" knowledge);

- Actions have attributes for associated procedural descriptions ("how" knowledge);

- Enquiries have attributes for sources (primarily "where" knowledge), and capture "what" knowledge.

By specifying available knowledge in shorthand form in these attributes (for example, encoding a clinical study that strongly supports CT scanning as "++CT: ref Kurabayashi"), and making some further knowledge available through hyperlinks (for example, the abstract of the Kurabayashi study and other clinical studies were hyperlinked to the HTML representation of the "Select Scan Type" Decision node), the PRO*forma* model acted as a very effective index to most of the relevant underlying knowledge. In addition, an expert system was implemented, based on the knowledge model, allowing the user the choice of browsing the available knowledge through a Web browser or being guided through it by an expert system.

6. Conclusions

We have argued that the two main technology challenges for knowledge management are to capture and represent knowledge assets accurately and accessibly. Knowledge engineering methods such as CommonKADS have come a long way towards meeting these challenges; they provide disciplined multi-perspective approaches to designing and building knowledge-based applications.

The six models from the CommonKADS methodology are a good starting point for the modelling of knowledge assets. However, these models were not defined with the goal of developing organizational memories. The Zachman framework helps us to define what aspects of organizational memory need to be represented; the necessary perspectives and detail will vary with the type of knowledge being acquired, the expected users of the system, and the purpose of the knowledge management effort. We suggest that knowledge engineers should apply whatever modelling techniques they prefer, as long as all the necessary perspectives are covered. We have suggested some techniques that are appropriate for particular perspectives or levels of abstraction.

We have further claimed that knowledge distribution systems based on the organizational memory can employ one of these perspectives as a user interface; which perspective is chosen will depend on the goal of the application. The individual elements of the chosen perspective provide a useful index for accessing organizational knowledge relevant to that element, as well as aiding the user in understanding the structure of the knowledge and the system. We have illustrated this argument by describing the Protocol Assistant, which represents, distributes, and reasons with a clinical protocol, along with its supporting evidence base, within a Web browser.

References

1. A.Th. Schreiber, J.M. Akkermans et al, Engineering and Managing Knowledge: The CommonKADS Methodology (version 1.0). University of Amsterdam, Amsterdam, 1998.

2. A. Macintosh, I. Filby and J. Kingston, Knowledge Management Techniques: Teaching & Dissemination Concepts. International Journal of Human Computer Studies (Special Issue on Organizational Memories & Knowledge Management), vol. 51, no. 3, Academic Press, September 1999.

3. G. van Heijst, R. van der Spek and E. Kruizinga, Organizing Corporate Memories. Proceedings of KAW '99, Banff, Alberta, November 1996. http://ksi.cpsc.ucalgary.ca/KAW/KAW96/vanheijst/HTMLDOC.html.

4. E.J. Conklin, Designing Organizational Memory: Preserving Intellectual Assets in a Knowledge Economy. http://www.gdss.com/DOM.htm, 1996.

5. J.K.C. Kingston, T.J. Lydiard et al, Multi-Perspective Modelling of Air Campaign Planning, Proc. AAAI-96, AAAI Press, 1996.

6. J.J. Sowa and J.A. Zachman, Extending and Formalizing the Framework for Information Systems Architecture. IBM Systems Journal, vol. 31, no. 3, 1992. IBM Publication G321-5488.

7. J. Zachman, The Framework for Enterprise Architecture. http://www.zifa.com/zifajz02.htm.

8. J. Fraser and A. Macintosh (eds.) Enterprise State of the Art Survey, The Enterprise Consortium, September 1994. Available from AIAI, The University of Edinburgh, http://www.aiai.cd.ac.uk.

9. P. Checkland and J. Scholes, Soft Systems Methodology in Action, John Wiley, 1990.

10. M. Ould, Process Modelling with RADs. IOPener: the newsletter of Praxis plc, 1-5 to 2-2, 1992-1993.

11. K.M. Ford and J.M. Bradshaw, Knowledge Acquisition as Modeling, chapter 1. John Wiley, 1993.

12. VITAL is the name of both a methodology project and its support tool. A good starting point is J. Domingue, "The VITAL Workbench", http://kmi.open.ac.uk/~john/vital/vital.html

13. J. Fox, N. Johns et al, Protocols for Medical Procedures and Therapies: A Provisional Description of the PRO*forma* Language and Tools. Proc. AIME'97, Springer Berlin, 1997.

14. UML Resource Center. Rational Software, http://www.rational.com/uml/, 1995-1999.

15. R.J. Mayer, P.C. Benjamin et al, A Framework and a Suite of Methods for Business Process Reengineering, http://www.idef.com/articles/framework/framework_pt1.htm, Knowledge Based Systems Inc., 1998.

16. M.A. Cook, Building Enterprise Information Architectures: Reengineering Information Systems, 1996. Prentice Hall PTR, New Jersey.

17. J. Simpson, J. Kingston and N. Molony, An Expert System for Best Practice in Medicine, Proc. Expert Systems 98, SGES Press, Cambridge 1998. Also published in Knowledge Based Systems, vol. 12, no. 5-6, October 1999, pp. 247-255. Elsevier Science.

18. J.E. Dobson, A.J.C. Blyth, J. Chudge et al. The ORDIT Approach to Requirements Identification, Technical Report 394, Computing Laboratory, University of Newcastle upon Tyne, 1992.

19. A. Waern and S. Gala, The CommonKADS Agent Model. Esprit Project Report P5248 (KADS-II), KADS-II/M3/TR/SICS, Swedish Institute of Computer Science, 1994

20. T.H. Davenport and L. Prusak, Working Knowledge: How Organizations Manage What They Know, Harvard Business School Press, 1998.

21. A.G. Maran, N.C. Molony, M.W.J. Armstrong et al. Is there an evidence base for the practice of ENT surgery? Clinical Otolaryngology 22 (1996) 152-157

22. A. Maclean, R. Young, V. Bellotti et al. Design Space Analysis: Bridging from theory to practice via design rationale. In *Proceedings of Esprit '91*, pages 720-730, Brussels, November 1991.

23. I. Nonaka and H. Takeuchi, The Knowledge-Creating Company: How Japanese Companies Create the Dynamics of Innovation. New York: Oxford University Press, 1995.

24. A. Casson, PLINTH: Integrating Hypertext, Semantic Nets and Rule-Based Systems in an Expertext Shell for Authors and Readers of Regulatory Information, Proc. CIKM'93 Workshop on Intelligent Hypertext, Arlington, Virginia. Also available as AIAI-TR-142, http://www.aiai.ed.ac.uk/

Ontology Assisted Process Knowledge Acquisition

Hugh Cottam and Nigel Shadbolt
University of Nottingham, AI Group, School of Psychology,
University Park, Nottingham NG7 2RD.
hdc@psychology.nottingham.ac.uk & nrs@psychology.nottingham.ac.uk
www.psychology.nottingham.ac.uk/research/ai/

Abstract: This paper explains how ontologies can be used in order to assist process oriented knowledge acquisition (KA). It explains what ontologies are and how they can be applied within the context of process oriented KA tasks such as Business Process Re-engineering (BPR) initiatives and the construction of company Intranets or knowledge repositories. In particular it explains the rationale behind the development of an ontology based methodology that accompanies the "Process Knowledge Editor" KA tool. The work described is part of the SPEDE project which aims to create a Structured Process Elicitation and Demonstration Environment.

1.   Introduction

In recent years there has been a growing awareness in business of the importance of knowledge. We increasingly hear terms such as knowledge assets, data warehouses, and knowledge management. The desire to make such knowledge entities more explicit and in turn more reusable is ever increasing. The experience of the knowledge based systems community in addressing knowledge issues is undoubtedly relevant to the construction of more general knowledge repositories. In this paper we explain how ontologies can be used to assist process oriented knowledge acquisition (KA). Section 2 contains a general definition of ontologies and their use. In section 3 we describe some major initiatives in the body of existing work on ontologies and the different roles that they can fulfil. Section 4 contains an exploration of the rationale for the use of ontologies. We describe in detail the analogy between our current work in constructing and using ontologies to support process oriented KA, and previous work in KA for the expert systems field. We then address more specifically how ontologies can be used to support process oriented KA. In section 5 we describe the development of an ontology based process KA methodology. This includes discussion of the General Process Ontology (GPO) and Knowledge Requirement Templates (KRTs). These approaches are supported within a new software tool, the Process Knowledge Editor which is described in section 6. In section 7 we discuss the results of several case studies and make conclusions.

2.   What are Ontologies?

A commonly used definition of an ontology is that it is an "explicit specification of a shared conceptualisation" [7]. This roughly outlines what an ontology is, but doesn't explain what it is for. A simple explanation is that the primary purpose of any ontology is to enable knowledge sharing. This can take on many different forms: knowledge sharing within software applications, between software applications, knowledge sharing in the form of re-use, knowledge sharing to arrive at a common understanding or to achieve integration. These many forms of knowledge sharing indicate the widely differing tasks and agents that ontologies can support.

Ontologies can be viewed as a structured approach to the representation of knowledge. They can be used to represent knowledge at a number of levels. Within SPEDE, ontologies are used to define the meta-level of process knowledge. By this we mean that the ontology defines the building blocks with which we can construct process models. The ontology can also define rules about how these building blocks fit together. We can use an analogy with language, whereby the ontology defines a language for process description. The ontology building blocks act like word categories in the vocabulary of a language. The rules as to how the blocks can fit together are similar to the grammar of a language. Within SPEDE ontologies can become progressively more specialised, and can be made specific to the requirements associated with performing a particular process KA task.

The term ontology is used both to refer to knowledge structures that define the meta-level nature of a conceptualisation, and knowledge structures that actually define the content. If we use a design process as a simple example, then the ontology can consist of definitions of meta-level entities used to describe a design process such as activity, data, component, resource, or role. However, the ontology can also consist of specific instances of such entities that describe an actual process performed in an organisation. This distinction between meta-level and content descriptions can become a source of confusion when discussing ontologies. There is no rigid distinction between the two, as whether an ontology is describing entities that are meta-level or content in nature depends on the use to which the ontology is put. It follows that an ontology that defines content in one context can form the basis of a meta-level definition for use in another context (this iterative nature to the use of ontologies is discussed in [17]). Within the SPEDE work we use the term "ontology" when referring to knowledge definitions used in a meta-level fashion.

3.   Existing Work on Ontologies.

In this section we outline a number of initiatives within the existing body of ontological research. In particular we explain the role that ontologies fulfil within the context of each initiative. We identify four categories of ontology from the existing body of ontological research. This is not an exclusive or exhaustive set of categories, and is motivated from a SPEDE perspective. There are a number of other important characteristics of existing ontological research. These include whether the work has an implemented system or tools associated with it, whether it is Web based and whether it supports collaborative construction of ontologies.

3.1 High Level Upper Ontologies.

High level upper ontologies attempt to provide a grand categorisation of everything. They can be powerful tools for the general purpose indexing of knowledge yet there is little consensus on which are the major distinguishing features that should be used as the basis of such ontologies. CYC [11] has been developed as a system providing encyclopaedic and common sense knowledge in operational form in a client-server fashion. It has its own high level upper ontology associated with it, but could also be included in the theory based formal ontology category. It is Web based but is not aimed at collaborative construction of ontologies. In the sense of its intended use it is not a meta-level definition but actual knowledge content. There are also a number of philosophically inspired upper level ontologies [18] that are not supported by systems or tools.

3.2 Theory Based Formal Ontologies.

Theory based formal ontologies are general compact, formal representations that provide deductive reasoning capability. They are oriented towards the construction of operational knowledge based systems. It should be noted that most of the ontologies that we have placed in this category are not used as a final system knowledge representation. Those that are not, are provided with translation capabilities to various operational formats. Some ontologies that we have placed in this category are constrained to particular domain areas, e.g. knowledge associated with enterprises or knowledge associated with engineering systems.

Ontolingua is both a language for ontology specification and a server based architecture for the construction and browsing of ontologies (defined using the language). The Ontolingua language uses formal ontologies as a means of specifying knowledge in order that it can be shared and reused across software entities [7]. The Ontolingua initiative is aimed at imposing an engineering rigour on the design of ontologies. In this context ontologies act as an on-line knowledge-base server that can be queried by a software client. The Ontolingua language is based on the Knowledge Interchange Format (KIF) [6] which was developed as a neutral format for knowledge representation.

KACTUS [9] is a project aimed at the development of methods and tools for the re-use of knowledge about technical systems. The KACTUS toolset is aimed less at facilitating the collaborative construction of ontologies and more directly at supporting KA for KBS construction. KACTUS attempts to combine domain specific ontologies with task type and problem solving method type indices, in order to provide a library from which users can select and configure reusable ontological components to construct a KBS.

PHYSSYS [1] is an ontology developed specifically for the area of engineering systems modelling, simulation and design. The ontology is used to represent physical systems. Despite being constrained to use within engineering domains it makes use of abstract ontological "super-theories". Examples of these are mereology, topology, graph theory and systems theory. The intention is that they can be used as reusable generic building blocks in ontology construction. The ideology behind PHYSSYS is similar to that behind KACTUS. They both support ontological component selection from libraries. The PHYSSYS approach is more domain oriented and does not contain the task type and problem solving method type indices found in KACTUS. Much of the work in PHYSSYS has focussed on the development and testing of the abstract "super-theories".

TOVE (the TOronto Virtual Enterprise project [8]) aims to create a common data model for enterprise databases that provides shared terminology for the enterprise that any agent can understand and use. The intention is that this will enable automated deduction to be carried out over the information in such enterprise databases. TOVE does not focus on collaborative ontology construction, but provides a logical framework for representing things such as activities, states and time in an enterprise integration architecture. This is formally specified in first-order logic. The TOVE focus on enterprises makes it highly relevant to SPEDE.

The Enterprise Ontology [20] has the broad goal of assisting the management of change within enterprises. The role of the ontology is to facilitate the inter-operation of software applications via a toolset for enterprise modelling.

3.3 Domain Rich Ontologies.

Domain rich ontologies are large scale and by nature they tend to be more application specific. They tend to be aimed less at the development of knowledge based systems and more at providing assistance with KA. Because of this emphasis they are less likely to be the final system format for knowledge representation.

Ontosaurus [19] is a sever based ontology browsing and editing system. Ontologies can be accessed by a standard Netscape client. The Ontosaurus server uses the LOOM knowledge representation format. Each object in an Ontosaurus ontology can include a natural language description as well as graphical documentation. Ontologies constructed in Ontosaurus tend to be large scale, domain rich knowledge bases aimed at task-specific applications. One of the large documented examples of the use of Ontosaurus is in the area of military air campaign planning. Ontologies in Ontosaurus are less in the form of logical theories and more in the form of highly structured extensive lexicons. The Ontosaurus system also facilitates the collaborative construction of ontologies.

3.4 Neutral Formats.

Neutral formats are aimed at defining a means of information exchange at a system level between software entities. They assist knowledge sharing in a more after the fact fashion by offering an accepted standard interlingua. PIF (The Process Interchange Format) [10] is an initiative to produce a neutral format for the exchange of process information. This can be thought of as an ontology that enables the sharing of process descriptions between a wide variety of software. A core set of objects has been developed that can be used to describe the basic elements of any process. This can be extended in order to include elements needed for more specific groups of applications. This work is relevant to SPEDE as many of the basic object types in PIF are also required within SPEDE. STEP is an international standard (ISO 10303) for the representation of product data. The data models are formally specified in the modelling language EXPRESS (ISO-94b). The relation between this work and ontologies is described in [13].

The MIT Process Handbook [12] does not easily fit into any of the categories we have used, though it is undoubtedly relevant to the subject of process oriented KA. Rather than being an ontology, it is a handbook of actual organisational processes.

4.   Ontologies to Assist Process Oriented KA.

There exist a number of methodologies to support the construction and population of expert systems. Such methodologies use structures that can be viewed as ontologies. Indeed, the KACTUS project has actually reworked the CommonKADS methodology into a more explicit ontological framework. Ontologies such as these guide and constrain KA for the population of expert systems. In recent years there has been a desire to improve the efficiency of expert systems projects and to identify where the bottlenecks lie. It became clear that the transfer of knowledge from human expert to computer system, was a critical and very labour intensive element of expert systems construction. Following the identification of this bottleneck the expert systems community has directed much effort to the problem of how to acquire, model, organise and reuse knowledge, in an efficient manner.

The focus upon knowledge in itself as opposed to its implementation in an operational system led to efforts to maintain a distinction between the two. One of the most influential of these was the identification of the "knowledge level" [15]. The concept of the knowledge level was introduced by Newell as a means of uniformly characterising natural and artificial systems. By describing the behaviour of a system in this manner he was able to distinguish between the rational behaviour of a system and it's implementation at the machine symbol level.

The concept of the knowledge level was embraced by the KA community for the purposes of KBS development. It emphasised the modelling of a human experts problem-solving knowledge in total independence from its later realisation as a computer KBS. This has lead to the construction of complete knowledge level methodologies for KBS development such as KADS [2], CommonKADS [3], and VITAL [16]. These methodologies not only embrace the principles of abstraction contained within Newell's "knowledge level"; the use of such abstraction principles within the modelling of expert problem solving behaviour has enabled the identification of standard types of building blocks for the construction of such models. The KADS methodology identifies a number of standard components. In particular it uses what are referred to as inference layer models whose components are either inference steps or domain roles. Example inference steps are abstract, match, and refine. Example domain roles are component, observable, and diagnosis. In addition to these basic components the originators and users of such methodologies have identified recurring patterns in the way these basic components can fit together. This has lead to the compilation of extensive libraries of what are referred to as generic problem-solving models. These models correspond to particular types of problem solving and offer great possibilities for knowledge re-use. Methodologies support the selection of one of these generic models from the library, that corresponds to the expert problem solving behaviour that is being observed (this in turn is constrained by the required functionality of the intended expert system). The generic model can then be modified if required and acts as a template that constrains and guides KA. Such generic approaches have achieved real success when applied to various domains.

The development of the knowledge level has been driven by motivations of improving the process of expert systems KA, and providing the possibility for knowledge re-use within such systems. By distinguishing between different ontological types of knowledge, the acquisition of knowledge has been improved. In the normal practice of performing KA in order to build an expert system the modelling activity is heavily constrained by the high level goals of the modelling endeavour. One of these high level modelling goals is the actual intent to construct an operational expert system. This provides a strong focus for the KA because of the fact that the knowledge acquired must enable the operationalisation of the relevant problem solving within a computer architecture. The ontological types that constitute knowledge level problem solving models reflect these goals.

It became clear within the SPEDE project that if we were to achieve similar efficiencies within process oriented KA to those that have been achieved in the expert systems field, then ontologies must be developed that reflect the goals of KA for process oriented tasks such as those associated with BPR. A number of requirements upon an ontology based process KA methodology can be outlined:

- Process oriented and enterprise ontologies already exist, yet they are aimed at enabling deductive reasoning capability rather than assisting KA for descriptive and knowledge mapping purposes. Our ontology must be less formal, more descriptive and more amenable to visualisation.
- The methodology must be very flexible as the goals of process KA can vary heavily from one initiative to another. It must therefore be capable of adaptation in a goal-oriented manner to each initiative.
- Because the operational task (as in KA for experts systems) is not present as a constraining factor, the ontologies used must focus on the process domains.
- Abstract ontological types will have to be identified that reflect this process domain focus. (see section 5.1).
- Ontologies must be constructed from the abstract ontological types that reflect the goals associated with process initiatives (see section 5.2).

5. An Ontology Based KA Methodology

5.1 A General Process Ontology (GPO).

A General Process Ontology (GPO) has been developed that lists a set of basic process concept and relation types that can be used for the definition of knowledge that is relevant to process description. The GPO is listed in Table 1. It is a base ontology that is designed to support process KA. We use the term KA here in a broad sense that embraces both knowledge elicitation and knowledge modelling. The GPO supports KA by enabling the definition of the structure of process knowledge prior to acquisition (though this structure may be modified during the acquisition task itself). Basic types are selected from the GPO and act as the building blocks for the construction of well structured process models. It forces the distinction between basic process concept types: e.g. Activity, Data, Result, Role, Organisational Group, Agent, Product Item, Cost, Location, Resource, Requirement. It also defines the basic relation types that can hold between the basic concept types: e.g. Sequence, Dataflow, Performs Role, Has Requirement, Uses Resource, Requires Skill, Has Sub-activity. These abstract basic types have been determined through an extensive analysis of existing ontologies, enterprise and process modelling formats (some of these were discussed in section 3 of this paper), and the knowledge requirements of the analysis activities conducted on process models. Additional basic types are being considered for inclusion in the GPO and it is envisaged that it will undergo modifications following further use.

A core sub-set of the GPO is hardcoded into the Process Knowledge Editor (see section 6), and the user may select additional basic types from the GPO dependent on the current KA task. The core subset of the GPO includes the basic process concept types, Activity, Data, Role, Skill, Resource, Result and Decision. It also includes the basic relation types, Sequence, Dataflow, Performed by Role, Requires Resource, Requires Skill, Requires Access to Data, and Acts as Support Role. All basic concept types can be organised in a taxonomy for that particular type using the "isa" relation. The local taxonomies are then linked via other relations, e.g. the Dataflow relation links an Activity concept with a Data concept.

Activity

Attributes:	Start Time, Finish Time, Duration
Hierarchy Relations:	Has Sub-Activity, Has Parent Activity
Sequence Relations:	Ends Before Starts, Starts Before Ends, Starts Before Starts, Ends Before Ends, Starts After Ends, Ends After Starts, Starts After Starts, Ends After Ends, Meets, Contains
Resource Relations:	Requires Resource, Produces Resource, Consumes Resource
Data Relations:	Has Data Input, Has Data Output, Requires Access to Data
Other Relations:	Is Performed By Role, Has Location, Has Result, Produces Product, Has Constraint, Has Cost, Requires Skill, Has Risk, Acts as Support Role, Cannot Start before Data Present.

Role

Relations:	Has Members, Has Constraint, Has Organisational Group, Has Authority Link, Is Empowered, Has Goal, Has Agent, Requires Skill

Organisational Group

Relations:	Has Role, Has Constraint, Has Group, Has Authority Link, Is Empowered, Has Goal, Has Location, Has Members

Agent

Relations:	Has Role, Has Constraint, Has Group, Has Authority Link, Is Empowered, Has Goal, Has Location, Has Skill

Location

Relations:	

Result

Type Attribute:	Fail, Pass, True, False, Continue, Return

Requirement

Relations:	

Data

Relations:	
Type Attribute:	Electronic, Paper

Product Item

Type Attribute:	Complete Product, Assembly, Component, Feature
Relations:	Has Sub-Part, Has Requirement, Has Constraint, By-Product of, Product of, Has Location

Resource

Type Attribute:	Raw Materials, Facility, Tool, Operator, Space
Motility Attribute:	Mobile, Stationary
Consumption:	Continuous, Discrete
Unit of Measure:	Length, Area, Volume, Weight, Time, Man-hours
Relations:	Has Location

Table 1: General Process Ontology (GPO).

5.2 Knowledge Requirement Templates (KRTs).

The GPO facilitates the adoption of a goal directed approach to process KA. The content and structure of a process model depends on the intended use of the model, such as the analyses that will be performed on the model or the knowledge that the model must contain in order for implementation of a re-engineered process. Re-engineering goals may be to minimise cost, minimise time, maximise quality, or more likely to combine a number of these goals within more specific requirements and constraints. The intended use of process knowledge thus defines high level knowledge requirements. The linking of high level requirements to the type of knowledge to be acquired can be explicitly supported using KRTs.

KRTs are configured subsets of the GPO and Table 2 shows a very simple KRT to support critical path analysis. This provides a definition of the knowledge required to perform critical path analysis on a process. Critical path analysis is used to detect activities that represent time "bottlenecks" in the process as a whole. For critical path analysis we only require knowledge relating to Activity, Sequence and Time.

Activity

Attributes:	Start Time, Finish Time
Hierarchy Relations:	Has Sub-Activity
Sequence Relations:	Ends Before Starts, Starts Before Ends, Starts Before Starts, Ends Before Ends

Table 2: A KRT for Critical Path Analysis

Table 3 shows a KRT to support Role Definitions. This is also a configured subset of the GPO, and defines the knowledge required to define the Roles associated with the Activities within a process. These Role definitions also make use of knowledge about Agents, Organisational Groups and the Locations, Constraints and Authority links that are associated with these. Activity sequencing knowledge is only required to ensure that too many Roles are not assigned to concurrent Activities.

Activity

Attributes:	Start Time, Finish Time
Hierarchy Relations:	Has Sub-Activity
Sequence Relations:	Ends Before Starts, Starts Before Ends, Starts Before Starts, Ends Before Ends
Other Relations:	Is Performed By, Has Location

Role

Relations:	Has Members, Has Constraint, Has Group, Has Authority Link, Is Empowered, Has Goal, Has Agent, Requires Skill

Organisational Group

Relations:	Has Role, Has Constraint, Has Group, Has Authority Link, Is Empowered, Has Goal, Has Location, Has Members

Agent

Relations:	Has Role, Has Constraint, Has Group, Has Authority Link, Is Empowered, Has Goal, Has Location, Has Skill

Location

Relations:	

Table 3: A KRT for Role Definition

A number of KRTs have been identified that correspond with particular process modelling tasks. Some of these have been populated and tested (e.g. critical path analysis, RADS, IDEF0 and IDEF3 are already defined). An interesting possibility for future work is to populate an extensive library of KRTs in conjunction with their use for process KA as a means of validation.

6. The Process Knowledge Editor.

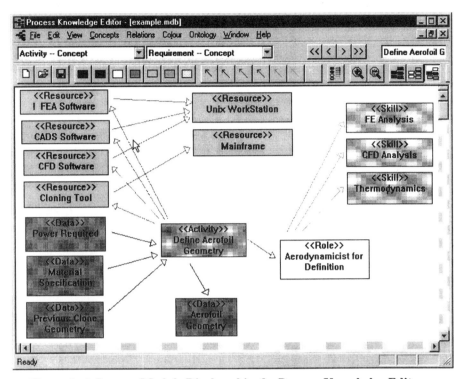

Figure 1: A Process Module Displayed in the Process Knowledge Editor.

The Process Knowledge Editor (PKE) is a software KA tool that supports process modelling in a goal directed manner. It is based around the methodology described in the previous section. The PKE and accompanying methodology are aimed at constraining process KA by ensuring that it is performed in order to meet specific goals and knowledge requirements. It is a PC based tool that runs on Windows 95, Windows 98 and Windows NT platforms. Process knowledge bases are constructed in the PKE and are saved in a Microsoft Access database format. The decision to house the knowledge bases in a standard database structure ensures the robustness associated with a well developed and ubiquitous database format. It also ensures the future openness of the knowledge base format, should further tools be developed.

The knowledge bases developed within the SPEDE project using the PKE are domain based and tend to be very large. There exists a need for some mechanism of modularisation and information hiding. To this end we have developed the notion of process modules (see figure 1). A process module is defined in order to index and visualise only that knowledge which is immediately related to an individual Activity. The modularisation is quite artificial in that relations still exist within the knowledge base across the partitions that are defined by the modules. This modularisation functionality is fully supported within the PKE.

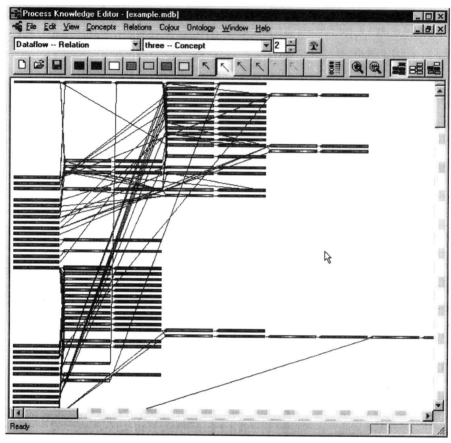

Figure 2: The Process Knowledge Editor Displaying a "Dataflow" network

Figure 2 shows a screenshot of the PKE being used to display a knowledge base from the viewpoint of a particular relation ("Dataflow" in this case). This enables the user to view the behaviour of a particular relation across the entire knowledgebase whilst being able to focus in particular areas using the modules. The PKE also allows the user to arrange concepts in hierarchies. Each basic concept type has a separate hierarchy. In the example shown there are separate hierarchies of Activity concepts, Data Concepts, Role concepts, e.t.c. As mentioned in section 5 most of the GPO is hardcoded into the PKE, though the user is at liberty to add any number of additional basic concept types and basic relation types (thus configuring the ontology to the current goals).

The PKE also supports the hypertext documentation of the concepts and attributes within the knowledgebase. By right clicking on any concept or attribute and selecting the "Notes" option a hypertext notes window opens. The hypertext notes facility allows the user to enter basic text documentation for the relevant object (either concept or attribute). The hypertext facility supports basic word processing functionality as well as allowing the user to enter hyperlinks within the documentation. The hyperlinks are used to access the hypertext entry for other objects within the knowledgebase. The PKE also has a "Hypertext Assistant Dialog" which provides context sensitive functionality for the automated generation of hypertext documentation based on the knowledgebase that has been constructed. If desired the hypertext associated with a particular knowledgebase can be exported directly to HTML files. Alternatively the PKE can store this hypertext information internally within the Access database.

The hypertext functionality of the PKE results in two potential modes of use. The PKE can be used to model processes with the hypertext merely used as a documentation feature. Alternatively the PKE can be used to model processes that are then used as a structure for constructing a Website within the PKE. This second use has proved particularly powerful for the population of company Intranets.

7.   Case Studies and Conclusions.

Case Study 1 involved the testing of the methodology and PKE within Rolls Royce within the area of turbine blade design. This involved a knowledge engineer using the methodology and PKE in order to capture an overview of the turbine blade design process. The knowledge engineer had access to existing documentation and also conducted a number of interviews.

Case Study 2 involved the application of the methodology and PKE within Rolls Royce. This project consisted of two Rolls Royce employees being directed in the use of the PKE and methodology over a twelve week period with the goal of constructing and populating the Rolls Royce Intranet site on issues relating to Transmissions and Structures Structural Analysis. An additional objective was to determine a structural analysis best practice for the analysis of static structures. Knowledge was gathered from experts at a number of Rolls-Royce sites. This knowledge was structured using the PKE, validated by the relevant company experts, and then exported into HTML. By the end of the project 175 web pages had been produced, and an analysis working practice had been established and presented within the Intranet site. The project was considered to be a great success and the approach was viewed as a major improvement on existing techniques.

The two case studies demonstrate the both the usability and efficiency of the approach. The PKE and accompanying methodology proved successful in enabling both knowledge engineers and novice users to partition a domain in a goal directed manner by defining an ontology (based on selection from the GPO) that matched the requirements of the KA task being undertaken. The defined ontologies can be considered as potential KRTs for inclusion in a library. The ontologies aided in both the organisation of the acquired knowledge and the planning of the KA work itself. Ontologies can be used to facilitate the application of KA tools, techniques and methodology to the task of acquiring and managing process knowledge. They confer significant advantages by:

- providing a means of indexing acquired knowledge thereby facilitating its later re-use. In particular this is possible within groups and organisations, but re-use may also be viable across organisations.
- providing a link from common clearly defined terms to process models gathered from a wide number of sources across the organisation. This facilitates the interpretation and analysis of the models.
- supporting the use of goal directed KRTs that guide KA.
- providing advice on how to carve up a description of a process, thereby managing the complexity of large models and the KA work itself.

As ontologies become more specific they can enable the construction of process descriptions from off-the-shelf components (this is where the distinction between meta-level and knowledge content becomes blurred). The methodology can also lead to the population of a library of KRTs that guide process KA and are indexed by the modelling goals.

References

[1]   Borst, W.N., Akkermans, J.M., & Top, J.L. (1997). Engineering Ontologies. International Journal of Human Computer Studies 46, 365-406. Special Issue on Using Explicit Ontologies in KBS Development.

[2]   Breuker, J., Wielinga, B., Van Someren, M., De Hoog, R., Schreiber, G., De Greef, P., Bredeweg, B., Wielemaker, L., Billault, J-P., Davoodi, M. & Hayward, S. (1987). Model driven knowledge acquisition: interpretation models. KADS-I Project Deliverable, University of Amsterdam, Holland 1987.

[3]   Breuker, J. & van de Velde, W.(Eds.). (1994) CommonKADS Library for Expertise Modelling. IOS Press, Amsterdam, September 1994.

[4]   Cottam, H., Shadbolt, N., & Milton, N. (1998a). Acquiring Knowledge for Business Process Re-Engineering, in: proceedings of AAAI-98 workshop on Using AI for Knowledge Management and Business Process Engineering, July 1998, (also available as technical report from AI Group, University of Nottingham).

[5]   Cottam, H., Shadbolt, N. & Milton, N. (1998b). The Use of Ontologies in a Decision Support System for Business Process Re-Engineering in Proceedings of IT& KNOWS Conference of the 15th IFIP World Computer Congress. Vienna/Budapest, August 1998.

[6]   Genesereth, M. R., & Fikes, R. E. (1992). Knowledge Interchange Format, Version 3.0 Reference Manual. Computer Science Department, Stanford University, Technical Report Logic-92-1, June 1992.

[7]   Gruber, T.R. (1993). Towards Principles for the Design of Ontologies Used for Knowledge Sharing, KSL-93-04, Knowledge Systems Laboratory, Stanford University.

[8]   Gruninger, M. & Fox,M.S. (1995). The Logic of Enterprise Modelling. In J. Brown and D.O.Sullivan (eds) Reengineering the Enterprise pp. 83-98. Chapman and Hall.

[9]   KACTUS Consortium. (1996). The KACTUS Booklet. ESPRIT Project 8145 - Technical Report. 1996.

[10]   Lee, J., Grunninger, M., Jin, Y., Malone, T., Tate, A., Yost, G., & other members of the PIF Working Group (1996), The PIF Process Interchange Format and Framework Version 1.1, Proceedings of Workshop on Ontological Engineering, ECAI '96. Budapest, Hungary. (Also available as MIT Center for Coordination Science, Working Paper #194, 1996; and at the following World Wide Web site: http://ccs.mit.edu/pif.)

[11]   Lenat, D. B. & Guha, R. V. (1990). Building Large Knowledge-Based Systems. Reading, MA: Addison-Wesley.

[12]   Malone, T. W., Crowston, K., Lee, J. & Pentland, B. (1993). Tools for inventing organizations: Toward a handbook of organizational processes. In Proceedings of the 2nd IEEE Workshop on Enabling Technologies Infrastructure for Collaborative Enterprises. Morgantown, WV, April 20-22.

[13]   Meis, E., & Ostermayer, R. (1996). Recommendations to the STEP committee. ESPRIT Project 8145 - Technical Report. 1996.

[14]   Milton, N. R., Shadbolt, N. R., Cottam, H. D., and Hammersley, M. (1999) Towards a Knowledge Technology for Knowledge Management, in special issue on Organisational Memories of The International Journal of Human Computer Studies. Fothcoming. 1999.

[15]   Newell, A. (1982). The knowledge level. Artificial Intelligence, 18:87-127, 1982.

[16]   O'Hara, K., Shadbolt, N. R., Laublet, P., Zacklad, M. & Le Roux, B. (1992). Knowledge acquisition methodology. VITAL deliverable DD212. Nottingham University, UK. 1992.

[17]   Schreiber, G., Wielinga, B., & Jansweijer, W. (1995). The KAKTUS View on the 'O' Word. In Proceedings of IJCAI95 Workshop on Basic Ontological Issues in Knowledge Sharing. Montreal, Canada.

[18]   Sowa, J. F. (1995) Top-Level Ontological Categories, in: International Journal of Human-Computer Studies, 43, p669-685. 1995.

[19]   Swartout, W. R., Patil, R., Knight, K., & Russ, T. (1996) Toward Distributed Use of Large-Scale Ontologies. In Proceedings of the Banff Knowledge Acquisition Workshop, Banff, Canada, Nov. 1996.

[20]   Uschold, M., & Gruninger, M. (1996) Ontologies: Principles, methods and applications. Knowledge Engineering Review, 11(2), 1996. Also available as AIAI-TR-191 from AIAI, The University of Edinburgh.

Web-Mediated Knowledge Servers: Some Technical Issues

Andrew Basden

The Centre for Virtual Environments, University of Salford, Salford, U.K.

Abstract

We are in the era of web-mediated knowledge, delivered by servers to distant clients. The initiative for obtaining knowledge is either with the client (searching the World Wide Web) or with the server, where automated (intelligent) agents proactively send messages. Between these are mixed initiative systems, where the knowledge server and client work together to seek, select and deliver relevant knowledge tailored to the user's needs. But this territory is, as yet, sparsely populated; true knowledge servers are rare, especially ones that deliver expert knowledge. It is a unique opportunity for traditional knowledge based systems, with their shared locus of control, their ability to tailor knowledge and advice precisely and dynamically to the needs of the user, and long experience in providing expert knowledge. Moreover, delivering their knowledge over the WWW might overcome some of the problems of knowledge isolation found with traditional KBS.

Though papers have been published on linking KBS to the Internet, none seem to have addressed the technical problems in detail in a way that would allow others to follow suit. This paper examines such problems and describes and discusses solutions as implemented in the Istar knowledge server.

Keywords: Knowledge servers, World Wide Web, knowledge distribution, concurrency, inference engines, Istar.

1. Introduction

1.1 Integrating Knowledge Based Systems and the Internet

In this era of knowledge management, an increasing volume of knowledge is distributed over the Internet, in various ways. In some, such as browsing the World Wide Web (WWW) or using WWW search engines, the locus of control resides with the user/client, in that they take the main initiative for selection of knowledge. In others, such as email mailshots compiled by intelligent agents, the locus of control resides with the server. In the former, the user receives little guidance on selection of relevant knowledge, while in the latter, though the modicum of knowledge in agents provides some guidance, it is relatively insensitive to the user's needs and context. However in between these two extremes are 'mixed-initiative' systems in which the locus of control is shared, and user and server might cooperate in the selection of knowledge.

Traditional knowledge based systems (KBS) technology (inference engines with knowledge bases) have always been mixed-initiative systems, and would seem admirably suited to occupying this middle ground. Because their backward chaining offers sensitive guidance, their forward chaining gives immediacy and their ability to handle uncertainty makes them particularly suited to responding well to human interpretations, the knowledge distributed can be of higher quality and greater relevance. If traditional KBS technology could be integrated with WWW technology then true 'knowledge servers' might be achieved and, as Sehmi and Kroening [1] suggest, "the future holds the promise of sophisticated and intelligent information delivery."

Such an integration might also benefit traditional KBS technology, which for some time has been hampered by problems knowledge isolation. Placing KBSs on the WWW as knowledge servers would distribute knowledge widely, making it available to a large usership in diverse contexts and cultures. Links to a wide variety of web pages could be inserted [1] that would aid contextual interpretation.

This paper discusses what is involved, technically, in effecting such an integration. In principle, integration can be achieved if the user interface modules of KBS technology are replaced by modules that seek and receive information via Internet connections (sockets). But the nature of the Internet requires changes in KBS technology itself which have not been fully discussed. Shankararaman, Poppon, Corley, Whittle, [2] describe an architecture for KBS-WWW connection but with little detail. Sehmi and Kroening [1] discuss the problem of persistence but bypass it rather than solve it. Cabeza, Hermenegildo and Varmaa [3] discuss some low level issues (their PiLLoW library for logic programming provides help with parsing WWW, handling forms, writing CGI scripts, active modules, client-server interaction, etc.). but many of the real problems occur at higher levels and require modification of the KBS architecture itself. Levy [4] discusses five issues, but not in the context of KBS.

What motivated us was: Given a knowledge base, previously built and used on a local machine, how can it be made available across the Internet for maximum beneficial use? The question we address in this paper is: In what ways must traditional KBS technology be modified to achieve useful knowledge servers by integration with the WWW?

1.2 Types of KBS-Internet Integration

Integration of KBS with the Internet opens up possibilities beyond that of knowledge service: "active WWW pages, search tools, content analyzers, indexers, software demonstrators, collaborative work systems, MUDs and MOOs, code distributors, etc." [3]. There are five main types of integration, shown in Fig. 1, where ovals indicate the KBS.

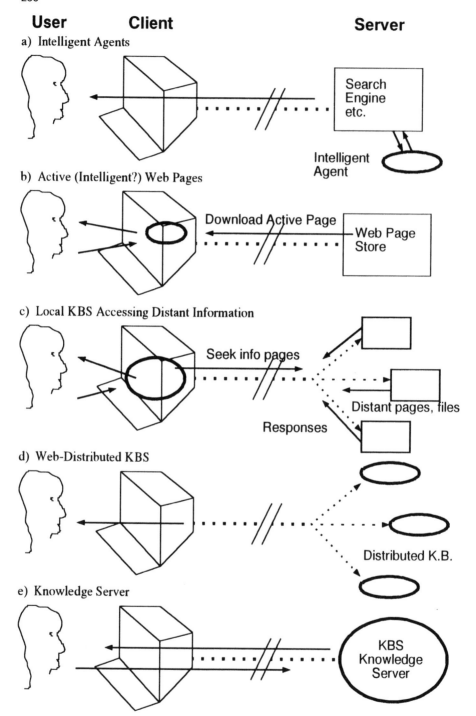

Fig. 1. Types of Integration of KBS with WWW

Type 1: Intelligent Agents. Type 1 is a KBS which runs automatically as an intelligent agent and helps WWW processes like search engines. It is activated when necessary and returns defined output without human intervention. Prolog or Horn logic can extend the power of web servers [5]. We do not consider this type here because we are concerned with serving knowledge to human users.

Type 2: Active Web Pages. LogicWeb [6], aims to use logic programming to achieve active WWW pages, by incorporating programmable behaviour and state. Boley [5] sees this as a natural extension from HTML-mediated document retrieval, through SQL-mediated data retrieval, to Horn-mediated retrieval of deduced knowledge on the WWW.

With appropriate programmable behaviour, active web pages could in principle be used to distribute expert knowledge. But, as was found early in the history of KBS, complex knowledge requires higher levels of representation than mere programmable behaviour and state. Though important, we do not consider it further.

Type 3: Local KBS Accessing Web-distributed Information. Type 3 is a KBS hosted on the user's own machine that seeks some of the information it needs for making inferences from distant WWW pages or files, rather than from the user. Time delays in obtaining the information means the normal strategy of waiting for information from one question before selecting the next is not realistic here. This problem is discussed in [3] and below.

Type 4: Web-distributed Knowledge Base. Type 4 extends the above concept from information to knowledge. Not only is (some) information distributed across the Internet but parts of the knowledge base are also distributed. The deduction engine is often run on the user's machine but is continually seeking parts of the knowledge base from distant sites. Obviously this type of distributed KB requires standard syntax in the KB fragments, with attendant problems of incompatibilities between versions. Time delays in obtaining information are more critical than in type 3 and this suggests that highly recursive portions should be kept locally rather than on distant sites [5]. Communication between the parts requires not just message passing but the active sharing of variables across the Internet, by shared variable and linda-based protocols [3].

Though often slow, type 4 deduction engines can be useful in collaborative KBs and might show promise for knowledge used in a variety of contexts or cultures where context sensitive knowledge can be kept locally. But we do not discuss it further here because it does not align with our motivation of being able to make existing knowledge bases more widely available.

Type 5: Knowledge Server. Type 5 is a KBS that runs on a server on behalf of a distant client, making some prepared knowledge available to them. The main function the Internet connection serves is as a user interface, though other possibilities are opened up that are discussed below.

1.3 Uses of Type 5 Knowledge Servers

There is some overlap between the types, of course, but it is type 5 knowledge servers that align most closely with our motivation of making complex or specialised knowledge more widely available over the Internet, so this is the type we mainly consider in this paper. Some aspects of type 3 (obtaining web-distributed information as input) can be integrated with type 5 knowledge servers, to provide a full service, so we discuss the issue of interleaving requests below.

Knowledge servers can fulfil most roles fulfilled by ordinary KBS [7]: providing expertise (consultancy role), amplifying expertise (training role), allowing experts to check they have not overlooked important factors (checklist role), and refining the knowledge of the user by a process of stimulation and clarification (knowledge refinement role). The PM-IES expert system [2] is used within BT to distribute advice on millennium compliance throughout the company's network. It is built on CLIPs [8] with a simple socket interface on the server side and a special bridge module on the client side. The demonstration system they reported aroused significant interest, but it is not known to what extent it has been used, and various technical limitations they mention suggest that scaling up for real use might be difficult. WebLS [1] is an embedded Prolog module designed to provide technical support of various kinds including fault diagnosis, query answering, clarification of common misunderstandings, rectifying deficiencies in documentation, and providing other technical advice. It is currently running a few type 5 knowledge servers.

1.4 Technical Issues

In spite of their potential, it is surprising how few type 5 knowledge servers are available and delivering expert knowledge over the WWW. Part of the reason for this is that few traditional KBS toolkits have been made Internet-friendly in such a way that the knowledge engineer needs only to concern him/herself with the knowledge at hand. Low-level libraries as described in [3], [9], [10] provide some Internet capability but require specialist programming and Internet knowledge on the part of the knowledge engineer. A possible exception is ART*Enterprise/Web [11] which provides an interface between ART*Enterprise and the Internet, but its claim to remove the need for such specialist knowledge has not been examined by this author.

There has been very little discussion of the higher level technical issues that arise when integrating KBS and WWW technologies. It seems to have been assumed that the major problem is merely to replace a human user interface of the KBS by a module that interfaces to TCP/IP sockets. Yet, as we have found, not only do the normal problems of distant communications manifest themselves, but there are fundamental inconsistencies between the very concept of KBS inference and that of the WWW. How to overcome these problems in a robust, usable manner does not yet seem to have been discussed in any detail.

2. Towards a Web-Mediated Knowledge Server

We envisage the type 5 knowledge server would operate via a standard WWW browser, typically as follows. The user would connect to the knowledge server via a link in an ordinary WWW page, and receive a welcome page either of a knowledge base or giving a selection of KBs. The selected KB would be loaded in the server, an inference session would start, and its first question would be sent to the user. Each question page would contain the means whereby the user answers with a value. Upon receiving this, the inference engine propagates the value, finds the second question and sends that to the user. This cycle continues until enough information has been received to satisfy the goals, and an end of session page is sent to the user which offers to display or explain results, restart the KB, etc.

(Note: In this paper we assume the client is the end user, not the knowledge engineer. Distant construction of KBs raises other issues not discussed here.)

2.1 HTML Pages

If these pages are composed of standard HTML, there is no need for esoteric technology, and the functionality of the knowledge server can be available to all. All that is required of the server's response by the client's browser is that the text of the question is contained within the standard HTML structure:

```
<HTML>
<HEAD>
 . .
</HEAD>
<BODY>
 . .
</BODY>
</HTML>
```

and whatever is sent by the server will be displayed on the client's screen in the form of a web page.

Because of the innate flexibility of HTML all pages sent by the knowledge server can include within themselves two types of hyperlink. One type is an ordinary URL (Universal Resource Link) which links to other web pages, e.g. for explanation and help, accesses to which the server never sees. The other type is a pseudo URL, which is a message sent to the server and interpreted by it. Since it is the server that has composed the page, the format of this pseudo URL can be anything the server requires.

2.2 HTTP Connections

HTML pages are transmitted by Hypertext Transfer Protocol, HTTP [12]. Being connection-orientated, it would seem, at first sight, to suit the passage of question pages and answer messages between inference engine and user. A

User/Client   **Server**

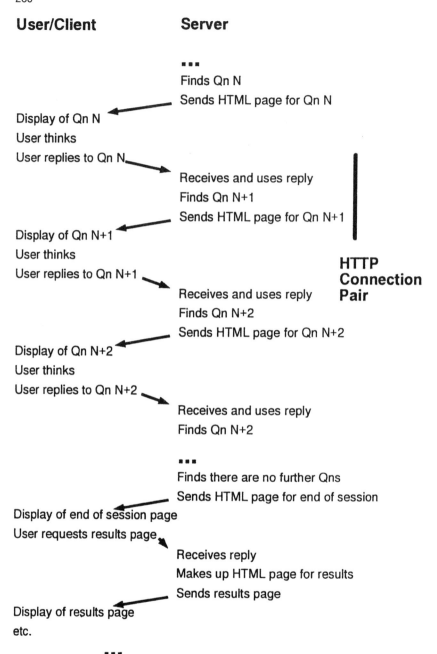

Fig. 2. HTTP Messages between Knowledge Server and Client

connection is a pair of messages: information request from the client of the general form

```
GET /[url] HTTP/1.0
```

(where '[url]' defines what information is to be obtained: a real or pseudo URL), followed by server response containing the requested information or an error message. On completion, both client and server close the connection.

This concept of a connection admirably meets all the normal requirements of web browsing, search engines and the like. In the case of web pages, the '[url]' is interpreted as the location of an HTML file on disk, which is sent whole to the client. In the case of search engines or CGI programs, the '[url]' is expected to contain parameters for the search or program, and the HTML page sent to the client is created from those parameters.

We can easily envisage how a KBS would fit this framework: when the inference session is underway, with a sequence of questions put to the client and answers received as replies, the client message that initiates an HTTP connection is the answer to question number N, and the response that the server sends to the client before closing the connection is the text of question number $N+1$. Because of backward chaining, which question is selected to be question $N+1$ can vary 'intelligently' according to the answer received for question N and knowledge held in the knowledge base; this is a very powerful concept in web access. Once all questions have been answered, then the server's response is the end of session page. The operation of HTTP connections to service this is shown in Fig. 2.

2.3 Technology Options for Server

A variety of technical mechanisms is available to operate a knowledge server in this way. CGI (Common Gateway Interface), which is designed to manage programs to act as servers of various kinds, has been employed by [1], [3] and others; the knowledge server would be one such program. Aided by the HTTP daemon (httpd) the CGI module listens for certain types of messages, in which '[url]' contains 'cgi-bin', the name of the program and various parameters for it. CGI loads the named program, runs it and passes the parameters to it. From them the program creates the contents of an HTML page which it returns to CGI, then it terminates. CGI sends this output to the client. See Fig. 3a.

CGI has two main disadvantages. Having to start and terminate a program on each client message imposes a huge overhead if the program is large [3]. Win 95 CGI imposes additional overhead by using files for CGI-program communication (rather than stdio as in Unix and Windows NT, or messaging as in Amiga) and this constrains the style of interaction allowed with the client [1]. The second concerns persistence of the state of the KB. While all server-side mechanisms must address persistence, the start-stop nature of CGI programs complicates this and makes it more error prone.

a) CGI Programs

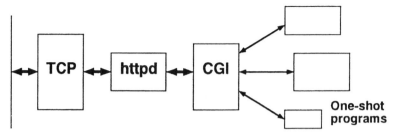

b) CGI with Bridge to Continuously Running KBS

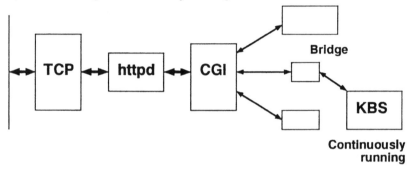

c) KBS listens directly to TCP port

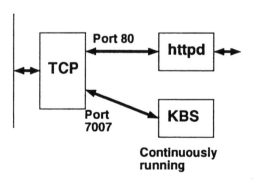

Fig. 3. Server Architectures

These problems can be overcome by using an 'active module' [3], a small bridge program between CGI and a continuously running KBS. The bridge program is loaded by CGI each time, sends a message to the KBS, awaits its reply (the next question), relays this back to CGI and terminates. Though it might reduce overheads, it is yet another step at which errors can be generated.

However, given that the knowledge server must parse and act on messages, why not parse HTTP messages directly, rather than ones constructed by CGI or the bridge program? Why not listen directly on a TCP/IP port, Fig. 3c? Not only does this remove all the overheads above, and fit more naturally the continuous running of the KBS, but it also can have advantages when running secure KBs; the standard modules between TCP/IP and the KBS are security loopholes. This is the solution we adopted.

3. Problems and Solutions

An existing KBS toolkit, Istar [13] was augmented with an interface to the Internet. Istar was deemed to be a good candidate for several reasons. It has a relatively clean modular architecture which would allow easy replacement of the normal user interface by an equivalent that composes HTML pages and responds to HTTP input. It is designed to work with several knowledge bases at one time, a prerequisite for multi-user access. Multi-user access also requires the interleaving of many concurrent activities; Istar already had a multi-threaded architecture. A selection of sophisticated knowledge bases is available for Istar, which can test the server's ability to immediately host existing KBs. One of these, from the INCA project [14], allows the user to write their own construction contract. Istar's inference engine operates on a goal list from which it backward chains to find questions to ask, then forward chains the answers given.

Here we examine some of the technical problems and solutions encountered in modifying Istar for WWW connection. The first two issues (3.1 and 3.2) mentioned are relatively easy to address, but there is one quite fundamental problem that lies at the root of several others, and posed quite a challenge.

3.1 The User Interface Module

The normal user interface of the KBS must be replaced with a two-way link to the Internet. Problems can arise if either the interface is graphically orientated (because HTTP assumes a stream) or much of the interface is hard coded into the KB (often true in logic programming). Istar proved remarkably easy to modify because it exhibited neither problem.

But two further topics require careful consideration, once the interface has been replaced: how the dynamic pages are constructed by the knowledge server [4], and how values and other user actions are sent to the server. We opted for a simple question page: the question text at the top, then a means of entering the answer value, followed by various user options like Help and Pause, and terminated by various notes (e.g. a hyperlink to the main Istar page). Question text is held with the question in the KB but generic text is held in companion files that can be easily edited.

Input of values is relatively easy using HTML, there being at least two methods one can use: either an HTML form or a small set of hyperlinks, each of which carries a different value. The user clicks either a 'Go' button or a hyperlink and a message is sent to the knowledge server with its attached value. For entering probabilities and degrees of belief sliders are best, but not available under HTML, so a pseudo slider is offered, being a scale of values 0..10, each with a hyperlink.

Questions can be asked either singly or in groups. Single questions use hyperlinks when it is appropriate to offer the user a selection (e.g. 'Yes', 'No'), but groups of questions always use HTML forms because all values must be set before the message is sent.

The results page is rudimentary at present, comprising a table of the goals and their values, or a document created from them (e.g. for the contract writing KB).

3.2 Linking to Other Knowledge

One of the benefits that WWW can bring to KBS is direct linking to a wealth of knowledge related to that in the KB [1]. Any page that the knowledge server sends to the client can include hyperlinks and pictures, for a variety of purposes: to provide help and explanation, to contextualize the information on the page, and to include access to other WWW functionality such as to invite emailed comments and queries. Even the question and help text can contain hyperlinks. This helps to overcome the problem of knowledge isolation.

3.3 Reversal of Roles

There is however a fundamental problem in modifying KBS for WWW access: the natural operation of an inference engine is directly opposed to that of HTTP. HTTP assumes atomic connections initiated by the client, but the inference engine assumes a sequence of related connections initiated by the server (asking the question, then awaiting answer). The inference message pair (page display, user action) is therefore out of phase with the HTTP pair (user action, page display); see Fig. 4. HTTP works extremely well for most types of page-by-page web browsing, for search engines and for anything that gives a single answer to a single request. But an inference engine wants to seek information from the client (distant human user), so the roles are reversed, and the client becomes the 'server', providing information (answers to questions) when requested, while the knowledge server becomes the 'client', requesting such information. This fundamental reversal of roles lies at the root of many of the problems we find.

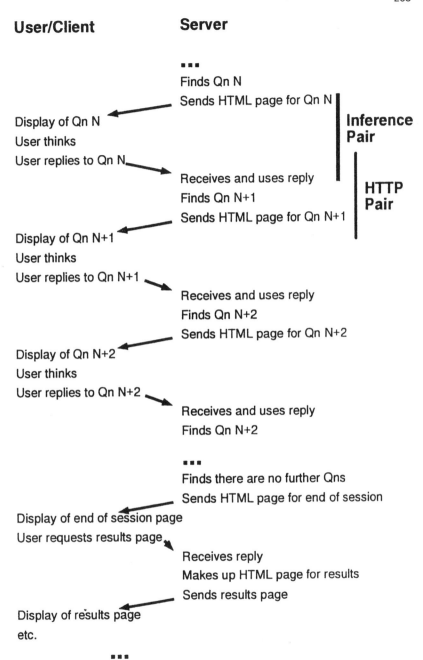

Fig. 4. Inference Pair out of phase with HTTP Pair

The server cannot initiate the connection with the client because the latter's URL is not known and often varies. Also, while the server is expected to be accessible continuously, the client's machine might have closed connections or even closed down. This asymmetry between client and server is important in giving indefinitely many clients access to collected information, but it poses a fundamental problem for inference engines.

3.4 Concurrent Inference Sessions

A knowledge server will have several different inference sessions operating at once, on behalf of different clients, and must progress each of them independently so that none is held up by the others. But some conventional inference engines are designed on the assumption of a single inference process. Istar has a multi-threaded architecture for its (local) user interface, which allows most of its operations to be interleaved, this was found to be only partially true of the inference session.

Istar treated the whole inference session as a single process with beginning, end, and points in between at which information was sought (Fig. 5a, where these points are labelled as questions). Based on graph traversal, this inference engine had quite an elegant architecture, in that the information seeking points were completely general, and instead of being questions put to a human user could be any other source such as a file, a web page, some operating system resource like time of day, etc. When (local) input is from the user, they can carry out other operations, owing to multi-threading in the user interface, and this proved a boon to the knowledge engineer because it allowed them to start a local inference session but, at any question during it, make modifications to the KB immediately they were thought of; see Fig. 5b. However, it was found that such in-session activities could not include starting a second inference session: because the second session would have to be completed before the next step could be taken in the first session. See Fig. 5c. This, of course, was useless for a multi-user knowledge server.

So the notion of inference as a process with start, end and generalised information points had to be modified, and broken up into individual steps; see Fig. 5d. But the steps were not those that are natural to inference, namely send question and await reply; rather, they had to be those that are natural to HTTP, namely receive reply, then find and send next question (Fig. 5e). The first and last steps were now different from all the others, and the whole inference engine became somewhat less elegant.

A related problem is interference between users; how this is dealt with is explained below.

3.5 Persistence

As the KBS puts the sequence of questions to the user, it builds up the state of the KB. The KBS in a knowledge server must retain some persistent memory of

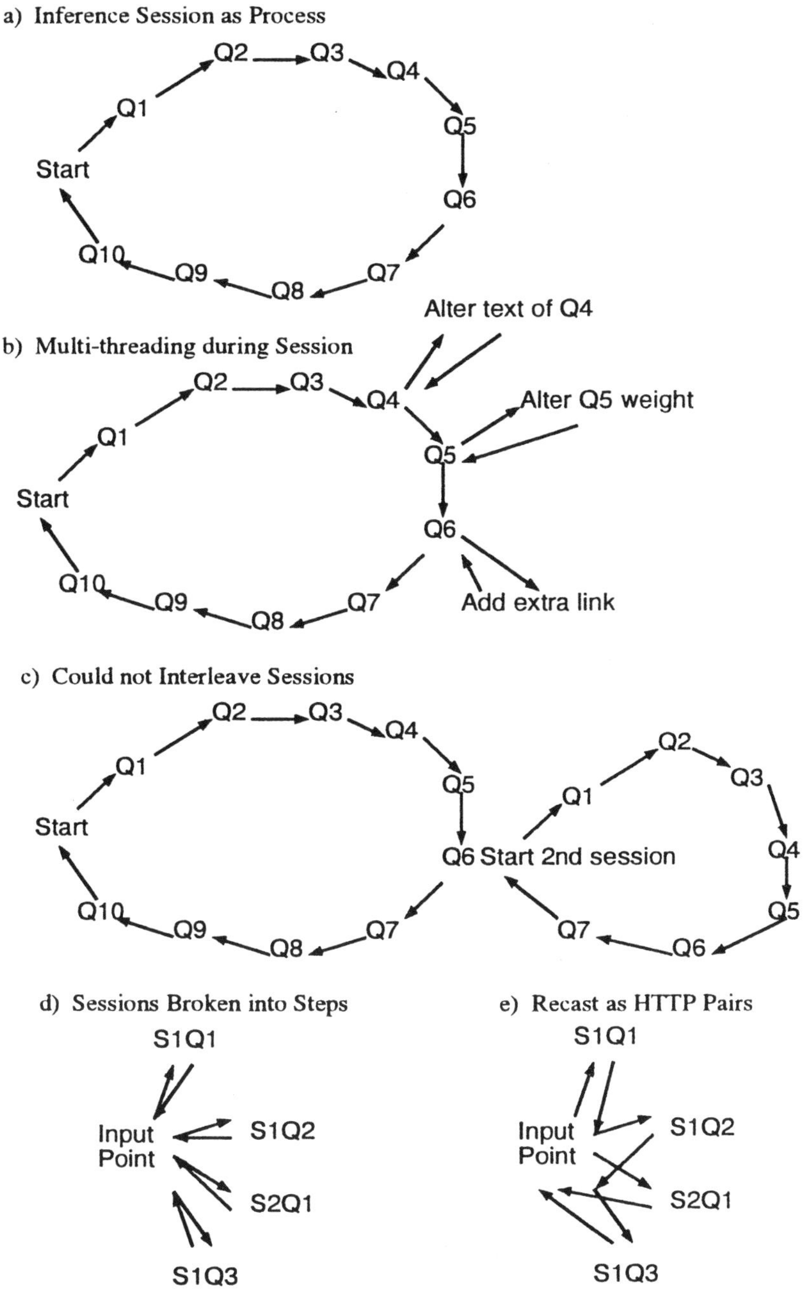
a) Inference Session as Process
Start
Q1
Q2
Q3
Q4
Q5
Q6
Q7
Q8
Q9
Q10
b) Multi-threading during Session
Start
Q1
Q2
Q3
Q4
Q5
Q6
Q7
Q8
Q9
Q10
Alter text of Q4
Alter Q5 weight
Add extra link
c) Could not Interleave Sessions
Start
Q1
Q2
Q3
Q4
Q5
Q6 Start 2nd session
Q7
Q8
Q9
Q10
Q1
Q2
Q3
Q4
Q5
Q6
Q7
d) Sessions Broken into Steps
S1Q1
Input Point
S1Q2
S2Q1
S1Q3
e) Recast as HTTP Pairs
S1Q1
Input Point
S1Q2
S2Q1
S1Q3

Fig. 5. Evolution of the Inference Session

the state of the KB from one connection to the next. The memory can be kept with either client or server.

Sehmi and Kroening [1] bypass this problem by putting all the questions of the KB to the user at once, so all answers are returned together. Only suitable for small KBs, this approach nullifies one of the distinct advantages of KBS backward chaining, the suppression of irrelevant questions. They acknowledge this and say these problems can be alleviated by splitting the KB into modules, but they do not say how they retain persistence between the modules.

Client-side persistence means the whole state of the KB is contained in cookies or in the page itself, such as in hidden fields in forms, as with [3] and the Assistum strategic thinking tool [15]. But each has problems. Cookies can be turned off by the user, and when the state is stored in the page the whole of it must be passed to and fro with each message between client and server. Both cookies and page fields can be interfered with. In general, client-side persistence is workable only for small KBs; large KBs which have thousands of variables would require too many cookies or hidden fields. Finally, client-side persistence would require the inference engine to instantiate all KB variables anew every message, an unacceptable overhead.

Server-side persistence is more natural, in that the KB state is kept within the KB itself on behalf of the client. It is less prone to interference, requires less messaging overhead, is more suited to large KBs, and allows usage to be monitored or controlled. In Istar a copy of the KB is loaded for each client. In its server module a table of clients is maintained, each client structure containing a pointer to the KB and a unique session identifier (which also uniquely identifies both client and KB). Arriving messages contain the session identifier (see below), so the table is searched for a match. If not found, a new client is assumed. If found, then the appropriate action is taken: such as propagating question values forward through the KB, and finding the next question to be asked.

However, for server-side persistence to perform reliably certain other issues must be addressed.

3.6 Correctly Identifying Input

Since HTTP 1.0 assumes atomic connections, the client's reply for question $N+1$ is completely unrelated to the reply for question N. The knowledge server must, therefore, have a means of reliably and uniquely identifying which question of which inference session a message relates to, irrespective of its source.

The client's URL cannot be used as identifier because the IP address is not unique and the port might change from one connection to the next. So a unique identifier must be created by the server and encoded into every reply. Other than cookies (which were ruled out above), this can be achieved either in HTML form fields or in the URL attached to hyperlinks. A unique session identifier is created for each client, which is retained throughout that session; currently it is the time at which the client started plus a monotonically increasing client count. In this way, the messages passed over the Internet when the user hits a server hyperlink or the form 'Go' button are relatively short and less subject to interference.

All HTTP requests related to an Istar inference session have the format:

GET /T37671a48_U37671a3d_32_P HTTP1.0

in which 'Txxx' is a timestamp, 'Uxxx_nn' is the unique session identifier and client count, 'P' indicates what type of message it is (in this case pause the inference session), and might have extra characters after it. Question answer messages have '?Q' in place of 'P', in the standard HTML parameter format, a question identifier, type of value returned and the value itself, such as:

GET /T37671a3e_U37671a3d_32_?Q23328_C=8 HTTP1.0

Several such parameters can occur in a single message.

(Note that HTTP 1.1 supports persistent connections, which would have solved some of this problem, but since many browsers do not yet use it, it seemed that reliance on it would jeopardise our aim of maximizing the availability of knowledge.)

3.7 Waiting for a Reply; Timing Out

Using persistent server-side memory raises the problem of when to remove it. Frequently the user does not hit the 'Finished' button, perhaps because they leave the terminal or the link breaks. There must be some way of detecting such situations and removing dead KBs.

Timing out is a common solution: if the client has not made connection within a given time then their copy of the KB is removed. Under HTTP 1.0, unfortunately, no 'five minutes left' warning can be sent.

Istar's standard time-out is 10 minutes. But often the user will browse other web pages during the inference session for longer than that, and would be annoyed to find the KB had timed out when they returned. So Istar invites the user to set a timeout between 1 and 60 minutes on each page by a small set of hyperlinks at the bottom of each page.

3.8 Seeking Distant Information

Though much of the information for the knowledge server comes from the human user, some could be obtained from Internet sources as part of the inference session, as a type 3 linking. Requests for such information must be made asynchronously, and can arrive in any order. This is like OR-parallel architectures [5] in which requests for and receipt of information are interleaved, and each piece received must be acted on appropriately. As long as each is identified uniquely, as above, KBS forward chaining is ideally suited to doing this.

But the power of traditional backward chaining is compromised by not having full information available on which to select the next question. The inference engine must be modified to bypass questions for which replies are awaited. Istar sets a 'waiting' flag for this purpose.

Sometimes the sought information does not arrive (page not available, wrong permissions, etc.), and an error message is sent instead. Sometimes only part of the page arrives. These situations must be detected and handled appropriately. The server software must recognise all possible error messages - and there are many of these, of different formats and styles, and covering different errors. Because these pages are designed for human readership some degree of natural language processing might be needed. Partial pages might still be usable, if only early portions are required. As far as possible, responsibility for detecting these cases should lie with the inference engine, rather than with the knowledge engineer.

But responsibility lies with the knowledge engineer for deciding what to do once it has been established that requested information is not available. Sometimes there may be other ways of obtaining the information. Istar variables have an 'unknown' flag, and can use a 'first known' inference method to allow for alternate information routes. However, seeking distant information is not yet fully implemented in Istar.

3.9 Browser Caching

Many browsers cache the pages they receive to reduce Internet message traffic. Before sending the HTTP 'GET /[url]' message the browser seeks '[url]' from the cache and, if there, displays it without sending the message. This presents both a problem and an opportunity for knowledge service.

The opportunity is that the user can bring up cached pages, such as that of an earlier question of the session to either review or change the answer. By hitting a different hyperlink a second answer to that question is sent. KBS forward chaining will normally cope well, but Istar's inference engine imposed an unnecessary ban on second answers, which was removed for the server version.

The problem is that running a KB several times, such as when wishing to vary the answers and see what effect that has on the results, can be unreliable. Sometimes a message is sent, but sometimes a cached 'page' is found and the user is presented with old information without being aware this has happened. One way of overcoming this is to insist that the user switches off browser caching while using the KB, but this would seem too harsh a constraint. Not only would many users not (know how to) do this, but during the session they might want to access other WWW pages in the normal, cached, manner. So the knowledge server should be designed so that every [url] reference in a page is unique, so that it will not be found in the cache. In Istar this is achieved by a combination of the unique session identifier with message timestamp.

Another problem is that browser users are free at any time to construct any URL. So a user might modify the URL of a previous question, and generate an inconsistency. For instance, a boolean question might receive an integer reply because the user has changed 'B' to 'I'. The server should be robust against any such eventuality.

More seriously, a user might change their user identifier to become that of another user, leading to interference between users, if the modified message happens to instantiate a question of a different user using the same KB. To overcome this, the session identifier should be unguessable; a random number is useful.

3.10 Integration with Local Use and Knowledge Engineer Facilities

Many commercial KBS toolkits offer two versions: for knowledge engineer and for user. Istar currently has only one version, and we decided to try to integrate local (graphical and window) input with server input. The elegant message port mechanism on the Amiga made this relatively easy to achieve.

So one running copy of Istar can be used by both distant clients and a local knowledge engineer at the same time. Though this would seldom happen in a main server, it offers practical usefulness. It allows quick checks to be made on the main server. And it aids preparation of KBs for server use: the knowledge engineer would build the KB, run it locally, then ask a colleague to connect to it via the server mechanism, and, working together, any changes necessary can be made immediately.

4. Results and Discussion

The Istar knowledge server has been running since summer 1999, quite robustly, and it feels fast to users. Currently, it offers around 6 KBs, but at the time of writing, all of them are draft versions, so a disclaimer is prominent on the welcome page. The KBs currently offered are those designed for local use, and no modification was required for server use. So the knowledge engineer does not need to know whether the KB is to be for local or Internet use, and thus can give full attention to domain knowledge. In this way, it has been possible to add knowledge server functionality that can make use of existing KBs. This is an advantage over, for instance, the Prolog engine described in [1] for which the knowledge engineer must write all the web-oriented interaction.

Users liked the simple hyperlink value input better than the forms input, because it was faster and more immediate. A trivial difference, perhaps, but it gave an impression of speed and a feeling of satisfaction. Allowing each user to alter their timeout period to suit their own needs also seemed user-friendly. The incorporation of hyperlinks in question, help and results pages seems useful, but the user probably needs strong cues to access such links. Placing hyperlinks in question texts would make them unsuitable for local use, so some versioning of texts would be desirable.

Provision of such knowledge servers allows KBS functionality on one platform to be made available on others. Until now, Istar could only be used on its native platform, the Amiga; now the knowledge in its KBs are available to all. Originally the knowledge server ran on a simple 6Mb 14MHz Amiga 1200, which could handle 4 to 6 concurrent clients comfortably. This is a tribute to the elegance and efficiency of the Amiga's multi-tasking operating system, its internal messaging, its lack of virtual memory overhead, and its Unix-like TCP stacks. (Istar itself consumes around 500k and each KB loaded consumes between 100k and 500k memory.) Being dedicated to the knowledge server, the machine can be run without TCP services like FTP and Telnet, so that security can be enhanced. Istar with Amiga provides a cost-effective, secure knowledge server hardware-software combination.

Giving Istar a server module has been relatively easy. But it has forced us to think about inference and generalise some concepts surrounding it, broadening and clarifying the concept of the inference session. It has helped us delineate more clearly the division of responsibility between knowledge engineer and KBS software.

4.1 Future Work

Provision of such a knowledge server opens up the possibility of making knowledge available to a variety of contexts and cultures, but little is known about the issues involved. So research is needed. Future development plans include more sophisticated results, password protection, multiple language texts, and full implementation of type-3 access to information pages. The latter is needed for the EPSRC project Intelligent Computation of Trust, which, it is hoped, will download Certification Practice Statements and analyse them.

Acknowledgements

Thanks are due to Tim Dean (DERA) and my colleague John Evans for stimulation and encouragement during development. I would also like to thank Martin Ansdell-Smith, network consultant, for technical guidance during development, my colleague Dave Chadwick for useful comments on this paper, and my wife, Ruth, for helping to check it. This project is partly funded by the EPSRC under grant number GR/L 54295.

References

1. Sehmi A, Kroening M. WebLS: A Custom Prolog Rule Engine for Providing Web-Based Tech Support. In: Proc. 1st Workshop on Logic Programming Tools for Internet Applications, in conjunction with JICSLP'96, Bonn, Germany, 2-6 Sep, 1996.
2. Shankararaman V, Poppon O, Corley S, Whittle B. An approach to intranet expert systems. In: Macintosh A, Milne R (eds.), Applications and

Innovations in Expert Systems V, SGES Publications, 1997, pp.197-206
ISBN 1 899621 19 9.

3. Cabeza D, Hermenegildo M, Varmaa S. The PiLLoW/CIAO Library for Internet/WWW Programming using Computational Logic Systems. In: Proc. 1st Workshop on Logic Programming Tools for Internet Applications, in conjunction with JICSLP'96, Bonn, Germany, 2-6 Sep, 1996.

4. Levy M R. Web programming in Guide. Software Practice and Experience, 1998, 28(15):1581-1603.

5. Boley H. Knowledge Bases in the World Wide Web: A Challenge for Logic Programming. Proc. 1st Workshop on Logic Programming Tools for Internet Applications, in conjunction with JICSLP'96, Bonn, Germany, 2-6 Sep, 1996.

6. Loke, S.W. Davison, A. Logic Programming with the World-Wide Web. Proceedings of the 7th ACM Conference on Hypertext, Washington DC, USA (Hypertext '96), pp 235-245. ACM Press, March 1996.

7. Basden A. On the application of Expert Systems. International Journal of Man-Machine Studies, 1983 19:461-477.

8. Johnson L B. CLIPS Reference Manual. NASA Software Technology Branch, 1993.

9. Cengeloglu Y. AGENT_CLIPS, http://users.aimnet.com/~yilsoft/yilsoft.html, 1999.

10. Maluf D. CKNP: CLIPS Knowledge Netowrking Protocol. http://www-db.stanford.edu/pub/ maluf/cknp/cknp.html, 1999.

11. Art*EnterpriseWeb. http://www.brightware.com/products/aeprodsum.html. 1999.

12. Berners-Lee T, Fielding R, Frystyk H. RFC 1945 Hypertext Transfer Protocol -- HTTP/1.0. 1996.

13. Basden A, Brown A J. Istar - a tool for creative design of knowledge bases. Expert Systems, 1996, 13(4):259-276.

14. Hibberd P, Basden A. Procurement and the use of intelligent systems of contract authoring. Proc. RICS COBRA Conference, Edinburgh September 1995.

15. Assistum. http://www.assistum.com. 1999.

CAPE: Extending CLIPS for the Internet

Robert Inder (R.Inder@ed.ac.uk)

Division of Informatics, University of Edinburgh

2 Buccleuch Place, Edinburgh EH8 9LW SCOTLAND

Abstract

This paper describes CAPE, a programming environment that combines Clips And Perl with Extensions. CLIPS is an efficient and expressive forward-chaining rule-based system with a flexible object system (supporting both message passing and generic functions). Perl is a popular procedural language with extremely powerful regular expression matching facilities, and a huge library of freely available software modules. CAPE closely integrates these two programming languages, and provides extensions to facilitate building systems with an intimate mixture of the two languages. These features make CAPE an excellent language for building knowledge-based systems to exploit the opportunities being presented by the Internet.

This paper describes the current version of CAPE and the facilities it offers programmers, including the demonstration systems and "component applications" that are distributed with it. The use of the system is then discussed with reference to DIME, a toolkit being developed to support identifying and coordinating the use of external knowledge sources, and illustrates its use in the construction of a system for retrieving images from the Internet on the basis of both the objective and subjective features of the content. Finally, planned developments of the system are indicated.

1 Introduction

Conventional Knowledge Based Systems (KBSS) involve the controlled manipulation of symbolic descriptions of the world. However, building those descriptions from raw data about the world is such a substantial challenge that work in KBSS has, as far as possible, sidesteped it.

Initially, KBSS worked with very restricted amounts of information (e.g. chess positions) presented in special formats. They started to achieve much wider use/acceptance when Expert Systems began asking questions, ("Has the patient got a rash?"), thereby exploiting the user's perceptual abilities and common sense to analyse the world into the abstract terms they required. Subsequently, KBSS began to access data, either statically (i.e. KBS linked to database) or by analysing real-time feeds (e.g. network monitoring). But while such systems determine what data is relevant, and when, they typically do so only within a fixed (or at least limited) range of data for which the format and semantics are known to their builders (or maintainers).

Now, we have the Internet, and ubiquitous global connectivity.

One effect of this is that any program has access to a previously inconceivable range of information from around the world—innumerable documents, including text, images and sound, plus a multitude of data sources offering everything from registered trade marks to dynamic feeds of stock prices. Conversely, that same program can easily be interrogated by huge numbers of both people and software systems, either synchronously (via the Web) or asynchronously by email.

Fully exploiting the opportunity that this presents—e.g. by building systems which can analyse and filter information for a particular purpose—will in several ways create a new breed of KBSS. The next section looks at some of the desirable features of a tool for building them. Section 3 then introduces CAPE, a programming system that provides many of these features and Section 4 describes DIME, a toolkit being developed in CAPE to support identifying and coordinating the use of external knowledge sources. Finally, Section 5 summarises the status of the system, and indicates directions for future work.

2 Objectives

The previous section highlighted the possibilities that the Internet offers the KBS builders. This section discusses the desirable features of a tool for exploiting those possibilities.

Clearly, whatever the features that may help work within an Internet environment, they should be *additions* to the features that make a good KBS development environment:

- Expressive language, with at least object-oriented information structuring

- Memory management

- Efficient symbolic reasoning mechanisms

- High-level tools (e.g. truth maintenance), and

- support for incremental program development and interactive debugging.

Any software system that starts to use the Internet will inevitably have to deal with a large, and rapidly growing, range of protocols and information formats. Fortunately, the Internet itself helps to solve this problem: by making software distribution easier, it has greatly increased the number of software packages which are readily accessible, including library components for more-or-less standard tasks, such as parsing standard document formats and mark-ups. It is particularly important that a tool for developing Internet-related systems has good support for incorporating code components of this sort.

The amount of material available on the Internet continues to grow at an astonishing pace. Only a tiny proportion of it is in a form that can be readily assimilated by a program: most is free text or "analogue" information (e.g. photographs) that a typical (symbolic) knowledge based system cannot directly handle. There has been a great deal of work done on data-intensive techniques which can handle material of this kind, such as neural nets, information retrieval, document clustering and other techniques for processing free text based on word occurrence statistics. But in a complex environment such as that of the Internet, there are clearly situations (e.g. when deciding what information to retrieve from which source) where techniques should be complemented by symbolic reasoning, within a so-called "hybrid" system. Building such a system on an existing implementation of such an algorithm will typically involve manipulating strings to construct control information and requests, and to analyse responses. It may also call for tools that support system-level operations, such as starting and stopping processes and managing files.

Even though most material on the Internet is best analysed within a hybrid system, there is still a huge amount that could be directly handled by a symbolic KBS. This information is typically in the form of tables and other more-or-less regular information presentations, such as lists, although this does not make it easy to access. Much of it is available as output from a search system, so that accessing it requires dealing with protocols, formats and exceptions. And almost all of it is designed for human readers to find attractive and concise, rather than for software to find straightforward or consistent. Moreover, its format is under independent control, likely to be subject to frequent revision without any meta data being available. While the ideal system for accessing this information would determine its structure for itself, any practical system must be easily configured by means of concise and comprehensible descriptions of sources of information. Analysing and handling material based on such descriptions will require powerful facilities for searching for words and phrases, recognising repeating structures and extracting content from them.

Finally, the Internet encourages one to make a system available as a "server" that users—or other programs (i.e. agents)—can contact as required. However, not all KBSS are well suited to starting on demand (e.g. for CGI), and many can require long periods of processing. An ideal KBS tool should support building processes that remain responsive while reasoning.

One way to achieve this is by extending an existing language which has some of the desired properties (e.g. by implementing a rule-based engine within Java, such as the Java Expert System Shell (Jess).[1]

The alternative is to combine two (or more) languages which each exhibit some of the desired properties into a single programming environment, in the manner of Poplog [1]. This is the approach adopted by CAPE.

3   CAPE

CAPE (**C**lips **A**nd **P**erl with **E**xtensions) is a programming environment which allows programs to be written in an intimate mixture of CLIPS (**C** Language Integrated **P**roduction **S**ystem [2]) rule-based and object-oriented language, and Perl [3], a very widely-used procedural programming language.

---

[1]See http://herzberg1.ca.sandia.gov/jess/

CLIPS was chosen because it closely integrates a very fast forward chaining rule-based system with a flexible object system (supporting both message passing and generic functions). CLIPS was initially a partial re-implementation, in C, of Inference Art [4], which was arguably the most powerful of the lisp-based "knowledge representation toolkits" that emerged during the nineteen-eighties. Its rule language features very powerful and efficient pattern matching facilities based on the RETE algorithm [5], and including the ability to match against the state of objects, and a truth maintenance mechanism. There is tutorial material for CLIPS in [6], and CLIPS itself is accessible via `http://www.ghgcorp.com/clips/`, along with detailed manuals and pointers to related software and information.

Perl was chosen because of its extremely powerful regular expression matching facilities, and its huge library of software modules freely available through the Comprehensive Perl Archive Network (CPAN).[2]. It also supports complex data structures, and (combinations of symbolic patterns), There are many books about Perl programming (e.g. [7]). The Perl system itself can be obtained via `http://www.perl.com/`, along with manuals and pointers to a huge quantity of related software and information.

Note that CAPE takes a fundamentally different approach to combining languages than that taken by Poplog. Poplog combined languages by creating a common virtual machine and implementing the various languages within it [8]. This allowed seamless integration with minimal performance overhead. In contrast, CAPE includes the standard language engines for both CLIPS and Perl. This has the advantage of ensuring that the functionality of these languages is provided correctly, so that all existing programs and libraries can be expected to work correctly. It also greatly reduces the implementation effort and maintenance effort, particularly when new features are added to the underlying languages.

3.1 Features of the Language

CAPE provides facilities for calling functions and exchanging basic data items between the two language sub-systems. CLIPS programs can call Perl subroutines, evaluate strings or match Perl regular expressions, on either the left- or right-hand side of a rule — that is, in either the condition or the action part — or from within the body of a CLIPS function or message handler. Perl programs can call functions defined in CLIPS—both normal functions and generic functions, send messages to CLIPS objects, and assert facts into CLIPS working memory. In addition, CAPE provides ...

Socket Handling CAPE provides a set of functions (in both CLIPS and Perl) for initiating and configuring Internet socket handling. The current state of port monitoring and socket connection is used to continually update a collection of CLIPS objects which are accessible from both languages and available for pattern matching in CLIPS rules. This means systems to provide services via an Internet port can be built using only CAPE alone.

---

[2]`http://www.perl.org/CPAN/CPAN.html`

The lowest level handling of socket activity is done in C within the core of CAPE. The relevant code is called after each rule firing by CLIPS's *run function* facility, which means that the CAPE application can remain responsive to socket activity while it is reasoning. Connections to any ports being monitored are accepted, and data from any current connections is buffered and passed to a connection-specific Perl function for filtering. This function could simply respond directly to the input received, but will typically map it into CLIPS working memory, thereby allowing the full power of the pattern matching to be used to decide when and how to respond.

CAPE Listener CAPE offers the user a read/eval/print loop, which prompts the user, reads a "chunk" of code, sends it for evaluation by either the Perl or Clips interpreter, and ensures that the result is printed. The appropriate interpreter for each "chunk" of code is selected purely on the selection of the first non-blank character, but CLIPS' lisp-like syntas means that this simplistic approach is adequate.

Pre-Processor Before CAPE passes any chunk of code to one of the underlying language systems for execution, it is first fed through a pre-processor, written in Perl, which can make arbitrary changes to the code. As yet, CAPE itself makes only limited use of this facility, to provide limited support for directly accessing Perl variables from within CLIPS code. However, because the pre-processor is written in Perl, it provides an easy way for CAPE programmers to use Perl's powerful pattern matching capabilities to extend CAPE (see Section 5).

The CLIPS rule engine has a very powerful mechanism for deciding which rule to fire at any point. This can be used to make extremely subtle and flexible decisions about the flow of control within the system—i.e. about what the CAPE application should do next. Doing this requires structuring the system as a whole as a rule-based system. Perl, supported by any relevant libraries, is then used to help analyse the information available to the system into symbols that CLIPS can then reason about, and to map the results of that reasoning into actions in the world. Such a system will also remain responsive to external events (e.g. socket activity), *provided* that the code executed by any particular rule does not take too long to run.

CAPE has been designed (and primarily tested and exercised) with this model of system operation in mind. However, there is no (known!) obstacle to building an "inverted" system — i.e. one in which overall control resides in a Perl program (or an interface generating call-backs into Perl), within which some subroutines specify or initiate rule-based reasoning.

4 DIME

Section 1 identified systems for retrieving and manipulating information as an important kind of application that the Internet makes possible. This section discusses implementing such a system in CAPE, and describes a set of tools being developed to support this process. It considers the specific example of a system to filter images on the internet on the basis of their content and subjective properties.

There is growing interest in the possibility of doing information retrieval (music, images, etc.) based on subjective features, or *kansei* [9–10]. Most work involves developing models that relate subjective terms to the properties of the object to which they are applied. For example, a system working with images might use a set of neural networks to map terms like "modern" or "romantic" to the objective properties of the images to which they apply [11]. Developing profiles or models of this kind is a substantial task, and it is essential that Internet-oriented system can incorporate or exploit existing work, rather than start from scratch.

However, a system for accessing images via the Internet must include much more than just a model of the relevant subjective properties. It must provide a range of further functionality:

- Supporting a user interface (e.g. via the Web), including result presentation
- Identifying the relevant information sources
- Formulating queries for a specific search engine
- Analysing responses to get URLs and details
- Tracking which results have been fetched
- Dealing with network errors
- Choosing to fetch more data, and how
- Keeping copies of information, to help system development and training learning algorithms.

These include a number of standard tasks, for which libraries are readily available: in particular, fetching information via the Web, storing and indexing local copies, and providing a user interface and service via the Web. One could simply add this functionality to an existing kansei modelling system. However, the need to exploit new types of model as they emerge argues for implementing it as a general framework within which arbitrary kansei models can be used.

DIME, the **D**istributed **I**nformation **M**anipulation **E**nvironment, is just such a framework. It is a collection of CAPE modules that are being developed into a general-purpose toolkit for coordinating the operation of external knowledge sources, or "oracles", in order to locate relevant information, retrieve it and filter it as required by the user. It is designed to allow further oracles—such as image databases or Kansei models—to be added easily.

It currently includes five main software components:

Web Server: This component supports listening for and accepting Web requests, analysing them, and mapping acceptable requests into CLIPS memory. It can also analyse HTML forms and map field contents into CLIPS facts. This makes it possible for an application to accept requests from the user simply using rules that match against the contents of a form. Finally, the Server will generate a standard Web (HTTP) error responses to unacceptable requests, and has functions to facilitate generating other HTTP responses (for example, re-directions), including sending files as replies.

Document Cache: The cache is intended to transparently support the development of Web-accessing software. It uses standard Perl libraries for fetching documents, but they are accessed through a particularly flexible caching mechanism which is designed to hold multiple versions of the same document, including the results of queries. The cache includes a number of functions for analysing cached documents in various ways. Moreover, its re-fetch behaviour can be controlled, which makes it easy to transparently run a piece of software repeatedly on a stable set of data from the Internet, but without loading (or relying on) the remote server. This is very useful for system development, or for training a learning algorithm.

Form Filling: This component provides a formalism for describing an HTML form, in terms of the fields it contains and the effects of completing them. Given a domain model, it can take a set of constraints and descriptions of a number of candidate search forms, and choose the best way of completing a form in order to express the given constraints. In doing so, it handles conflicting ways of completing the same form, including choosing values for fields which affect the behaviour of other fields (e.g. specifying whether to search for all or any of the words given)

Remote Information Retrieval: This code controls the process of fetching batches of information from remote sources, such as indexing engines. It provides a framework for specifying the properties of a remote search interface. This includes the way a query must be formatted and the address (URL) to be used to submit it; regular expressions and customised functions for analysing the results obtained; and functions (methods) for extracting the contents of the pages of results.

Test Suite: The test suite supports regression testing of CAPE systems. It takes a declarative definition of a set of tests and then executes them produce a file of test results. These results are compared with two "reference" sets, with the differences reported. Each test is defined in terms of one or more functions to be called, and one or more facts to be asserted. Test specifications also include limits to the expected number of rule firings that should occur, with failure to stay within limits being taken as an indication of a major problem.

The Web Server and Test Suite are already parts of the CAPE distribution: the others will be added as they become stable.

DIME is currently being used to develop two research systems. One is Maxwell, a "smart" agent intended to both query and combine the results from a number of book vendors databases on behalf of the user. An initial version of Maxwell was implemented in Emacs Lisp (see [12] and [13]), and

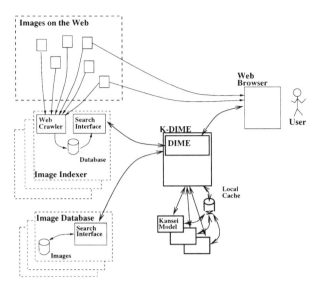

Figure 1: The K-DIME System

a more powerful version is currently being implemented in CAPE using DIME. The other is K-DIME, or Kansei DIME [14], which is concerned with fetching and filtering images based on subjective criteria, or kansei.

Both systems act as a bridge between users, databases and domain-specific processing—"black box" kansei models for K-DIME, and knowledge of book identification for Maxwell. The core of both systems coordinates the use of the various components of DIME in order to identify relevant items from range of sources and assess their properties appropriately for the user. They are designed to allow further knowledge sources—such as databases or filtering "oracles"—to be added easily.

Figure 1 shows the overall architecture of K-DIME, and a broadly similar diagram would also apply to the highest level of Maxwell. Both systems are accessed via the Web, via a user interface supported by the DIME Web Server component. They provide HTML forms with which users can identify themselves and specify their interests/requirements. The forms are sent directly to CAPE (i.e. without involving a conventional Web server) using the Hypertext Transfer Protocol (HTTP), the normal Web information transfer protocol.

On receiving a query, the systems will analyse it and use DIME's form-filling module to generate a query to one or more existing search engines or databases. DIME's Remote Information Retrieval module then submits these queries through the search engine's normal (human-oriented) Web interface—i.e. CAPE appears to these systems as just an "ordinary" user. The results from the search system are typically split across a number of normal (HTML) Web pages which are designed to appeal and communicate to a human reader.

The pages are added to DIME's document cache, which can be easily config-

```
! initial_port('http-request',1200, 1210);

(deffacts configuration
  (allowed-request query "^/query" 100 no-op user-query))

;;;

(defrule make-a-query-object
  (http-request-info
      (id ?req-id)
      (time ?t)
      (connection ?conn))
  (form-field ?req-id ?conn user-query UserEmail ?email)
  (form-field ?req-id ?conn user-query SearchTerm ?term&~"")
  (test (p-match-p ?email ".+\\@.*\\.[A-Za-z]+$"))
  =>
  (make-instance (gensym query) of query
(status new)
(http-request ?req-id)
(email-address ?email)
(search-term ?email))
```

Figure 2: A rule for starting to process a web query

ured to allow queries to be re-run during software development without loading the remote system. The document cache can also analyse documents on the basis of Perl regular expressions, for instance, to extract the parameters the Remote Information Retrieval module needs to control paging through a batch of results. Applications will also use these mechanisms to extract information such as the URLs, descriptions or other details of the items that the remote image database or search engine has identified. The information extracted from the documents is then available to (i.e. can trigger CLIPS rules in) the domain-level part of the system.

DIME aims to ensure that, as far as possible, CAPE systems can be written in terms of rules that focus purely on the domain level, without reference to the mechanics of fetching or searching documents. To illustrate the extent to which this is being achieved, Figure 4 shows the rule used for accepting a request from a user via the Web Server component. For this to work, the system must first be configured, as shown by the first two lines in the figure. The first line tells CAPE to listen at the first free port in the range 1200–1210, and tag input from any connections received as an http-request. The second line tells DIME's Web Server that HTTP requests sent to URLs starting with /query should be accepted, and forms they contain should be tagged as user-query. Once this has been done, the rule shown will fire whenever a form is submitted that contains a legitimate UserEmail field and a non-blank SearchTerm field. Note the use of a Perl regular expression to validate the email address given.

5 Status & Future Work

CAPE is a new tool which brings together two very different programming systems. As such, there are inevitably a number of minor inconsistencies and omissions that reveal the immaturity of the system. Nevertheless, the core functionality of the current version of the system has been stable since the spring of 1998, and, as described above, the system itself has been used for the development of substantial research systems since the following summer.

Since CAPE is available free-of-charge, it does not come with any support. This is a drawback compared to broadly comparable commercial products. Against this, both Perl and CLIPS are long established and widely used, and support of them is available through active mailing lists. Moreover, CAPE itself is very small (the core CAPE environment comprises 3000 lines of C code, plus 600 lines of Perl or CLIPS) and all source code is distributed with the system. As a result, CAPE is a sound choice for system developers who have the IT skills needed to exploit these resources, or can call on support from those who do, or on a commercial basis.

CAPE comes with a thirty-one page manual [16]. The distribution currently also includes 1500 lines of CAPE code in two standard CAPE "component applications", or "Capplets" (support for regression testing CAPE applications and a simple Web server), and three demonstration applications:

Handshaking: A minimal demonstration of communication between a pair of CAPE processes. An "interface agent" accepts user requests (via HTTP) for commands to be executed, and forwards them to the relevant "execution agent", which executes them in due course. The execution agent then contacts the interface agent with the results, which it then forwards to the user.

Web server This application operates as a simple web server. It accepts a limited set of HTTP requests, locates the relevant file and then replies with either an appropriate HTTP response—either an error, or the contents of the requested file (along with appropriate HTTP header information). However, the server also allows users to specify ((using an HTML form that it generates) required transformations to pages, which are then subsequently applied to the pages being served. This demonstration system, which uses the "webserve" component application, is about 350 lines of code.

"Dungeon" This application, which was build from scratch in five days (and pre-dates the web-server component) provides a real-time multi-user "dungeon" simulation. One can use a web browser to direct the actions of one of a number of "characters", moving about, manipulating objects and encountering other characters, either controlled by other players, or by the computer. All descriptions of situations are generated from information structures (i.e. there is no "canned" text) based on the objects and locations known to the user. Computer-controlled characters can generate and follow multi-step plans.

CAPE runs under a number of versions of UNIX, including Solaris and Linux. A version was first made available by FTP and announced on the Web in February 1999, and has been being downloaded by about one person per day since then.

The main shortcoming of CAPE is the fact that CLIPS and Perl have different syntaxes, CLIPS being lisp-like and Perl being generally C-like. This unfortunately means that fully exploiting CAPE requires achieving reasonable proficiency in both languages, *and* in working with more than one language at a time (when programming, it is easy to write fragments of the "wrong" language). A single "unified" syntax is therefore clearly desirable, although defining it is non-trivial, since Perl syntax is already complex and very "dense" (in the sense that a great many characters and character combinations are already assigned meanings).

There are a number of other obvious extensions to CAPE, some of which will be added to the system in the near future.

- Use a combination of CLIPS's ability to handle references to external data structures, and its generic functions, could be used to give CLIPS procedural code access to Perl's flexible data structuring.

- Use the newly-added pre-processing mechanism to give CLIPS backward chaining and relationships properties (e.g. symmetry, inverses).

- Provide tighter integration in those areas where CLIPS and Perl provide closely related functionality: modules, object and I/O systems.

- Support the implementation of autonomous agents by supporting timed events, the KQML agent-communication standard, and the controlled mapping of specific kinds of information between CLIPS working memory and (ideally shared) persistent store

- Exploit Perl's ability to support multiple threads.

6 Conclusion

CAPE is a powerful tool for building a new generation of KBSS. It provides powerful mechanisms to support a number of key activities:

Symbolic reasoning CLIPS offers a very efficient forward chaining rule-based system with extremely expressive pattern matching, coupled with a highly flexible object-oriented system and supported by a truth-maintenance system.

Data analysis/manipulation Perl has extremely powerful regular expression matching coupled with very concise string handling and easy-to-use hash-based index-building and data structuring.

Service Provision CAPE's socket monitoring mechanisms allow a rule-based program to remain responsive to external activity even while it is reasoning.

Standard languages/libraries CAPE programs can use any of the enormous range of software available in CPAN, the Comprehensive Perl Archive Network (accessible via http://www.perl.com/).

Interaction with software packages Perl provides very concise and flexible mechanisms for controlling and processing the results obtained from system commands and other external programs. CAPE programmers can also exploit the tools for generating Perl "wrappers" for software components written in C, and make use of Perl's ability to dynamically load compiled code at run-time.

CAPE is a powerful tool for building KBSS that can exploit the opportunities offered by the Internet. Download it now!

Acknowledgements

CAPE was developed while the author was supported by a NEDO Visiting Researcher fellowship at the Electrotechnical Laboratory (ETL) in Tsukuba, Japan. Matt Hurst helped greatly with bug hunting in the early stages, and [7] was invaluable!

References

[1] A. Sloman and S. Hardy. "Poplog: A Multi-Purpose Multi-Language Program Development Environment" AISB Quarterly, Vol 47, pp26–34, 1983.

[2] Gary Riley, "Clips: An Expert System Building Tool". Proceedings of the Technology 2001 Conference, San Jose, CA, 1991

[3] L. Wall, T. Christiansen and R. Schwartz, *Programming Perl (2nd Edn.)* O'Reilly and Associates, 1996.

[4] R. Inder, "State of the ART: A review of the Automated Reasoning Tool." In *Expert System Applications*, S. Vadera (ed), Sigma Press, Wilmslow, 1989. Also available as AIAI-TR-41.

[5] Charles L. Forgy, "Rete: A Fast Algorithm for the Many Pattern/Many Object Pattern Match Problem", Artificial Intelligence 19(1982), 17-37.

[6] J. Giarratano and G. Riley, "Expert Systems: Principles and Programming, 2nd Edition". PWS Publishing Company, 1994

[7] S. Srinivasan, "Advanced Perl Programming". O'Reilly and Associates, 1997.

[8] Robert Smith, Aaron Sloman and John Gibson, "POPLOG's Two-level Virtual Machine Support for Interactive Languages". Cognitive Science Research Paper 153, School of Cognitive and Computing Sciences, University of Sussex, 1983.

[9] S. Lee and A. Harada. "A Design Approach by Objective and Subjective Evaluation of Kansei Information". In *Proc. Intl Workshop on Robot and Human Communication (RoMan'98)*, Hakamatsu, Japan (pp. 327–332). IEEE Press, 1998.

[10] T. Shibata and T. Kato. "Modeling of Subjective Interpretation for Street Landscape Image." In G. Quirchmayr, G, Schweighofer and T.J.M Bench-Capon (eds) *Proc. Intl Conference on Database and Expert Systems Applications*, Lecture Notes in Computer Science, pp501–510. Springer, Austria, 1998.

[11] N. Bianchi-Berthouze, L. Berthouze, and T. Kato, T. "Towards a Comprehensive Integration of Subjective Parameters in Database Browsing." In Y. Kambayashi et. al (Eds.), *Advanced Database Systems for Integration of Media and User Environments.* pp.227-232). World Scientific, Singapore, 1998.

[12] Robert Inder and Toshikazu Kato, "Towards Shoppers' Assistants: Agents to Combine Information". In *Advanced Database Systems for Integration of Media and User Environments 98*, Y. Kambayashi (ed.), World Scientific, February 1998.

[13] Robert Inder, Matthew Hurst and Toshikazu Kato, ``A Prototype Agent to Assist Shoppers'' in *Computer Networks and ISDN Systems*, V30 (1998), pp 643–645. Also appeared as a short paper in *Proceedings of WWW7*. Full version available as *Technical Report ETL-TR98-3*, Electrotechnical Laboratory, Tsukuba, Japan.

[14] Robert Inder, Nadia Bianchi and Toshikazu Kato, "K-DIME: A Software Framework for Kansei Filtering of Internet Material" Proceedings of IEEE Systems Man and Cybernetics, 1999.

[15] N. Bianchi-Berthouze and T. Kato "An Interactive Visual Environment to Understand, Model and Exploit User Subjectivity in Image Retrieval". In *Proc. ICIAP'99*, Venice, Italy, September 1999.

[16] Robert Inder. CAPE *Users Manual.* ETL Technical Report ETL-TR98-3,[3] Electrotechnical Laboratory, Tsukuba, Japan.

---

[3]The most recent version is always available via http://www.hcrc.ed.ac.uk/~robert/CAPE/manual.ps

SESSION 5
KNOWLEDGE REPRESENTATION AND REFINEMENT

Approach to Active Knowledge Based Scene Exploration

U. Ahlrichs, J. Fischer, D. Paulus, H. Niemann
Lehrstuhl für Mustererkennung (Informatik 5)
Universität Erlangen-Nürnberg
Martensstraße 3, 91058 Erlangen, Germany

Abstract

In almost every knowledge based image analysis system the knowledge base serves as model for the application domain and is used during the interpretation of the images. However, in visual based scene exploration a system needs the ability to perform camera movements, because objects may not be visible with the initial camera setting. Nevertheless, most of the known systems lack a representation of such movements which are necessary to acquire missing information. In this paper we will show how to integrate these (camera) movements into a conventional knowledge base using a semantic network formalism. To use the knowledge during the interpretation, an iterative control algorithm is applied which has any-time capabilities. This control algorithm was extended in order to deal with the actions which have been integrated into the knowledge base.

The suitability of the approach is verified by experiments in which an office scene is explored with an active camera. These experiments revealed, that in 93 % of all cases the objects were found correctly.

1 Introduction

In the near future autonomous mobile systems which use visual information will become more and more important for daily life. Examples for systems which carry out simple routine tasks like the transportation of mail, books or dishes can be found in [1]. In order to fulfill such tasks the system has to be able to interpret an image and perform actions to acquire information which is not available in the current image, but is needed for the task to be accomplished. If, for example, the robot wants to localize an object and this object is not visible in the initial camera set-up, the camera parameters have to be changed and the object localization starts with the new image. Another example is the modification of focus, if the image is blurred, or the modification of zoom, if small objects cannot be reliably recognized. The strategy which suggests these adaptations of camera parameters is called *active vision* [2]. The goal is to change the camera parameters such that they are suitable for following processing steps, e.g. the image interpretation. The criterion of suitability has to be defined according to the task of the system.

In order to explore the environment autonomous systems use knowledge about the objects which are important for the task to be performed, and about the scene. In this paper a new approach is presented which combines the traditional representation of knowledge about objects and the scene with camera actions as suggested by the strategy of active vision. A camera action corresponds to a selection of new camera parameters or the move of the camera. The knowledge about scene information and camera actions is *uniformly* represented in *one* knowledge base using a semantic network formalism.

In classical image analysis, of course, many systems like VISIONS [3], SPAM [4] or SIGMA [5] are known which use information represented in a knowlegde base. But all these systems lack a representation of camera actions. Related work on the selection and performance of actions using Bayesian networks can be found in [6, 7]. Examples of approaches for uniform representation of actions and knowledge about the task domain are the situation calculus or decision networks, see [8, 9] for an overview or [10] for an example using Bayesian networks. We found the semantic network representation formalism particularly suitable for the description of objects [11], of medical decisions [12], and of a dialogue system [13], and prefer this formalism to a uniform description using e.g. Bayesian networks which give a less obvious object representation [10].

In order to make use of the represented knowledge about the scene, a control algorithm has to be provided. We proposed an iterative control algorithm which is particularly suitable for the application domain because of its any-time capabilities [14]. This algorithm was originally developed for pattern interpretation tasks. Here we demonstrate how we extended this control algorithm in order to handle the camera actions represented in the very same framework and allow an active scene exploration.

After an outline of the problem we deal with in section 2 we describe the knowledge representation formalism in section 3. In section 4 we explain the representation of actions. We outline the iterative control used in section 5 and its extension to actions in section 6. Finally, we demonstrate the feasibility and efficiency of our approach by means of experiments with a system for office scene exploration (section 7).

2 Problem Description

The problem which has to be solved by our system is the exploration of arbitrary office scenes with static objects, i.e. motion of objects is not modelled. The goal is to find pre–defined objects in these scenes where the location of the objects is not restricted. Since the main contribution of the approach is on the conceptional work to integrate the camera actions into the knowledge base, only a simplified task for object recognition is choosen in the experiments. Three red objects, a punch, a gluestick and an adhesive tape are used as shown below. These objects need not be visible in the initial set-up which makes it necessary to perform camera movements to search for the objects. Since these movements are time-consuming, efficient strategies are needed to choose the next camera setting or to determine if a camera movement should be performed at all. The decision where to look next relies heavily on the objects which have been found already in the scene. This motivated the design of a knowledge base which contains both, the knowledge which is needed for identifying the objects, and the information about search strategies.

3 The Knowledge Representation Scheme

For the representation of task–specific knowledge we propose our semantic network formalism [15, 16] which provides the following types of network *nodes*:

- *Concepts* representing abstract terms, events, tasks, actions, etc.;

- *Instances* representing actual realizations of concepts in the sensor data;

- *Modified Concepts* representing concepts that are modified by restrictions arising from intermediate results (i.e., the interpretation of part of the sensor data leads to restrictions on the interpretation of the remaining sensor data).

There are also the following network *links*:

- *Part Links* connecting concepts to the parts they consist of;

- *Concrete Links* connecting concepts on different *levels of abstraction*;

- *Specialization Links* establishing inheritance relations from general concepts to more specific ones.

Thus, our *knowledge model* is a network of concepts linked to each other by the various types of links.

Since there may be many different possibilities for the realizations of a concept, *modalities* have been introduced[1] with the implication that each individual modality may define the concept. Examples will follow in section 4. Furthermore, parts of a concept may be defined as being *obligatory* or *optional*.

For the definition of properties or features, a concept has a set of *attributes*. There may also be *relations* between the attributes of a concept. Each attribute references a function which computes its value and a judgment function which computes a measure of confidence for the attribute value. During the computation of an instance (i.e. the instantiation of a concept) values for all attributes, relations and the corresponding judgment values are calculated; therefore a concept can only be instantiated if instances for all obligatory parts and concretes of the concept have been computed before in previous analysis steps.

Due to errors in the image segmentation (arising from noise and processing errors) and ambiguities in the knowledge base (arising, for example, from the various modalities), competing instances may be computed for a single concept. In order to measure the degree of confidence of an instance, a *judgment* function is needed (and included into the definition of a concept). In most cases this judgment function combines the judgment of the attributes, relations, and the instances of the parts and concretes of a concept.

The goal of the analysis is represented by one or more concepts, the *goal concepts*. Subsequently, an interpretation of the whole sensor data is represented

---

[1] Another possibility for the representation of different concept realizations is to define a concept for each realization; this, however, inhibits a compact knowledge representation.

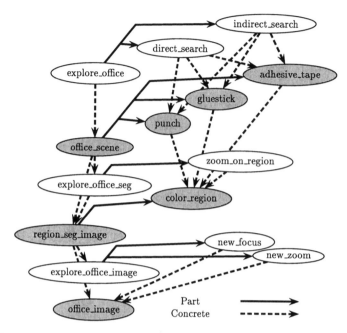

Fig. 1: Semantic network which combines the representation of camera actions (white ovals) with the representation of the scene (gray ovals). In addition, the network contains generalizations for some concepts, which are left out to keep up clarity.

by an instance of a goal concept. Now, in order to find the 'best' interpretation, the computation of an *optimal instance* of a goal concept with respect to the judgment function of the corresponding concept is required. In our approach the interpretation problem is viewed as a combinatorial optimization problem and solved as such (section 5).

4 Embedding Camera Actions into the Knowledge Base

4.1 Declarative Knowledge

The structure of the knowledge base of our application domain is shown in Fig. 1. As we have motivated in the introduction, the knowledge base unifies the representation of objects and their relations and the representation of camera actions on different levels of abstraction. The gray ovals represent information which would be found in almost any conventional knowledge base on this matter. This set of concepts contains, for example, the objects of the application domain, e.g. the concepts "punch", "gluestick" or "adhesive_tape" and their concrete representation which modelled by the concept "color_region".

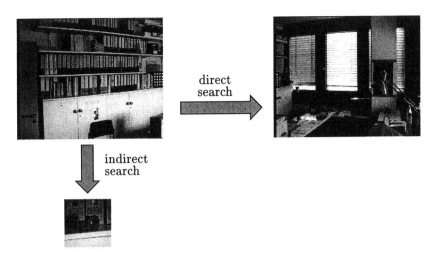

Fig. 2: Difference between indirect and direct search.

The concepts representing the objects are parts of the concept "office_scene"[2].

In addition to the representation of scene concepts, concepts for camera actions are integrated into the knowledge base. On the highest level of abstraction one can find camera actions which are equivalent to search procedures and which are used to find objects in a scene. The first example is the concept "direct_search". Each instantiation of this concept computes a new pan angle and a new zoom for the camera in such a way, that overview images, which are images captured with a small focal length, are obtained. If we look at all overview images as one image, we get a scan of the whole scene. The second example is the concept "indirect_search". This concept represents an indirect search [17], that is the search for an object using an intermediate object which is the punch in our application domain. Usually, large objects like tables or book shelves are used as intermediate objects. These objects have in common that they are relatively large and therefore can be found in an image captured with a small focal length. This is advantageous because less images are necessary to scan a whole scene. An example for the effect of direct and indirect search is depicted in Fig. 2. Using direct search a second overview images is taken, using indirect search with the cupboard as an intermediate object a close-up view of an area above the cupboard is generated. In our application the indirect search is performed only if we have already found an adhesive tape and a punch and we are searching for the gluestick. Recall that the punch is choosen as intermediate object in our application.

On the intermediate level of abstraction in Fig. 1, the camera action "zoom_on_region" can be found. The effect of this action is the fovealization of regions which are hypotheses for the objects the system is searching for. During the fovealization the pan angle and the zoom of the camera are adjusted in such a way that the region can be found in the middle of an image afterwards and

---

[2]In the following the "_seg" part of the concept names stands for segmentation.

is larger than before fovealization. The fovealization bases on the observation that the regions which are found in the overview images are too small for a good verification. Images taken after fovealization are called close-up views.

On the lowest level of abstraction camera actions are modelled which are performed data-driven and are independent of the application domain. The focus of a camera, for example, has to be adjusted in order to get sharp images. Furthermore, the zoom setting has to be chosen in such a way that not only one homogeneous region is in the image.

Recall that the instantiation of a camera action concept leads to the selection of new camera parameters or the performance of a camera action. So, only one of the camera action concepts can be instantiated in a single step. In order to represent competing camera actions, i.e. actions which can not be performed at the same time, we make use of modalities (section 3). For example, the concept "explore_office" has as parts the concepts "direct_search" and "indirect_search", each of them is represented in one modality of "explore_office". The concept "region_seg_image" is another example for a concept which contains two modalities, one for "explore_office_image" and one for "office_image". In section 5 we explain how we deal with the ambiguities arising from the modalities.

4.2 Procedural Knowledge

In addition to declarative knowledge, each concept contains procedural knowledge which consists of the functions for value and judgment value computation of attributes, relations, and instances (section 3).

In the concepts of our scene representation, for example, functions for attribute value computation are defined which compute the color of a region (in the concept "color_region") or the height and the width of an object (in the concepts "punch", "gluestick" and "adhesive_tape"). In addition, each of these concepts contains attributes for the focal length and for the distance of the represented object refering to the close-up views of the objects.

A management of uncertainty is provided by the control based on the judgment functions (section 5). In order to rate the different camera actions, a utility-based approach is applied [18]. Probabilities are used to estimate the instances of the scene concepts "punch", "gluestick" and "adhesive_tape" because the utility measure relies on the evidence if an object has been found during analysis. The probabilities are calculated using a priori trained normal distributions for the individual attributes, the height, and the width of the objects. During training we calculate the mean and variance of these attributes for each object using 40 images.

5 Parallel Iterative Control

Our control algorithm [13, 14] treats the search for an optimal interpretation and for optimal camera actions as a *combinatorial* optimization problem and solves it by means of *iterative* optimization methods, e.g. simulated annealing, stochastic relaxation, and genetic algorithms. One advantage of this algorithm is its *any–time* capability. After each iteration step a (sub–)optimal solution is available and this solution can be improved by performing more iterations.

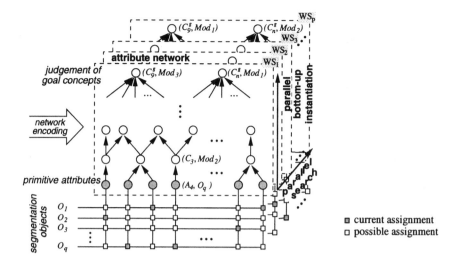

Fig. 3: Scheme of the parallel iterative control algorithm.

If we have got enough time for analysis, the optimal solution is always found. Another advantage is that the algorithm allows an efficient exploitation of *parallelism* by automatically compiling the concept–centered semantic network into a fine–grained task–graph, the so–called *attribute network*. This network represents the dependencies of all attributes, relations, and judgments of concepts to be considered for the computation of goal instances. In Fig. 3 a schema of the parallel iterative control is shown. In following we explain how the control works principally. The attribute network is automatically generated in two steps from the semantic network:

- **Expansion** First the semantic network is expanded top-down such that all concepts which are necessary for the instantiation of the goal concepts exist. Concepts which have more than one predecessor in the network like the concept "color_region" in Fig. 1 are duplicated.

- **Refinement** The expanded network is refined by the determination of dependencies between sub–conceptual entities (attributes, relations, judgments, etc.) of all concepts in the expanded network. These sub–conceptual entities are represented by the nodes of the attribute network and the dependencies between them by the links.

Both steps are executed automatically in advance to search and depend only on the syntax of the semantic network representation. Nodes without predecessors (*primitive attributes* in Fig. 3) represent attributes that provide an interface to the initial segmentation (for example color regions), and nodes without successors (*judgment of goal concepts* in Fig. 3) represent the judgments (i.e. confidence measures) of goal concepts. Now, for the computation of instances of the goal concepts, all nodes of the attribute network are processed in a single bottom–up step. Therefore the flow of information is fixed from the primitive attribute node to the judgment nodes of the goal concepts. This bottom–up instantiation corresponds to a single iteration of the iterative optimization.

Parallelism can be exploited on the network and on the control level. Each node of the network for example may be mapped to a multiprocessor system for parallel processing (depicted in Fig. 3 as *parallel bottom–up instantiation*). In addition, several competing instances of the goal concepts may be computed in parallel on several workstations. This is shown in Fig. 3 as *parallel search* on p workstations $WS_1, \ldots, WS_p$.

The search space the control algorithm has to deal with is determined by the competing segmentation results which arise, for example, from an erroneous segmentation, and by the different modalities of the concepts in the knowledge base (section 3). Recall that in our application domain the segmentation results are the color regions and the modalities determine which camera action is performed, e.g. the indirect or the direct search. In addition, we define the *current state of analysis* of our combinatorial optimization as a vector r which contains the assignment of segmentation results to primitive attributes and the choice of a modality for each (ambiguous) concept:

$$r = \left[(A_i, O_j^{(i)}); (C_k, Mod_l^{(k)}) \right]^T$$
$$\text{with } i = 1, \ldots, m \; ; \; k = 1, \ldots, n \; .$$

where m denotes the number of primitive attributes, j the index of the segmentation results, k the number of concepts in the semantic network, and l the index of the modality for each corresponding concept. In each iteration step judgments for the goal concepts are computed for the actual state of analysis. After an iteration step one randomly chosen entry of the analysis vector is changed. For example another segmentation result is bound to a primitive attribute node. Furthermore, a *performance function* for the state of analysis vector is introduced. The task of the control algorithm is now to optimize the performance function, i.e. to find *that* state of analysis which leads to the best interpretation, i.e. to an optimal instance of a goal concept.

Fig. 3 shows, for example, that in the current state of analysis for which the attribute network is computed on the first workstation (WS_1), the segmentation object O_q is assigned to the primitive attribute node A_4, modality 2 is assigned to the concept C_3, and modality 3 and modality 1 are assigned to the concepts C_9 and C_n, respectively, which are goal concepts (thus stated as C_9^g and C_n^g). Furthermore, it is shown that different instances (recall that the computation of instances depends only on the current state of analysis) are computed on the several workstations: the current state of analysis for which instances are computed on workstation p (WS_p) differs from that on WS_1 at least by the assignment of different modalities to the goal concepts C_9^g and C_n^g.

In our current application we have only one goal concept, which is "explore_office", and the performance function corresponds to the judgment function of this concept.

6 Expanding the Control to Actions

The goal in our application is to instantiate the concept "explore_office". Therefore we *alternately* have to interpret the image data and perform camera ac-

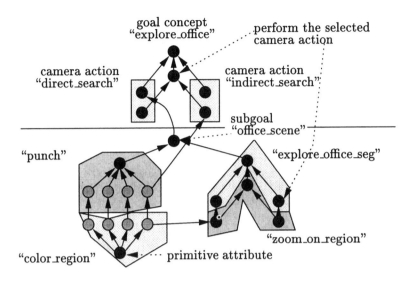

Fig. 4: Excerpt of the attribute network for the knowledge base depicted in Fig. 1 showing a subset of the network for the concepts "explore_office" and "office_scene". Only the most important arrows are shown.

tions. This alternating computation cannot directly be expressed by either the syntax of the semantic network nor by the attribute network. This means that we have to extend the *control algorithm.*

If we compute the whole attribute network for our goal concept in one bottom–up step as described in section 5, we select the camera actions "direct_search" or "indirect_search" possibly without an optimal interpretation of the concepts "punch", "gluestick" and "adhesive_tape". This makes no sense, because we first need to find an optimal interpretation for the view under the actual camera setting, before deciding which camera action has to be performed next. In addition, if we instantiate the concept "new_zoom" and then go on with the bottom–up computation of the attribute network we get an instance of "explore_office" based on image data which was taken with the old zoom.

In order to solve these problems, the control for the bottom–up instantiation of the attribute network is extended as it was already successfully demonstrated for an application with a speech dialog system [13]. The instantiation is divided into several data driven instantiations of subnets of the attribute network. The division is initiated by specifying subgoals prior to the computation of the attribute network which has to be done by the user once before the system is run. From these subgoals, the subnets can be automatically derived by the network encoder. This induces a partial order of the subgoals in the attribute network. Initial subgoals are chosen from the lowest level in the network. Analysis starts by the instantiation of the initial subgoal. This means that the bottom-up computation of the corresponding subnet is iterated until an optimum is found. Afterwards, the control chooses the next subgoal to be instantiated, and so on. This process continues until an optimal instance of the "explore_office" is found.

To give an example: If the user chooses, for example, the concepts "region_seg_image" and "office_scene" as subgoals, the control starts finding the best instance of "region_seg_image". Afterwards, it searches for the best instance of "office_scene". Once this instance has been found, the subnet which belongs to the goal concept "explore_office" is instantiated. This is done until the goal concept, that is "explore_office", is reached or a camera action is performed. If the judgment of the instance of the "explore_office" is below an application dependent threshold, the control starts again with the subgoal "region_seg_image". In Fig. 4 the subnets belonging to "explore_office" and to "office_scene" are depicted. The excerpt of the attribute network shows a part of the expanded knowledge base described in Fig. 1. Thus, we have three modified concepts of "color_region" which are bound to the concepts "punch", "gluestick" and "adhesive_tape". The highlighted areas contain the attributes which belong to the corresponding concepts. In addition, camera actions are performed by computing the attribute pan of concept "explore_office" and concept "explore_office_seg".

Fig. 4 depicts two subnets, one above the horizontal line, one below. The upper subnet belongs to the concept "explore_office" and shows the attributes required for the instantiation of that concept. Attributes originating from one concept are boxed and highlighted. The lower subnet explains the relations of attributes used to instantiate the subgoal "office_scene". Three modified concepts of "color_region" are bound to the concepts "punch", "gluestick" and "adhesive_tape"; only one ("punch") is depicted in the figure for simplicity. Depending on the state of analysis, a zoom camera action is performed if the color region assigned to the primitive attribute is too small.

7 Experimental Results

So far the lower part of the knowledge base in Fig. 1 is provided as one module. This part contains the concepts "office_image", "new_zoom", "new_focus", "explore_office_image", "explore_office_seg", and "zoom_on_region". In this module hypotheses for the red objects are computed by a histogram backprojection [19] which is applied to an overview image taken with the minimal focal length of the camera (cf. Fig. 5). In order to verify these hypotheses they are fovealized by moving the camera and varying the camera's focal length. This is exactly the task of the lower part of the knowledge base shown in Fig. 1. The hypotheses correspond to color regions which are the input of the primitive concept "color_region" of the semantic network. Thus, the primitive concept serves as interface to the module performing the task of the lower part of the knowledge base.

The suitability of the approach has been tested in 20 experiments while performing explorations in two different offices. In each experiment the objects were positioned at different places. Ten experiments took place in office_1 and

Fig. 5: Overview images of two different office scenes (office_1 on the left, office_2 on the right). The close-up views below the overview images show fovealized object hypotheses.

	number of iterations N_i				
	10	30	50	100	150
office_1	57 %	82 %	93 %	93 %	93 %
office_2	13 %	46 %	54 %	70 %	79 %

Table 1: Percentage of correct recognized objects.

the other ten in office_2. In the experiments, seven red objects are used, where three of them are modelled in the knowledge base. These three objects which are interesting for the interpretation step were hypothesized in 54 cases of 60 possible ones by the data driven hypotheses generation module using histogram backprojection. On average six close-up views were generated, that is, six object hypotheses were found in each overview image. The search space for the iterative control algorithm was reduced by restrictions concerning the color of the objects. These restrictions were propagated once from the higher concepts to the primitive concepts at the beginning of analysis. However, the task gets not trivial due to the propagation of the restrictions because on average between 43 and 66 color regions fulfill the restrictions. Therefore the system needs the ability to detect the objects in this set of hypotheses which is done by making use of the knowledge represented in the knowledge base. In Table 1 the results are shown for the two different offices. The recognition rates give the ratio between the number of correctly recognized objects and the total number of verified objects, performing N_i iterations. One can see that the recognition rate increases with the number of iterations up to a maximum of 93 % for office_1 and 79 % for office_2. Currently we use only 2D features which are view-point dependent. Because the objects' pose is more restricted in office_1 the recognition rate is higher than for office_2.

The increase with the number of iterations shows particularly well the any-time capability of the algorithm. The results revealed furthermore that 50 iterations for office_1 and 150 iterations for office_2 are sufficient to achieve an optimal result for a specific camera setting. The number of necessary iterations depends upon the number of hypotheses which are generated by the data driven module. For office_2 eight hypotheses were found on average, whereas for office_1 only five hypotheses were found. Therefore, more iterations had to be performed for office_2.

As optimization method the stochastic relaxation was used. The processing cycle for one camera setting for interpretation (i.e., from the data driven hypotheses generation up to the computation of an optimal instance of "explore_office") lasts around five minutes. The major time need arises by moving the camera axes, waiting until the goal position is reached, for the median filtering in the histogram backprojection, and the segmentation of the color regions. One iteration, that is one bottom-up instantiation of the attribute network for the scene part of the knowledge base, takes on average only 0.015 s, that is, 2.25 s for 150 iterations.

8 Conclusion and Future Work

In this paper, we proposed an integrated formalism for representing and using knowledge about an application domain combined with the various camera actions the system needs to perform in order to explore a scene. The application domain is the exploration of office scenes. The current task of the system is the localization of three pre-defined red objects. In order to use the knowledge and actions represented we employed a parallel iterative control algorithm with any-time capabilities. Initial experiments have proved the feasibility of the approach.

Future work will concentrate on completing the implementation of the approach for the application presented. This includes a systematic determination of the subgoals by a goalconcept estimation and a reduction of processing time.

References

[1] K. Kawamura and M. Iskarous. Trends in Service Robots for the Disabled and the Elderly. In *Intelligent Robots and Systems*, pages 1647–1654, München, 1994.

[2] J. Aloimonos, I. Weiss, and A. Bandyopadhyay. Active vision. *International Journal of Computer Vision*, 2(3):333–356, 1988.

[3] A. Hanson and E. Riseman. Visions: A computer system for interpreting scenes. In A. Hanson and E. Riseman, editors, *Computer Vision Systems*, pages 303–333. Academic Press, Inc., New York, 1978.

[4] D. McKeown, W. Harvey, and J. McDermott. Rule-based interpretation of aerial imagery. *IEEE Trans. on Pattern Analysis and Machine Intelligence*, 7(5):570–585, 1985.

[5] T. Matsuyama and V. Hwang. *SIGMA. A Knowledge-Based Aerial Image Understanding System*, volume 12 of *Advances in Computer Vision and Machine Intelligence*. Plenum Press, New York and London, 1990.

[6] R. Rimey. Control of Selective Perception using Bayes Nets and Decision Theory. Technical report, Department of Computer Science, College of Arts and Science, University of Rochester, Rochester, New York, 1993.

[7] T. Levitt, T. Binford, G. Ettinger, and P. Gelband. Probability based control for computer vision. In *Proc. of DARPA Image Understanding Workshop*, pages 355–369, 1989.

[8] S. J. Russell and P. Norvig. *Artificial Intelligence. A Modern Approach.* Prentice-Hall, Englewood Cliffs, NJ, 1995.

[9] J. Pearl. *Probabilistic Inference in Intelligent Systems. Networks of Plausible Inference.* Morgan Kaufmann, San Mateo, CA, 1988.

[10] B. Krebs, B. Korn, and F.M. Wahl. A task driven 3d object recognition system using bayesian networks. In *International Conference on Computer Vision*, pages 527–532, Bombay, India, 1998.

[11] A. Winzen and H. Niemann. Automatic model–generation for image analysis. In W. Straßer and F.M. Wahl, editors, *Graphics and Robotics*, pages 207–219, Berlin Heidelberg, 1995. Springer.

[12] H. Niemann and G. Sagerer. A model as a part of a system for interpretation of gated blood pool studies of the human heart. In *Proc. 6th ICPR*, pages 16–18, München, 1982.

[13] Fischer, J. and Niemann, H. and Noeth, E. A Real–Time and Any–Time Approach for a Dialog System. In *Proc. International Workshop Speech and Computer (SPECOM'98)*, pages 85–90, St.–Petersburg, 1998.

[14] H. Niemann, V. Fischer, D. Paulus, and J. Fischer. Knowledge based image understanding by iterative optimization. In G. Görz and St. Hölldobler, editors, *KI-96: Advances in Artificial Intelligence*, volume 1137 (Lecture Notes in Artificial Intelligence), pages 287–301. Springer, Berlin, 1996.

[15] H. Niemann, G. Sagerer, S. Schröder, and F. Kummert. ERNEST: A semantic network system for pattern understanding. *IEEE Trans. on Pattern Analysis and Machine Intelligence*, 12(9):883–905, 1990.

[16] G. Sagerer and H. Niemann. *Semantic Networks for Understanding Scenes.* Advances in Computer Vision and Machine Intelligence. Plenum Press, New York and London, 1997.

[17] L. Wixson. Gaze Selection for Visual Search. Technical report, Department of Computer Science, College of Arts and Science, University of Rochester, Rochester, New York, 1994.

[18] F. V. Jensen. *An Introduction to Bayesian Networks.* UCL Press, London, 1996.

[19] M. J. Swain and D. H. Ballard. Color indexing. *International Journal of Computer Vision*, 7(1):11–32, November 1991.

Object Location in Colour Images Using Fuzzy-Tuned Scanpaths and a Neural Network

M. J. Allen, Q. H. Mehdi, I. J. Griffiths, N. E. Gough and I. M. Coulson
University of Wolverhampton,
Wolverhampton, United Kingdom
ex1215@wlv.ac.uk

Abstract: The ability of our machine vision system to efficiently locate specific object(s) present within a dynamic environment is essential in a host of practical applications, e.g. security surveillance, robot football, navigation of mobile robots and applications within the military area. In this paper a method for scanning an image and identifying objects in a controlled environment using fuzzy logic and neural networks is described. The ability of a neural network to correctly classify objects under varying lighting conditions using colour data is tested. Results are presented which illustrate how the proposed system can efficiently monitor the position of moving and stationary objects.

1. Introduction

The Multimedia & Intelligent Systems Research Group (MIST) at the University of Wolverhampton is currently developing a Machine Vision System (MVS) that will efficiently analyse each frame of a video sequence to identify and monitor the position of mobile and stationary objects contained within a dynamic environment. This builds upon work previously undertaken by the group into the navigation of Autonomous Guided Vehicles (AGVs) and integrates with other on-going lines of research, such as co-operation between agent teams [1]. Research already undertaken by the group includes path planning using genetic algorithms and fuzzy logic [2], trajectory and kinematic modelling for AGV navigation [3], fuzzy tuned stochastic scanpaths for AGV vision [4][5] and object recognition using colour data [6][7]. Intelligent tools have been employed in each vein of the group's research.

The development of a MVS will enable data relating to an object's environment to be captured for analysis using the tools and processes already developed by the group [1] - [7]. The environment may be virtual or real and will be dynamic, i.e. environmental conditions and the position of objects may change with respect to time. The MVS will be required to overcome the problem of changing conditions and provide *robust* information regarding the relative position of a variety of different objects. The environment will be monitored by overhead camera(s) that relay data to a central database that communicates with the various agents.

The MVS must operate in real time. The idea of using Fuzzy Tuned Stochastic Scanpaths (FTSSs) was proposed by Griffiths *et al* [4] and further developed by Allen *et al* [5]. It provides a means of reducing the amount of processing required by the MVS by identifying areas of significance within the captured images.

In Section 2, the use and classification of FTSSs within the MVS is examined. An overview of FTSSs is provided in Section 3. Colour data is used in this work for object recognition. The application of colour data for object recognition and how it can be used in conjunction with FTSSs is examined in Sections 2 and 4. Section 5 describes the experimental work undertaken and Section 6 reports on the results obtained. Section 7 contains the conclusion and further work.

2. Machine Vision and Fuzzy-Tuned Scanpaths

A *Machine Vision System* recovers useful information about a scene from its two-dimensional projections - Jain *et al* [8]. The operations used in a MVS can be catagorized in number of different ways. In this discussion the MVS under development has been broken down into various sections as shown in Figure 1.

Image capture makes use of an electromagnetic transducer, e.g. a CCD camera, to convert the electromagnetic waves produced by a scene into an electrical signal that can be digitized to produce numerical values. The low, medium and high level image processing elements identified in Figure 1 relate to colour images and are loosely based on those defined by Low [9] for the processing of intensity images:

- *Low Level Processing:* improving the initial image and identifying areas of significance. This category may include: morphological operations, edge detection, image smoothing, image sharpening etc..
- *Medium Level Processing:* the identification of regions and the extraction of data relating to these regions.
- *High Level Processing:* relating the data extracted from the different regions to a knowledge base to identify these regions of the image as real objects.

The element '*Action*' makes use of the information extracted from the image data, e.g. to relay the position of a specific agent or object back to the central database and to provide information to the MVS. The input of *Strategic Information* and *Antecedent Information* enables prior knowledge of the environment to be used to identify areas of significance. The strategic information would relate to areas of significance that will not change with time, e.g. the location of doorways from which agents might enter into the environment. Antecedent Information identifies areas of initial significance that may change with time, e.g. the position of an agent or non static object when the MVS system was shut down. The *Feedback* loop uses a saccade map (see Section 3) to identify which parts of the image are significant at a point in time, e.g. the position of a mobile agent.

The image sequence used in this experimental work was captured at 25 frames/second using a Canon MV-1 digital video camera and downloaded to a PC as a set of individual images through an Adaptec Firecard (IEEE1394 interface board). The image sequence was captured using a progressive scan - as opposed to an interlaced scan - so that the CCD chip read every line from top to bottom to ensure that no image data was overlooked. The image frames were downloaded from the camera and initially stored as 640x480, 24-bit colour files. For hardware/software compatibility reasons the images were then converted to 8-bit indexed colour images and stored as bitmap files.

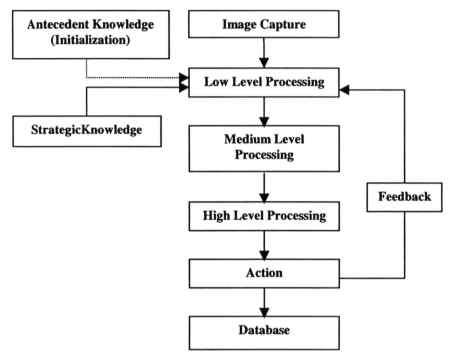

Figure 1: A Machine Vision System using Fuzzy-Tuned Stochastic Scanpaths

In order to efficiently analyse the image sequence it is proposed that areas of significance within each image frame are identified in order to pinpoint the on-going positions of two objects (one mobile and the other stationary). Scanpaths, see Section 3, are used to systematically select significant areas within the image. The scanpath is directly influenced by the saccade map which biases the search. The saccade map, see Section 3, is constructed using historical data and can be tuned to suit the requirements of the tracking system. This process is catagorized as a low level process as it identifies areas of significance within the image. Figure 2 relates the FTSS cycle to the elemental layout of the MVS presented in Figure 1.

The saccade map contains the feedback data used in the scan process. A saccade map is essential right from the outset and, therefore, one must be constructed at the beginning of the process. All the elements of this initial saccade map can be initialized to the same value and this will induce a totally random search over the whole of the image surface. Alternatively, prior knowledge regarding the environment can be applied. If a static camera is used to relay image data to the system then strategic information and/or antecedent information can be used to construct the map. In this work antecedent and strategic information is used. The initial positions of different objects were given to the system and the saccade map was initialized based on this information. Strategic information was also used to initialize and update the saccade map to adjudge its effect on the system as a whole.

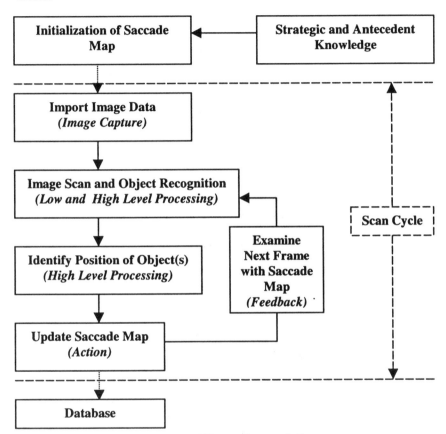

Figure 2: Structure of Fuzzy Scanpath System

To reduce the dimensionality of the image an $(X \times Y)$ matrix is used to identify sub-regions of $(x \times y)$ pixels in each of the image frames (see Figure 3). The image scan runs for n iterations and during each iteration one sub-region is selected and examined to identify which object is prominently represented by the pixels within it. This identification process is based on the classification of colour data (see Section 4).

The scan process identifies sub-regions in which objects are present. Where more than one region is identified as containing an object the centroid of these regions is used to identify the position of the object on the $(X \times Y)$ grid. The position of the object is required to determine the input parameters to the fuzzy inference system that is used to construct the saccade map.

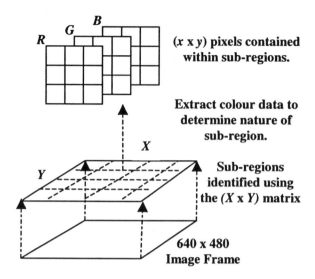

R G B

(*x* x *y*) pixels contained within sub-regions.

Extract colour data to determine nature of sub-region.

X

Y

Sub-regions identified using the (*X* x *Y*) matrix

640 x 480 Image Frame

Figure 3: Sub Division of Image frame and Data Extraction

3. Fuzzy Tuned Stochastic Scanpaths

When using a camera to monitor a dynamic environment *Fuzzy-Tuned Stochastic Scanpaths* (FTSSs) were proposed by Griffiths et al (1997) [4] to determine a camera's next orientation, i.e. the next area of the environment to be examined. The aim of this process was to identify areas of interest within the scene and to ensure that these areas received comparatively more attention. The use of FTSSs was inspired by the scan processes employed by the human eye. It has been found that humans use repetitive patterns of saccades (a series of rapid eye movements) to inspect scenes and these have been labelled *scanpaths* or *eye contour maps* [10][11]. The eye must move to ensure that the area of interest within the scene is focused on the fovea which is the only part of the retina that is capable of defining fine detail [12][13]. The use of FTSSs allows the pattern of saccades to be defined statistically using a *saccade map*. The saccade map is a 2D stochastic transition state matrix. In the initial work each cell within this 2D matrix represented a particular orientation of a camera. The value contained within a particular cell represented the possibility that the camera would be orientated to examine that cell on the next iteration. To evaluate the system a 10x10 binary image matrix was used where the object was represented by a '1' in an otherwise zero matrix.

In the method described here the FTSSs have been adapted to systematically scan the (*X* x *Y*) matrix which refers to the different sub-regions of each image frame (see Figure 3). The nature of the sub-region is determined using the process described in Section 4.

A Mamdani style *Fuzzy Inference System* (FIS) has been used to determine the probabilities contained within the saccade map by evaluating historical data, i.e. *distance, attention, bias* and *strategic data*. In this instance a 20x20 saccade map is used and each element refers to one of the sub-regions of the image. The map assigns a possibility value to each region and this determines the likelihood that a sub-region will be examined on the next iteration, i.e. a high possibility value indicates a region of high significance.

The *'distance'* parameter is measured in terms of map cells using the *chessboard* measure and is normalized between 0 and 1, i.e.:

$$dist = \frac{\max(|i_{object} - i_{exam}|, |j_{object} - j_{exam}|)}{D}$$

where (i_{object}, j_{object}) and (i_{exam}, j_{exam}) are the row and column dimensions of the nearest cell known to contain an object and the cell under examination, and D is the maximum distance possible. If the cell is close to an object it will be assigned a higher possibility value. The 'distance' input determines the probabilities for all those sub-regions local to an object. *'Attention'* measures the time elapsed in terms of examination cycles and is also normalized between 0 and 1:

$$attention = \frac{C_{current} - C_{(i,j)}}{C_{current} - C_{min}}$$

where $C_{current}$ is the current cycle count, $C_{(i,j)}$ is the cycle number when cell (i, j) was last examined and C_{min} is the cycle number of the cell that has not been examined for the longest period, i.e. has received the least attention. The 'attention' parameter determines the probabilities for those sub-regions that are not local to an object. The aim of this input is to promote a systematic scan of pixels in areas of low significance in order to search for new objects. The *'strategic'* parameter identifies areas of constant significance. A strategic map is created during the initialization of the system and areas of constant significance can be identified on this map, i.e. a significant region is assigned a '1' whereas a non significant area is assigned a '0'. The *'bias'* is used to determine which rules are used and has a direct effect on the systems behaviour. The 'bias' parameter is used to reduce the probabilities in the saccade assigned to those regions not local to an object. It is activated if the system fails to identify an object on a particular iteration of the scan cycle. The consequence of invoking the bias is that more attention is paid to those sub-regions local to the objects in order to relocate them on the next scan.

There are thirteen fuzzy rules in a verbose form. Each rule carries the same weighting of '1' and triangular membership functions (MFs) are used throughout. The fuzzy inputs for 'distance' and 'attention' are each defined using sets of four MFs. The inputs 'bias' and 'strategy' just act as switches which are either on or off, i.e. '0' or '1'. The fuzzy output set that results from implication is defined using seven MFs.

The transition of attention from one sub-region to another is determined by using a *weighted roulette wheel* and the stochastic probabilities contained within the saccade map [4]. In this system, once a sub-region has been selected for examination in respect of a particular image frame its possibility value is changed to zero to ensure that it is not examined again during that scan. Naturally, when a new saccade map is constructed for use with the subsequent frame the probabilities relating to all the cells are updated.

4. Colour Object Recognition using a Neural Network

An object recognition technique was required to classify the sub-regions of an image surface (see Figure 3). These regions could contain areas of a single object or areas of different objects and these objects could be either stationary or mobile. The use of *colour* appears to be an obvious feature to use in the classification process because a region can be classified as belonging to one object, or a reduced set of objects, based exclusively on the data compiled from pixels it contains.

In this work a single image sequence has been used that was captured under mixed lighting conditions. The scene was lit from one side so that shadows were produced. A neural network with its ability to generalize is used to classify the colour data extracted from the image regions.

The data extracted from the image frames are represented in terms of red, green and blue (the *RGB model*). However, the RGB model does not really describe how colour is actually perceived. The *HIS model* (hue, intensity and saturation) better approximates to the psycho-physiological characteristics of colour, i.e. how colour is actually perceived [14]. Equal geometric distances in the RGB space do not generally correspond to equal perceptual changes in colour. Hence the RGB colour space is inappropriate for applications requiring direct colour comparisons [15]. A number of colour models have been developed that define colour in terms of hue, saturation and intensity, and a number of reviews and comparisons have been made [16][17][18]. In this work the HSV model contained within the MATLAB environment was used to transform the data from the RGB space.

The HIS data extracted from each region of the image was summarized statistically. The mean and the standard deviation were used as summaries to define the position and dispersion of the input point in the HSV space. In this work a competitive neural network was used to classify the HIS data. This network was chosen because of its speed of operation and relative simplicity. The Group intends to make more use of self-organizing networks, such as networks based on the Adaptive Resonance Theory (ART)[19], in future work in order to make the MVS more flexible. However, in this experiment, the network weights were calculated from a training set of image segments taken from each object. The HIS data from each segment was summarized to produce six input parameters in the form of a six element vector. The data from all the vectors representing a particular object were summarized by calculating a robust mean for each element. The resulting vector pin-points the centre of the cluster of values that represents a particular object and it is this vector that was used as the weight vector. The network was simulated using the competitive network routine contained within MATLAB.

In addition to colour a parameter is also used to filter the classified data and remove misclassified cells using a distance measure. If a cell is classified as a specific object that is more than N cells from that object's predicted position then the system treats this as a rogue classification and reclassifies it as part of the background. The distance N is known as the 'Rogue Threshold'.

5. Experimental Work

The video sequence analysed here contains fifty six frames and three objects are contained within each frame: the textured blue, white and grey background, a green pyramid and a yellow ball. The pyramid is static whereas the ball is always mobile. As the background never changes the system is designed to locate the position of the ball and pyramid in each frame. The environment is constrained so that:

- The camera is held in a stationary position throughout the whole sequence.
- No more than three objects, including the background, are present within the image at any one time. The size of each object remains constant.
- Clearly the background is static. The green pyramid remains stationary whilst the balls crosses the environment.

The scene was illuminated from one side to create areas of shadow to more closely align with conditions encountered in a real environment. Some parts of the background are in shadow and one side of the green pyramid is completely in shadow (see Figure 4).

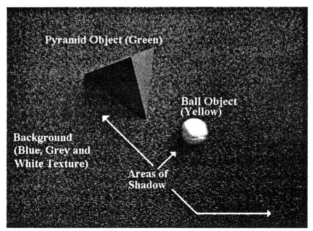

Figure 4: Sample Frame from the Image Sequence

When tuning this MVS to operate in a particular environment the neural network used for object classification must be specifically designed to classify all the objects, including the background. At present, the Rogue Threshold, the size of the

experimental system - the 'estimated positions'. The centroid of the pyramid was calculated from the known position of the three points on its base.

Measures	Analysis of all Data	Analysis of Data with Outliers Removed[*]
Longitudinal Error	18.56 pixels (3.9%)	12.44 pixels (2.3%)
Latitudinal Error	74.70 pixels (11.7%)	17.20 pixels (2.7%)
Euclidean Error	80.75 pixels (10.1%)	23.59 pixels (3.0%)
Identification Failure	30.75 iterations (54.9%)	25.82 iterations (46.1%)
Instant Recovery	8.63 iterations (28.1%)	10.30 iterations (40.0%)

Table 1: Scan Data regarding the Rolling Ball

Measures	Analysis of all Data	Analysis with Outliers Removed[†]
Longitudinal Error	17.82 pixels (3.7%)	16.10 pixels (3.4%)
Latitudinal Error	24.30 pixels (3.8%)	23.03 pixels (3.6%)
Euclidean Error	33.67 pixels (4.2%)	31.58 pixels (3.9%)
Identification Failure	7.23 iterations (12.9%)	6.46 iterations (11.5%)
Instant Recovery	5.50 iterations (76.1%)	5.56 iterations (86.1%)

Table 2: Scan Data regarding the Green Pyramid

The system was tested forty times and the results of each test were summarized. A number of different measures have been employed to grade the success of the system:

- *Longitudinal Error:* measures how far the estimated position is from the actual position along the y axis. The results are presented in terms of pixels and as a percentage of the maximum possible error, i.e. 480 pixels.

---

[*] Seven cycles were removed from the analysis as the system had failed to locate the ball during the first five iterations of the scan cycle and, due to the operation of the Rogue Threshold and the antecedent information, the system could never recover.

[†] One value was removed that was obviously a rogue as it appeared to have no correlation with the other values.

sub-regions, the number of sub-regions selected during each scan and, where applicable, strategic and antecedent information have to be set manually.

As described in Section 2, for this work, the image frame was sub-divided into *400* equally sized sub-regions using a *20x20* matrix. Consequently, each sub-region is *32x24* pixels. During one iteration of the scan cycle a sub-region is selected and classified based on the colour of the pixels it contains and using the rogue threshold. Each cycle lasts for *20* iterations during which time 20 cells are examined, i.e. *5%* percent of the total image. These parameters were chosen based on the size of the objects and some initial experimentation.

As described in Section 3 a competitive network is used for the classification of the sub-regions. The network in question has been designed to classify the sub-regions as being part of the background, the pyramid or the ball. Data from *250* image samples of each object from a range of image frames were used to calculate the weights in the network (see Section 4). An initial test of the input data revealed that some areas of the background located in shadow were misclassified as the pyramid object, i.e. the input vectors representing shadowed areas of the background were more closely matching with the feature template (weight vector) that characterizes the pyramid object. To overcome this problem the area of carpet in shadow and the area not in shadow were treated as two separate objects. A second test showed that this had overcome the problem of misclassification regarding pyramid. However, some image data of the background not in shadow was misclassified as that being in shadow. As there is a gradual progression from shadow to the non-shadow area this is not surprising and, as the two outputs from the network are treated in the same way, this was not deemed to be a problem.

In this experiment the Rogue Threshold used to discard misclassified cells (see Section 4) was set to *3* cells and antecedent and strategic knowledge regarding the initial positions of the pyramid object and the ball object were given to the MVS.

6. Results

The progress of the ball was first analysed using an exhaustive system designed to accurately calculate the position of the ball in each frame by identifying its centre of mass (centroid). This process examined every pixel in each image and classified each one using a threshold approach to produce a binary image, i.e. those pixels representing the ball were set to 1 and those representing the background were set to zero. The threshold values were based upon the hue, saturation and intensity value of each pixel. The morphological operation of *opening* was employed to remove isolated rogue pixels that had been incorrectly classified and finally a test was made to remove all remaining outlying pixels statistically to ensure only those pixels representing the ball remained. The centroid was then calculated to ascertain the x and y position of the ball in each frame. The results returned from this system were finally checked with results ascertained visually by a human operator. The positions of the ball, calculated using this exhaustive system, were classed as 'actual ball positions' and are compared here with those returned by the

- *Latitudinal Error:* measures how far the estimated position is from the actual position a long the x axis. The results are presented in terms of pixels and as a percentage of the maximum possible error, i.e. 640 pixels.
- *Euclidean Error:* measures the Euclidean distance between the actual position and the estimated position. The results are presented in terms of pixels and as a percentage of the maximum possible error, i.e. 800 pixels.
- *Identification Failure:* the number of times during one test (56 cycles) the system failed to identify the object on a particular cycle. If the system fails to locate an object or object during the examination of a particular frame the system puts forward the location of that object in the previous frame as its estimated position.
- *Instant Recovery:* the number of times after failure that the system relocated the object on the next iteration. The percentage error is calculated as proportion of the Identification Failure.

The results presented in Tables 1 and 2 represent the mean results extracted from all the tests for the ball and pyramid respectively.

In seven of the forty tests the system failed to locate the ball within the first five iterations. The operation of the Rogue Threshold meant that the system could never recover. The two sets of results presented in Table 1 grade the system with these seven results included and without them. In Table 2 the two sets of results represent one analysis using all the data and one with a rogue result removed.

Tests on the object recognition system revealed that the network reliably classified sub-regions when only one object was represented. However, it did misclassify sub-regions on occasions when data from two objects were present in the same sub-region.

7. Conclusion and Further Work

In this paper we have demonstrated the potential of the MVS under development. The MVS makes use of intelligent tools to improve the efficiency with which an image can be scanned and to classify colour data. As part of this demonstration the use of FTSSs as a low level image processing tool has been proposed.

An analysis of the results showed that when the system successfully located the ball object in the first five iterations it identified its position throughout the cycle with a mean error of 3.0% (Euclidean measure). This reflects the validity of the system as only 5% of the total image was analysed in each case.

The 'Identification Failure' of the ball object was nearly four times greater than it was on the pyramid object: the average failure rate on the ball was about 26 iterations compared with about 6 for the pyramid object. As the position of the ball object changes from frame to frame it confronts the MVS with a more challenging problem than the stationary pyramid object and the results reflect this. However, on average the system located the centroid of the ball object with more accuracy than that of the pyramid object . This may relate to the relationship between the size of the object and the dimensions of the matrix used to sub-divide the image. It would appear that the size of the sub-regions has a direct effect on the accuracy of the system when locating an object's centroid. This needs to be examined further.

The FTSSs are currently tuned manually (see Section 5) but scope exists to develop a self-tuning system using the bias as a variable control rather than a switch. The 'bias' parameter currently selects the fuzzy rules but could be used to change other factors within the system, for example the number of sub-regions that are examined during one cycle. Using an optimization tool, such as a genetic algorithm, the system could optimize the combination of factors for a given set of parameters.

The object recognition system using 'colour' and 'distance' worked reliably once the scanning system had located the object. The MVS as a whole makes much use of 'distance' and it would appear to be an obvious feature to use. It proved to be very successful. The use of the 'Rogue Threshold' improved the reliability of the recognition system and work will be needed to develop and integrate it further.

In future work it is proposed that the complexity of the experimental environments are gradually increased to reflect the complexity of a real environment. Different lighting scenarios will be used to identify how well the system can handle factors such as: changes in the ambient light source, the presence of multicoloured objects and variations of illumination intensity. It is proposed that low and medium level image processing techniques (see Section 2) are included to refine and segment the image data from each selected sub-region. Data from the main region can be used to determine the nature of that sub-region. More sophisticated methods of summarizing the image data, prior to classification, will also be examined, e.g. color indexing [20].

Unknown objects will be added to the environment in order to investigate if the classification process can identify them as new objects and subsequently classify them. As discussed in Section 4 a self-organizing neural network is envisaged for this task. As part of this investigation it is proposed that parallel processing systems are examined as a means of monitoring the position of each individual object, i.e. each subsystem could monitor a different object.

References

[1] Wang, T., Mehdi, Q. H., Gough, N. E. (1998). Cooperation and competition in AGV systems. Proceedings of the 12th European Simulation Multiconference on Simulation; Past, Present and Future – ESM '98, Manchester, UK.

[2] Griffiths, I. J., Mehdi Q. H., Wang, T., Gough, N. E., (1997). A Genetic Algorithm for Path Planning. Proceedings of the 3rd IFAC Symposium on Intelligent Components and Instruments for Control Applications – SICICA '97, Annecy, France, pp 531-536.

[3] Wang, T., Mehdi, Q. H., Gough, N. E., (1996). Kinematic Models for Autonomous Guided Vehicles and their Applications. Proceedings of the ISCA 5th Int. Conf., Reno, Nevada, pp 207-211.

[4] Griffiths I. J., Mehdi, Q. H., Gough, N. E. (1997). Fuzzy Tuned Stochastic Scanpaths for AGV Vision. Proceedings of the Int. Conf. on Artificial Neural Networks and Genetic Algorithms - ICANNGA '97, Norwich, UK.

[5] Allen M. J., Griffiths, I. J., Coulson, I. M., Mehdi, Q. H., Gough, N. E., (1999). Efficient Tracking of Coloured Objects using Fuzzy-Tuned Scanpaths. Proceedings of the Workshop - Recent Advances in Soft Computing, Leicester, UK.

[6] Allen M. J., Coulson, I. M., Gough, N. E., Medhi, Q., (1998). Identifying Coloured Objects under different Lighting Conditions using a Radial Basis Neural Network, Proceedings of the Workshop - Recent Advances in Soft Computing, 1, pp 47-52.

[7] Allen M. J., Coulson, I. M., Gough, N. E., Medhi, Q. H., (1999). Classifying Coloured Objects under different Lighting Conditions using the HSV Colour Model and a Neural Network, Proceedings of the 5th European Control Conf. - ECC '99, Karlsruhe, Germany.

[8] Jain R., Kasturi, R., Schunck, B. G., (1995). Machine Vision. McGraw Hill.

[9] Low A., (1991). Introductory Computer Vision and Image Processing. McGraw-Hill Int..

[10] Zuber, B., (1981). Model of Oculomotor Behaviour and Control. Boca Rotan, FL CRC Press.

[11] Norton, D., Stark, L., (1971). Scanpaths in eye movements during pattern perception. Science, 171, pp 308-311.

[12] Ditchburn, R., (1973). Eye Movements and Visual Perception. Oxford University Press.

[13] Carpenter, R., (1989). Eye Motion Machinery, Physics World, 2.

[14] Salmon, R., Slater, M., (1987). Computer Graphics: Systems and Concepts, Addison Wesley Publishing Company, p 493.

[15] Gong Y., Chuan, C. H., Xiaoyi, G., (1996). Image Indexing and Retrieval Based on Colour Histograms. Multimedia Tools and Applications 2, pp 133-156.

[16] Foley, J. D., Dam, A. V., Feiner, S.K., Hughes, J. F., (1995). Computer Graphics: Principles and Practice. Addison Wesley Publishing Company.

[17] Power W., Clist, R., (1996). Comparison of supervised learning techniques applied to the colour segmentation of fruit images. Proceedings of the Spie - The International Society for Optical Engineering, 2904, pp 370-381.

[18] Palus H., Bereska, D., (1995). The comparison between transformations from RGB colour space to IHS colour space, used for object recognition. Proceedings of the 5th Int. Conf. on Image Processing and its Applications, Edinburgh, UK, pp 825-7.

[19] Carpenter G. A., Grossberg, S., (1988). The ART of adaptive pattern recognition by a self-organizing neural network. Computer, 21, pp 77-90.

[20] Swain, M. J., Ballard D. H., (1991). Color Indexing. Int. Journal of Computer Vision, 7:1, pp 11-32.

An Algebraic Approach to KBS. Application to Computer Network Selection*

L.M. Laita
Dept. Artificial Intelligence, Univ. Politécnica de Madrid
Madrid (Spain)

E. Roanes-Lozano
Dept. Algebra, Univ. Complutense de Madrid
Madrid (Spain)

M.A. Henares
School of Computer Science, Univ. Politécnica de Madrid
Madrid (Spain)

A. Esteban
School of Computer Science, Univ. Politécnica de Madrid
Madrid (Spain)

L. de Ledesma
Dept. Artificial Intelligence, Univ. Politécnica de Madrid
Madrid (Spain)

E. Roanes-Macías
Dept. Algebra, Univ. Complutense de Madrid
Madrid (Spain)

Abstract

This article deals with an implementation of a theoretical result that relates tautological consequence in many-valued logics to the ideal membership problem in Algebra. The implementation is applied to automated extraction of knowledge and verification of consistency in Propositional KBS expressed in terms of many-valued logics formulae. As an example, a small KBS expressed in Lukasiewicz's three-valued logic (with modal operators), describing how to select a computer network, is studied.

1 Introduction

This article outlines a theoretical result relating Logic and Computer Algebra and describes an implementation of that result which is very well fitted to

---

*Partially supported by Project DGES PB96-0098-C04 (Ministerio de Educación y Cultura de España).

automate both verification and knowledge extraction in Knowledge Based Systems (KBS) based on many-valued logics. A small KBS describing a computer network, expressed in Lukasiewicz's three-valued logic with modal operators, is studied as example. The example intends to be both an illustration of the method and an illustration of how the logic used is an appropriate tool for representing imperfect knowledge.

Our program runs on a standard 128 Megabytes Pentium based PC. It checks for consistency and automatically finds consequences in KBS containing 200 propositional variables under bivalued logics (it has not be tested with more variables), KBS containing from 120 to 150 variables under three-valued logics, and KBS containing about 40 variables under five-valued logics. It has also been applied to seven-valued logics. The example in this paper refers to just 27 variables under three-valued logic.

The first proof of the theoretical result was produced in [1] and improved in [3]. Another approach by the authors of this article, based on Algebraic Geometry, appears in [5]. A new proof and a better setting for implementation appears in [4].

In Section 2 we outline some notions of Logic and Algebra, in order to prepare the reader for a better understanding of the result that relates Logic and Algebra.

Section 3 deals with the application of the mentioned result to automated proving and verification in KBS. An advance about how to implement this application using the computer language CoCoA [2] is also presented in this section.

In Section 4 the example above mentioned is studied.

2 Basic concepts and notations

2.1 Basic logical notions

2.1.1 $P_C(X_1, X_2, ..., X_n)$

$P_C(X_1, X_2, ..., X_n)$ represents the set of well formed propositional formulae from a set of propositional variables $X = \{X_1, X_2, ..., X_n\}$ and a set of connectives $C = \{c_1, c_2, ..., c_t\}$. The letter A (with or without subscripts) represents a generic element of $P_C(X_1, X_2, ..., X_n)$ and s_j represents the "arity" of the connective c_j.

2.1.2 p-valued propositional logic

We use the following restricted concept of a "p-valued propositional logic", based on the idea of "tautological consequence". We only deal with the case when p is a prime number.

A p-valued propositional logic PL_p consists of:

- A set $P_C(X_1, X_2, ..., X_n)$ of well formed formulae.

- A set $L = \{0, 1, ..., p-1\}$. The elements $0, 1, ..., p-1$ are considered as the truth values of the p-valued logic; $p-1$ represents the value "true", 0 represents "false", and the other elements represent intermediate truth values.

- A set of truth tables defined by functions $H_j : L^{s_j} \longrightarrow L$ (for each connective $c_j \in C$).

- A function v called "valuation" $v : X \longrightarrow L$.

- For each v another function $v' : P_C(X_1, X_2, ..., X_n) \longrightarrow L$

  recursively defined as follows:

  i) $v'(A) = v(A)$ if $A \in X$

  ii) $v'(A) = H_j(v'(A_1), ..., v'(A_{s_j}))$ if A is well formed from c_j and $A_1, ..., A_{s_j}$.

- A relation named "tautological consequence", defined in 2.1.3. That A_0 is a tautological consequence of $A_1, A_2, ..., A_m$ is denoted as $\{A_1, A_2, ..., A_m\} \models A_0$.

Example 1 *A three-valued logic (Lukasiewicz's logic with modal operators). The set of connectives is* $C = \{c_1 = \neg,\ c_2 = \Diamond,\ c_3 = \Box,\ c_4 = \vee,\ c_5 = \wedge,\ c_6 = \rightarrow,\ c_7 = \leftrightarrow\}$; $\Diamond$ *and* $\Box$ *are modal logic connectives,* $\Diamond$ *means "it is possible that" and* $\Box$ *means "it is necessary that". The other connectives have the usual meaning.* $Z_3 = \{0, 1, 2\}$ *is the field of integers modulo 3, where 0 represents "false", 1 represents "indeterminate" and 2 represents "true". The truth value functions H are given by the following truth tables:*

$H_\neg$	
0	2
1	1
2	0

$H_\Diamond$	
0	0
1	2
2	2

$H_\Box$	
0	0
1	0
2	2

$H_\vee$	0	1	2
0	0	1	2
1	1	1	2
2	2	2	2

$H_\wedge$	0	1	2
0	0	0	0
1	0	1	1
2	0	1	2

$H_\rightarrow$	0	1	2
0	2	2	2
1	1	2	2
2	0	1	2

2.1.3 Tautological consequence

A propositional formula A_0 is a tautological consequence of the propositional formulae $A_1, A_2, ..., A_m$, denoted $\{A_1, A_2, ..., A_m\} \models A_0$ iff for any valuation v such that $v'(A_1) = v'(A_2) = ... = v'(A_m) = p - 1$, then $v'(A_0) = p - 1$.

2.1.4   Contradictory domain

A set of formulae $\{A_1, A_2,...,A_m\}$ is a "contradictory domain" iff $\{A_1, A_2,..., A_m\} \models A$, where A is any formula of the language in which A_1, A_2, ..., A_m are expressed. This is equivalent to state that a "logical contradiction" can be inferred from $\{A_1, A_2,..., A_m\}$.

2.2   Basic algebraic concepts and notations

In order to manage the information contained in the KBS, we translate this information into polynomials (we suppose the KBS based on a p-valued logic, being p a prime number).

$Z_p[x_1, x_2,...,x_n]$ is the polynomial ring in the variables $x_1, x_2,...,x_n$ with coefficients in Z_p. These lower case letters correspond to the upper case letter in the set X of 2.1. The letters q and r, possibly with subscripts, are variables that range over the elements (polynomials) of $Z_p[x_1, x_2,...,x_n]$.

I is the ideal $< x_1^p - x_1, x_2^p - x_2,...,x_n^p - x_n >$ of $Z_p[x_1, x_2,...,x_n]$ generated by the set of polynomials $\{x_1^p - x_1, x_2^p - x_2,...,x_n^p - x_n\}$.

A polynomial is assigned to each logical formula. This is achieved by defining a function

$$f_j : (Z_p[x_1, x_2,...,x_n])^{s_j} \longrightarrow Z_p[x_1, x_2,...,x_n]/I$$

for each connective c_j.

The effect of working in the residue class ring $Z_p[x_1, x_2,...,x_n]/I$ is that the system, any time that finds an x_i^p, reduces it to x_i (see the whole development in [5]). A translation of formulae to polynomials for the three-valued case is:

$$f_\neg(q) = (2 - q) + I$$

$$f_\diamond(q) = 2q^2 + I$$

$$f_\square(q) = (q^2 + 2q) + I$$

$$f_\vee(q,r) = (q^2r^2 + q^2r + qr^2 + 2qr + q + r) + I$$

$$f_\wedge(q,r) = (2q^2r^2 + 2q^2r + 2qr^2 + qr) + I$$

$$f_\rightarrow(q,r) = (2q^2r^2 + 2q^2r + 2qr^2 + qr + 2q + 2) + I$$

$$f_\leftrightarrow(q,r) = (q^2r^2 + q^2r + qr^2 + 2qr + 2q + 2r + 2) + I$$

2.3   Main result

The main theoretical result is that *"a formula A_0 is a tautological consequence of other formulae $A_1,..., A_m$ iff the polynomial that translates the negation of A_0 belongs to the ideal J generated by the polynomials that translate the negations of $A_1,..., A_m$, and the polynomials $x_1^p - x_1, x_2^p - x_2,..., x_n^p - x_n$".*

3 Automated proving and consistency in KBS

3.1 Automated proving in KBS

Let the formulae $A_1, ..., A_m \in P_C(X_1, X_2, ..., X_n)$ in the main result above be the formulae that represent the rules, facts, additional information (denoted as ADIs), and negations of integrity constraints (denoted as NICs) of a KBS. Let J be the ideal generated by these formulae, denoted for the sake of simplicity as:

$$J = IDEAL(NEG(Rules), NEG(Facts), NEG(NICs), NEG(ADIs)).$$

Thus, a formula A_0 follows from the information contained in the KBS iff the polynomial translation of the negation of A_0, $NEG(A_0)$, belongs to $J + I$.

Now, the way to check whether a polynomial belongs to an ideal is to ascertain whether the Normal Form (NF) of the polynomial, modulo the ideal, is **0**. In our case:

$$NEG(A_0) \in J + I \quad \text{iff} \quad NF(NEG(A_0), J + I) = 0.$$

Normal forms of polynomials, modulo some ideal, are well-known constructs in Computer Algebra (see for instance [8]).

3.2 Application to the study of KBS consistency

Let $A_1, ..., A_m$, be as in 3.1. We shall say that the KBS is inconsistent when $\{A_1, A_2, ..., A_m\}$ is a contradictory domain.

Thus a KBS is inconsistent iff

$$1 \in J + I$$

(because 1 belongs to the ideal iff the ideal is the whole ring, which holds iff all formulae are tautological consequences of the KBS). Moreover, a well known result in Computer Algebra is that 1 belongs to an ideal iff its (reduced) Gröbner Basis is $\{1\}$ ([1] in CoCoA's notation).

Example 2 *An elementary example based on bivalued logic.*
Rules:
    R1: $\neg x1 \wedge x2 \wedge \neg x3 \to x4 \vee \neg x5$
    R2: $x6 \wedge x7 \to \neg x4$
    R3: $x8 \wedge x9 \to x10 \vee \neg x11$
    R4: $x12 \to x5$
Facts:
    F1: $\neg x1$
    F2: $x2$
    F3: $\neg x3$
    F4: $x6$
    F5: $x7$
    F6: $x8$

F7: x9

F8: x12

Consistency:

Let us consider all potential facts as facts (so that all rules are fired). When firing R1 and R2, ¬x5 is obtained. On its side, when firing R4, x5 is obtained, which is a contradiction with ¬x5.

Another contradiction is obtained by firing R1 and R4 (x4 is obtained) which contradicts ¬x4 (obtained from rule R2).

3.3 Implementation in CoCoA 3

How can the theoretical results above be transferred to a computer? The Computer Algebra language CoCoA [2] is very well suited for this purpose. CoCoA includes the commands GBasis(ideal) and NF(polynomial,ideal) that calculate the Gröbner Basis and the Normal Form, respectively.

The process of implementation consists of taking a series of steps, of which the more important are as follows.

Translate rules, facts, and negations of integrity constraints and any other additional information into polynomials (this process is automated).

In order to check whether or not the KBS is consistent, ask the computer for the Gröbner basis of the ideal generated by these polynomials. If the result is [1], the KBS is inconsistent, if the result is different from [1] (it may be a large set of polynomials, but the computer response time is quite fast), the KBS is consistent.

In order to check whether any information follows from a consistent subset, K, of the set of rules, facts, ICs and ADIs of the KBS, translate the information into a logical formula; then ask for the normal form of the polynomial that corresponds to the negation of that formula, modulo the ideal of polynomials that corresponds to K (plus I). If this value is 0, the information follows from K, otherwise, it does not.

4 An application to a decision problem

4.1 Introduction

The aim is to built, as illustration of the method, a KBS capable to decide what type of computer network is the adequate one regarding the needs of some company, according to some provided data [7, 6].

The initial process, even though more complex, is basically the same as in Example 2. Rules and facts are stated and then rules are fired and consistency is studied. In addition, in the next example the KBS is debugged and inconsistencies are eliminated. Then consequences can also be extracted.

4.2 The KBS

4.2.1 Variables

(Remark: the nets of not specified type can be of local or broad areas).

$x1$: distance $<=$ 500 m.
$x2$: Vt $<=$ 10 Mbps.
$x3$: local Ethernet net.
$x4$: moderate budget.
$x5$: low traffic.
$x6$: distance $<=$ 200 m.
$x7$: Vt $=$100 Mbps.
$x8$: local net, Ethernet high speed net.
$x9$: medium-high traffic.
$x10$: medium-low traffic.
$x11$: distance $<=$ 2000 m.
$x12$: FDDI net.
$x13$: medium budget.
$x14$: maximum efficiency.
$x15$: very low efficiency.
$x16$: local Token Ring net.
$x17$: high tolerance to failures.
$x18$: simultaneous information transmission.
$x19$: extremely long distance.
$x20$: very low BER.
$x21$: frame relay.
$x22$: ATM net.
$x23$: Vt $>$ 100 Mbps.
$x24$: Vt $=$ 64 Kbps.
$x25$: RDSI net.
$x26$: broad net.
$x27$: high budget.

4.2.2 Logical rules

Among the many rules that may be built, let us present the following 15 ones, based on Lukasiewicz's three-valued logic.

Rule 1: if distance $<=$ 500 m and Vt $<=$ 10 Mbps then Ethernet.

$x1 \wedge x2 \rightarrow x3$

Rule 2: if necessarily Vt $<=$ 10 Mbps and necessarily moderate budget and low traffic then Ethernet.

$\Box x2 \wedge \Box x4 \wedge x5 \rightarrow x3$

Rule 3: if distance $<=$ 200 m and possibly Vt $=$ 100 Mbps then Ethernet high speed net.

$x6 \wedge \Diamond x7 \rightarrow x8$

Rule 4: if possibly Vt = 100 Mbps and medium-high traffic and possibly moderate budget then Ethernet high speed net.

$\Diamond x7 \land x9 \land \Diamond x4 \rightarrow x8$

The next two alternative rules will be considered (the one suggested by the expert is Rule 5b). Only one of them is consistent with the rest of the KBS, as will be detected below.

Rule 5a: if medium-low traffic and moderate budget then not Ethernet net or not Ethernet high speed net.

$x10 \land x4 \rightarrow \neg x3 \land \neg x8$

Rule 5b: if medium-low traffic and moderate budget then Ethernet net or Ethernet high speed net.

$x10 \land x4 \rightarrow x3 \lor x8$

Rule 6: if Vt = 100 Mbps distance $<=$ 2000 m then FDDI.

$x7 \land x11 \rightarrow x12$

Rule 7: if Necessarily Vt = 100 Mbps and medium budget and maximum efficiency then FDDI.

$\Box x7 \land x13 \land x14 \rightarrow x12$

Rule 8: if medium budget and very low efficiency and distance > 2000 m and high Vt then not Ethernet net and necessarily not Token Ring net.

$x13 \land x15 \land x11 \land \Diamond x2 \rightarrow \neg x3 \land \Box \neg x16$

Rule 9: if high tolerance to failures and distance > 2000 m and Vt = 100 Mbps then FDDI.

$x17 \land x11 \land x7 \rightarrow x1$

Rule 10: if necessarily simultaneous transmission and necessarily Vt = 100 Mbps and medium-high traffic and medium budget then Ethernet high speed net and FDDI or necessarily Ethernet high speed net.

$\Box x18 \land \Box x7 \land x9 \land x13 \rightarrow (x8 \land x12) \lor \Box x8$

Rule 11: if necessarily Vt = 2 Mbps and extremely long distance and very low BER then frame relay.

$\Box x2 \land x19 \land x20 \rightarrow x21$

Rule 12: if necessarily simultaneous transmission and distance > 2000 m then necessarily not frame relay or ATM.

$\Box x18 \land x11 \rightarrow \Box \neg x21 \lor x22$

Rule 13: if maximum efficiency and Vt > 100 Mbps and high budget then ATM.

$\Diamond x14 \land x23 \land x27 \rightarrow x22$

Rule 14: if Vt = 64 Kbps and high efficiency and simultaneous transmission and medium-low budget then RDIF.

$x24 \land \Diamond x14 \land x18 \land x4 \land x13 \rightarrow x25$

Rule 15: if Vt = 64 Kbps and low budget and high BER then X.25.

$x24 \land x4 \land \Box x20 \rightarrow x26$

4.2.3 Potential facts

Once inconsistencies have been eliminated, the potential facts are:

Fact 1: distance $\leq$ 500 m (x1).
Fact 2: necessarily Vt $\leq$ 10 Mbps ($\Box$x2).
Fact 3: necessarily budget moderate ($\Box$x4).
Fact 4: traffic low (x5).
Fact 5: distance $\leq$ 200 m (x6).
Fact 6: necessarily Vt = 100 Mbps ($\Box$x7).
Fact 7: traffic medium–high (x9).
Fact 8: traffic medium-low (x10).
Fact 9: distance $\leq$ 2000 m (x11).
Fact 10: budget medium (x13).
Fact 11: maximum efficiency (x14).
Fact 12: high tolerance to failures.(x17).
Fact 13: necessarily simultaneous information transmission ($\Box$x18).
Fact 14: extremely long distance (x19).
Fact 15: very low BER (x20).
Fact 16:Vt $>$ 100 Mbps (x23).
Fact 17: budget high (x27).
Fact 18: Vt = 64 Kbps (x24).
Fact 19: not distance $\leq$ 2000 m ($\neg$x11).
Fact 20: possibly not Vt $\leq$ 10 Mbps ($\Diamond\neg$x2).
Fact 21: necessarily not BER low ($\Box\neg$x20).

4.3   Syntax of the KBS using CoCoA

4.3.1 Introduction

The paragraphs written in normal fonts are explanations of the example and those written in `typewriter` font are the CoCoA expressions of the program and its results.

The first thing to do is to declare the ring of polynomials with 27 variables, to which the formulae of the KBS are to be translated, and the ideal I (see section 2.2).

```
A::= Z/(3)[x[1..27]];
USE A;
I:=Ideal(x[1]^3-x[1],x[2]^3-x[2],..., x[50]^3-x[50]);
```

Notation: NEG = negation, POS = possible, NEC = necessary, OR1 = or, AND1 = and, IMP = implies, NF = normal form, GBasis = Gröbner basis.

The rules must be written in prefix form.

```
R1:=IMP( AND1(x[1],x[2]) , x[3] );
R2:=IMP( AND1( AND1(NEC(x[2]),NEC(x[4])), x[5]) , x[3] );
R3:=IMP( AND1(x[6],POS(x[7])) , x[8] );
R4:=IMP( AND1(AND1(POS(x[7]),x[9]), POS(x[4])) , x[8] );
```

```
R5a:=IMP( AND1(x[10],x[4]) , AND1(NEG(x[3]),NEG(x[8])) );
R5b:=IMP( AND1(x[10],x[4]) , OR1(x[3],x[8]) );
R6:=IMP( AND1(x[7],x[11]) , x[12] );
R7:=IMP( AND1(AND1(NEC(x[7]),x[13]),x[14]) , x[12] );
R8:=IMP( AND1(AND1(AND1(x[13],x[14]),NEG(x[11])),
    POS(NEG(x[2]))),AND1(NEG(x[3]) , NEC(NEG(x[16])))));
R9:=IMP( AND1(AND1(NEG(x[11]),x[17]),x[7]) , x[12] );
R10:=IMP( AND1(AND1(AND1(NEC(x[18]), NEC(x[7])),
    x[9]),x[13]) , OR1(NEC(x[8]),AND1(x[8],x[12])) );
R11:=IMP( AND1(AND1(NEC(x[2]),x[19]),x[20]) , x[21] );
R12:=IMP( AND1(NEC(x[18]),NEG(x[11])),OR1(NEC(NEG(x[21])) ,
    x[22])));
R13:=IMP( AND1(AND1(POS(x[14]),x[23]), x[27]), x[22] );
R14:=IMP( AND1(AND1(AND1(POS(x[14]),x[24]),x[18]),
    AND1(x[4],x[13])) , x[25] );
R15:=IMP( AND1(AND1(x[24],x[4]),NEC(NEG(x[20]))) , x[26] );
```

For example, Rule R1 is automatically translated into the following polynomial

$$x[1]\hat{\ }2x[2]\hat{\ }2x[3] + x[1]\hat{\ }2x[2]x[3]\hat{\ }2 + x[1]x[2]\hat{\ }2x[3]\hat{\ }2 +$$
$$x[1]\hat{\ }2x[2]\hat{\ }2 - x[1]\hat{\ }2x[2]x[3] - x[1]x[2]\hat{\ }2x[3] - x[1]x[2]x[3]\hat{\ }2 +$$
$$x[1]\hat{\ }2x[2] + x[1]x[2]\hat{\ }2 + x[1]x[2]x[3] - x[1]x[2] - 1$$

Potential facts are declared next

```
F1:=x[1];
F2:=NEC(x[2]);
F3:=NEC(x[4]);
F4:=x[5];
F5:=x[6];
F6:=NEC(x[7]);
F7:=x[9];
F8:=x[10];
F9:=x[11];
F10:=x[13];
F11:=x[14];
F12:=x[17];
F13:=NEC(x[18]);
F14:=x[19];
F15:=x[20];
F16:=x[23];
F17:=x[27];
F18:=x[24];
F19:=NEG(x[11]);
F20:=POS(NEG(x[2]));
F21:=NEC(NEG(x[20]));
```

4.3.2 Consistency verification

The ideal generated by the negation of all rules and the maximal set of facts formed by all facts except F19, F20 and F21 (see Sections 3.1 and 4) is:

```
L:=Ideal(NEG(F1),NEG(F2),NEG(F3),NEG(F4),NEG(F5),NEG(F6),NEG(F7),
    NEG(F8),NEG(F9),NEG(F10),NEG(F11),NEG(F12),NEG(F13),NEG(F14),
    NEG(F15),NEG(F16),NEG(F17),NEG(F18),NEG(F18),NEG(R1),NEG(R2),
    NEG(R3),NEG(R4),NEG(R5b),NEG(R6),NEG(R7),NEG(R8),NEG(R9),
    NEG(R10),NEG(R11),NEG(R12),NEG(R13),NEG(R14),NEG(R15) );
```

(note that rule R5a has not been included).

Let us check for consistency using Gröbner bases (see Sections 3.2 and 4)

```
GBasis(I+L);
```

The output is

$$[x[15]^3 - x[15], x[16]^3 - x[16], x[26]^3 - x[26], x[1] + 1, x[5] + 1,$$
$$x[6] + 1, x[9] + 1, x[10] + 1, x[11] + 1, x[13] + 1, x[14] + 1, x[17] + 1,$$
$$x[19] + 1, x[20] + 1, x[23] + 1, x[27] + 1, x[24] + 1, x[18] + 1, x[7] + 1,$$
$$x[4] + 1, x[2] + 1, x[12] + 1, x[3] + 1, x[8] + 1, x[22] + 1,$$
$$x[21] + 1, x[25] + 1]$$

which means consistency (it is not $[1]$).

Let us substitute Rule 5b in ideal L by Rule 5a, and let us denote by J the resulting ideal. In this case the Gröbner basis of (I+J) results to be

```
[1]
```

which means inconsistency.

The following procedure checks for consistency adding element by element of the KBS:

```
Define CONSIST(J_,N_)
N_:=N_-1;
GB_:=[0];
While N_ < Len(J_) And Not GB_=[1] Do
  N_:=N_+1;
  GB_:=GBasis(Ideal( First(J_,N_) ));
  If GB_=[1]
    Then Print 'In element';Print N_;Print 'of the list';
      PrintLn 'INCONSISTENCY exists'
    Else Print 'Up to element'; Print N_; Print' of the
    list';PrintLn 'there is CONSISTENCY'
    End;
  End;
End;
```

Let us find the element that produces this new inconsistency

```
CONSIST(List(I+J),1);
```

The answer is a list of statements:

```
. . . . . . . .
Up to element 48 of the list, CONsistency
Up to element 49 of the list, CONsistency
Up to element 50 of the list, INCONsistency
```

As there are 27 elements in the ideal I, counting the elements of the ideal J from **F1** as element 28, it means that the element 50 is **R5a** (it can be seen by a logic manipulation that R5a is in contradiction with R2 and R3).

So the erroneous rule has been detected.

4.3.3 Automated proving

Once the KBS has been made consistent (ideal K) let us ask the KBS the following questions:

1) If distance $<= 500$ m and moderate budget, then type of net local Ethernet?

   $x4 \wedge x1 \rightarrow x3$?

2) If $10 <= Vt <= 100$ Mbps and medium budget, then type of local net Ethernet high speed?

   $\neg x2 \wedge \neg x23 \wedge x13 \rightarrow x8$?

3) If $Vt = 100$ Mbps and medium budget and distance > 2 Km, then type of net FDDI?

   $x7 \wedge x13 \wedge \neg x11 \rightarrow x12$?

4) If $Vt > 100$ Mbps and high budget and distance > 2 Km, then type of net ATM?

   $x23 \wedge x27 \wedge x11 \rightarrow x22$?

5) If maximum efficiency and medium budget, then type of net ATM?

   $x14 \wedge x13 \rightarrow x22$?

6) If very low BER and $Vt <= 10$ Mbps, then necessarily not type of net frame relay?

   $x20 \wedge x2 \rightarrow \Box \neg x21$?

In order to find the answers to the above questions, the following commands, using Normal Forms (see Sections 3.1 and 4), are given to CoCoA:

```
NF( NEG( IMP( AND1(x[4],x[1]) , x[3]) ), I+J );
NF( NEG( IMP( AND1(AND1(NEG(x[2]),NEG(x[23])),x[13]) , x[8] ) ) ,
    I+J);
NF( NEG(IMP( AND1(AND1(x[7],x[13]),NEG(x[11])) , x[12] )) , I+J);
```

```
NF( NEG(IMP( AND1(AND1(x[23],x[27]),NEG(x[11])) , x[22] )) , I+J);
NF( NEG(IMP( AND1(x[14],x[13]) , x[22] )) , I+J);
NF( NEG(IMP( AND1(x[20],x[2]) , NEC(NEG(x[21])) ) ), I+J);
```

CoCoA gives as outputs, respectively, 0, 0, 0, 0, 0 and 1, which means that the five first questions are automatically proved and the sixth question disproved.

5 Conclusions

A Computer Algebra based method has been applied to the processes of verification and knowledge extraction in KBS. As an example, we have studied a decision problem regarding a small KBS that helps to take decisions about how to select a computer network. Such a study has been intended to be an illustration of the method and an illustration of the usefulness of many-valued logic in knowledge representation, when imprecise knowledge is involved.

References

[1] J.A. Alonso, E. Briales, A. Riscos, Preuve Automatique dans le Calcul Propositionnel et des Logiques Trivalentes, Proceedings Congress on Computational Geometry and Topology and Computation in Teaching Mathematics, Universidad de Sevilla, 1987.

[2] A. Capani, G. Niesi, CoCoA User's Manual (v. 3.0b). Dept. of Mathematics, University of Genova, 1996.

[3] J. Chazarain, A. Riscos, J.A. Alonso, E. Briales, Many-valued Logic and Gröbner Bases with Applications to Modal Logic, Journal of Symbolic Computation, 11, 181-194, 1991.

[4] L.M. Laita, E. Roanes-Lozano, L. de Ledesma, J.A. Alonso, A Computer Approach to Verification and Deduction in Many-valued Knowledge Systems, Soft Computing, 3 (1), 7-19, 1999.

[5] E. Roanes-Lozano, L.M. Laita, E. Roanes-Macías, A Polynomial Model for Many-valued Logics with a Touch of Algebraic Geometry and Computer Algebra, Mathematics and Computers in Simulation, 45 (1), 83-99, 1998.

[6] W. Stallings, Comunicaciones y Redes de Computadores, 5th edition, Prentice Hall, 1997.

[7] J. García-Tomás, S. Ferrando, M. Piattini, Redes de Alta Velocidad, RA-MA, Madrid, 1997.

[8] F. Winkler, Polynomial Algorithms in Computer Algebra, Springer, Wien, 1996.

Qualitative Reasoning with Complex and Composite Regions in 2D Space

Alia I. Abdelmoty and Baher A. El-Geresy

School of Computing, University of Glamorgan

Treforest, Wales, UK

Abstract

A new approach is proposed in this paper for the representation and reasoning over complex and composite regions in space. Complex regions are non-simple, irregular shaped regions with possible holes. Composite regions are regions defined through multiple separate regions. Both types exhibit different behaviour in space which is also distinct from simple regions. Spatial databases are currently limited to treating both types as simple, and approaches to qualitative reasoning are also limited to handling simple regions only. The approach proposed in this paper is general, where any type of region is treated uniformly, and flexible, where different levels of representation could be devised. A general reasoning approach is presented based on the representation formalism. It is shown how the composition of spatial relations is achieved between different types of regions.

1 Introduction

A need is emerging in many application domains for handling spatial and spatio-temporal data. This is evidenced by the spatial extensions developed in large database management systems [10]. Geographic information systems are the main driving force behind these developments, but other significant applications can also be found in many domains, including, medical and multimedia systems. Complex decision making tasks typically required in such systems depend to a large extent on data modelling and representation. The set of basic spatial data types used are between, vector; points, lines, and regions and raster; point-sets. However, it is well recognised that more complex data types need to be handled, typically made from specialisations or aggregations of the basic types.

Queries in these systems involve the derivation of different types of spatial relationships which are not explicitly stored. It is generally agreed that it is neither practical nor efficient to store the substantial amount of different types of spatial relationships that can exist in space [15]. Qualitative spatial reasoning has been proposed as a complementary mechanism for the automatic derivation of spatial relations which are not explicitly stored. It is based on the manipulation of qualitative spatial relationships such as, **near** and **touch**, as opposed to quantitative information such as, **at a distance of 10 m.** and **intersect in point(x,y)**. Queries involving qualitative spatial relationships are common in spatial decision support systems when no precise geometric information is needed. Spatial reasoning has also been proposed to maintain the consistency of the database [13].

In this paper, a representation and a reasoning approach is proposed for handling complex and composite regions in space. Complex regions are non-simple, irregular shaped areas, and composite regions are those defined by multiple, possibly, disconnected regions. Several works have been proposed for representing those object types. However, they are mostly limited to handling very specific, well-defined cases, or quite complex to form the basis for reasoning mechanisms. The method proposed in this paper is simple, based on a straightforward decomposition strategy for representing object and space topologies. It is also general and can be applied uniformally to regions with random complexity, and flexible, where different levels of representations can be readily devised. It is shown how topological relationships can be uniquely defined between the different region types. Two general rules and constraints are used for reasoning over those objects. A major advantage of the method is that reasoning between objects of any complexity can be achieved in a definite limited number of steps. Hence, the incorporation of spatial reasoning mechanisms in spatial information systems becomes plausible.

The rest of this paper is structured as follows. The representation formalism is presented in section 2. Examples are given for the representation of regions with variable complexity. The representation of spatial relationships is presented in section 3 and section 4 describe the general reasoning formalism. Comparison with other related approaches are given throughout the different sections and conclusions are given in section 5.

2   Representing Object and Space Topologies

2.1   The Underlying Representation

The method used for representing the space and the objects is similar to the space vocabulary described in [14] where objects of interest and their embedding space are divided into components according to a required resolution. The connectivity of those components is explicitly represented.

Let S be the space in which the object is embedded. The object and its embedding space are assumed to be *dense* and *connected*. The embedding space is also assumed to be infinite. The object and its embedding space are decomposed into components which reflects the objects and space topology such that,

1. No overlap exist between any of the representative components.

2. The union of the components is equal to the embedding space.

The topology of the object and the embedding space can then be described by a matrix whose elements represent the connectivity relations between its components. This matrix shall be denoted *adjacency matrix*. In the decomposition strategy, the complement of the object in question shall be considered to be infinite, and the suffix 0, e.g. (x_0) is used to represent this component.

Hence, the topology of a space S containing an object x is defined using the following equation.

$$x \ = \ \bigcup_{i=1}^{n} x_i \tag{1}$$

$$S_x \ = \ x \cup x_0 \tag{2}$$

where S_l is used to denote the space associated with object l.

In figure 1(a) different possible decompositions of a simple convex region and its embedding space is shown along with their adjacency matrices. In 1 (a), the object is represented by two components, a linear component x_1 and an areal component x_2 and the rest of the space is represented by an infinite areal component x_0 representing the surrounding area. In 1(b), only one areal component is used to represent the region. Both representations are valid and may be used in different contexts. Different decomposition strategies for the objects and their embedding spaces can be used according to the precision of the relations required and the specific application considered. The higher the resolution used (or the finer the components of the space and the objects), the higher the precision of the resulting set of relations in the domain considered.

The fact that two components are connected is represented by a (1) in the adjacency matrix and by a (0) otherwise. Since connectivity is a symmetric relation, the resulting matrix will be symmetric around the diagonal. Hence, only half the matrix is sufficient for the representation of the object's topology and the matrix can be collapsed to the structure in figure 1(c) and (d).

In the rest of this section, the method is applied for representing complex and composite regions.

2.2 Representing Complex Regions

Different types of regions may be of interest in different application domains. Several works have addressed the problem of representing irregular or concave regions [6], regions with holes [12] and regions with indeterminate boundaries [7, 8]. The examples shown in figure 2 and 3 demonstrate how the approach proposed above is used for representing the first two cases.

As can be seen from the figures, the same methodology of object and space decomposition is used uniformly in the different cases. In the case of the concave region, the cavities in the region are represented as separate (virtual) components. They are initially identified using the convex hull of the object (the minimum convex polygon that can enclose the object), as demonstrated in 2 (b). Any number of cavities can be distinguished depending on the degree of precision required, Also, more precise relations will be distinguished if the boundary of the cavity is distinguished.

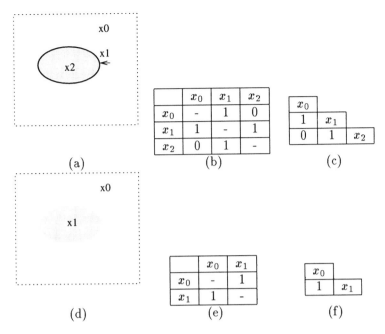

(a)

	x_0	x_1	x_2
x_0	–	1	0
x_1	1	–	1
x_2	0	1	–

(b)

x_0		
1	x_1	
0	1	x_2

(c)

(d)

	x_0	x_1
x_0	–	1
x_1	1	–

(e)

x_0	
1	x_1

(f)

Figure 1: (a) and (d) Possible decompositions of a simple convex region and its embedding space. (b) and (e) Adjacency matrix of the two shapes in (a) and (d). (c) and (f) Half the symmetric adjacency matrix is sufficient to capture the object representation.

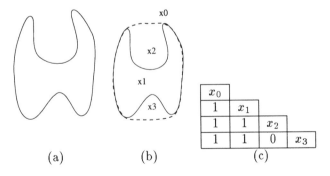

(a)   (b)

x_0			
1	x_1		
1	1	x_2	
1	1	0	x_3

(c)

Figure 2: (a) Irregular (concave) region. (b) Representation of virtual components using convex hull. (c) Its corresponding adjacency matrix.

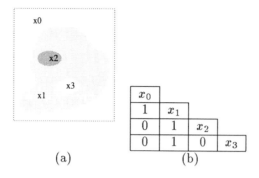

(a)   (b)

Figure 3: (a) A region with several holes. (c) Its corresponding adjacency matrix.

2.3   Representing Composite Regions

Composite regions are used here to denote regions with multiple separate components. This type of objects is needed in many application contexts. For example, a university may be built on different sites in a city; a country may consist of separate islands, etc. There is a need in spatial databases to model those aggregate objects as wholes, and hence enabling the representation of their relationships in space. This need has been identified in many works [2, 17]. However, so far, few works addressed this representation problem [5].

One possible method for representing a composite region, proposed here, is by using its convex hull, as shown in figure 4(a). The region is defined by the union of its separate component regions as well as their complement which lies within the convex hull, x'. A coarse level of representation is used initially. Further refinement of the object details may be used later for exact determination of relationships, as shall be shown later on in the paper.

3   Representing Topological Relations between Regions

Distinction of topological relations is dependent on the strategy used in the decomposition of the objects and their related spaces. For example, in figure 5 different relationships between two objects representing a ship (y) and an island (x) are shown, where in 5(a) the ship is inside the bay and in 5(b) the ship is outside the bay. The concave region representing the island (x) is decomposed into two components x_1 and x_2 and the rest of the space associated with x is decomposed into two components (x_3 representing the bay and x_0 representing the rest of the ocean). The component x_3 is a virtual component, i.e. with no physical boundary to delineate its spatial extension. It is the identification of this component that makes the distinction between the two relationships in the figure.

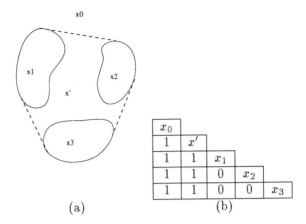

(a)

(b)

Figure 4: (a) A composite region formed of multiple, separate, parts, x_1, x_2 and x_3, defined using its convex hull. (b) Its corresponding adjacency matrix.

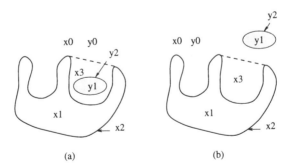

(a)

(b)

Figure 5: Different qualitative spatial relationships can be distinguished by identifying the appropriate components of the objects and the space.

	y_0	y_1	y_2
x_0	1	0	0
x_1	1	0	0
x_2	1	0	0
x_3	1	1	1

(a)

	y_0	y_1	y_2
x_0	1	1	1
x_1	1	0	0
x_2	1	0	0
x_3	1	0	0

(b)

Figure 6: The corresponding **intersection matrices** for the relationships in figure 5 respectively.

The complete set of spatial relationships are represented by combinatorial intersection of the components of one space with those of the other space.

If $R(x, y)$ is a relation of interest between object x and object y, and X and Y are the spaces associated with the objects respectively such that n is the number of components in X and m is the number of components in Y, then a spatial relation $R(x, y)$ can be represented by one state of the following equation:

$$
\begin{aligned}
R(x, y) &= X \cap Y \\
&= \left(\bigcup_{i=1}^{n} x_i \right) \cap \left(\bigcup_{j=1}^{m} y_j \right) \\
&= (x_1 \cap y_1, \cdots, x_1 \cap y_m, x_2 \cap y_1, \cdots, x_n \cap y_m)
\end{aligned}
$$

The intersection $x_i \cap y_j$ can be an empty or a non-empty intersection. The above set of intersections shall be represented by an intersection matrix as follows.

$$R(x, y) =$$

	y_0	y_1	y_2	$\cdots$
x_0				
x_1				
x_2				
$\vdots$				

For example, the intersection matrices corresponding to the spatial relationships in figure 5 are shown in figure 6. The components y_1 and y_2 have a non-empty intersection with x_0 in 6(a) and with x_3 in 6(b).

Different combinations in the intersection matrix can represent different qualitative relations. The example in figure 7 shows an example of spatial relationships between composite regions and between composite and simple regions. The set of sound, or physically possible, spatial relationships between objects is dependent on the particular domain studied. Also, properties of the objects would affect the set of possible spatial relationships that can exist between them. For example, if one object is solid and the other is permeable, there cannot be any intersection of the inside of the solid object with any other component of the other object.

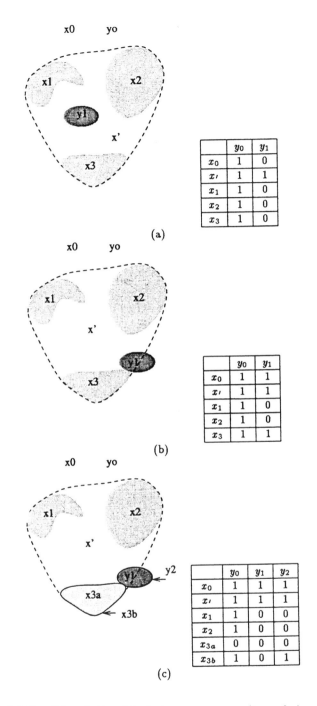

Figure 7: (a) Possible relationship between a composite and simple region. (b) A different relationship, distinguished by y connecting to x_3. (c) Exact nature of relationship is revealed by considering finer object detail.

4 Reasoning over Regions in Space

The reasoning approach consists of: a) general constraints to govern the spatial relationships between objects in space, and b) general rules to propagate relationships between the objects.

4.1 General Constraints

The intersection matrix is in fact a set of constraints whose values identifies specific spatial relationships. For example, the constraints used to represent the relationship in figure 5(a) are $x_1 \cap y_1 = 0, x_1 \cap y_2 = 0, x_1 \cap y_3 = 0, x_1 \cap y_4 = 1, \cdots$

The process of spatial reasoning can be defined as the process of propagating the constraints of two spatial relations (for example, $R_1(A, B)$ and $R_2(B, C)$), to derive a new set of constraints between objects. The derived constraints can then be mapped to a specific spatial relation (i.e. the relation $R_3(A, C)$).

A subset of the set of constraints defining all spatial relations are general and are applicable to any relationship between any objects. These general constraints are a consequence of the initial assumptions used in the definition of the object and space topology. The identification of these constraints is useful and can be used in checking the correctness of the relations and shall be used later in the paper to give some insight in the propagation of spatial relations.

The two general constraints are:

1. Every unbounded (infinite) component of one space must intersect with at least one unbounded (infinite) component of the other space.

   Intuitively this rule says that it is impossible for an infinite component in the space to only have an intersection with finite component(s). In this case the infinite component becomes a subset of the finite component(s) which is not possible.

2. Every component from one space must intersect with at least one component from the other space.

   If one component of one space does not intersect with any component of the other space, either the two spaces are not equal or the spaces are not *connected*. Both conditions are excluded by the initial assumptions. This implies that there cannot exist a row or a column in the intersection matrix whose elements are all empty intersections, hence the combinatorial cases in the matrix where this case exists can be ignored.

4.2 General Reasoning Rules

Composition of spatial relations is the process through which the possible relationship(s) between two object x and z is derived given two relationships: R_1 between x and y and R_2 between y and z. Two general reasoning rules for the propagation of intersection constraints are presented. The rules are characterised by the ability to reason over spatial relationships between objects of arbitrary complexity in any space dimension. These rules allow for the automatic derivation of the composition (transitivity) tables between any spatial shapes [1]- a task considered to be a challenge to automatic theorem provers [21].

Reasoning Rules

Composition of spatial relations using the *intersection-based* representation approach is based on the transitive property of the subset relations. In what follows the following subset notation is used. If x' is a set of components (set of point-sets) $\{x_1, \cdots, x_n\}$ in a space X, and y_j is a component in space Y, then $\sqsubseteq$ denotes the following subset relationship.

- $y_j \sqsubseteq x'$ denotes the subset relationship such that: $\forall x_i \in x'(y_j \cap x_i \neq \phi) \wedge y_j \cap (X - x_1 - x_2 \cdots - x_n) = \phi$ *where* $i = 1, \cdots n$. Intuitively, this symbol indicates that the component y_j intersects with every set in the set x' and does not intersect with any set out-with x'.

If x_i, y_j and z_k are components of objects x, y and z respectively, then if there is a non-empty intersection between x_i and y_j, and y_j is a subset of z_k, then it can be concluded that there is also a non-empty intersection between x_u and z_k.

$$(x_i \cap y_j \neq \phi) \wedge (y_j \subseteq z_k) \rightarrow (x_i \cap z_k \neq \phi)$$

This relation can be generalised in the following two rules. The rules describe the propagation of intersections between the components of objects and their related spaces involved in the spatial composition.

Rule 1: Propagation of Non-Empty Intersections

Let $x' = \{x_1, x_2, \cdots, x_{m'}\}$ *be a subset of the set of components of space* X *whose total number of components is* m *and* $m' \leq m$; $x' \subseteq X$. *Let* $z' = \{z_1, z_2, \cdots, z_{n'}\}$ *be a subset of the set of components of space* Z *whose total number of components is* n *and* $n' \leq n$; $z' \subseteq Z$. *If* y_j *is a component of space* Y, *the following is a governing rule of interaction for the three spaces* X, Y *and* Z.

$$
\begin{aligned}
(x' \sqsupseteq y_j) \quad &\wedge \quad (y_j \sqsubseteq z') \\
&\rightarrow \quad (x' \cap z' \neq \phi) \\
&\equiv \quad (x_1 \cap z_1 \neq \phi \vee \cdots \vee x_1 \cap z_{n'} \neq \phi) \\
&\qquad \wedge (x_2 \cap z_1 \neq \phi \vee \cdots \vee x_2 \cap z_{n'} \neq \phi) \\
&\qquad \wedge \cdots \\
&\qquad \wedge (x_{m'} \cap z_1 \neq \phi \vee \cdots \vee x_{m'} \cap z_{n'} \neq \phi)
\end{aligned}
$$

The above rule states that if the component y_j in space Y has a positive intersection with every component from the sets x' and z', then each component of the set x' must intersect with at least one component of the set z'.

The constraint $x_i \cap z_1 \neq \phi \vee x_i \cap z_2 \neq \phi \cdots \vee x_i \cap z_{n'} \neq \phi$ can be expressed in the intersection matrix by a label, for example the label a in the following matrix indicates $x_1 \cap (z_2 \cup z_4) \neq \phi$ (x_1 has a positive intersection with z_2, or with z_4 or with both). A $-$ in the matrix indicates that the intersection is either positive or negative.

	z_1	z_2	z_3	z_4	$\cdots$	z_n
x_1	$-$	a	$-$	a	$-$	$-$

Rule 1 represents the propagation of non-empty intersections of components in space. A different version of the rule for the propagation of empty intersections can be stated as follows.

Rule 2: Propagation of Empty Intersections

Let $z' = \{z_1, z_2, \cdots, z_{n'}\}$ be a subset of the set of components of space Z whose total number of components is n and $n' < n$; $z' \subset Z$. Let $y' = \{y_1, y_2, \cdots, y_{p'}\}$ be a subset of the set of components of space Y whose total number of components is p and $p' < p$; $y' \subset Y$. Let x_i be a component of the space X. Then the following is a governing rule for the spaces X, Y and Z.

$$(x_i \sqsubseteq y') \quad \wedge \quad (y' \sqsubseteq z')$$
$$\longrightarrow \quad (x_i \cap (Z - z_1 - z_2 \cdots - z_{n'}) = \phi)$$

Remark: if $n' = n$, i.e. x_i may intersect with every element in Z, then no empty intersections can be propagated. Rules 1 and 2 are the two general rules for propagating empty and non-empty intersections of components of spaces.

Note that in both rules the intermediate object (y) and its space components plays the main role in the propagation of intersections. Indeed, it shall be shown in the next example how the above two rules are applied a number of times equal to the number of components of the space of the intermediate object. Hence, the composition of spatial relations using this method becomes a tractable problem which can be performed in a defined limited number of steps.

4.3   Reasoning with Composite Regions

The example in figure 8 demonstrates the composition of relations using composite regions. Figure 8 shows the relationship between a composite region y and a simple region x in (a) and a concave region z in (b). The intersection matrices for both relations in shown in 8(c).

Given the relationships between the composite region y and the simple region x in 8(a) and its relationship with the concave region z in 8(b), it is required to derive the possible relationships between x and z.

The reasoning rules are used to propagate the intersections between the components of objects x and z as follows. From rule 1 we have,

- y_0 intersections:

$$\{x_0\} \sqsupseteq y_0 \quad \wedge \quad y_0 \sqsubseteq \{z_0, z_1, z_2, z_3\}$$
$$\longrightarrow \quad x_0 \cap z_0 \neq \phi \wedge x_0 \cap z_1 \neq \phi$$
$$\wedge \quad x_0 \cap z_2 \neq \phi \wedge x_0 \cap z_3 \neq \phi$$

- y_1 intersections:

$$\{x_0, x_1, x_2\} \sqsupseteq y_1 \wedge y_1 \sqsubseteq \{z_3\} \longrightarrow x_0 \cap z_3 \neq \phi \wedge x_1 \cap z_3 \neq \phi \wedge x_2 \cap z_3 \neq \phi$$

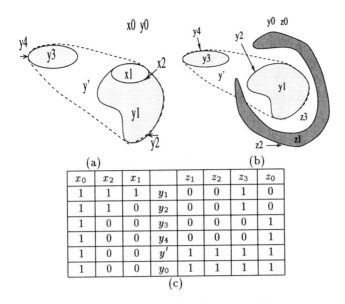

x_0	x_2	x_1		z_1	z_2	z_3	z_0
1	1	1	y_1	0	0	1	0
1	1	0	y_2	0	0	1	0
1	0	0	y_3	0	0	0	1
1	0	0	y_4	0	0	0	1
1	0	0	y'	1	1	1	1
1	0	0	y_0	1	1	1	1

(c)

Figure 8: (a) and (b) Spatial relationships between different types of regions. (c) Corresponding intersection matrices.

- y_2 intersections:

$$\{x_0, x_2\} \sqsupseteq y_2 \quad \wedge \quad y_2 \sqsubseteq \{z_3\}$$
$$\rightarrow \quad x_0 \cap z_3 \neq \phi \wedge x_2 \cap z_3 \neq \phi$$

- y_3 intersections:

$$\{x_0\} \sqsupseteq y_3 \quad \wedge \quad y_3 \sqsubseteq \{z_0\}$$
$$\rightarrow \quad x_0 \cap z_0 \neq \phi$$

- y_4 intersections:

$$\{x_0\} \sqsupseteq y_3 \quad \wedge \quad y_3 \sqsubseteq \{z_0\}$$
$$\rightarrow \quad x_0 \cap z_0 \neq \phi$$

- y' intersections:

$$\{x_0\} \sqsupseteq y_0 \quad \wedge \quad y_0 \sqsubseteq \{z_0, z_1, z_2, z_3\}$$
$$\rightarrow \quad x_0 \cap z_0 \neq \phi \wedge x_0 \cap z_1 \neq \phi$$
$$\wedge \quad x_0 \cap z_2 \neq \phi \wedge x_0 \cap z_3 \neq \phi$$

Applying rule 2 we get the following,

- $x_1 \sqsubseteq \{y_1\} \wedge \{y_1\} \sqsubseteq \{z_3\} \rightarrow x_1 \cap z_1 = \phi \wedge x_1 \cap z_2 = \phi \wedge x_1 \cap z_0 = \phi$
- $x_2 \sqsubseteq \{y_1, y_2\} \wedge \{y_1, y_2\} \sqsubseteq \{z_3\} \rightarrow x_2 \cap z_1 = \phi \wedge x_2 \cap z_2 = \phi \wedge x_2 \cap z_0 = \phi$
- $z_1 \sqsubseteq \{y', y_0\} \wedge \{y', y_0\} \sqsubseteq \{x_0\} \rightarrow z_1 \cap x_1 = \phi \wedge z_1 \cap x_2 = \phi$
- $z_0 \sqsubseteq \{y_3, y_4, y', y_0\} \wedge \{y_3, y_4, y', y_0\} \sqsubseteq \{x_0\} \rightarrow z_0 \cap x_1 = \phi \wedge z_0 \cap x_2 = \phi$

Refining the above constraints, we get the intersection matrix in figure 9(a) which maps to one definite relation 9(b).

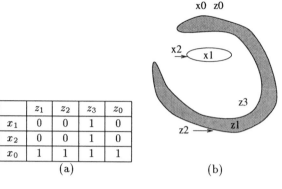

	z_1	z_2	z_3	z_0
x_1	0	0	1	0
x_2	0	0	1	0
x_0	1	1	1	1

(a)   (b)

Figure 9: (a) Resulting intersection matrix for the composition in figure 8 (b) Its corresponding definite relation.

4.4 Comparison with Related Approaches

Approaches to spatial reasoning in the literature can generally be classified into a) using *transitive propagation* and b) using *theorem proving*.

- Transitive propagation: In this approach the transitive property of some spatial relations is utilised to carry out the required reasoning. This applies to the *order relations*, such as before, after and $(<, =, >)$ (for example, $a < b \wedge b < c \rightarrow a < c$), and to the subset relations such as contain and inside (for example, $inside(A, B) \wedge inside(B, C) \rightarrow inside(A, C)$, $east(A, B) \wedge east(B, C) \rightarrow east(A, C)$).

  Transitive property of the subset relations was employed by Egenhofer [11] for reasoning over topological relationships. Transitive property of the order relations has been utilised by Mukerjee & Joe [19], Guesgen [16], Chang & Lu [4], Lee & Hsu [18] and Papadias & Sellis [20].

  Although order relations can be utilised in reasoning over point-shaped objects, they cannot be directly applied when the actual shapes and proximity of objects are considered.

- Theorem proving (elimination): Here, reasoning is carried out by checking every relation in the full set of *sound* relations in the domain to see whether it is a valid consequence of the composition considered (theorems to be proved) and eliminating the ones which are not consistent with the composition [9].

  Bennett [3] have proposed a propositional calculus for the derivation of the composition of topological relations between simple regions using this method. However, checking each relation in the composition table to prove or eliminate is not possible in general cases and is considered a challenge for theorem provers [21].

In general the limitation of all the methods in the above two approaches are as follows:

- Spatial reasoning is studied only between objects of similar types, e.g. between two lines or two simple areas. Spatial relations exist between objects of any type and it is limiting to consider the composition of only specific object shapes.

- Spatial reasoning was carried out only between objects with the same dimension as the space they are embedded in, e.g. between two lines in 1D, between two regions in 2D, etc.

- Spatial reasoning is studied mainly between simple object shapes or objects with controlled complexity, for example, regions with holes treated as concentric simple regions. No method has yet been presented for spatial reasoning between objects with arbitrary complexity.

The method proposed here is simple and general - only two rules are used to derive composition between objects of random complexity and is applicable to different types of spatial relations (topological and order).

5 Conclusions

A general approach is presented for the representation and reasoning over regions in space. The approach is general and can be used for regions with random complexity and for composite regions formed from multiple separate components. It is based on a uniform representation of the topology of the space as a connected set of components. A structure called adjacency matrix is proposed to capture the topology of regions with different complexity. It is shown how topological spatial relations can be uniquely defined between different types of regions. The reasoning method consists of a set of two general constraints to govern the spatial relationships between objects in space, and two general rules to propagate relationships between objects in space. The reasoning process is general and can be applied on any types of objects with random complexity. It is also simple and is based on the application of two rules for the propagation of empty and non-empty intersections between object components. Finally, the method is applied in a finite known number of steps (equal to the number of components of the intermediate objects) which allows its implementation in spatial information systems.

References

[1] A. I. Abdelmoty and El-Geresy B. A. A General Method for Spatial Reasoning in Spatial Databases. In *Proceedings of the Fourth International Conference on Information and Knowledge Management (CIKM'95)*. ACM, 1995.

[2] Alia I. Abdelmoty, Norman W. Paton, M. Howard Williams, Alvaro A.A. Fernandes, Maria L. Barja, and Andrew Dinn. Geographic Data Handling in an Deductive Object-Oriented Database. In D. Karagiannis, editor, *Proc. 5th International Conference on Database and Expert Systems Applications (DEXA)*, pages 445–454. Springer Verlag, Sep 1994.

[3] B. Bennett. Spatial Reasoning with Propositional Logics. In *Principles of Knowledge Representation and Reasoning (KR94)*, pages 51–62. Morgan Kaufmann, 1994.

[4] S.K. Chang and S.H. Liu. Picture Indexing and Abstraction Techniques for Pictorial Databases. *IEEE Transaction on Pattern Analysis and Machine Intelligence*, PAMI-6(4):475–484, 1984.

[5] E. Clementini, P. Di Felice, and G. Califano. Composite Regions in Topological Queries. *Information Systems*, 20(7):579–594, 1995.

[6] A.G. Cohn, B. Bennett, J. Gooday, and N.M. Gotts. Qualitative Spatial Representation and REasoning with the Region Connection Calculus. *Geoinformatica*, 1(3):1–42, 1997.

[7] A.G. Cohn and N.M. Gotts. Expressing Spatial Vagueness in Terms of Connection. In *GISDATA Specialist Meeting: Spatial Conceptual Models for Geographic Objects with Undetermined Boundaries*. Taylor & Francis, 1994.

[8] A.G. Cohn and N.M. Gotts. The "Egg-Yolk" Representation of Regions with Indeterminate Boundaries. In P.A. Burrough and A.U. Frank, editors, *Geographic Objects with Indeterminate Boundaries, GISDATA*, pages 171–187. Taylor & Francis, 1996.

[9] A.G. Cohn, D.A. Randell, Z. Cui, and B. Bennet. Qualitative Spatial Reasoning and Representation. In P. Carrete and M.G. Singh, editors, *Qualitative Reasoning and Decision Technologies*, 1993.

[10] Oracle   Corporation. http://www.oracle.com/database/options/spatial/index.html. 1999.

[11] M.J. Egenhofer. Deriving the composition of Binary Topological Relations. *Journal of Visual Languages and Computing*, 5:133–149, 1994.

[12] M.J. Egenhofer, E. Clementini, and Di Felicem P. Topological Relations Between Regions With Holes. *Int. J. Geographic Information Systems*, 8(2):129–142, 1994.

[13] M.J. Egenhofer and J. Sharma. Topological consistency. In P. Bresnahan, E. Corwin, and D. Cowen, editors, *Proceedings of the 5th International Symposium on Spatial Data Handling*, volume 2, pages 335–343, Charleston, 1992. IGU Commission of GIS.

[14] K. D. Forbus, P. Nielsen, and B. Faltings. Qualitative Kinematics: A Framework. In D. S. Weld and J. De Kleer, editors, *Qualitative Reaoning About Physical Systems*, pages 562–574. Morgan Kaufman, 1990.

[15] K.D. Forbus, P. Nielsen, and B. Faltings. Qualitative Spatial Reasoning: the CLOCK Project . *Artificial Intelligence*, 51:417–471, 1991.

[16] Guesgen, H.W. Spatial reasoning based on allen's temporal logic. Technical Report TR-89-049, International Computer Science Institute, Berkeley, California, 1989.

[17] Th Hadzilacos and Tryfona N. An extended entity-relationship model for geographic applications. In *SIGMOD RECORD*. ACM, 1997.

[18] S-Y Lee and F-J Hsu. Picture Algebra for Spatial Reasoning of Iconic Images Represented in 2D C-string. *Pattern Recognition*, 12:425–435, 1991.

[19] A. Mukerjee and G. Joe. A Qualitative Model for Space. In *Proceeding of the 8th National Conference on Artificial Intelligence, AAAI, 1990*, pages 721–727, 1990.

[20] D. Papadias and T. Sellis. Spatial reasoning using symbolic arrays. In *Theories and Methods of Spatio-Temporal Reasoning in Geographic Space*, LNCS 716, pages 153–161. Springer Verlag, 1992.

[21] D.A. Randell, A.G. Cohn, and Z. Cui. Computing Transitivity Tables: A Challenge for Automated Theorem Provers. In *CADE*, Lecture Notes In Computer Science, 1992.

AUTHOR INDEX